P9-DMG-453

A Jewish Social Studies Reader

Emancipation and Counter-Emancipation

A Jewish Social Studies Reader

Emancipation and Counter-Emancipation

WITHDRAWN

Selected Essays from

Jewish Social Studies

Edited by

Abraham G. Duker and Meir Ben-Horin

with an Introduction by

Salo W. Baron

KTAV PUBLISHING HOUSE, INC.

CONFERENCE ON JEWISH SOCIAL STUDIES

© COPYRIGHT 1974
CONFERENCE ON JEWISH SOCIAL STUDIES

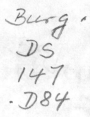

Burg.
DS
147
.D84

c.2

Library of Congress Cataloging in Publication Data

Duker, Abraham Gordon, 1907-   comp.
  Emancipation and counter emancipation.

  (A Jewish social studies reader)
  Bibliography: p.
  1. Jews—Emancipation—Addresses, essays, lectures. 2.
Antisemitism—History—Addresses, essays, lectures. I. Ben-
Horin, Meir, 1918-   joint comp. II. Jewish social
studies. III. Title. IV. Series.
DS147.D84   301.45'19'24   70-147927
ISBN 0-87068-160-5

MANUFACTURED IN THE UNITED STATES OF AMERICA

Table of Contents

OCT 1 8 1976

DEDICATED

To the Memory of

DAVID ROSENSTEIN

1895–1963

Distinguished Philanthropist and Communal Leader.

For many years Treasurer and Chairman of the Board of the Conference on Jewish Social Studies. He gave the Conference and its publication, JEWISH SOCIAL STUDIES, years of dedicated, loving, and attentive service.

Editors' Preface

This collection of articles which originally appeared in JEWISH SOCIAL STUDIES begins in 1939, its first year of publication, and comes down to 1957. The Editors hope that this *Reader* will provide an anthology of scholarly writing on aspects of modern Jewish life suitable for university courses and seminars in modern Jewish history, sociology, Christian-Jewish relations, and antisemitism. In addition, the readings cover developments in modern Jewish history that are pertinent to the teaching of nationalism, minority life and culture, and revolutionary and reform movements. The subjects of Emancipation and Counter-Emancipation were selected for their inherent importance, as well as for the number and variety of articles about them which have appeared in the quarterly. Other subjects have also been covered intensively in JEWISH SOCIAL STUDIES and hopefully will be treated in future volumes. Abraham Duker's Bibliography is intended as an additional resource. The following contributors have graciously supplied some bibliographical and textual corrections and changes: Baron, Barzilay, Duker and Karbach.

The selection was made by the Editors and Professors Lloyd Gartner of Tel Aviv University and Arthur Hertzberg of Columbia University and Brooklyn College. Professor Salo W. Baron has not only consented to write the introduction, but has always been ready with valuable suggestions. Ben-Horin edited the articles for the printer. The introductions to individual articles were written mainly by Duker and looked over by his daughter, Sara Rivkah, and Arthur Hertzberg. The Editors are aware that other articles could and perhaps should have been included. Selection is a difficult and sometimes subjective process. The Editors apologize for the omissions and hope that amends will be made in another volume. They also wish to express their thanks to Mr. Bernard Scharfstein of Ktav Publishing House, Inc., for his cooperation and above all for his patience.

ABRAHAM G. DUKER
Brooklyn College
City University of New York

MEIR BEN-HORIN
Dropsie University

The Journal and the Conference
of Jewish Social Studies

by Salo W. Baron

The essays included in this volume are but a small selection of articles which have appeared in JEWISH SOCIAL STUDIES over the last thirty years. The Editors had a genuine embarrassment of riches in trying to select studies representative of the various areas covered by this quarterly. This is the first in what we hope will be a series of several *readers* culled from the pages of JEWISH SOCIAL STUDIES. Its theme is Emancipation and Counter-Emancipation, the field of modern Jewish scholarship on which perhaps most work has been done. As it is, Jewish social research has not yet become the subject of intensive and specialized preoccupation of many scholars throughout the world. Even Jewish schools of higher learning have no chairs in Jewish sociology, economics, or political science comparable with the traditional professorships for Bible, Talmud, Medieval Jewish philosophy, and Hebrew language and literature. Within the very field of Jewish history, the traditional concentration on the ancient and Medieval periods has but slowly been giving way to research in modern Jewish history, particularly in its social aspects. On the other hand, general scholarship in the social sciences, even if cultivated as it now is by increasing phalanges of Jewish academic teachers,

1

has paid relatively scant attention to Jewish phases of these disciplines. It was a truly pioneering effort for the Conference on Jewish Social Studies from its inception to try to stimulate competent research in these novel areas. A small measure of its success may be gleaned from the respective essays submitted in this volume.

I

It has been said that the Conference and the journal came into being as a reaction to the Nazis' rise to power in Germany. This is only partially true. Long before 1933, I may testify, I had felt the need, and advocated the establishment, of a journal of this kind in the United States. During the years of my association with the Jewish Institute of Religion in 1926-30, I intensively negotiated on this subject with the late Drs. Stephen S. Wise and George A. Kohut. I submitted to them several memoranda, urging the foundation of a new organ for research in modern and contemporary Jewry. While these distinguished leaders and their associates evinced considerable interest in such a project, the Institute, then still a young growth, was fully preoccupied with its numerous other tasks connected with developing a training program for rabbis and teachers and its quest to influence the religious life of the Jewish community outside the range of the three religious divisions. The Great Depression of 1929 and after made financing of such a new program of research and publication wholly unrealistic. Yet even in the depths of the Depression I had often discussed the need of such a journal, for instance with Professor Koppel S. Pinson, then a youthful Associate Editor of the *Encyclopedia of Social Sciences* and subsequently an active collaborator and co-editor of our journal.

A decisive turn came in April 1933. I still vividly recall the morning on which the distinguished philosopher, Morris Raphael Cohen, appeared in my office at Columbia University to discuss with me what the American Jewish intelligentsia could do to counter-act the growing world-wide Nazi propaganda. We realized, of course, that major Jewish defense organizations had taken up the cudgels in the struggle against Nazism. However, we felt that beyond the day-to-day political actions, there was a need of more searching and far-ranging investigations about the "position of the Jew in the modern world." If, for one example, Mr. Goebbels, the Nazi propaganda minister, was shouting from the rooftops then and later that there were seventeen million American Jews who were in the vanguard of anti-German "warmongering" and the source of the main American attacks on Nazism and the Third Reich, it was clear to us that merely referring to any figure counted by the United States Census of Religious Bodies would not do. All informed persons knew that the figures underlying that census were often based upon "guesstimates," rather than on scientifically ascertainable facts. Professor Cohen and I decided on the spot that there was a need for a new scholarly organization which would attract theretofore Jewishly unaffiliated professionals and members of the academic community, and thus help to marshal the vast Jewish scholarly resources for the ascertainment of objective facts about Jewish life in this country and abroad.

Moreover, quite apart from correcting the misinformation spread by the Nazis, we believed that such precise and detailed data about Jewish life in the present and more recent past would in themselves be a vital contribution to Jewish culture and learning. These long-neglected tasks were to be undertaken by Jewish scholars in America, whether or not they were specializing in any aspect of Jewish affairs. On the contrary, we felt that, for instance, specialists in anthropology like Professor Franz Boas of Columbia or Professor Edward Sapir of Yale would be able to bring to bear some fruits of their great anthropological scholarship on the understanding of many hidden phases of Jewish life today and throughout history. Both of these men indeed joined our work; the former as a contributor of the first article in JEWISH SOCIAL STUDIES, the latter as one of the early Vice-Presidents of the organization.

Not unexpectedly, the work of organizing the new society progressed very slowly. Although Professor Cohen invested much time and energy in promoting the idea and enlisting active and interested co-workers, it took about three years before the new association received its name, Conference on Jewish Relations (later changed to Conference on Jewish Social Studies) and was formally incorporated.

The final step was made early in 1936 at a dinner meeting, presided over by Albert Einstein and addressed by Professors Cohen, Harold Laski, and myself. After the speeches, Henry Morgenthau, former U.S. Ambassador to Turkey, and father of the then U.S. Secretary of the Treasury, made an appeal for funds to the small group of some two-score leaders of the Jewish community assembled at the dinner. Slowly recovering from the Depression, that group responded generously, and through its contributions laid the financial foundation for the formal establishment of the Conference.

No sooner was the organization set up and formally incorporated in the State of New York in 1936, than we resumed the discussion on the need of a journal. Once again, I prepared a lengthy memorandum detailing its program, the financial possibilities, and, most importantly, the problems of securing competent and willing collaborators. Notwithstanding immense difficulties, the first group of editors and an Editorial Board were assembled and a number of articles secured. As a result, the first issue of JEWISH SOCIAL STUDIES saw the light of day in January 1939. It has since appeared regularly, and the full contents of the first twenty-five volumes of this publication may be gleaned from the *Cumulative Index,* prepared by Dr. Max M. Rothschild.

II

The Conference did not limit itself, however, to this publication. From the outset, it engaged in some research activities and held public symposia and conferences intended to open up new vistas for both modern Jewish scholarship and the management of Jewish affairs. Quite early, the Conference dispatched at its expense two younger scholars to Geneva. At that time, James MacDonald, serving as High Commissioner for Refugees at the League of Nations (later he was appointed by President Truman as the first American Ambassador to Israel), required considerable assistance in dealing with the complicated aspects of the Jewish refugee problem. Some work of the League of Nations in this area was subsequently aided by the facts and ideas presented to Mr. MacDonald by these younger scholars, Professor Oscar I. Janowsky and Melvin M. Fagen. The fruits of their research were also published, with the aid of the Conference, by the Oxford University Press in a volume entitled, *International Aspects of German Racial Policies* (New York, 1937).

Refugee adjustment in this country likewise engaged the attention of the Conference. In general, the after-effects of the Great Depression caused long-lasting, widespread unemployment, and it was extremely difficult for Jewish refugees to secure paid work. Among other projects, the Conference succeeded in assembling an almost complete list of Jewish physicians practicing in this country, together with their backgrounds and qualifications. It was able on the basis of this research to present to the National Refugee Service a large list of American cities and towns with populations of over 10,000 which at that time had no Jewish doctors, and where some of the new arrivals could find work without exacerbating the then tense relations with non-Jewish neighbors. These and other data assembled by the Conference were also to help combat the extensive anti-Jewish discrimination in admission to medical schools. A distinct aspect of this problem was the paucity of opportunities for Jewish doctors to secure residencies in preparation for specialization in one or another branch of medicine. The situation has changed since; but in the 1930 and early 1940s, there was a genuine threat that even Jews able to overcome the serious difficulties in obtaining training for general practice would be almost totally barred from becoming specialists, some of whom have always given luster to the entire profession. The Conference began by reviewing the existing facilities for specialized training at Jewish-sponsored hospitals, and urged the Jewish communities to enlarge these facilities for future use. A brief summary of these findings was presented by a Subcommittee of the Conference in its report on "Facilities of Jewish Hospitals for Specialized Training," JEWISH SOCIAL STUDIES, vol. iii, no. 4 (October 1941), pp. 375-86.

Medicine was, of course, but one of many occupations from which both new arrivals and older Americans could earn a living. The Conference also made the first study of Jewish lawyers in the City of New York. A brief study to this effect, summarized by Melvin

M. Fagen under the title, "The Status of Jewish Lawyers in New York City," in JEWISH SOCIAL STUDIES, vol. 1, no. 1 (January 1939), pp. 73-104, was merely intended to open up the problem rather than furnish definitive answers. Unfortunately, because of the intervening Second World War and other reasons, this study could not be continued, and hence the more comprehensive country-wide investigation, to be periodically repeated, has remained a mere desideratum.

Finally, in this area, the Conference was trying to look ahead toward what occupational opportunities might be expected to be available to the growing Jewish youth in future years. A conference of experts in economic trends, vocational guidance, and related fields contributed much to the clarification of objectives for such research and guidance. As a result, under the stimulus of the Conference, a Jewish Occupational Council was founded, whose task was to assemble the necessary data and communicate the fruits of its investigations to various schools and agencies for use in guiding candidates in search of suitable careers. Needless to say, the situation here, too, has changed radically, and until the recent recession our society had been suffering more from shortages of skilled labor than of qualified personnel unable to find work.

III

Economic discrimination was but a phase of general antisemitism. Despite the availability of an enormous literature, the fundamental aspects of the psychology, sociology, and even history of antisemitism had theretofore never been examined in full and illuminating detail. The Conference on Jewish Social Studies has always been concerned with all aspects of anti-Jewish prejudice. In some of its public meetings, it explored the legal facets of the Nuremberg Laws adopted by the Nazis in 1935 and their possible bearing on the legislation in one or another American state. A very stimulating Conference on the history of antisemitism, held under the auspices of the Conference on Jewish Relations, resulted in a fine volume of *Essays on Antisemitism,* edited by Koppel S. Pinson and re-edited by him several years later in an enlarged and revised edition. A more recent Conference on Antisemitism in the Post-War Era, however, brought about the publication of four essays by Professors Paul Tillich, A. Roy Eckardt, Arieh Tartakower, and Melvin Tumin in JEWISH SOCIAL STUDIES, vol. xxxiii, no. 4 (October 1971) pp. 253-316.

Population studies were another area of considerable interest to the Conference leadership. After arranging for surveys of a number of Jewish communities which, in many ways, were fairly representative of the Jewish settlements in various parts of the country and in larger or smaller urban centers, the Conference published a summary volume of *Jewish Population Studies,* edited by Professor Sophia M. Robison in collaboration with Dr. Joshua Starr. Here was not only a pioneering collection of detailed and reliable facts concerning these particular communities, but also a thorough airing of both the theory and practice of methods employed in Jewish demographic research. I am happy to say that these new approaches have proved very fruitful in the numerous local surveys conducted since by various communities, in some of which Professor Robison and other Conference associates have often taken an active part.

Still dissatisfied with the progress in this field, the Conference, in cooperation with the American Jewish Committee and the Council of Jewish Federation and Welfare Funds, called together in December, 1945 a conference devoted to Jewish demography in this country. As a result there emerged an Office for Jewish Population Research with membership recruited from almost all important national Jewish organizations. It was to coordinate the divergent efforts in ascertaining facts pertaining to the size and composition of the Jewish population. Because of these basic divergences, even the existing local surveys, sometimes covering the same communities in different years, are not completely comparable and hence do not shed sufficient light on important trends in the Jewish community such as rising or declining birth and death rates, the ratio of mixed marriages, the age and sex distribution, and so forth. However, for reasons beyond the control of the Conference, the Office for Jewish Population Research has not developed as planned. Yet work along these lines still is a major desideratum on the agenda of the Jewish community in America.

IV

Understandably, after the Second World War the Conference turned much of its attention to the problems of the reconstruction of European Jewry and to healing the wounds inflicted upon the Jewish community and culture by the Nazi barbarians. In pursuing its primary scholarly objectives, the Conference organized a Commission for European Jewish Cultural Reconstruction, consisting of some of the most distinguished Jewish scholars in this country, to investigate the changes wrought in Jewish culture by the Second World War. The Commission prepared a number of studies surveying the Jewish cultural treasures preserved in libraries, museums, and archives, Jewish educational institutions, the Jewish press, and the Jewish publishing firms which had existed in Nazi-occupied Europe before the War. On the basis of these studies, which appeared as supplements to our quarterly, we could not only demonstrate the vast and irretrievable losses suffered by the world Jewish community, but also place in the hands of the various military administrations in Germany reliable reference works for whatever was still salvageable of that millennial heritage.

Since immediately after the War there was an imminent danger that the remaining cultural treasures in private and public possession would be further destroyed or at least vanish from sight, the Commission organized in 1947 a new group, Jewish Cultural Reconstruction, Inc., of which the major Jewish national and international organizations became active members. In protracted negotiations with the State Department, the military occupation forces, and the Allied governments, the JCR persuaded the United States Military Government in the American Zone in Germany to issue a decree ordering all military personnel to deliver Jewish cultural objects wherever found to a new central depot established in Offenbach. At one time, that depot included a collection of one and a half million books and a multitude of Jewish art and ceremonial objects. According to an Inter-Allied agreement, cultural objects of identifiable provenance had to be returned to the respective countries of origin. But there still remained approximately half a million books, some seven thousand ceremonial objects, eleven hundred Scrolls of the Law, and so forth whose origin was uncertain and which could either be returned to their owners or their heirs, later to be verified, or else be used for the cultural upbuilding of the Jewish communities in Israel and other rising centers of Jewish life.

Just at the point when the JCR was supposed to be appointed the trusteeship corporation representing the Jewish people in the American Military Zone in Germany and entrusted with the salvage and distribution of that Jewish cultural property, the important organizations constituting its membership decided that the same general principles relating to the restoration and reconstruction of world Jewry ought to apply to Jewish property other than cultural as well. By general agreement, therefore, a new organization, called the Jewish Restitution Successor Organization, was called into existence. It basically had the same national and international membership as the JCR, but it engaged in a broader action of recapturing as much as possible of Jewish property for the benefit of the Jewish people at large. In that organization, the Jewish Agency for Palestine (subsequently, the Jewish Agency for Israel) and the American Jewish Joint Distribution Committee (JDC) became responsible for the salvage of non-cultural property, whereas Jewish Cultural Reconstruction, Inc., remained the agent of rescue and redistribution of the cultural treasures saved from the Holocaust. The dramatic story of this recapture of much of the irreplaceable heritage of many centuries has never yet been told in detail. However, it is one of the noteworthy chapters of the work initiated by the Conference on Jewish Social Studies, the ongoing results of which are still being felt today. As a matter of fact, it might not be too venturesome to suggest the following organizational genealogy: (1) Commission on Jewish Cultural Reconstruction; (2) Jewish Cultural Reconstruction, Inc.; (3) Jewish Restitution Successor Organization, Inc.; (4) Conference on Jewish Material Claims Against Germany; (5) Memorial Foundation for Jewish Culture.

Leaving this area of combined research and practical work, one other undertaking of the Conference ought to be mentioned. Jewish scholarship the world over has long been suffering from the growing diffusion of publications by both Jews and non-Jews in the vast variety of areas relating to Jewish life, past and present. Even specialists sometimes find it difficult not to overlook significant research done in their own fields by scholars working in different lands and publishing their writings in general organs in a variety of languages. A good bibliography of Jewish social studies, we felt, would not only prevent duplication of effort, but would also assist many scholars— both beginners and more advanced students—to engage in Jewish social research with fewer handicaps. As a sample of such an undertaking, I have personally devoted some two years of my life to preparing a bibliography of this kind for the years 1938-39. Although not unprepared for it, I was amazed by the richness, variegated nature, and high quality of the Jews' intellectual creativity in many communities which subsequently suffered destruction. It was a mere coincidence that this bibliography, which first appeared in JEWISH SOCIAL STUDIES, vol. iii, nos. 3 and 4 (July-October 1945), pp. 305-388, 481-605, and was subsequently reprinted with many additions in a separate volume, became a monument for European Jewish cultural effervescence on the eve of the Great Holocaust, which also marked the end of the great European epoch in Jewish history. Our hopes, that such current bibliographies would be continued on a more or less permanent basis, have thus far, however, not been fulfilled.

V

These examples of unfinished items on the agenda of the Conference and the community at large can easily be multiplied. Nonetheless, looking back upon three and a half decades of achievement, the Conference and its journal may derive much satisfaction from their manifold accomplishments. If some of the work initiated and set in motion was not always continued because of lack of communal response, it still stands out as a clarion call to further efforts. The studies selected for this volume may serve as an inkling of the type of Jewish social research which ought to prove of great interest to scholars, students, and intelligent layman alike, and which, I hope, will be cultivated and expanded ever more fruitfully in the fourth and fifth decades of our journal's publication.

EDITORS' PREFACE

Philosophies of Jewish History

The broad lines of interpretation of Jewish history have rarely been presented and analyzed by competent modern scholars who are not specialists in the field. An exception is the essay by Morris Raphael Cohen (1880–1947). A "Litvak" of White Russian birth and orthodox background, Cohen came to the United States as a youth, to become Professor of Philosophy at the College of the City of New York (1912-1938), a rare feat at the time.

At City College, Cohen was known for his sceptical views on Jewish continuity, attitudes typical of Jewish academicians in those days. Stories circulated of his denial of the existence of a Jewish problem. However, with the coming of Hitler to power, Cohen became interested in the struggle against antisemitism, and particularly in the role that science and scholarship could play in that battle. This eventually led to the establishment of the Conference on Jewish Relations, now the Conference on Jewish Social Studies.

Cohen's article reprinted here not only offers an interesting approach to the subject, but is also significant as a late 1930s credo of a perceptive and critical scholar, very much at home both in the secular culture of the university and in Jewish life. The religious

13

interpretation of history, Cohen holds, eschews nationalism. He traces its beginnings to the Jewish people's belief in responsibility before God, in punishment for transgressions, and in the promise of universal messianic peace. He believes that these prophetic and pharisaic conceptions of history endowed the travail of the Jewish people with a universal meaning: the expiation of its sin would make possible the inauguration of the messianic days.

Cohen briefly traces attempts to adjust the philosophy of history to the prevailing views in the environing societies. He sketches the literary approaches of Zunz, Geiger, and Frankel, who urged that the religious conception of history be supplemented by western methods and learning. His coverage of autonomism is terse, but he is more explicit in his estimate of political interpretations. He argues that the relatively brief period of Jewish experience with statehood and Judaism's emphasis on religious autonomy rather than political independence make it difficult to apply political factors to Jewish history. For Cohen, independent peoplehood is not the "supreme good," and, without criticizing Zionist aims or activities, he restates the emancipationist position, which despite the German "reversion to medieval barbarism," he views as still valid. After a lengthy evaluation of the "geographic" interpretation and a critique of economic and Marxist views, Cohen advocates a pluralistic approach in the search for solutions to mankind's problems.

In this essay, Cohen, for most of his life a liberal anti-nationalist and secularist-culturist, emerges as a neo-emancipationist non-Zionist.

An eminent figure, widely respected in the academic world, and one of the most dynamic and influential teachers of philosophy of his time, MORRIS RAPHAEL COHEN was the first President of the Conference on Jewish Relations and a founding Editor of JEWISH SOCIAL STUDIES. Fittingly, this article, one of Professor Cohen's few contributions to Jewish learning, appeared in the first issue of the journal.

Cohen's numerous works include: *Reason and Nature: Studies in the Philosophy of Law; The Faith of a Liberal; Reflections of a Won-*

dering Jew; and his autobiography, *A Dreamer's Journey.* His biography, *Portrait of a Philosopher: Morris R. Cohen in Life and Letters*, has been written by his daughter, Lenora Cohen Rosenfield. In 1951, the Conference on Jewish Relations published a tribute to him, *Freedom and Reason: Studies in Philosophy and Jewish Culture in Memory of Morris Raphael Cohen.*

Philosophies of Jewish History

by Morris R. Cohen

That a knowledge of the past is necessary for an understanding of the present and as a guide to the future, has now become a maxim that needs no defense or even reiteration. Rather is it important for clarity's sake to consider carefully its limitations, as a great legal historian has indicated.[1] For if social conditions do change with time, history can at best be a necessary but not a sufficient condition for an adequate solution of contemporary problems. This is true quite apart from the fact that it is always difficult to get at the exact course of past events, and hence our actual knowledge of the past is always fragmentary and seldom free from unverifiable guesswork. Unless men's beliefs have nothing to do with their conduct, however, prevailing views as to the course of history are an integral part of the contemporary social scene. Indeed, works of history may throw more light on the period in which they were written than on the era they profess to describe.

Such works as those of Flint, Paul Barth, Fueter, Gooch, and Croce, have indicated how conceptions of history are molded by prevailing philosophies, and Paul Janet[2] has shown how the interpretation of a single event, namely the French Revolution, has varied according to the different outlooks of the various writers on that theme. Despite the vast amount that has been written about the sufferings, achieve-

Reprinted from JEWISH SOCIAL STUDIES, Volume I, 1939

ments, and contributions of the Jews, however, we have not as yet, so far as I know, any adequate systematic survey of the different philosophies or modes of interpreting the general meaning of their history and of the principal events in it. Such a survey would certainly throw light on the various schools of thought that are concerned with the contemporary problems of the Jewish people. The hope of stimulating more thorough study along this line has suggested the following reflections.

Professor Baron has elaborated the point that the Jewish religion has progressively turned to historical explanations of its ritual or cultus.[3] Without subscribing to any sharp distinction between history and nature, which would make the former unnatural or supernatural, and passing over such questions as whether the Deuteronomic explanation of the Sabbath as a commemoration of the Exodus (Deut. 5:15) is not of a more historical character than the later cosmologic one (Gen. 2:3), we may in the main agree with Professor Baron's thesis. Certainly not only biblical but all Hebrew literature is dominated by reference to certain events like the Exodus from Egypt, the Davidic kingdom, the destruction of the temple, and the dispersion among the nations. We may add that this emphasis on historicity has also been a dominant note in Christianity since St. Augustine realized that a religion that aims to organize the life of a human society, needs concrete images or stories and not merely an abstract doctrine for philosophers in the manner of neo-Platonism.

It is well, however, to note in this connection that there have been currents, in Jewish thought as elsewhere, which have tended to minimize the importance of the actual course of temporal events. We see this in the Book of Ecclesiastes, in the allegoric exegesis of the Bible which begins with Philo, and in the course of qabbalistic speculation. Indeed, one may maintain that rabbinic thought as a whole was predominantly unfavorable to genuine historical studies. In the course of more than seventeen centuries a vast mass of impressive legends and homilies was produced but no major work of history. Contrasted with the great epics of the Jewish people, in the Bible, Josephus, or Graetz, the total amount of genuine historical work contributed by talmudic Judaism previous to the nineteenth century seems pitiably small.[4] We must, however, distinguish between actual historical writings and philosophies or general interpretations of the course of human events.[5] Our concern is only with the latter.

Unhistorical Philosophies of Life

The idea of progress, including the wider idea that human events take place according to some all-embracing design or law, has taken such a hold on Western thought that we forget the relative infrequency with which this view was held before the eighteenth century. While old men often sigh for the good old days and younger folk look more to the future, most people do not think that everything they and others do is the necessary unfolding of a definite world plan. The seasons come and go, men are born and struggle and die, but the sea of human events remains the same despite the changing waves. This widespread attitude found philosophic expression in various forms of Hindu and Greek theories of an eternal return, and these doctrines were revived in recent times by Nietzsche, by Anatole France in the concluding paragraphs of his *Penguin Island,* and by Bertrand Russell in the conclusion to his famous essay, entitled *A Free Man's Worship.* History has no real significance; for in the succession of the ages nothing is permanently achieved. Various forms succeed each other, but after a certain period the whole process starts all over again. This is particularly true of philosophies like the Epicurean, in which there are no constants or invariants with which to weave the fortuitous combinations of atoms into an objective pattern embracing the whole of time. The writer or writers of Ecclesiastes apparently were influenced directly or indirectly by these Hellenistic views. All is vanity because there is no goal. Things come and go, but in the end there is no real difference. In any case, as in the Book of Job, there is no inclination to inquire whether the history of the Jews or of any other people offers any guidance or direction in the conduct or understanding of life. Koheleth, King of Jerusalem, is an imaginary type, not an historical figure.

The recent tendency to see everywhere man's creative or myth-making activity has been most elaborately expressed by a gifted but ill-fated German Jew, Theodor Lessing, whose chief work, *Geschichte als Sinngebung des Sinnlosen,* has gone through four editions. In the

United States, with its tendency to emphasize the practical and prospective at the expense of the contemplative and retrospective, Jews are not the only ones who share the sentiment (although they may hesitate at the language) of Henry Ford, that "history is bunk." And no candid student will deny that a good deal of what passes as authentic history deserves that appellation.

At the other extreme there are the spiritualistic philosophies which exalt mind or spirit to an unchangeable essence which can have no genuine commerce with the altogether illusory or contaminating realm of matter and flesh. Thus Philo Judaeus, without going as far as Hindu philosophies in denying any significance at all to what happens on our earth—that would prevent insistence on the priority of Moses to Plato—is primarily concerned with eternal truths about the soul rather than with the actual trials of Israel through the ages preceding his own. Philo's allegoric interpretation does not deny the existence of the events in the Pentateuch, but it minimizes their importance by treating them as esoteric expressions for a non-empirical psychology. Philo himself was, to be sure, devoted to the interests of his people, and his historical accounts, such as of his mission to Rome, have a good deal of vividness in them. In his philosophy, however, all national interests, such as prosperity or political power or independence seem altogether irrelevant. It has sometimes been alleged that Philo stands outside of the main current of Jewish thought. But without trying to indicate here the extent to which elements of Philo's version of Platonism are present in talmudic and later Hebrew philosophy (particularly in Ibn Gabirol), we may readily point to his unquestioned influence on the emanational mysticism of the qabbala and on doctrines of the ecstatic union of the soul and God. And these have certainly been powerful elements in Jewish thought throughout the centuries, by no means confined to the relatively modern hasidic sect. Of course, those who have been devoted to the qabbala, have, like other mystics, taken an interest in mundane affairs and have even, since the days of Isaac Luria, tried to use it as a means not only for computing but actually bringing about the advent of the messiah. Some have even tried to use it for less lofty purposes (as can be seen in such works as the *Qab ha-Yashar*). But even in the purest form of qabbalistic thought there is no interest in, or attempt to explain, the career of Israel as a people in various lands and ages. Nor indeed can there be any bridge between its arbitrary procedure and such attempts at temporal history as can claim any scientific or objective validity.

While talmudic thought has a great deal in common with the qabbala—many teachers and expounders of the Law adhered to both —it is not so consistently unhistorical. Broadly speaking it sees no significance and has no interest in the struggle between nations other than Jews.[6] And as for the latter, the only important events are those which can be used to illustrate or expound the Law. But preoccupation with the conduct of an actual people and a reverence for the Bible which contains so much spirited history, make it impossible utterly to disregard the actual course of temporal events.

The Orthodox Religious Interpretation

Because of the wide dispersion of the Jews throughout the world and the absence of any central authority to determine what is and what is not Judaism, there is a wide variation of beliefs even among those who call themselves orthodox Jews. For our limited purpose, however, we may overlook these differences and fix our attention on the main stream of tradition, beginning with the Bible, the Talmud, and the Midrashim, and terminating in the later rabbinic works, such as the commentaries of Rashi, the *Mishneh Torah* of Maimonides and Joseph Karo's *Shulhan Arukh*. The majority of Jews still accept this tradition as authoritative, and the conception or conceptions of history found in this literature may properly be called orthodox.

If we recognize that the Bible is not a single book but that which remains of the entire literature of the Hebrews, produced during a single period of over eight centuries, we must not expect to find in it a single unitary point of view as to history. Three main strands, however, may be clearly distinguished within it. There is, first, the great epic of the Jews from creation to the united monarchy—an epic which has made the Bible a great work of literature as well as a model for historical writing. Its central theme is the origin and adventures of the "chosen people," a people that despite sufferings in Egypt, wanderings in the desert, and misfortunes in the promised land, nevertheless succeeded in overcoming its enemies, establishing a victorious kingdom, and dominating its neighbors such as Edom. Although Yahweh is often enough invoked, the history is distinctly temporal, often military, and predominantly nationalistic. It celebrates, in such songs as those of Miriam and Deborah or the oracles of Balaam, the triumph of the Israelitish people.

Prophetic literature however, strikes a different note. It glorifies the justice, love or grandeur of Yahweh and justifies the terrible calamities of the Jewish people as a proper punishment for infidelity and unrighteousness.[7] The hope of the future, the messianic kingdom of peace is one for all humanity, even though its central light will come from Zion. Egypt and Assyria, the oppressors of Israel, are also children of the one true God (Isa. 19:24).

To these two points of view is added that of the later editors, who wrote at a time when the Jews had lost their independence and were subject to foreign powers. In their day priests rather than kings were the heads of the Jewish community. To them the history of the Jews was the history of the cultus, especially the temple ritual. This shows itself most characteristically in the treatment of the reign of Jeroboam II. The older history had recorded that Israel had recovered its old dominions and enjoyed a period of great prosperity following the relief from the oppression of the Arameans. But the final editor of the second Book of Kings is slightly interested in such matters. What is of primary importance to him is the fact that Jeroboam continued to allow the worship of the two golden "calves" at Dan and Bethel.

The legal-religious phase of biblical history dominated the thought of Pharisaism, from which the orthodox Judaism of today directly stems. In this connection, it is significant to note the indifference of talmudic literature to the national Maccabean rulers. The festival of Hanukkah celebrates the miracle of the cruse of oil that kept on burning after the cleansing of the temple. The martyrs of the Syrian persecution and the priest Mattathiah are remembered for their resistance to those who wished to pervert the true worship of God. But the subsequent nationalist movement, which led to the liberation of the Jews from foreign rule, receives little commendation. More regard is paid to the rebuilding of the temple by the Idumean, Herod. There is, similarly, little regard for the national uprising under Bar Kochba, although it had the support of Akiba.[8]

Talmudic Judaism is centered around the Law, which existed even before creation and was given to Abraham personally and to all the Jews through Moses on Mt. Sinai. According to one of the leading talmudic scholars of to-day, "the Law is not a means but an end in itself."[9] David is viewed as a student of the Law who prepared for the building of the temple in accordance with its provisions. Even soldiers like Joab and his cousin Amasa are regarded as occupying themselves with the study of the Torah.[10] Not the destruction of the commonwealth but the suspension of the temple service is the crucial fact of our history. The various persecutions of the Jews under Hadrian and others, by which attempts were made to prevent them from living according to their religion, form the kernel of a tradition which makes our subsequent history a long martyrology. Rabbinic Judaism did produce some important historical documents such as Sherira's account of the schools in which the oral law was developed. Its main energy, however, has been devoted to legal and homiletic considerations, and the course of temporal events has been regarded as of little significance. Thus scant attention is given to the social changes effected by the shifts of Jewish centers from Palestine to Babylon and from Babylon to Africa and Spain, or by the turn from agricultural and industrial to commercial life. After all, "this world is but a corridor to the world to come." Perhaps the best illustration of the characteristic attitude to secular history on the part of rabbinic Judaism is found in David Gans' apology for writing on secular affairs and in his effort to prove that it is not against the Law to read such writings on the Sabbath. In this he is faithful to the talmudic tradition which centers on the verse of Isaiah (43:18): "Remember not former things nor pay heed to things long past."[11] When God's chosen people are continually harassed and persecuted and His enemies rule the world, how else can we keep the faith if we do not systematically minimize the importance of earthly affairs?

Yet the explanation of the suffering of the faithful presents a problem which must be faced by any religious philosophy of history. In the earliest portions of the Bible the explanation is very simple. When Yahweh is angry because His people have neglected Him, He turns His face away from them and they become helpless before their enemies. Sometimes He sends plagues or famines. According to this view, the destruction of the Northern Kingdom is due to the idolatry at Dan and Bethel, and idolatry is likewise the explanation for the destruction of the Kingdom of Judea and of the temple. The prophets, beginning with Amos and Micah, emphasized the neglect of social righteousness as a reason for the imminent destruction of the Kingdom; and the talmudic sages attribute the destruction of the second temple to fraternal enmity, i.e., to an excessive tendency to civil strife.

The view that the misfortunes of the Jews are attributable to some form of religious neglect is still very much alive today. Not long ago I received a letter from a rabbi in which he pointed to the suffering of the German Jews since the advent of Hitler as God's punishment for the Reform movement and for the general "assimilationist" tendencies of the German Jews.

The view which regards all suffering as directly due to sin involves too many difficulties, however, to be universally accepted. Jewish history itself cannot overlook the fact that the righteous, too, suffer; and they who oppress the saints of Israel seem to prosper. The Psalms are full of this complaint. In the Book of Job, the traditional view which makes suffering naught but the consequence of sin is categorically rejected, and God pronounces judgment against Job's friends who cling to that view. The Book of Job itself, as indicated before, is not directly concerned with the problem of the suffering of the Jews as a people. It does, however, suggest two answers which have been incorporated into the orthodox conception of Jewish history.

The first is that suffering may be merely temporary and a trial of faith. This is, after all, but a modified form of the older view held by the prophets, to wit, that since the Jews as the chosen people stand in a peculiar relation to God they must be judged by a higher standard (Amos 3:2). The high priest is subject to more laws and therefore to more punishment; but such punishment is only an indication of a higher position in the eyes of God. From this point of view there is an easy transition to the view found in the poems on the suffering servant of God, in Deutero-Isaiah. Israel suffers not for its own sins but for the sins of humanity, just as the pain of the entire body may be concentrated in a sensitive organ. Thus all humanity is purified and its sins atoned for by the sufferings which the Jewish people willingly bear to glorify God's name. And by this means will Zion be exalted and all the nations of the earth be blessed.

This view of vicarious suffering, which plays such an important role in Christianity and which forms an integral part of Reform Judaism's conception of the world-mission of Israel, is a view which cannot be universally accepted so long as our ordinary disinclination to suffer for others or cherish those who wrong us asserts itself. There is, therefore, among orthodox Jews, as among other religious people, great reliance upon a different theory of suffering, expounded dramatically in the Book of Job in God's answer in the whirlwind. Human intelligence is too limited to grasp God's entire plan. Who are we to pass judgment on the whole cosmic drama? We must accept our fate and trust God. Logically the latter view would give us no interpretation of any specific event in history. But no people have ever been ruled entirely by the logical development of a single doctrine. In fact, therefore, rabbinic Judaism relies on different sources for the interpretation of specific events of Jewish history, invoking after all the authority of revelation and tradition. While the qabbalists try to penetrate into the plan of the Almighty so as to predict the time of the coming of the messianic age, the stricted talmudists are satisfied to have it come in God's good time, meanwhile making Israel worthy by prayer, fasting, good deeds, and the study of the Law (Sanh. 97b).

Few Jewish historians of recent generations have escaped the influence of the modern spirit, which minimizes, if it does not avoid, the biblical miracles, and which regards worldly affairs as worthy of interest. Nevertheless, the orthodox religious interpretation, with its emphasis on religious fidelity, martyrdom, and the superiority of the Jews to idol-worshipers, has influenced the works not only of conservatives like Graetz, Marx, and Margolis, but also of those who, like Dubnow and Zinberg, are avowedly modern and sociological in their approach. This is due largely to the nature of the source materials at the disposal of the historians up to recently,[12] and also to the cumulative force which the traditional interpretation has acquired through the ages. It must be admitted that some of the vivid accounts of the sufferings of the Jews because of their religion, found in such chronicles as the *Emeq ha-Bakhah* of Joseph ben Joshua Hacohen, are most impressive. Also, despite its other-worldliness, or perhaps because of it, the orthodox view of Jewish history has proved the most

powerful factor in disciplining the Jewish people and enabling them
to weather the fearful storms which have pursued them through the
ages. For it provides the Jews not only with a hope for divine restoration but also with a sustaining pride in being the favorites of God—
the only people to serve the one true God while all the other peoples
are sunk in the mud of ignorance and idolatry. But few of the orthodox consider whether this pride is not a source of resentment on the
part of other peoples, and whether it is justified in the forum of historical truth. Was the Greek and Roman worship of idols really so
different from the respect of the Jews for the *sacra* of their own
religion? The absence of statuary or graven images is an artistic loss.
It reduces the number of religious symbols. But does it of itself prove
a superior conception of God's righteousness in human history?

As to technical methods, the difference between the orthodox and
the more modern Jewish historians consists not only in the difference
in attitude towards the miraculous events recorded in the Bible but
also in the different approach towards supplementing our scant material in regard to the period following the return from the Exile.
While the modernists try to interpret the events on the basis of
analogies in general political and international relations, orthodox
historians like Javetz try to read these events in the light of talmudic
traditions. But even Javetz, in the arrangements of his materials, has
not altogether escaped modernism.

The Philosophy of History in Modernistic Judaism

By modernistic Judaism I wish to denote the general movement to
modify the old customs, ritual law, and the beliefs or dogmas on which
they are based, to the end that they may be better adapted to the
mental and material conditions of modern or Western civilization. It
thus includes Reform Judaism in Germany and the United States, the
Liberal Judaism of men like Israel Abrahams and Claude Montefiore
in England, as well as the Haskalah or Enlightenment of eastern
Europe. It is often regarded as the outcome of Jewish emancipation,
but it might be viewed more broadly as the consequence of the
anterior industrial revolution and the resulting expansion of European
commerce, which created openings for Jewish enterprise. When Jews

came into greater contact with Western civilization it became more difficult for them to regard all non-Jewish learning as entirely heathenish. Even before the time of Moses Mendelssohn, the need for bringing Western learning into Jewish life, "the beauty of Japhet into the tents of Shem," was felt even in eastern Europe. Such a pillar of orthodoxy as Elijah the Gaon of Vilna encouraged the study of geometry and other sciences.[13] As a religious movement, however, Reform and Liberal Judaism went much further. Accepting the modern idea of progress and evolutionary history, Reform Judaism broke with the dogma of the immutability of the Jewish Law, at any rate, of the ritual part of it. Although it rejects the use of miraculous intervention it remains, however, a religious interpretation of history, maintaining that there is a divine direction for human affairs in which a special role or mission is assigned to the Jewish people.[14] Naturally, the representatives of Reform Judaism in western Europe and the United States, enjoying greater opportunities for education along Western lines, were more influenced by the methods of critical historiography prevailing in nineteenth-century European universities.

France, as the first country to emancipate the Jews and to give them full rights as citizens, produced the first essay on Hebrew history from the point of view of the French Revolution, *La loi de Moïse* (1822) by the French half-Jew, Joseph Salvador. The humanistic and rationalistic writers of the eighteenth century were, with a few exceptions like Toland, hostile to orthodox Judaism because of the latter's claim to a privileged position in regard to true religion, based on special revelation. Moreover, the French *philosophes* like Voltaire saw in the priestly legislation of the Old Testament the antecedents of the Christian church with its intolerance of new learning and with its persecution of free thought. Mendelssohn had tried to meet this point by representing Judaism as a religion free from all dogmas and thus identical with what was then called natural religion. But this attempt failed to convince men like Kant. Indeed in his effort to represent Judaism as free from dogmas Mendelssohn so stressed the restricted or national character of the Torah as a system of laws for Jews only ("an inheritance of the house of Jacob") that the philosophers of the Enlightenment remained convinced that Judaism was not a religion at all but only a ritual or legal system particular to the

Jews. True religion they held must appeal to the universal sense of truth and morality of all mankind.[15] The significance of Salvador's essay is that he made the Mosaic legal institutions his starting point and tried to show that they were all permeated with the principles of the French Revolution, liberty, equality and fraternity. He represented Hebrew legal prescriptions as founded on right reason and natural equity, in that they banished polytheism and the regime of castes, abolished slavery, and preserved the natural rights of the people. Moreover, the entire law was not merely inherited or imposed by force but was voluntarily received by the people in the form of a covenant at Mt. Sinai. By systematically minimizing the role of the priests in Israel, Salvador was able to present its commonwealth not as a priest-ridden theocracy but as a government by law (nomocracy), which is the essence of what Spinoza called democracy and Kant a republic. The history of Jewish persecutions was thus attributed to the efforts of the Christian clergy to fan the flames of bigoted hatred because the Jews denied the dogmas of Christianity and were thus dangerous in arousing free thought. In consonance with the positivistic tendency of the time, Salvador, apparently unfamiliar with the role of rationalistic and mystic doctrines in Judaism, represented the Hebrew religion as free from metaphysical dogmas and as entirely concerned with the ethical conduct of life.

This essay of Salvador, like his subsequent work on the Jews under Roman rule,[16] is not to be taken seriously from the point of view of critical historical scholarship. Like so many other French works on history, such as those of Bossuet, Lamartine, and Renan, it lets rhetoric or romance fill in the lack of adequate historical research. Its great merit, however, lay in the fact that it raised ideas which stirred men's minds. It not only helped to break down the hostility of the liberal philosophers of the eighteenth century but emphasized that element in Judaism which nineteenth-century biblical scholarship served only to re-enforce, namely the role of the prophets—not as the preachers of an established Law or as mere foretellers of the future, but as revolutionary innovators who stressed universal ideas of social justice as against mere adherence to national cultus. Reform Judaism adopted this interpretation of the role of the prophets in the history of Judaism. Indeed it may be said that the leading characteristic of

Reform Judaism is the setting of the ethical message of the prophets above the legal system as developed in the priestly code and in the Talmud.

The vitality of the point of view represented by Salvador can be seen in the essay on the Hebrew prophets by the accomplished scholar, James Darmesteter. Darmesteter regards the message of the prophets as the saving moral gospel for an age that can no longer accept any theological supernatural dogmas. When the theological elements in the Hebrew prophets and their references to miracles are interpreted as merely poetic discourse, they cannot impede the progress of science. The spirit of God thus becomes simply the spirit present whenever men are moved to heroic and philanthropic deeds. But Reform Judaism as a whole is much more theological. Indeed, its most outstanding recent figures, Hermann Cohen and Claude Montefiore, have a much more intense conviction of a personal deity than many of those who put orthodox ritual observances above theological doctrine.

There is a general impression today that the renaissance of Jewish historical literature in the nineteenth century, the essence of the *Wissenschaft des Judentums,* is the great achievement of the Jews in Germany. This is true, however, only if Germany is meant to include Galicia as well as Austria. Certainly the great pioneers in this direction were Krochmal and his younger friend, Rapoport.

It may seem to be violently straining a point to connect as pious and conforming a Jew as Nachman Krochmal with Reform Judaism in any way. Yet he certainly was the first to formulate the view of history centering around the mission of Israel. A more profound, if less clear, thinker than Mendelssohn, Krochmal realized much more than the latter how necessary it was to have a coherent view of the temporal development of the Jewish spirit or character in order to obtain an intelligent conception of Judaism. Inspired by Azariah de' Rossi, he saw that this could not be done without a critical attitude towards the talmudic sources and chronology. Critical or scientific history is impossible if, on arbitrary authority, we accept miracles or events which are contrary to those observable regularities of experience generally referred to as laws of nature. Hence no such history was possible when even a man as rational and methodical as Maimonides accepted the chronology which put the Persian kings from

Cyrus to Alexander of Macedon all within a period of thirty-four years, and saw no difficulty in Phineas, the grandson of Aaron, living hundreds of years. For expressing such sceptical views in the third part of his *Me'or Enayim,* de' Rossi was almost excommunicated in the sixteenth century. But Krochmal lived in a more propitious time and he worked out a more constructive theory for a Jewish religious history, which took account of natural laws. In his reaction against the superstitions of the *hasidim* and their belief in the magical powers of their *tsadiqim,* he fully accepted the faith of the Enlightenment in the natural course of events.

Assuming that every nation is endowed with a special genius of its own which determines its mission in history, Krochmal tried to show that the special genius and historical mission of Israel is to envisage, and to testify to the existence of, a God of truth and righteousness. Jewish history is interpreted as an effort in this direction, subject to the laws of natural growth, maturity, and decline. This is embodied in a cyclical view of history. The Jewish people have, by virtue of their devotion to an ideal or spiritual end, been able to survive periods of decay or destruction and to start on a new cycle of history. In the first of these cycles, the period of growth ends with the entrance into Palestine, the period of maturity with the death of Solomon, and the period of decay terminates with the murder of Gedaliah. In the second cycle, growth takes place from the beginning of the Babylonian Exile until the Macedonian rule. The period of maturity extends to the Roman conquest under Pompey. And the period of decline follows, until the development of the Mishnah ushers in a new period of growth in a new cycle.

The Hegelian origin of Krochmal's view of history has been maintained by Zunz and his followers and has been vehemently controverted by Dr. Rawidowicz, the latest and most careful editor of Krochmal's *Guide to the Perplexed of Our Time.* There can be no doubt that Krochmal was much impressed with Hegel's view of the nature of the absolute Spirit and its necessary unfolding. But passing over the fact that Hegel's lectures on the philosophy of history were published in 1837, some time after Krochmal's work was practically finished, careful reading shows that there is really nothing in any of Hegel's writings similar to the foregoing cyclical view. Hegel's Absolute expresses Himself in one people at a time, after which the latter cannot play any further role in world history, so that the Jews can have no history after the advent of Christianity. The three stages of growth, maturity, and decay have nothing in common with the trinity of thesis, antithesis, and synthesis. Some rather slight resemblance to Krochmal's cyclical view of history is to be found in Vico, but although the *Scienza nuova* was translated into German in 1821, it was so little known outside of Italy before Michelet's version of it[17] that it seems improbable that Krochmal was even indirectly familiar with, much less indebted to, the latter work. It seems, on the whole, that his specific views were original with him.

Krochmal was only a pioneer. The men who first showed what could actually be done in the way of critical Jewish history on an impressive scale were Rapoport and Leopold Zunz. Rapoport, especially in his biographies, showed how much scattered but available material could be organized into full life-like history. His conception of the mission of Israel is stated in his letter to Luzzatto: "God scattered us over the world . . . to be both pupil and teacher." Although rather conservative in religion, Zunz's principal work, *Gottesdienstliche Vorträge,* was a great support for the Reform movement by showing that the sermon in the vernacular was historically a part of the worship of the synagogue. Zunz did not consider that a general history of the Jews was possible for a period since the Bar Kochba rebellion, for the Jews have had no land and state of their own. "We need not be surprised if the Jewish Middle Ages can boast of no historian. A nation *in partibus* performs no feat. Her sufferings may produce chroniclers and poets, but no historian. Scientific faculty, yea even the necessity thereof, was wanting for historical investigation." Thus, not only the work of Zunz but also the works of Abraham Geiger, Zacharias Frankel, and the other luminaries of the *Wissenschaft des Judentums* were concerned for the most part with literary history, which is predominantly the history of the religious writings which have kept up the spirit of the synagogue, the centre of Jewish life in the diaspora.

It has been repeatedly charged, especially by Zionists, that the historical writings of the German Jews were purely archaeological, that they had no bearing on the problems and conditions of the Jews of their, much less our, time, because the writers lacked a philosophy of Jewish nationalism. To this, however, two answers have been made. The first is the one intimated above. Jewish sacred literature and the history of the Jewish religion still represent such a central interest to a majority of the Jewish people that they cannot be regarded as belonging entirely to the past. The second answer is to be found in the philosophy of Judaism worked out by the great Kantian, Hermann Cohen, who insists that nationalism is ruled out by prophetic Judaism as a religion of universal truth and righteousness. Nor is Cohen satisfied to put his case on the general philosophic ground that there cannot be such a thing as true religion or truth of any kind that is not valid for everyone. In his various writings, he insists on the universal elements not only in the prophets, but in the Psalms and even in talmudic literature.[18]

The insistence that religion must contain some doctrines or beliefs that can claim to be true is inconsistent with the view of liberals from Mendelssohn to Claude Montefiore that all religions express the same truth. Monotheism, Buddhistic atheism, Hindu polytheism, and Christian trinitarianism cannot all be equally true. If that were the case, what would be the need of having the Jews teach the world ethical monotheism?

There is something decidedly noble in the idea that Jewish history is the realization of the religion of the prophets, that the Jews have been chosen to be torn away from their land and scattered over the world to teach mankind by fidelity and suffering, the higher righteousness. But in the court of critical history, little evidence has been presented as to whether the Jews, by clinging to their separateness, have actually been teaching mankind. If ethical monotheism were the gospel, has not Islam insisted on it for over thirteen centuries?

In the light of recent terrific calamities it is easy, all too easy, to scorn Hermann Cohen's enthusiasm for pre-Nazi German culture and his hope that the messianic age will be realized in a League of Nations of the kind sketched in Kant's "Essay on Universal Peace." But an earthquake or a fire does not prove that what it destroys was valueless. Barbaric reactions against enlightenment do not disprove the supreme worth of the latter, although they do hit the blind faith in inevitable and continuous progress.

Despite his early talmudic training, Hermann Cohen was too much of an abstract and aprioristic a thinker to throw light on the specific and always more or less contingent events of history; and it may be claimed that few of his many enthusiastic Hebraic disciples have done so except on the basis of their own ideas. It is men like Israel Abrahams, equipped with more historical scholarship and imagination, that have made the liberal point of view fruitful for the understanding of the actualities of Jewish history.

Although modernistic or liberal Judaism is popularly supposed to have revolted against talmudic law, Abrahams has shown the continuity of talmudic with biblical law and even the extent to which early Christianity was indebted to Pharisaic Judaism. Like his friends Schechter and Montefiore, he has shown the untenability of the neo-Pauline view of romantic theologians that the Law is only a heavy burden. He has shown that not only in the Psalms, but throughout Hebrew literature, we have the expression of delight in the Law, and that the Law has been progressive and has thus enabled the Jews to adapt themselves to their various environments. It does not, however, seem in consonance with actual historical fact to deny that such progress, while adhering to the dogma of an immutable law, has been possible only through fictional interpretations which, as among other peoples, has led to a lot of unsavory casuistry, *e. g.,* the selling of all *hamets* on the eve of the Passover.

The charge that Reform Judaism has taken its conception of ancient Hebrew history from Protestant theologians, such as Wellhausen (an admired friend of Hermann Cohen), has been met by the observation that Jews, like other people, have always been influenced in periods of growth by foreign intellectual currents, and that this can be seen in the Bible, Philo, Saadia, Maimonides, and emphatically so in the writings of all the recent Jewish nationalists. A difficulty, however, with liberal or modernistic Judaism arises precisely from its too great reliance on history (taking refuge in the past). How can we justify progressive departures from traditional faith or practice on a philosophy which has no support for Judaism but its history, on the assumption that a knowledge of the past will breed loyalty to it? With all their interest in ethical monotheism, men like Montefiore and Cohen have, in fact, failed to develop any new support for the Jewish religion or for the claim that the Jews are in the possession of some supreme moral or religious wisdom to teach the world. Nor has progressive Judaism developed any rational criterion by which to judge which parts of the Torah may be disregarded as obsolete and for which parts we must be ready to suffer martyrdom. If the significance of the Sabbath is merely that of a day of rest and peace, why Saturday, rather than Sunday, and why not every fifth, rather than every seventh, day? Thus Reform Judaism presents the spectacle of a progressively retreating army that has no natural fortification behind which it can take a definite stand.

The Political Interpretation of Jewish History

When historians are monks or theologians, the periods they describe seem to be mainly concerned with religious ideas and practices. But when they are interested in affairs of state, history becomes political, i. e., concerned with forms of government, regional or party strife, dynastic changes, wars, and international relations. An amazingly large proportion of all Western historical writings has, up to recently, been the latter kind. Jewish thought has naturally been influenced by this fashion. It is urgent, if we really wish to understand the career of the Jewish people, that we should supplement our hitherto predominantly religious history with a knowledge of the secular life of our people through the ages. The invasion of Palestine, the establishment of the united Kingdom and its disruption, were not purely religious affairs. They were conditioned by the decline of the Egyptian power. David began as a vassal of King Achish of Gath, made a marriage alliance with the king of Geshur and began the alliance with Tyre. Solomon seems to have tried to come to terms with Egypt by another marriage, but failed, judging by the way the revolt of Edom and Israel was encouraged by the court of the Pharaoh—not to mention the later invasion by Sheshonk. The history of Israel, also, is unintelligible if we do not consider its relation with Tyre and Damascus. Omri seems to have made Israel a power by alliances with Tyre and some sort of commercial treaty with Damascus; and the revolt of Jehu and the prophetic opposition to the Omrides seems to have been a part of a nationalistic uprising (probably supported largely by the country people such as the Rechabites) against undue foreign influence in the cities, Samaria and Jezreel, just as the Maccabean revolts arose in small towns like Modin against the Hellenism of the large cities such as Jerusalem. The strong anti-Egyptian attitude in Deuteronomy may well be a reflection of the popular attitude immediately before and after the death of Josiah. In the second commonwealth, the rise of the Maccabeans was largely conditioned by Roman desire to break up the Seleucid empire. And the successors of Caesar for a time favored the Jews as a point of support against the Parthians. The friendly attitude to the Jews on the part of Cyrus was part of the general policy of building an empire with more internal peace than that of Assyria and Babylonia.

But while the political factor is thus indispensable for understanding the past as well as the present, an exclusively political view receives a peculiar challenge when applied to the history of the Jews. For not only have the Jews for the larger part of their career been scattered among the various nations without a state of their own, but even when they lived in Palestine they were only for a short period a politically united and independent people. The united monarchy under David and Solomon lasted little more than seventy years, and the same is true of the Hasmonean rule from the days of Simon Maccabeus to the time when his great-grandsons called in the Romans under Pompey to settle their civil war. Moreover, the development of prophetic and Pharisaic Judaism prevented ordinary political conceptions such as independence and extended dominion from receiving the attachment which moderns are apt to assume as the normal life of a people. For prophets like Amos not only exalt Yahweh as the god of all humanity, and obedience to His law as superior to allegiance to king, nation or country, but they are quite prepared to accept the complete destruction of Israel as leaving His glory untarnished.[19] Despite the fact that the Babylonians had destroyed the temple, ravaged Judea most horribly, and taken away its leading citizens, Jeremiah asked the exiles to pray for the welfare of the cities of their captors. And this has become a characteristic custom of orthodox Judaism to this day. In their prayers they invoke God's blessing on the rulers of their country wherever they are. In this connection it is well to note the hostility of the Pharisees to the national Maccabean kings. The Jews were willing to be governed in their political relations by some outside power like Persia or Rome, by Syrian or Egyptian Greeks, so long as the religious customs were unmolested. In fact, they preferred to be ruled by a Roman procurator rather than by the half-Jew Archelaus.

Politically minded historians, like those who regard Judaism as but a preparation for Christianity, have found it convenient to terminate Jewish history with the destruction of the temple in 70 C.E. or at any rate with the suppression of the Bar Kochba rebellion in 137 C.E. But tragic and significant as were these events from several points of view, they really do not denote any great *political* change. If political independence were the important consideration, the Jews lost it long before these dates. To be sure, Jerusalem ceased to be the Jewish centre after 70 C.E., but the rabbinical assembly at Jabneh and later in Galilee seems to have exerted the same kind of influence as was formerly exercised by the Sanhedrin. It must also be remembered that the Jews continued to be a major part of the population of Palestine and had a certain amount of self-government under their *nesi'im* or patriarchs (hereditary in the house of Hillel). Origen testifies to the quasi-royal dignity of these rulers. Even after Constantine made Christianity the religion of the empire and his successors actively persecuted Judaism, large multitudes of Jews continued to live in Palestine. We can see this in the Emperor Julian's plan to rebuild the temple or in the large support which the Jews gave to the Persians against Heracleius. Even centuries after the Moslem conquest, the Jews formed sufficiently large communities in Jerusalem and other Palestinian cities to be the object of special massacres by the Crusaders. Moreover, even in the Diaspora Jewish communities up to the middle of the eighteenth century generally enjoyed a certain amount of cultural autonomy. But although their fate has naturally depended upon the political conditions of the countries which they have inhabited, the orthodox majority of the Jews has been much more concerned about religious observances than about political issues. Thus their emancipation in western Europe and the United States was the result of a general movement of liberation rather than of any political organization of their own.

The mode of thought which attaches supreme importance to an

organized state is largely a consequence of the French Revolution and the philosophy of Hegel, which glorified the state as God on earth.[20] But Greek as well as Jewish history show how a people can be spiritually united by the possession of common traditions without a common territory or a national state of their own. Homeric and biblical literature may thus be of greater historical significance than the political organizations of their respective peoples.

Against the last suggestion we have the philosophy of those political Zionists who maintain that only in a Palestinian Jewish state can the Jews live a "normal" life. Under the influence of Western nationalism they assume that the perpetuation of the Jews as a separate and independent people is a supreme good to which everything must be subordinated.[21] The return to Erets Yisrael through messianic intervention has of course always been the hope of orthodox Judaism. Even to be buried in Palestinian soil has always been deemed a privilege by the pious. What distinguishes modern Zionism as founded by Herzl is its emphasis on political rather than the traditional religious motives. Many of its younger adherents are even antireligious. To regard the Jews merely as a religious sect is from the nationalist point of view anathema, the utter degradation to which Reform Judaism has led. From this point of view the great events in Jewish history are naturally the political ones: the establishment and the destruction of the kingdom of David, the return from the Babylonian exile, the restoration of Jewish independence by the later Maccabeans, the destruction of the second commonwealth by the Romans, the dispersion of the Jews, the emancipation from the restrictions of ghetto life, and finally the renaissance of political nationalism.

The Maccabeans are thus viewed by political Zionists as the great national heroes, although to as sympathetic an historian as George Foot Moore the methods by which Jonathan and Simon acquired the high priesthood seem unscrupulous.[22] Not only the rule of the Maccabean kings but the whole political history of the Jews in Palestine with its bloody and cruel civil strife, from the Benjamite war narrated in the Book of Judges, to the siege of Jerusalem under Titus, is hardly an especially inspiring story. Certainly, the prophets and talmudic sages took no pride in it. But hope and pride are stronger than memory and love of truth. Moreover, consistent adherents of the nationalist philosophy of history regard the emancipation as a calamity; for a regime of individual rights tends to weaken the communal bonds which held the Jews together in the ghetto. Thus, Dr. Weizmann, the official leader of Zionism, insists that the position of the emancipated Jew is more tragic than that of his oppressed brother,[23] and Mr. Leon Simon, one of the leaders of that movement in Great Britain, quotes with approval Ahad Ha-Am's preference for the condition of the "unutterably poor, persecuted, ignorant and degraded" Jews in tsarist Russia over the state of their emancipated brethren.[24] As an individual preference, it may have a certain nobility and one may admire its eloquent rhetoric. But the thesis that those Jews who prefer emancipation have no freedom or that they lack self-respect is certainly not the expression of an historical imagination or of adequate understanding. The fact is that the Western Jews as a body do prefer their condition of emancipation, and the main tide of migrating has been from the East to the West. Even in Russia, Poland, and Rumania large masses have indicated, whenever they were free to do so, a similar preference for Western ways of dress, occupation, language, education, recreation, and all the intellectual and material things that constitute Western culture.

The reason given by Weizmann and others in support of their view is that antisemitism is not wiped out by assimilation. The historic fact, however, is that antisemitism is not restricted to countries where the Jews have been emancipated. It has a past of over two thousand years. Nor is the recent reversion of Germany to medieval barbarism an argument against the value of emancipation, although it is a blow to those who try to cover the uncertainty of the human future with the dogma of inevitable progress. But, does Jewish or other history offer any support for the view that any political arrangement can free us from the uncertainty of human affairs?

It may prevent misunderstanding to insist that the foregoing is not intended as a critique of the Zionist practical program or even of its entire ideology, but only as a critical reflection on the political philosophy of history which is implicit in some of its forms. It is only fair to add that, as a practical movement, the Zionist organization has found its strongest support among the unemancipated. Exception of course has to be made for extreme orthodox groups like the Agudath Israel, which cannot identify themselves with a movement that does not put the Torah to the forefront and the leaders of which, like Herzl, Nordau, Zangwill[24a] and others, married non-Jews. As a rule, however, an oppressed people grasps at anything which seems to offer some hope of salvation. And the more oppressed the less likely a people is to consider the common humanity of which our oppressors are part. Certainly, no critic of Zionist philosophy can deny that it has developed the energies not only of those who have gone to Palestine and have drained marshes and built human habitations on the sands of the Mediterranean shore, but has also strengthened those who hope to do likewise. This, however, does not prove the adequacy of its interpretation of history.

The Geographic Interpretation of Jewish History

The influence of climate on the civilization and character of a people was recognized by Greek philosophers since the time of Hippocrates. It was under the influence of nineteenth-century materialism, however, that the geographic interpretation of history assumed a dominant role. Many came to think it a "scientific" duty to believe that man and his social institutions are the product of the physical environment, including topography, soil, climate, and other geographic factors.[25] This theory too exercised its influence on Jewish historians who found rather mystic connections between the land of Palestine and the Jewish soul. Rapoport explained the Jewish temper by the fact that Palestine is between Africa and Asia. But if so it should also explain the temper of present-day Arabs! Graetz says: "A country situated on the shore of a surging sea and offering a diversification of mountains and valleys, hills and dales, will impel its inhabitants to the performance of uncommon deeds." But should this not also be true for Albania?

Taken by and large, geographic determinism seems especially inapplicable to Jewish history, since the Jews have for the longer period of their history lived outside of Palestine. Jewish communities were located in Babylonia and Egypt as far back as the sixth century B.C.E. and in the course of time they had an important influence on the development of Judaism. Whether we accept the biblical account or not, it is clear that the Hebrews were a people with definite characteristics before they invaded Palestine. If their sojourn in that country for a thousand years or so molded their character, why should not their subsequent sojourn in other lands be of equal influence? And do not the Jews of different lands today differ? Certainly, that which distinguishes the culture of the Polish Jews from that of the rest of the Polish population cannot be due solely to geographic reasons.

The continuous longing of the Jews to return to Palestine is a psychological fact which has several different roots. All of them, however, are conditioned by the fact that the Old Testament and its literary outgrowths have all glorified the land of Palestine. David complained that when driven out by Saul he was forced to worship other gods, and the Babylonian captives wondered how they could sing the songs of the Lord in foreign lands. While this is no longer the prevailing view, the orthodox still do in their daily prayers complain that the full worship of the Lord through the temple ritual in Jerusalem is no longer possible. But quite apart from religious motives, Zionists take the position that Jewish civilization was not only developed in Palestine but can thrive only there, and this on sentimental grounds, quite apart from material and economic considerations. This can be seen in the way in which the Zionist Organization rejected the British offer of Uganda and other plans for settling Jews anywhere but in Palestine.

The insistence that only in Palestine can the Jewish genius express itself would, if logically developed, lead to a systematic disparagement of Jewish achievements in the Diaspora—which includes talmudic and midrashic literature, Jewish philosophy, and all other achievements in the arts and sciences. This is a very difficult position for those Zionists who are not orthodox and cannot regard the Bible as outweighing all other Jewish achievements. Besides, it is not certain that some of the grandest parts of the Bible, such as Job and the other Wisdom books, parts of Deutero-Isaiah, and some of the Psalms were not written outside of Palestine. More serious, however, is the difficulty that such a glorification of Palestine involves an altogether helpless and hopeless attitude in regard to the great mass of Jews who are bound to remain outside of Palestine.

Because of the realization of this latter point, a group of historians led by Simon Dubnow, began to emphasize cultural autonomy as the factor which has maintained the Jewish people throughout the centuries outside of Palestine.

The Economic Interpretation

The traditional view of Jewish history as essentially concerned with religion has so long dominated the stage that the mere suggestion that one might give a purely economic account of it seems at first rather strained or far-fetched. Yet, it would be surprising if a point of view which has been so extensively applied in so many other fields were entirely kept out of this particular domain of history. The interesting point, however, to note is that this mode of interpretation has been applied not only by professed Marxists but also by liberals such as Marvin Lowenthal, Eli Ginzberg, and Selig Perlman; by Hebraists like Yehezkel Kaufmann; and even by conservative rabbinical scholars such as Professor Louis Finkelstein, not to mention the history of Jewish commerce by Rabbi Levi Herzfeld. It is obviously impossible to leave the economic factor out of account if Jews are to be viewed as human beings who have to earn their living by some economic activity. When the economic is combined with other factors, many of the familiar incidents in biblical history receive substantial illumination.

The extreme emphasis on the economic factor as *the* determining one—all others such as religion, culture, and political institutions being but reflexes of the economic—belongs of course to the Marxian groups, socialists, Bundists, communists, and at times Poale-Zionists. Marx himself, to whom all racial and national feelings and his own Jewish descent were thorns in the flesh, wrote on the Jewish question and referred to the peculiar economic position of the Jews "in the interstices of Polish society." But he scarcely touched on the long history of the problem. His knowledge of ancient Hebrew history was hardly adequate for the purpose. The nestor of socialist theory, Kautsky, starts from the biological or anthropological fact that the Jews are not a race and tries to show that it is not necessary to assume that they are possessed of any special soul to explain why their economic activities have brought about their special development or their conflicts with their neighbors. More specifically, Max Beer tried to show that the struggle between the 'anavim and the resha'im (so often referred to in the Psalms) represented a class struggle between the poor and their rich oppressors, and that the Deuteronomic legislation represents the triumph of the former party. On the whole, however, few socialist writers have been equipped with sufficient knowledge of the sources of Hebrew history to make any substantial contributions in this field. Communist writers are satisfied with the dogma that the economic class struggle is the key to all history and therefore also to that of the Jews. Thus Nikolsky has tried to prove (on inadequate evidence) the absence of private ownership of land in the early stages of Israel's history. Many believe that the messianic ideal of a classless society has actually been attained in the U.S.S.R. of today, and the Jewish problem has thus been definitely solved—though for a time they claimed that additional salvation was to come from Birobidjan. Socialists have explained the growth of modern antisemitism and the feeling of the followers of Ahlwardt and other forerunners of the nazi party as the socialism of fools who think that they can abolish capitalism by getting rid of the Jews.

Socialist-Zionists like Ber Borochov start with the idea that the historically necessary breakup of modern capitalism must compel Jewish laborers to go to an undeveloped country and hence to Palestine— although to an outsider it seems hard to see why on purely economic grounds Palestine should be preferred to other undeveloped regions.

For some time, the distinction between the nomadic and the agricultural elements in Hebrew society has been much emphasized by historians and often treated as the key to the prophetic movement and the struggle for a restoration of a purer form of religion. This has sometimes been used as a support by those who wish to maintain the historicity of the sojourn in the desert and the Mosaic authorship of Hebrew law. But it is difficult to determine to what extent the few references in the prophets to Israel's life in the desert may be utopian idealizations, like the early histories of Rome and Sparta. Certainly, on an analysis of the Pentateuchal laws, the references to slaves, to houses, to oxen, and the like, all point to an agricultural society. The stories of the patriarchs, the festivals of sheep-shearing, the elaborate meals for guests, and the abundance of jewels testify to a settled society, in which, to be sure, cattle form a large part of wealth. Even the Negev was a more or less settled country. The prophet, Amos of Tekoah, is not only a herdsman but also a tender of sycamore trees. The Rechabites, like the Nazirites, are not a typical section of the people but represent something exotic, so that they are pointed to as remarkable examples.

It is also well to remember that a transition from semi-nomadic life to that of settled agricultural and even town life takes place very readily in our own day, and there is no reason to assume any long period for it in Jewish history. An interesting point in this connection is the absence of smiths in the period of the Judges. This has been interpreted as the position of an immigrant-nomad people or an attempt on the part of the Philistines to monopolize that occupation, and by others as an attempt to prevent the Jews from being armed. Discoveries at Ezion Geber tend to indicate that Solomon developed iron foundries at that point, and the fact that the Kenites were smiths may help to explain why their incorporation into Judah gave such strength to David.

In regard to the dogma about the class struggle, it may be observed that the main class distinction among the Jews seems to have been that between the larger landowners and the poorer people. The servants do not seem to have been at any time a separate class. There is no hint of any servile restlessness or uprising. Possibly the number of such servants was not very large, for the number of rich landowners does not seem to have been great, because of the relative paucity of large tracts of rich land. But both Jeremiah and Nehemiah refer to the oppression of the poor by rich money lenders. The priestly class seems to have had a quite definite organization of its own. At any rate, they possessed a continuous tradition and kept elaborate genealogical, as well as other, records.

Discussion of the possibilities of Jewish immigration into Palestine has raised the question as to how many people lived in that land in historical times. The numerous references to sheep grazing, and several references to lions infesting the roads, point to a sparsely settled land. But this may have been the case at certain intervals, after famines, plagues or desolating wars, such as those with Damascus. It is counterbalanced by definite testimony to periods of prosperity.

We also have numerous references to a victorious people living in a land "flowing with milk and honey." There is evidence of festivals, of the possession of much wealth (providing booty for invaders) and of extensive trade, although the Jews never had a seaport before the Maccabeans captured Jaffa.

The Kingdom of Judah seems to have been impoverished after the reign of Solomon. Possibly Jehoshaphat and his immediate successors were merely vassals of the house of Omri. It was only under Uzziah that Judah recovered sufficient strength to dominate Edom and to challenge Northern Israel. Still if we are to believe even a part of Sennacherib's testimony to the fact that he conquered 46 Judean cities and carried away captive 200,000 inhabitants, Judea must have become a populous country in the reign of Hezekiah. If the battle of Megiddo represents an attempt on the part of King Josiah to oppose the power of Egypt, the natural implication is that the Judean kingdom had absorbed a large part of what had formerly been the Israelitish kingdom. The Book of Jeremiah clearly points to a developed court and a group of people who stood above the lowly multitude—people who had servants, signet rings, and readily wrote on various subjects.

Whether we hold the traditional view that the Second Temple was built by returning exiles from Babylonia or whether we adopt the newer view that it was really much more due to the native population that had remained in and around Jerusalem, it seems that under Persian and Greek rule Judea continued to grow in population and wealth. Nor can there be any doubt that under Roman rule (up to the revolt in 67 B.C.E.) the Jewish population increased to a remarkable extent. This would indicate that under settled rule and the safe pursuits of agriculture and industry, the food supply of Palestine proved adequate to support a large population.

After the decline of Palestinian Jewry, the great Jewish communities of the dispersion adapted themselves to the diverse economic conditions of their respective countries. But in only exceptional circumstances could the Jewish masses become tillers of the soil (as today in Carpatho-Russia). This meant that the Jews became a predominantly urban people, so that trade and special kinds of handwork have been their main source of revenue. A number of writers have regarded this urban psychology as the key to Jewish history in the dispersion.

One form of the economic interpretation offers an historical explanation of the present crisis which faces the Jewish people throughout the world. According to this view, as expounded by Professor Perlman, the period of liberalism was the result of the expanding commercial economy in which the Jews found a place. But as a period of recession is replacing that of expansion, there is no more need for Jewish enterprise, and hence the movement to restrict their rights and even to eliminate them altogether. There can be no doubt that in the time of scarcity people are less tolerant. Liberality is a virtue of those who have something to spare, not of those who must live on a very narrow scale. Yet the purely economic interpretation has not, because of its obvious limitations, found universal acceptance. What country, for instance, was more in need of commercial development than Russia? Yet, can the persecution of the Jews and the organized riots against them be said to have had a purely economic motive? Race friction involves certain psychological factors which cannot be reduced to questions of economics alone. Political considerations, questions of prestige, and religious prejudice enter into the picture and sometimes seem to be independent elements. The nationalistic wave spreading over Europe today is certainly not altogether an economic one: it would have been economically more profitable for the greater part of Poland to have remained within the Russian empire and to have continued to sell goods in the Russian market. The break-up of the Austrian empire was certainly not economically profitable to the constituent elements. Men under the influence of religion or certain waves of nationalistic feeling are willing to sacrifice their economic welfare, and indeed, their very lives. That is a fact richly illustrated in the history of the Jews. You may call it irrational or by any other name but you cannot deny it is an historical fact.

The Cultural Interpretation

The various interpretations so far discussed are extreme points of view. It may be admitted that relatively few cling to one of these exclusively and that most people are inclined towards intermediate and eclectic positions. Thus the fact that Geiger is a typical representative of Reform Judaism certainly does not prevent his making acute and illuminating observations on the political differences between Pharisees and Sadducees. Still it is well to consider the separate points of view somewhat analytically to clarify their meaning. For they are ideals actually applied more or less clearly by Jewish thinkers today in determining the meaning of our past. In recent times, however, there has been a notable turn away from monistic theories and a general recognition that nothing is really explained if we rely on any one principle, and that, certainly in dealing with human affairs, a pluralistic point of view must be adopted. It is this view which dominates what is frequently called the cultural interpretation in history, and has been worked out in the general field of anthropology by men such as Boas and his followers.

By culture, we mean nothing more than the customary social arrangements according to which people work and live. These are naturally conditioned by their physical environment. But, as we have already noted, different types of culture can co-exist in the same physical region, for example, Jewish and Catholic Poland. Against those who take refuge in the theory that culture is completely determined by race, it is for scientific purposes sufficient to show that there are no pure races and that a people like the Jews and Germans may go through great cultural changes without any pronounced mixture of foreign blood. In this connection, it is well to draw a distinction between race theories of history and laws prohibiting marriage to foreigners, which play such a large role in the books of Ezra and Nehemiah. Race theories are modern and sophistical inventions. Laws of endogamy are ancient and almost universal and rest on simple considerations of preventing alienation of property or interference with old mores or customs, especially of family worship. That theories of heredity have nothing to do with the case is shown by the fact that most of the ancient peoples, having rigorous laws against marriage with foreigners, have no objection at all to adoption whereby a stranger becomes a member of the family. The convert to Judaism thus becomes Abraham ben Abraham.

While attempts to explain natural events as due to the soul, mind or spirit of Israel, Rome, or America, are often mythological and at best only metaphorical, we need not deny that history may be illumined by careful study of the mental traits manifested in the peculiar customs of any group such as the Jews. And while the work of Steinthal and Lazarus in this field was somewhat premature and insufficiently critical, they did raise important issues and gave impetus to the collection of the materials which, treated by more scientific methods, should help historical understanding and diminish the amount of irresponsible vagaries in this field.

One of the great facts of our history which such psychological study should illumine is a fact often regarded as quasi miraculous, viz. the persistence of the Jewish people despite their scattered condition and long record of terrible persecution. Actual records, of course, show that other people, for instance the Armenians, have endured long series of persecutions and that the Jews have also enjoyed periods of prosperity. Indeed, there was hardly ever a time when in some place or other the Jews were not at least as comfortable as the average of the rest of the population. But ignoring this, it is well to note that social cohesion and opposition from without are closely connected. No one factor will explain the persistence or recurrence of antisem- itism. For it is after all a name for a number of different forces mil- itating against the Jews either on religious, political, or economic grounds, as a result of the universal social-psychological prejudice against the fellow who is near you and yet strangely different. By and large, Jews like others tend to become absorbed in any larger com- munity that is willing to receive them. But this process is retarded not only by religious differences, but by natural group loyalty, especially when its members are dependent upon each other. General social cohesion, resulting from the persistence of customary ways of thought and action, will keep a group together although it may be melting on the periphery. Yet the history of scattered Sephardi communities or of the Samaritans shows that racial pride and religious convictions may preserve small groups for many generations.

Throughout their dispersion, the Jews have had not only a common ritual and common observances, but also the common language involved in their prayers and Bible reading. And in any social history a very large role must be assigned to the influence of literature in helping to maintain the cohesion of a group. If common traditions, especially those of common suffering help to keep people united, books and writings which preserve traditions must be regarded as a powerful force. Hence we must regard the Bible and more specifically the legends concerning the patriarchs, the exodus, the Judges and the "good" kings of Judah, as one of the factors to explain the cohesiveness of the Jews first in Babylonia and then in other lands of their exile. And it is to be observed that it is not necessary for every individual to be familiar with such traditions. Anyone born in a marked group naturally associates more with its members than with those of any other group, will be readily identified as such, and will seldom escape all consciousness of it.

It is the great merit of historians like Dubnow and Baron to have pointed out that despite the absence of a political state or land of their own the Jews have lived in communities that have been more or less autonomous, although they have been influenced by the social, economic, and political conditions of their environment. And this is true of all groups. Dubnow, especially, deliberately rejects the quasi-Hegelian attitude of Graetz which assumes that one community, first Palestine, then Babylon, then Spain, and then Poland, carried the torch of Judaism and that that is the whole of Jewish history. Jewish, like other, communities are dependent upon those general factors which determine the fate of all peoples, and hence on what has been called general history. Certainly, the Jews of Babylonia do not disappear because of the closing of the schools of Sura and Pumpedita, nor does the Jewish community of Egypt suddenly come into being to produce a Saadia. The hegemony of prestige which various Jewish communities have enjoyed has been due not only to religious learning, but to general world conditions. And we must study the latter to understand the history of any one people.

The historian, according to Friedrich Schlegel, is a prophet looking backward, and those who have followed these reflections will perceive how the various philosophies of Jewish history see in the past something which they expect in the future. Those who remain true to the Orthodox tradition center their hope on a messianic redemption which will come in God's good time and for which we can prepare by living according to His law, trusting that His promise will not fail. Reform

Judaism differs from this only as regards the content of the law, the observance of which by all mankind will bring about the messianic age. Marxists also hope that universal salvation will come to all mankind by means of a revolution which will abolish once and for all the root of all evil, namely, economic exploitation. Political Zionists hope that at least a large part of the Jews, a saving remnant, can be redeemed by establishing a Jewish state in Palestine. Pluralists, however, need not hope for any definitive revolution or messianic state. The future is at least as uncertain as the remote past. The best we can do is to pursue all those ways which experience shows to be helpful in making life more viable under known conditions. To determine what these are, at any one time and place, and by what means the maximum good may be promoted and unavoidable evil minimized, we need not only to study history and the causes of social change but to reflect critically on what things we shall regard as good and what we shall banish from our hearts as evil.

NOTES

[1] Holmes, O. W., *Collected Legal Papers* (1920), p. 303. *See also* Cohen, M. R., *Reason and Nature* (1931), book iii, ch. iii.

[2] *La Philosophie de la Révolution française* (Paris 1875, 4th ed. 1892).

[3] Baron, S. W., *A Social and Religious History of the Jews,* vol. i, ch. i. *Cf.* Finkelstein, L., in *Jewish Quarterly Review,* vol. xxii, pp. 169–70.

[4] This, of course, does not deny the many valuable features in the various rabbinic chronicles, and it is highly regrettable that no complete collection of them is available in any modern language. Two moderate volumes would contain them all. Some glimpse of them can be had in extracts, translated into German, and collected by Winter and Wünsche. For general accounts *see* the sections on historical writings in M. Waxman's *A History of Jewish Literature,* Zinberg's *Geshikhte fun der Literatur bay Yidn,* and Karpeles' *Geschichte.* An interesting collection of historical references in the Talmud is found in the fifth part of the *Monumenta Talmudica.*

[5] "The philosophy of history is the work of the Jews," Renan, Joseph Ernest, *Revue de Deux Mondes* (October 15, 1860).

[6] For homiletic purposes, it sometimes attributes the worldly success of a great empire to some virtuous act on the part of its supposed progenitor. Thus the triumph of the Greek, Roman and Arabic empires is attributed to the virtues of Japhet, Esau, and Ishmael in showing filial respect to Noah, Isaac, and Abraham *(Seder Eliahu Rabba* [ed. Friedmann], pp. 65, 114, 115).

[7] Ezekiel and even Jeremiah regard the Jews as always a sinful people (Ezek. 16:20–23; Jer. 3:24–25).

[8] The fall of Bethar is a punishment for his causing the death of Rabbi Eliezer of Modin *(Ekha Rabba* at 2, 2).

[9] Ginzberg, L., *Students, Scholars and Saints,* p. 205.

[10] Baba Batra 21b; Sanhedrin 48b, 49a; *Yalkut Samuel,* 131 and Rashi's comment on II Samuel 20:17. *See also* Zunz, *Gesammelte Schriften,* vol. i, p. 162, and Ginzberg, *Legends of the Jews,* vol. iv, p. 97.

[11] For the anti-historical influence of Maimonides *see* the essay by S. W. Baron in the *Proceedings of the American Academy for Jewish Research,* vol. vi (1935), p. 9.

[12] When Dubnow comes to the Polish-Russian period, for which he has done so much to gather available sources, he conforms more to his explicit program and less to the traditional attitude.

[13] Prof. Ginzberg attaches great value to the Gaon's critical attitude not only in the matter of manuscript readings, but also as to the relation between reason and religious conscience. It is curious that the Gaon was willing to regard the wearing of hats in the synagogue as but a custom which might be disregarded while Graetz was shocked by it *(Jewish Encyclopaedia,* vol. ii, pp. 530–33, and Graetz, *Volkstümliche Geschichte,* vol. iii, p. 731).

[14] *See* Montefiore, C., *Liberal Judaism.*

[15] Kant, *Religion,* pp. 186 ff., 206n., 252n. (Hartenstein ed. vol vi, pp. 224ff., 225n., 264n.).

[16] The first edition of Salvador's essay was entitled, *Essai sur la loi de Moïse et la système religieuse et politiques des Hébreux* (1822), the second ed., *Histoire des institutions de Moïse et du peuple hébreu,* 3 vols. (1828). In this book he quotes Fleury, *Moeurs des Israélites ou Modèle d'une politique simple et sincère,* but I have not been able to see a copy of it. In 1846 Salvador published his *Histoire de la domination romaine en Judée.* Eight years before that he published *La Vie de Jésus Christ,* which had a great influence on Renan. *See* Salvador, V. G., *Joseph Salvador, sa vie, ses oeuvres et ses critiques* (Paris 1881).

[17] On the knowledge of Vico outside of Italy, *see* the second appendix to Croce, B., *La filosofia di Giovanni Battista Vico* (3d ed. Bari 1933), tr. by R. G. Collingwood (London 1913). The cyclical view of general history is, of course, much older. It can be seen in the cycles of the various forms of government sketched by Plato in his *Republic* and by Aristotle in his *Politics.* Plato's theory of "the great year" in which all the heavenly bodies returned to their original position influenced the astrological interpretation of history of the Arabs and, through the latter, Jewish writers like Bar Hiyya. The periodicities of Midrashic literature, such as the *Pirqe Rabbi Eliezer* and the *Seder Eliahu,* seem to be of a different kind, and the same is true of the view of Volney's *Ruins* or Rückert's poem, *Chider,* which, although published in 1838, expresses an older popular view.

18 The universalist view in rabbinic literature is well expressed in the Midrash Rabba on the second chapter of Deuteronomy. "Every distress in which Israel and the other races share is a distress. But every distress that is only Israel's is no distress."

19 Throughout the Bible there is a persistent demand that we rely on faith in Yahweh rather than on material means for our protection. *Cf.* I Sam. 17:47, Isa. 37:21–22; Zech. 2:5.

20 In this he was partly anticipated by Kant. Aristotle, too, glorified the state, but he made it distinctly a means to the good life, the end being the enjoyment of the vision of God.

21 "Anything is valuable from the national standpoint if it preserves Judaism, even if like mysticism it has admittedly pernicious consequences" (Greenstone, J., *The Messiah Idea in Jewish History* [Philadelphia 1906], p. 159).

22 *Judaism,* vol. i, p. 53. The orthodox of the time regarded the Maccabean kings as usurpers. *See* the *Psalms of the Pharisees,* ed. by Ryle and James.

23 *Zionism and the Jewish Future,* ed. by H. Sacher (1916), pp. 6, 7, 9.

24 *Op. cit.,* pp. 55–56. Quoting Ahad Ha-Am, *Selected Essays* (1912), pp. 193–94. This quotation does not, of course, identify Ahad Ha-Am with political Zionism. He indeed protested that "it would be a ridiculous anti-climax if the struggle of the ages should produce a picayune state in an Arab world, a parvenu in international diplomacy." Rabbi Silver, who regarded himself as a follower of Ahad Ha-Am, referred to secular nationalism as neo-Sadduceeism. Pharisees and orthodox Judaism, generally, believe in the immortality of the soul and in a world beyond the temporal one since the messianic restoration may not come in our own lives. But nationalistic Zionism, like the Sadducees, is concerned with preserving the national body on earth. To many of the orthodox the demand for a *Judenstaat* appears very much like the demands of the Israelites of Samuel: Give us a king; we want to be like other nations.

[24a Herzl was married to a Jewess. Eds. (1971)].

25 The following criticisms do not deny that an adequate interpretation of the Palestinian period in Jewish history requires a knowledge of its geography. The scarcity of roads in the hill regions shows the difficulties in the way of a centrally-organized kingdom replacing cantonal or tribal society. And to the extent that Palestine is on the highway from Egypt to the east, an independent commonwealth in it is even more difficult. The paucity of sizable rivers indicates the moderate rainfall and consequently limited vegetation as well as the great importance of wells. A consideration of the geography of the wilderness at Paran and the region of Kadesh will indicate what possibility there was of such a large group of people as is mentioned in the Bible being able to maintain themselves there for forty years. In regard to the post-Palestinian period, it is a significant inquiry as to what effect the wanderings in different lands and exposure to different climates has had on the physique and temperament of the Jewish people.

EDITORS' PREFACE

Privileged Jews

Like other political émigrés in history who felt impelled to examine the causes behind their forced exodus, Jewish refugees from Nazi Germany, too, have engaged in such stock-taking. As Jews, they have dwelled particularly on the causes behind the failure of Emancipation and assimilation. Professor Arendt's article combines such soul-searching with a scholarly scrutiny of the past, a critique of the present, and implied lessons for the future. In a wider sense, it is an important study of the position of the Jew in Western society and a reflection of the search for psychological security of a generation of westernized Jews. Written some thirty years ago, her theses will continue to be debated. The essay remains the challenging intellectual exercise that it was some thirty years ago.

Professor Arendt poses in her trenchant essay the preference of some pre-Emancipation advocates of the "improvement" of the Jews for granting privileges to individuals as rewards for achievement or usefulness rather than for granting equality to all Jews as their right as human beings. She holds that the practice of dividing Jews into categories of "exceptional" and others has served to weaken the solidarity of the community and even functioned as preparation for

53

massacres. She traces this divisive approach to the influence of the Court Jew in the Central European states.

Because of their usefulness to the rulers, such individuals were exempted from the usual restrictions. In turn, they were dependent on their patrons, to whom they were useful only as long as they remained Jews. Therefore, they had a vested interest in the status quo of the privileged and unprivileged. This relationship with the authorities, maintains Arendt, made the Court Jew the intermediary between the Jewish community and the state, and consequently turned the "notables" into the virtual rulers of community government with a resultant weakening and demoralization of the traditional Jewish communal autonomy. Marriages between the rich and the powerful of different countries eventually turned the Court Jews into an aristocratic caste with its own life style and interests. Despite their wealth and acculturation, they remained outsiders in both the Jewish and Christian worlds.

Initially, the Court Jews played significant roles in the defense of the Jews. They were instrumental in establishing new communities, in an age when exile and restriction were the lot of the Jew in Europe. They provided jobs and the right of residence for clerks, bookkeepers, servants, and teachers. Because of their education, the latter became privileged Jews in another sense. The educated and eventually westernized arrivals from the small towns of Germany or Poland presented the image of a new type of Jew to the Christian world. Some newcomers frequented the common meeting places of the enlightened intelligentsia, both Jews and Christians—the rich Jewish women's salons. As they became more immersed in German culture and less involved in the Jewish one, such persons increasingly resented the situation that cast them in the same public image and subjected them to the same restrictions as those of the backward Jewish masses. The privileged had to remain Jews because of their economic position and communal leadership. For the new, poor, intellectuals, conversion was the answer to the frustrating search for privileges. The solution for the educated daughters of wealthy families was intermarriage. The baptized Jews faced problems in social acceptance. They disliked identification with rich and reactionary

Jews, and were held in contempt by the "old" Christians. They formed small social enclaves of their own and continued to marry among themselves for several generations.

Professor Arendt also points out the connection between modern social antisemitism and assimilation. In order to emphasize the distinction between themselves and the "Jew in general," culturally emancipated Jews cultivated a life style that came to be viewed by Christians as "typically Jewish." As Arendt puts it, "Judaism became Jewishness—a psychological quality—and the Jewish question became a personal problem." Every Jew had to choose "whether to remain a pariah or to become a parvenu." Ambivalence became the condition of the assimilated Jew as "the Jewish question projected in their individual psychological situation."

HANNAH ARENDT served for many years on the Board of the Conference on Jewish Social Studies, and as Executive Director of Jewish Cultural Reconstruction. A holder of many honorary degrees and the recipient of numerous awards and fellowships, she has been a Professor at Princeton University, at the University of Chicago, and at other universities, and is now University Professor at The New School for Social Research in New York. Her many works include *The Origins of Totalitarianism; On Revolution; Eichmann in Jerusalem; Men in Dark Times;* and *On Violence.*

Privileged Jews *

by Hannah Arendt

The Moral of History

Wilhelm von Humboldt, one of the rare genuine German democrats who played a big part in the emancipation of Prussian Jewry in 1812 and a still bigger part in the intervention in behalf of the Jews at the Congress of Vienna, looked back in 1816 to the days of his public battle for Jewish rights and his many years of personal intercourse with Jews and said: "I love the Jew really only *en masse; en détail* I strictly avoid him."[1] This amazing and paradoxical utter-

---

* This essay was written about twenty-five years ago and translated from the German for publication in *Jewish Social Studies*. (When I wrote it, the facts of the Final Solution were not yet known.) Some of the material dealt with here was later used by me in "Antisemitism," the first part of *The Origins of Totalitarianism*, first published in 1951. This part which tries to give an abbreviated history of antisemitism throughout the 19th century, is now available in a separate paperback edition—Harvest Book 131.

Subsequent literature on the subject is too voluminous to be added. Jacob Katz's studies: *Exclusiveness and Tolerance, Jewish-Gentile Relations in Medieval and Modern Times* (New York 1961); *Die Entstehung der Judenassimilation in Deutschland und deren Ideologie* (Frankfurt 1935); and Selma Stern's *The Court Jew* (Philadelphia 1950), and especially *Der preussische Staat und die Juden*, 2 vols. (Tübingen 1962), are indispensable.

> "Die nämlich, welche zu gleicher
> Zeit Juden sein und Juden
> nicht sein wollen . . ."
> H. E. G. Paulus, 1831.

Reprinted from JEWISH SOCIAL STUDIES, Volume VIII, 1946

ance, standing as it does in extreme contrast to the personal history of Humboldt—he had many personal friends among Jews—is unique in the history of the arguments presented for Jewish emancipation. Since Lessing and Dohm in Prussia, since Mirabeau and the Abbé Grégoire in France, the advocates of the Jews always based their arguments on the "Jews *en détail,*" on the notable exceptions among the Jewish people. Humboldt's humanism, in the best traditions of Jewish emancipation in France, aimed to liberate the people as a whole, without bestowing special privileges upon individuals. As such, his viewpoint was appreciated very little by his contemporaries, and it had still less influence on the later history of emancipated Jewry.

More in keeping with the sentiments of the time were the views of H. E. G. Paulus, a liberal Protestant theologian and contemporary of Humboldt. Paulus protested against the idea of emancipating the Jews as a group. Instead, he urged that individuals be granted the rights of man according to their personal merits.[2] A few decades later, Gabriel Riesser, the Jewish publicist, vented his irony upon the sort of official Jewish propaganda which based its appeal upon stories of "virtuous Jews" who saved Christians from drowning.[3] The basic principle of granting special privileges to individuals and refusing civic rights to the Jewish people as a group had successfully asserted itself.

In the minds of the privileged Jews such measures taken by the state appeared to be the workings of a sort of heavenly tribunal, by whom the virtuous—who had more than a certain income—were rewarded with human rights, and the unworthy—living in mass concentration in the eastern provinces—were punished as pariahs. Since that time it has become a mark of assimilated Jews to be unable to distinguish between friend and enemy, between compliment and insult, and to feel flattered when an antisemite assures them that he does not mean them, that they are exceptions—exceptional Jews.

The events of recent years have proved that the "excepted Jew" is more the Jew than the exception; no Jew feels quite happy any more about being assured that he is an exception. The extraordinary catastrophe has converted once again all those who fancied themselves extraordinarily favored beings into quite ordinary mortals. Were history a closed book, sealed after each epoch, we would not be much interested in the story of the privileged Jews. The vitality of a nation, however, is measured in terms of the living remembrance of its history. We Jews are inclined to have an inverted historical perspective; the more distantly removed events are from the present, the more sharply, clearly, and accurately they appear. Such an inversion of historical perspective means that in our political conscience we do not want to take the responsibility for the immediate past and that we, together with our historians, want to take refuge in periods of the past, which leave us secure in terms of political consequences.

Behind us lies a century of opportunist politics, a century in which an unusual concurrence of circumstances allowed our people to live from day to day. During the same period scholars and philologists have succeeded in estranging history from the people in the same manner as opportunist statesmen alienated them from politics. The sublime concept of human progress was robbed of its historic sense and perverted into a simple natural fact, according to which the son is always presented as better and wiser than his father, the grandson as more enlightened than his grandfather. Or, it was degraded to an economic law, according to which accumulated wealth of the fore- bears determines the well-being of the sons and grandsons, making each of them advance further in the unending career of the family. In the light of such developments, to forget has become a holy duty, inexperience a privilege, and ignorance a guarantee of success.

Since the circumstances under which we live are created by man, the deceased force themselves upon us and upon the institutions that govern us and refuse to disappear into the darkness into which we try to plunge them. The more we try to forget, the more their influence dominates us. The succession of generations may be a natural guar- antee for the continuity of history but it is certainly not a guarantee of progress. Because we are the sons of our fathers and the grandsons of our grandfathers, their misdeeds may persecute us into the third and fourth generations. Inactive ourselves, we cannot even enjoy their deeds for, like all human works, they have the fatal tendency to turn into dross, just as a room painted white always turns black if not repainted frequently.

History in this sense, has its moral, and if our scholars, with their impartial objectivity, are unable to discover this moral in history, it means only that they are incapable of understanding the world we have created; just like the people who are unable to make use of the very institutions they have produced. History, unfortunately, does not know Hegel's *"List der Vernunft";* rather does unreason begin to function automatically when reason has abdicated to it.

The automatism of events, reigning since the beginning of the nineteenth century in place of human reason, prepared with incomparable precision for the spiritual collapse of Europe before the bloody idol of race. It is no mere accident that the catastrophic defeats of the peoples of Europe began with the catastrophe of the Jewish people, a people in whose destiny all others thought they could remain uninterested because of the tenet that Jewish history obeys "exceptional laws." The defeat of the Jewish people started with the catastrophe of the German Jews, in whom European Jews were not interested because they suddenly discovered that German Jews constituted an exception. The collapse of German Jewry began with its splitting up into innumerable factions, each of which believed that special privileges could protect human rights—*e.g.,* the privilege of having been a veteran of World War I, the child of a war veteran, or if such privileges were not recognized any more, a crippled war veteran or the son of a father killed at the front. Since Jews *"en masse"* seemed to have disappeared from the earth, it was easy to dispose of Jews *"en détail."* The terrible and bloody annihilation of individual Jews was preceded by the bloodless destruction of the Jewish people.

The European background against which Jewish history appears is complicated and involved. Sometimes the Jewish thread is lost in the maze but most of the time it is easily recognizable. The general history of Europe, from the French Revolution to the beginning of World War I, may be described in its most tragic aspect as the slow but steady transformation of the *citoyen* of the French Revolution into the *bourgeois* of the pre-war period. The stages of the history of this period of nearly 150 years are manifold, and often present magnificent and very human aspects. The period of *enrichissez-vous* (get-rich-quick) was also that of the flowering of French painting; the period of German misery was also that of the great age of classic literature; and we cannot imagine the Victorian age without Dickens. At the end of the era, however, we are confronted by a strange de-humanized kind of humanity. The moral of the history of the 19th century is the fact that men who were not ready to assume a responsible role in public affairs in the end were turned into mere beasts who could be used for anything before being led to slaughter. Institutions, moreover, left to themselves without control and guidance by men, turned into monsters devouring nations and countries.

The Jewish phase of 19th century history reveals similar manifestaitons. While reading Heine and Börne, who, just because they were Jews, insisted on being considered men and were thus incorporated into the universal history of mankind, we forgot all about the tedious speeches of the representatives of the special group of privileged Jews in Prussia at the same time. In the country which made Disraeli its Prime Minister, the Jew Karl Marx wrote *Das Kapital,* a book which in its fanatical zeal for justice carried on the Jewish tradition much more efficaciously than all the success of the "chosen man of the chosen race."[4] Finally, who does not, in thinking of the great literary work of Marcel Proust and the powerful bill of indictment by Bernard Lazare, forget those French Jews who filled the aristocratic salons of the Faubourg St. Germain and who, unconsciously following the unseemly example of their Prussian predecessors of the beginning of the 19th century, endeavored to be "Jews yet at the same time not Jews?"[5]

This ambiguity became decisive for the social behavior of the assimilated and emancipated Jewry in western Europe. They did not want and could not belong to the Jewish people any more, but they wanted and had to remain Jews—exceptions among the Jewish people. They wanted to and could play their part in non-Jewish society, but they did not desire to and could not disappear among the non-Jewish peoples. Thus they became exceptions in the non-Jewish world. They maintained they were able to be "men like others on the street but Jews at home."[6] But they felt they were different from other men on the street as Jews, and different from other Jews at home in that they were superior to the masses of the Jewish people.

The Privileged of Wealth

During the 17th and 18th centuries Jews succeeded, in exceptional cases, in escaping from the ghettos of western Europe. By the middle of the 18th century conditions had developed so that Jews with a lot of money and great ability were able to enter the paradise of rights and liberties, and Jews without money and business still continued to live in dire poverty and without civic rights. In Austria and in all the south-German states—Bavaria, Württemberg, Baden—the Jews belonged to the court-household of the more or less enlightened despots of the times. They were usually called *Hofjuden,* but in Prussia they were characteristically named *Generalprivilegierte Juden.* This name was no exaggeration. The *Hofjuden* enjoyed all privileges, they could live wherever they liked, they could travel anywhere within the realm of their sovereigns, they could bear arms and demand the special protection of all local authorities. Their way of life was on a much higher level than that of the middle class of the period. The *Hofjuden* possessed greater privileges than the majority of the population of their homelands, and it would be erroneous to believe that this state of things escaped the attention of their contemporaries. Dohm, in his *Denkwürdigkeiten,* complains of the practice in force since the time of Frederick William I to grant those Jews who became rich "all sorts of favors and support," often "at the expense of and with the neglect of diligent and legal citizens."[7]

The Jews of that time still lived for the most part in small villages. All these small Jewish communities of provincial Jews, peddlers, artisans and the like had their *Hofjude* as protector, who brought all local grievances directly to the ruler. The Jews were thus better protected than the surrounding non-Jewish population, which was left helpless to the exploitation of the feudal landowners. This right of entering petitions through the *Hofjude* was such an enormous advantage for the local communities that for its sake they agreed to all sorts of radical changes in the formerly democratic constitution of the communities and often accepted as formal heads of the community rich Jews who did not even live among them. The price which the Jewish people had to pay for the short-lived advantages brought to them by the *Hofjuden* during the first years of their miraculous rise was the domination of the community by the "notables," a condition which was already firmly established at the beginning of the 18th century.

The *Hofjuden* were "exceptional Jews," because the princes made exceptions in their favor. Even if a prince was an enemy of the Jews,

the disastrous condition of the state finances in the 18th century and
the fact that the nobility was encumbered with debts forced him to
suppress his inner feelings and to grant privileges to one or another
Jew. It would be naive, however, to believe that one can make exceptions in laws without experiencing an exception in feelings. The
cordial relations between *Hofjuden* and their principals proved that
feelings toward them had changed. The "exceptional Jews," moreover soon began to adapt themselves to the opinions of their rulers.
In the Jewish communities, over which they reigned from afar, their
exercise of power soon began to resemble, in its good and bad effects,
the government of the absolute monarchs. There was one decisive
difference however; they never once dreamed that they were installed
"by the grace of God," but knew very well that they had ascended the
throne by the grace of the princes and their own money.

The first *Hofjude* with monarchical aspirations among his own
"nation" was a Jew of Prague, who was purveyor of supplies to the
Elector Maurice of Saxony in the 16th century. He demanded that all
rabbis and community heads should be selected only from members
of his family.[8] The practice to install *Hofjuden* as dictators in their
communities became general in the 18th century. The *Hofjuden,* like
all still unspoiled upstarts, showed themselves, in their relations with
the princes, to be proud of their dark background of misery, misfortune and pariah-existence. Against that background their glory as
exceptions shone more brilliantly. Later, these Jewish notables took
great care to see that this dark background of poverty, misery and
rightlessness be continued. It is rather due to their efforts and not so
much to the hostility of the Prussian government that poor Jews of
Posen in the first decades of the 18th century received citizenship
rights only as exceptional cases. Similarly the emancipation of the
Jews during the French Revolution took place against the remon-
strances of the rich Jews of Bordeaux and Avignon, the "privileged
Jews" of the French monarchy. The more the wealthy Jews moved
away from Jewish morals and religious custom, the more orthodox
they became for the people.[9] Thus the Rothschilds in the 1820's
withdrew a large donation from their native community of Frankfurt,
in order to counteract the influence of reformers who wanted Jewish
children to receive general education and thus to create possibilities

for advancement for the poorer classes.[10] This "double dependence" of the poor Jews, dependence on "both the state and their wealthy brethren,"[11] became more oppressive with the growing power of the privileged Jews. As their wealth increased, the Jewish bankers had greater need for the poverty of the Jewish masses as a protective argument. The poorer the masses became, the more secure the rich Jews felt and the brighter their glory shone.

The *Hofjuden* owed their rise from the ghetto not only to favorable circumstances but also to their personal merits, their self-earned wealth, and their self-created social relations. They were particularly gifted, clever men, with a high degree of initiative. With their special privileges and their special position also came exceptional achievements. The privileges they received were a reward for past services and a prize for future and still greater efforts. The needs of the growing nation states increased much more rapidly than the understanding on the part of the people for the necessity of building up an efficient state machinery. The financial needs of the princes, influenced solely by political factors, created new fields of economic activity which, separated from the economic development of the countries, remained state monopolies. Jews penetrated into the economy of the state everywhere: in France as farmers of taxes, in Prussia as mint coiners or operators in the state works, in Bavaria as lessees of the royal salt mines, and everywhere as purveyors of military supplies.

It is a characteristic aspect of the rise of the *Hofjuden* that it was due everywhere to political conditions and remained relatively independent of the economic developments of the time. States and princes did not pay any attention to the economic capacity of their privileged Jews and forced them into doing business on a basis of pure speculation. On the other hand, the Jews had little inclination to integrate themselves into the normal economic life of their home countries. Jewish money played a role in the state factories of the mercantilist age inasmuch as Jews figured as the suppliers of credit to the state and to its business enterprises. However, the Jews hardly ever tried, even if offered opportunities, to enter into manufacturing and industries independent of the state.[12] The Jewish positions created by the *Hofjuden* in the 17th and 18th centuries remained decisive for Jewish economic life as late as the 20th century. They remained outside the

real capitalistic development and outsiders in the capitalistic bourgeoisie which developed within the nation states but independent of
the state machinery and often antagonistic to it. In contrast to the
non-Jewish bourgeoisie they felt that they were under the special
protection of the state and that their business interests depended on
the political interests of their sovereigns.

These Jews who were treated as exceptions and had made brilliant
individual careers stood outside all social connections. They were
separated from the ghettos and Jewish districts. At court, they were
appreciated by the princes, but naturally despised by the court society.
They had no business connections and no social relations with other
circles of the non-Jewish population. Their economic rise remained
independent of contemporary economic conditions, and their social
contacts remained outside the laws of society. Friendships between
princes and *Hofjuden* were not at all rare, but they never created a
social atmosphere.

We know relatively little about the personalities of these early privileged Jews of wealth. The fact that the *Hofjuden,* until the end of the
18th century, used their power in favor of their communities, leads
to the conclusion that they did not yet fear to be identified with
ordinary Jews. The stubbornness with which they carried on the fight
to have Eisenmenger's *Entdecktes Judentum,* that last compendium of
medieval Jew-hatred, prohibited (1701), shows that they still felt that
attacks on all Jews were also a direct threat to themselves. Their
power was very great at the time and never became so great again in
the coming century of emancipation. It is true that behind the credit
of every prince stood the credit of his *Hofjude* (when the Vienna
court-Jew Oppenheimer died in 1703, the credit of the Austrian state
was seriously impaired),[13] that no war could be carried on without
Jewish purveyors (only Jews could buy victuals in entire provinces
with the aid of Jewish peddlers), and that the Jews had the largest
part in the state monopolies, such as mints, lotteries, salt and tobacco-
monopolies. All this, however, was not the true foundation of their
power. The decisive factor was that they were completely isolated
from the population and had to give no consideration to any of the
important classes in the country. It was their social independence that
gave them the feeling of an independent political factor.[14]

This feeling of power was enhanced by the distance that separated this little group of privileged Jews from the masses of the Jewish people, without any Jewish middle class or larger strata of well-to-do Jews bridging the gap. They ruled as absolute princes among the people, but they still felt themselves to be *primi inter pares*. They still were single individuals risen to great splendour; as yet they formed no caste within their people.

Class arrogance among privileged Jews developed but slowly. It was held in bounds for a long time by the terrible loneliness in which these men were forced to live. In the capitals, in which they were not only allowed to live but obliged to dwell because of the proximity to the court, there were no Jewish communities. At that time, more than in later periods, there was no possibility of leaving Judaism and being absorbed in the non-Jewish surroundings. The whole existence of the *Hofjude* depended upon his being a Jew and not a Christian, this fact giving him the opportunity of disposing of international connections which at that time no Christian banker and no Christian agent could mobilize. The enlightened despots needed people who, on the one hand, could procure war supplies over vast territories and, on the other hand, stood outside a society and a population that could not even imagine themselves taking part in operations like the granting of state credits.[15] Only a Jew could mobilize the Jewish peddlers all over the country, use them as business agents and through them buy up in a few weeks all the food-products in whole provinces. Very soon the most important favor a prince could confer upon "his Jew" was the right to employ other Jews as servants and agents. It is evident that the first *Hofjuden* had no social ambition and no desire for social relations with non-Jews. This made it comparatively easy for them to endure the general hostility of the population. These conditions can be most clearly observed in the imperial cities, in which the Jews were not subject to the authority of the town councils but directly dependent on the emperor. Here they remained quite unconcerned with the rising hostility of the commoners, their neighbors.[16]

These Jews could have ever so many business relations with their prince; all that business did not bring them a step nearer to the strange environment around them. Let us take Samson Wertheimer as an example. In the first three decades of the 18th century, Wertheimer lent to the Austrian state more than six million florins. He could be counted as a confidant of the court and had access to all the diplomats and distinguished noblemen of his time. Yet all this did not imply any social relations, and he did not even think of being treated as an equal by the courtiers. He was much more proud of his dignity as "a privileged Rabbi of all Jewry," and of his title of "Prince of the Holy Land."[17] Up to the middle of the 18th century the *Hofjuden* would have agreed with the saying of the Dutch Jew, reported by Schudt in his *Merkwürdigkeiten,* viz: *"Neque in toto orbi alicui nationi inservimus."* Neither then nor later would they have understood fully the answer of the "learned Christian," who replied: "But this means happiness only for a few persons. The people, considered as a *corpo (sic)* is hunted everywhere, has no self-government, is subject to foreign rule, has no power and no dignity, and wanders all over the world, strangers everywhere."[18]

The pride of those who, because of the privileges granted to them, were equal to the most highly privileged inhabitants of the states they served had a very real political and economic basis. Their privileges were based upon their Jewish connections, and they had neither the ambition nor the possibility to assimilate to any class of non-Jewish society or to establish connections with such a class.[19] Slowly the fact appeared that wealth and privilege had rendered them just as remote from their own people as from their non-Jewish surroundings. This isolation did not lead them any closer to their environment but to the establishment of more intimate connections between the families of the various *Hofjuden* who often lived far apart. The business relations and the international correspondence between the leading *Hofjuden* families were soon followed by intermarriage, resembling in all details the international marriage relations of the aristocracy. This culminated in a real caste system, unknown thus far to Jewish society. Non-Jewish circles noticed this establishment of a new caste all the more as it took place at a time when the European castes began to disappear into newly developing classes. The Jewish people did not have any such classes; there were no peasants among them and they did not participate in the development of capitalism as employers or workers. In the 19th century, when the process of the establishment of classes in the non-Jewish world and the establishment of a caste

in Jewry was nearly completed, the Jewish people as a whole came to
be regarded as a caste, although only the former *Hofjuden* were a
caste within the Jewish people.[20]

The Privileged of Education

In order to protect themselves against too risky business operations
and exorbitant demands from the princes, the *Hofjuden* began to
allow more prosperous ghetto dwellers to participate in their state
affairs. In this way they not only secured influence over the material
welfare of wider groups of Jews but also drew them out of the narrow
ghetto life and got them to become interested in the welfare of the
states in which they resided. By force of circumstances the princes, in
turn, also became interested in the well-being and rights of this group
of Jews. The *Hofjuden* in this way helped to pave the way for Jewish
emancipation in Europe. The edicts of emancipation later promulgated by the various European states were not intended to do more
than to grant privileges to those Jews who, by their wealth and their
business activities, already had come to be counted among the most
trustworthy supporters of the nation states, and who in Prussia had
been called *Schutzjuden*.

From the somewhat larger strata of the well-to-do but not generally
privileged *Schutzjuden* came a new type of privileged Jew—the Jew
who was exceptional because of culture and education. Of this group
Moses Mendelssohn became the prototype. In contrast to the exceptional Jews of wealth, these Jews had very little influence upon the political development of the Jews of western Europe, but they did play an
important role in the discussion of the Jewish question. Whereas the
court-Jews had proved to the state that Jews were useful, the first
western-educated Jews convinced society that Jews were human
beings. In contrast to the policy of the *Hofjuden,* the educated Jews
tried, from the very beginning, to receive recognition from the non-
Jewish world. But just as the princes no longer considered their
Hofjuden as Jews when they proved to be useful and, therefore, relieved them of disabilities in force against other Jews, so contemporary society admitted the educated Jews for the express reason that
they no longer considered them to be Jews. "Who in the world,"

wrote Herder, "when reading the philosophic works of Spinoza, Mendelsohn and Herz, would give any thought to the fact that they were written by Jews?"[21]

For the enlightened Berlin of Mendelssohn's time as for the Berlin of Humboldt and Schleiermacher the Jews served as living proof that all men were human. That they could be friends with Markus Herz or with Mendelssohn was for them the salvation of the dignity of the human race. Jews were "new types of humanity" and, because they were scions of a despised and oppressed people, they were a purer and more exemplary model of humanity. Social relations with Jews not only exhibited freedom from prejudice (called "tolerance" in the 18th century) but served as an example of the possibility of intimacy with all species of humanity. Herder, a great friend of the Jews, first used the phrase, "a strange people of Asia, driven into our regions,"[22] which was later misrepresented by antisemites. These humanists wantonly alienated themselves from neighbors of many thousand years standing, from one of the basic nations of European culture, because they were eager to stress the basic unity of humanity, and the more alien the origins of the Jewish people were made out to be, the more effective would be the demonstration of this universal principle.

During a short period, which however proved very important for the history of Europeanized Jewry, Prussia's enlightened intelligentsia —under the impression made by Lessing's *Nathan the Wise*—arrived at the conclusion that the "new types of humanity," because they had become examples of humanity, must also as individuals be more intensely human. Mirabeau was strongly influenced by this tenet and powerfully proclaimed it—again with reference to Mendelssohn's personality—in pre-revolutionary Paris. Herder once more may be considered the representative spokesman of this school of thought. He hoped that educated Jews would show a greater freedom from prejudice, because "the Jew is free of certain political judgments which it is very hard or impossible for us to abandon."[23] Above all, protesting expressly against "concessions of new mercantile advantages," Herder proposed to the German Jews that education was their way out of Judaism and out of "the old and proud national prejudices . . . customs that do not belong to our age and constitutions." Through education they, more than any others, would become "more purely humanized" and of great value for the "development of the sciences and the entire culture of mankind."[24]

This kind of judgment concerning the exceptional Jews of education turned out to be disastrous for the normalization of the Jewish situation. The educated Jews, faced with the ludicrous demand to be not only exceptional Jews but also exceptional specimens of humanity, did their best to fulfill it. This does not, however, apply to Mendelssohn, who hardly knew Herder and the thoughts of the younger generation. Mendelssohn was revered because he really was an extraordinary and unique individual. His firm adherence to his Jewish religion made impossible for him that ultimate break with the masses of Jewry, which became a matter of course for his successors. He felt himself to be "a member of an oppressed people which must beg for the good-will and protection of the governing nation."[25] Mendelssohn always was aware of the fact that the extraordinary esteem given to his person only corresponded to the extraordinary contempt in which his people were held. He was not yet among the number of those who shared in this contempt and, therefore, did not consider himself an exception.

The first European-educated Jews had this in common with the court-Jews: they owed their extraordinary career to themselves only and to their uncommon individual talents. The rewards for education, however, were quite different from those reaped by the wealthy.

In contrast to the privileged Jews of wealth, the educated Jews enjoyed no political privileges. Mendelssohn himself wrote ironically to Lavater that he, friend of all educated Germany, would be subject to the same tax levied upon an ox led to the market if he wanted to visit Lavater in Leipzig. On the other hand, the educated Jews, as soon as they appeared on the scene, were granted access to society, made friends and enjoyed special esteem in intellectual circles. It is true the middle class of the time refused to enter into social contact with them, but this was of very little importance to them and their social career since, for the greater part of the 19th century, and particularly in Prussia, it was the nobility and not the bourgeoisie that decided social standards. It was because bourgeois society in Prussia had no social standards and because the German intelligentsia, therefore, was socially homeless that Jews and Jewish salons could become the centers of German intellectual life.

A kind of social upheaval in Prussia seemed to act as a substitute for the French political emancipation. While France was the land of political glory, Prussia seemed on the way to become the land of social splendor. At the turning point from the 18th to the 19th century "Jews all over the world turned their eyes to the Jewish community in Berlin" and not to Paris.[26] "Intellectual Berlin," where Mendelssohn established close connections and exchanged letters with nearly all the famous men of his time, was only a beginning. True, Jewish scholars in many periods of European history since the time of Charlemagne had relations with their Christian colleagues. The novel and surprising aspect of Mendelssohn, however, was that this friendship was used for political purposes, as by Dohm and Mirabeau, or as an example of true humanity, as by Lessing and Herder. Mendelssohn himself never took any interest in the political battles of his time, not even in the fight for Jewish emancipation. The Prussia which his friend Lessing described as "Europe's most enslaved land" was to Mendelssohn "a state in which one of the wisest princes who ever ruled men has made the arts and sciences to flourish, has made national freedom of thought so general that its beneficent effects reach even the lowliest inhabitants of his domain."[27] A generation later, in the Jewish salons where Mendelssohn's daughter Dorothea Schlegel, Henriette Herz, and Rachel Levin-Varnhagen reigned amidst a truly mixed society, Jewish political interests had become completely extinguished. Here the dominant view was that public discussion of the Jewish question and, above all, those measures by the state which would liberate by force the educated Jewish individuals together with the "backward" Jews, could only make their situation worse. When such emancipation seemed to be on the verge of reality, after Napoleon's victory over Prussia and the beginnings of Prussian reforms, the number of Jewish conversions increased rapidly. It looked as if the educated Jews of Prussia tried to escape emancipation by baptism.[28]

The first Jewish "salon" in Berlin was in the house of the physician and philosopher, Markus Herz, a disciple of Kant, who held a series of private lectures in his home in the 1780's. Markus Herz still belonged to the older generation of Mendelssohn, and for him, as for Mendelssohn, contacts with non-Jews were less a social program than a simple and agreeable fact, a matter of personal friendship with learned men and disciples. His wife, however, very much younger than Herz, soon gathered around her a social circle of pupils. In Henriette Herz's salon, too, the atmosphere of personal friendship still prevailed. She tried, however, to organize the friendships into the so-called *Tugendbund,* which counted the brothers Humboldt, both Counts Dohna, and Schleiermacher among its members. In her hands, the purely personal and intimate social relations were transformed into a program. Assimilation had begun.

Ten years later nothing remained of the *Tugendbund.* The enlightened nobles, the romantic intellectuals and the middle-class characters who formerly frequented Henriette Herz's house moved into the famous "attic" of Rahel Levin. Here a new element—the actors—soon joined them. In contrast to Henriette Herz's salon, Rahel's attic remained at the very fringe, sometimes even outside society and its conventions. While the glamor of Henriette came from her wide knowledge, Rahel was proud of her "ignorance" and celebrated because of her native cleverness and social talent. Rahel's salon which, as she herself declared, foundered after the Prussian defeat of 1806 "like a ship containing the highest enjoyment of life,"[29] was a unique and original manifestation in the history of Jewish assimilation. In her circle each person really counted only for what he represented. Here judgment was based only on personality. Neither rank (although Louis Ferdinand was a Hohenzollern prince and von der Marwitz a scion of one of the oldest aristocratic families), nor money (although Abraham Mendelssohn, son of Moses Mendelssohn and father of Felix Mendelssohn-Bartholdy was a rich banker), nor success in public life (although Friedrich Gentz was already a well-known political writer), nor even an exceptional literary career (Friedrich Schlegel, despite growing fame, was never very much liked) had any influence. Likewise Rahel's salon was not, like so many later Jewish salons, a mixed society only in name, but in fact Jewish with a few "exceptional non-Jews"; it was also, however, not non-Jewish with a few specially admitted Jews. It was naively undenominational and represented a short period of flowering of German-Jewish social relations which produced more mixed marriages than any subsequent period.

There was one remarkable point about these mixed marriages; they were nearly always concluded between Jewish women and German noblemen. Except for the case of Mendelssohn's daughter, Dorothea Veit, who left her Jewish husband and eloped with Friedrich Schlegel, there is hardly an instance of intermarriage with middle-class Germans. During a whole decade it looked as if the Jewish girls of Prussia would be snapped up and married by noblemen. What the Jewish women of the period thought was the beginning of a new "enlightened" era was in reality the end of the centuries-old economic relations between Jewish money-lenders and debt-burdened feudal nobility. It was the end. Wealthier Jews had withdrawn from the business of lending money to private persons among the nobility, and the medium and small businessmen had their hands full with investments in the loans floated by the states at the time, so that they too had lost interest in personal loans. The endeavor to replace loans by dowries remained for some time the economic basis for the spiritual and social tolerance of the Prussian aristocracy. It is not unimportant to note, in this connection, that the policy of the Rothschilds to refuse them personal loans and to substitute "gifts" is one which they have followed since the time of the Congress of Vienna,[30] while their own family law, which permitted their girls to marry non-Jewish aristocrats but kept the male line Jewish, is of much more recent date.

While the period of intermarriages between Jews and aristocrats was a short one in Prussia, close relations between nobility and Jewry lasted in Austria until the end of the Hapsburg monarchy. In general, it may be said that the extraordinary aversion shown by the European nobility toward the bourgeoisie and its fear of the steadily growing political power of this class offered certain opportunities to the Jews. It certainly was more agreeable and less dangerous for an aristocrat to be helped by a Jewish banker's money than to accept as a father-in-law one of the big industrialists, who either wanted to get into parliament himself or whose sons were out for a political career. They were sure that no such ambitions reigned among the Jews.

It was a characteristic feature of the social idyll in Rahel Levin's attic that such social and economic interests were still completely hidden; her aristocratic friends were driven by a powerful yearning for individual emancipation, a feeling which had been present in a stronger measure only among the French nobility of the *ancien régime*. The peculiar intimacy, the atmosphere of real comprehension in friendship which connected the scions of noble families and the daughters of the Jewish middle class, were but indirectly due to the spread of ideas of the Enlightenment. The essential thing was that the personal problems of these educated Jews were fundamentally identical with those of the young and intellectually starved aristocrats. Both wanted individual and not political emancipation; for both the greatest hindrance to such emancipation was their rigid family relationship according to which they were first of all links in the family structure and only secondarily independent individuals. Individual assimilation for the Jews and individual emancipation for the nobles meant escape from this family association and transformation into a person independent of family.[31] What bound these individuals to each other was the purely personal; this period of high development of social life in Prussia was due to the total absence of political aims among the Jewish women and the noblemen. They were preoccupied only with the development of their personality and their *"éducation sentimentale."*

Rahel's salon, its cultural atmosphere and its cult of Goethe, continued to exercise for a long time a strong influence on the Jews and the middle class of Berlin. These exceptional Jews of education who considered Germany their home, could well have said that they were Germans by the grace of Goethe. The ideas of *Bildung* expounded by Goethe particularly in his *Wilhelm Meister,* became the spiritual element of German-Jewish assimilation. In *Wilhelm Meister* education is clearly tied up with social advancement and it actually aims at the transformation of the burgher into the nobleman.[32] Through education these Jews became "personalities" and as such found open doors to society. Through culture, and not through political means like emancipation, did Jews seek to escape from the lowly status of their people.

The enthusiasm for culture of these first Jews to escape from the ghetto had much more in common with the great enthusiasm of the *Haskalah* than with the educational philistinism of later decades which did so much to make the German Jews unpopular. What distinguished Rahel from all her female and male successors was the fact that she was a real "personality," an exceptionally courageous, clever, and entirely natural human being. With her, the "individual solution of the Jewish question," which later became a tradition and a tenet of the philistines of learning, was still a pure form of individual development. It turned out to be an ironical fact in her life, that the spiritual, social, and psychological means with which she tried to escape from Judaism, became a Jewish tradition. But her personality was so much imbued with a great sense of honesty that she, as the only one among the women of her age, could die in peace as a self-conscious Jewess, consoled by the knowledge that the young "rebel Heinrich Heine" would be her true heir.[33]

While the privileged Jews of wealth had to remain Jews by force of circumstances and acquired power as political representatives and rulers of the Jewish communities, the exceptional Jews of education, in their first and second generations, nearly all followed the way that led to baptism. Heine's celebrated saying that "baptism is the entrance ticket to European culture" does not properly apply to these converts, who were already steeped in European culture before they were baptized. The Jewish intelligentsia had no other choice if it wanted to escape from the traditional Jewish way of life. Another saying by Heine, not so well known, that he would never have become converted "if the law permitted one to steal silver spoons," is much nearer the truth. Just as Jewish businessmen were compelled to remain Jews in order to acquire more wealth, so Jewish intellectuals had to abandon Judaism so as not to starve.[34] The law which prohibited the stealing of silver spoons punished only the Jewish intellectuals with starvation; it took liberal care of the business interests of court-Jews and state-bankers.

Even though nearly all the educated Jews in Prussia followed the road to the baptismal font, this fact did not make them cease to be Jews, neither in their own opinion nor in that of their environment. Many years after his baptism and after having changed his name, Börne wrote: "Some reproach me with being a Jew, some praise me because of it, some pardon me for it, but all think of it."[35] The forced conversion, by which they could not and did not want to lose their Jewishness, placed the Jewish intelligentsia in bitter opposition to a state of things which put a premium on lack of character and punished simple human dignity with starvation. The "new specimens of humanity" all became rebels. When the rich Jews not only recognized the very constitutions and states which humiliated and insulted them but also supported and financed the most reactionary tendencies of European politics (first, English intervention against Napoleon on the continent, then Metternich's policy of "stability" and reaction), this rebellion was carried over to the Jewish scene. When one reads Karl Marx's *Zur Judenfrage,* a work which is historically false and in many points unjust, one should not forget that Marx's voice was that of the Jewish intelligentsia, full of hate against the machinations of the rich Jews who had sold universal human rights for the sake of the special privileges of their own class. This is a fact which Börne, writing a few decades before Marx, expressed as follows: "Rothschild kissed the Pope's hand. . . . At last the order has come which God had planned originally when he created the world. A poor Christian kisses the Pope's feet, and a rich Jew kisses his hand. If Rothschild could have gotten his Roman loan at 60 per cent instead of 65, and could have sent the cardinal-chamberlain more than ten thousand ducats, they would have allowed him to embrace the Holy Father."[36]

The contrast between rich Jews and educated Jews was plainly visible only in Germany. In Austria, a Jewish intelligentsia did not appear before the end of the 19th century and immediately felt the whole impact of antisemitic pressure. After World War I educated Jews in Austria became Social Democrats, but before this they, together with the Jewish middle class, sought refuge in the protection of the Hapsburg monarchy. A significant exception to this rule was Karl Kraus, the last representative of a tradition created by Heine and Börne, who converted to Catholicism as a young man. In France, where the emancipation decree survived all changes of regimes and where even the *décret infâme* affected "only" poor Jews and not educated Jewish circles, there were individual Jewish intellectuals but not a Jewish intelligentsia as a new and socially recognized class. In all these countries there never existed the short period, so decisive for the history of German Jews, in which the very vanguard of society not only accepted Jews *nolens volens,* but in a fit of strange enthusiasm wanted to assimilate them immediately. The well-known remark by Bismarck that he wanted to see "German stallions paired off with

Jewish mares," is but the last and most vulgar expression of his readiness.

A little known fact, though very important for the history of German Jewry, is that assimilation as a program led much more often to baptism than to mixed marriage. We know that there were families in Germany who were baptized for generations and yet remained purely Jewish.[37] The converted Jew left his family only in very rare cases, still more rare were instances of baptized Jews leaving their Jewish surroundings. The Jewish family proved to be a more durable and conserving force than the Jewish religion. This peculiar phenomenon is only partly due to the Jewish will to survive. Such a will for continued existence is active in all nations, and, if it is frustrated politically, it triumphs over any individual tendency on the part of individual members of the nation. Equally important was the fact that Jews who were baptized because they found it opportune, soon learned that society, insofar as it accepted Jews at all, wanted to have Jews and not Christians. At best, society desired "new specimens of humanity" and not silly mimicry. Thus, a convinced humanist like Wilhelm von Humboldt arrived at his above-mentioned remarks about "Jews *en détail"* only when good old friends, like Rahel Levin, Henriette Herz, and the physician Koreff, began to make a career by abandoning Judaism. Both Humboldt and Schleiermacher became such zealous protagonists of emancipation because they hoped that full and unmistakable equality would stop the mimicry and the parvenu aspirations of the former pariahs.[38] This hope was not fulfilled because emancipation did not liberate the existing Jewish people. Imitating the edicts of toleration for the various Christian sects, the emancipators invented the "believers in the Mosaic faith," in order to be able to confer upon them human rights. Thus were created among the Jewish people a class of men and women who gladly accepted such a designation, but the Jewish people remained a nation of pariahs and continued to produce its parvenus. Even Humboldt, in the last analysis, believed that assimilation had to be, if not a condition, a necessary consequence of emancipation. For him also, the political task presented only the aspects of a social problem. It is one of the most unfortunate facts in the history of the Jewish people that only their enemies, but never their friends, could understand that the Jewish question was "a political problem."[39]

Nothing could be more favorable for the development of privileged Jews both of wealth and of education than this social ("liberal") concept, which was dominant during the 19th century. The defenders of emancipation presented the problem as one of education, originally applying to Jews as well as non-Jews.[40] Deprived of its political significance, it was considered preparatory for assimilation. It was taken for granted that the vanguard in both camps would consist of particularly educated, tolerant, cultured people. This meant that particularly tolerant and cultured non-Jews could enter into social relations with exceptional Jews of education. The demand for the abolition of prejudice soon became a very one-sided affair and only the Jews were called upon to become "educated."

The social paradise for Jews in Prussia—that brief period, when ancient Jew-hatred had really disappeared and modern antisemitism had not yet been born—came to a definitive end in the same year when Napoleon's *décret infâme* temporarily abolished political freedom for the Jews. The proclamation of human rights by the French Revolution would never have been a really revolutionary act if the wishes of the rich Jews of Bordeaux and Avignon had been fulfilled and the Ashkenazim, the poor Jews of Alsace, had been excluded. The *décret infâme*, referring to Alsatian Jews only, reestablished the old order by creating, on the one hand, privileged Jews and, on the other, a class which from that period to our own tragic times has come to be called *Ostjuden*.

Prussia in the period of reforms, after it had lost Posen and the provinces with the largest number of Jews, could, without risk of complications, carry through the type of emancipation which would benefit the "loyal" wealthy elements without the inclusion of the masses of Jewish peddlers and artisans. Thus in 1808, the government of the enlightened despot, Frederick William III, promulgated, immediately after the cession of Posen, the Prussian municipal law, which gave civic but not political rights to the former *Schutzjuden*. Four years later the same Prussian government, under the pressure of the liberal bureaucracy, had to grant a decree of emancipation. When Prussia, after the Congress of Vienna, regained Posen and with it the greatest part of its Jews, the government rescinded the emancipation decree but left the municipal law in force. This provided civic, non-political rights for those Jews who were useful to the state.

During the short period when Prussia lost Posen to the Duchy of Warsaw, *Schutzjuden,* numbering about 20 per cent of the Jewish population before, lost the broad background of poor, uneducated Jews against which these privileged Jews stood out so advantageously. The interest the state evinced in the welfare of its remaining Jews showed clearly to society that the problem was not that of individual exceptions but rather of a collective group that was most intimately bound up with the interests of the monarchy.[41] The vague foreboding, which had been shown by the exceptional Jews of education in their protestations against state interference indeed proved justified; society drew apart from the individual Jews as soon as it noticed that they were members of an officially protected group. The state, often under the pretext of its "Christian character," supported, during the entire 19th century the separation of Jews from the non-Jewish society around them.[42] The administration carried out this aim by over-privileging the wealthy Jews and, after granting emancipation to the Jewish middle class, raising them into the ranks of the nobility, and by wilfully under-privileging the Jewish intelligentsia. Only a class of Jews completely dependent on the state, because it was ostracised by society, could be trusted by the government to be completely loyal and ever ready for any service. Changes in the political ideas of the changing state administrations did not have any influence on the service given by these Jews. Like the civil services which usually survived all changes in government, the rich Jews definitely were a part of the state machinery. The history of the house of Rothschild proves that Metternich was wrong when he said to the Austrian Rothschilds a few years before the Revolution of 1848: "If I go to the devil, you will go with me."[43]

The paradox of the history of the Jews in western Europe—and this can best be studied in the history of Germany—consisted of the fact that they always had to pay for social glory with political misery and for political success with social insult. Social assimilation in the sense of full recognition by non-Jewish society was granted to them only so long as they appeared distinctly as exceptions from the Jewish masses. When these dark masses disappeared for a few years, the exceptional Jews became once again simple Jews, not exceptions from, but representatives of the despised people. After the Prussian defeat in 1807 Berlin society left the Jewish salons with unmatched rapidity and turned to the houses of the titled bureaucracy and the upper middle classes. The Brentanos, the Arnims, Kleist, even the older generation of Schlegel and Gentz, all these became more or less antisemitic, and their contempt for the Jews was directed toward the Berlin Jews they knew and not against the unknown Jews of Posen. Since the time of political romanticism the educated circles of Germany did not show any too great discretion in handling the Jewish question. Their tact became so pitiful that it almost looked like an insult. No ever-so-large mass of *Ostjuden,* within or without the German borders, could again help the poor heap of assimilated Jews to the collective consciousness of being exceptions. Every one of them had henceforth to prove that, although he was a Jew, yet he was not a Jew. They were thus forced to betray not only sections of their "backward brethren" but their entire people as well as themselves.

This social transformation so unfavorable for the Jews was noted by contemporaries only in a few isolated cases, and historians took almost no notice of it. The edict of 1812 and the frank pro-Jewish attitude of the state during the period of Prussian reforms subsequently caused the antisemitic feelings in society to be forgotten. At that time, however, state and society were very far from being identical, and the absolute monarchy still remained absolutely separated from the people even when it carried through measures in behalf of the people, such as the emancipation of the Prussian serfs. The Prussian state granted emancipation to the Jews when sympathies for the Jews in society had disappeared; no class in the nation stood behind the new pro-Jewish measures. It now turned out that social antisemitism remained politically of as little effect as the philosemitism and assimilation tendencies of the preceding decade.

Modern social antisemitism is as old as assimilation. The discussion of the emancipation of the Jews and the assimilation of individual Jews to non-Jewish society was in full swing when Grattenauer's publication, *Wider die Juden,* appeared in 1802.[44] It was clearly written and intended not so much to impress the government as Berlin society. In this Grattenauer was thoroughly successful. It is interesting to note in this pamphlet for the first time the expression "the Jew," that is to say, "not the Jewish individual, but the Jew in general, the Jew everywhere and nowhere."[45] This and similar phrases regarding the Jews as a "principle," recur as stereotypes during the entire course of the 19th century.[46] In Grattenauer's pamphlet it is still an isolated occurrence. His phrase shows, however, that the antisemites sensed what the ideological protagonists of emancipation did not know and what educated Jews vaguely feared, namely, that the coming emancipation, as conceived by the state, was to be a reward for the individual services of the *Hofjuden*, tending to create a select group under the protection of the state as reward for its unconditional support. This ended the period when society considered only the individual Jew; now every Jew became once again a member of a collective which society viewed as part of the state machinery, and which at times it resisted. Never again did society accept the Jews with free mind and pure heart.

In the pre-emancipation era in Berlin of the 1780's when Shakespeare's *Merchant of Venice* was produced, a little, charming prologue was presented, which explained to the public that Shylock the Jew should not be identified with the Jews in the audience and requested the Jews in the theatre not to take amiss the presentation of the character of Shylock. After emancipation, such a show of good will and courtesy can hardly be imagined. In the earlier period society still cherished the naive opinion that the Shylocks lived in Posen or faraway Poland. When this background had disappeared, society created something new, viz.: "the Jew in general." This Jew looked very similar to Mr. Shylock.

The Personal Problem

In order to escape the pariah situation in society, emancipated Jewry had to differentiate itself from this "Jew in general," and this completely changed its character. It perverted their self-reliance and created a peculiar set of manners that soon came to be regarded as "typically Jewish." Jews ceased to appear to themselves and to their neighbors as men of a certain origin and certain religion. Instead, they became a group of people with certain attributes called Jewish.

Judaism became Jewishness—a psychological quality—and the Jewish question became a personal problem.

In its tragic endeavor to differentiate itself from the specter of the "Jew in general," assimilated Jewry did indeed develop a Jewish type with a definite and fixed personality. This type had little in common with the picture of the Jew invented by Jewish apologetics and used to combat the caricature of the "Jew in general." The invented Jewish type was endowed with attributes that are the privilege of pariahs and which Jews really possessed: humanity, kindness, freedom from prejudice, rebellion against injustice. The type of "Jew in general" created by antisemites was endowed by them with certain qualities which the *parvenu* must acquire if he wants to be successful and which Jewish *parvenus* really showed: inhumanity, greed, insolence, cringing servility, and ambition. So long as defamed peoples and classes exist, such attributes will be produced anew by every generation with incomparable monotony.

The problem which confronted every Jewish individual in every generation was the decision whether to remain a pariah or become a *parvenu*. Ever since the middle of the last century the key to the so-called complex spiritual and psychological state of mind of the average Jew is to be found in the regret of the pariah not to have succeeded in becoming a *parvenu* and the bad conscience of the *parvenu* who knew that he had betrayed his people, denied his origin, and exchanged universal justice for personal privilege. The character of generations of Jews has been influenced by the simple fact that every Jew belonged either to an over-privileged upper class or to an under-privileged mass and that the only way out of the dilemma was the questionable one of abandoning Judaism. In some cases under-privilege and over-privilege were strangely intertwined in the same person. A good instance is the case of Salomon Maimon, the philosopher, whom Kant esteemed more than all his other pupils. Maimon was born in bitter poverty in a small Polish-Jewish town. He could never have made his career as an adventurer and a scholar had he not been a Jew and helped by Jews; but he died in the castle of a Prussian count without a penny in his pocket. A Polish non-Jew of his circumstances could hardly have attained the status of a well-known commentator of Kant; however, in the unlikely case that he did succeed, he would have died a full professor, leaving a small fortune. Salomon Maimon knew well that he was a pariah, and Heinrich Heine would never have risen above the ranks of the mediocre talents which German Jewry produced by the dozens if he had not adhered from the very beginning to the "accident of his birth." *"Geldjuden,"* whom Heine and Börne derided so bitterly, came to participate in high politics even though they secretly knew that as Jews they had no right to do so. The great rebels of the 19th century raised their voices on all the affairs of their time just because they were Jews and because they could produce the telling credentials of oppression.

The fate of the average Jew, however, was that of eternal lack of decision. Society, moreover, never compelled him definitely to make a choice. The average assimilated Jew lived in a twilight of favor and misfortune, with a presentiment that both success and failure were inextricably connected with the fact that he was a Jew. For him the Jewish question had lost all political importance, but it haunted his private life and hence influenced all the more tyrannically his private decisions. It was by no means a simple task to behave in such a manner as not to resemble the image of the "Jew in general" pictured by society and yet remain a Jew. The average Jew, neither a *parvenu* nor a rebel, could only stress an empty sense of "being different," which later was interpreted in many psychological variations as innate strangeness. The chief point in this unhappy self-anaylsis was the conviction that one was as widely different from the "simple and naive *Goy,"* as from the "backward east-European Jew."

The strangeness of the individual Jews, of which they were so proud, was nothing but the Jewish question projected into their individual psychological situation. It is hard to decide whether this psychological projection was of greater harm to a reasonable discussion and solution of the Jewish question or to the individual Jews themselves. A political task becomes only distorted if a psychological solution is sought for, and the souls of men are strangely transformed when politics is converted into inner experience and the reality of public affairs into private emotion. If even today a Jew, when asked what he thinks he is and what he wants, answers with a description of his emotions and inward experiences, one should not forget that this peculiar behavior has been the *modus vivendi* of generations; it does not disappear overnight. After all, when the world was in a somewhat peaceful state, this attitude did not work out so badly. While sentiments are harmful in political life, where they choke the passions, they can be useful in individual life. At all times society has appreciated people who could express their emotions directly, such as the actor and the virtuoso. The assimilated Jews, half proud and half ashamed of their "Jewishness," clearly were in this category.

NOTES

[1] *Wilhelm von Humboldt und Karoline von Humboldt in ihren Briefen* (Berlin 1900), vol. v, p. 236.

[2] Paulus, H. E. G., *Beiträge von jüdischen und christlichen Gelehrten zur Verbesserung der Bekenner jüdischen Glaubens* (Frankfurt 1817). "The separation of the Jews will only be encouraged if the governments continue to treat them as a whole, in a bad or good sense. If however every one of them is given individual treatment, with justice for every one, according to his behavior, this separation will be dissolved through action." The attack is directed particularly against Humboldt, who defended the cause of the Jews at the Congress of Vienna. Humboldt's argument for the liberation of the Jews *"en masse"* and against a slow method of amelioration, is clearly outlined in his "Expert Opinion" of 1809: "A gradual abolition confirms the separation which it intends to destroy. In all points which are not abolished, it draws attention—by the very fact of the new liberty—to all still existing restrictions and thereby acts against itself" (cited in: Freund, Ismar, *Die Emanzipation der Juden in Preussen* [Berlin 1912], vol. ii, p. 270).

[3] Riesser, Gabriel, *Gesammelte Schriften* (Leipzig 1867), vol. iv, p. 290.

[4] *Cf.* Samuel, Horace B., *Modernities* (London 1914), pp. 50 ff.

[5] Paulus, H. E. G., *Die jüdische Nationalabsonderung nach Ursprung, Folgen und Besserungsmitteln* (1831), pp. 6–7.

[6] It is not without its irony that this excellent formula which may serve as a motto for western European assimilation as a whole, was propounded by a Russian Jew and first published in Hebrew. It comes from Judah Leib Gordon's Hebrew poem, *Haqitsah ammi* (1863).

[7] Dohm, Christian Wilhelm, *Denkwürdigkeiten meiner Zeit* (Lemgo 1814–19), vol. iv, p. 487.

[8] *Cf.* Bondy-Dworsky, *Geschichte der Juden in Böhmen* (Prague 1906), vol. ii, p. 727.

[9] Paulus, *op. cit.*, already made a very just remark: "The mighty ones (leading Jewry) . . . endeavor only to get more influence for themselves, but would like to keep the others in their national isolation, pretending that this separation

is part of their religion. Why? . . . Because the others should depend on them even more and be put to the sole use of the powerful ones under the name 'Unsere Leute.' "

¹⁰ *Cf.* Jost, Isaak Markus, *Neure Geschichte der Israeliten,* vol. x (1846), p. 102.

¹¹ *Op. cit.,* part ix, p. 38.

¹² Priebatsch, Felix, "Die Judenpolitik des fürstlichen Absolutismus im 17. und 18. Jahrhundert," in *Forschungen und Versuche zur Geschichte des Mittelalters und der Neuzeit,* in honor of Dietrich Schaefer (1915). In this work, we find a typical example from the early 18th century: "When the manufactory of mirrors in Neuhaus, Lower Austria, which was subsidized by the administration, did not produce results, the Jew, Wertheimer, gave the emperor the money to buy it. When asked to take over the manufactory, he refused, stating that his time is too much taken up with his financial transactions."

Corresponding to this tradition, which kept the rich Jews from the real positions of power in capitalism, is the fact that the Paris Rothschilds in 1911 sold their share in the oil wells of Baku to the Royal Shell Group, after having figured for a while as the biggest petroleum tycoons at Rockefeller's side *(see* Lewisohn, R., *Wie sie gross und reich wurden* [Berlin 1927]).

André Sayous' statement in his polemic against Sombart's identification of Jews and capitalist development, may be taken as a general rule: "The Rothschilds and other Israelites who were almost exclusively engaged in launching state loans and in the international movement of capital did not try at all . . . to create great industries." "Les Juifs," in *Revue Economique Internationale* (1932).

¹³ *Cf.* Grunwald, M., *Samuel Oppenheimer und sein Kreis* (1913), p. 150. Conditions in Bavaria were very similar. *See* Sundheimer, Paul, "Die jüdische Hochfinanz und der bayrische Staat im 18. Jahrhundert," in *Finanz-Archiv,* vol. xli (1924).

¹⁴ Johann Jacob Schudt reports in his *Jüdische Merkwürdigkeiten* (Frankfurt a.M. 1715–1717) as follows: "A certain Jew . . . when a noble and cultured medical man reproached him gently that they (the Jews) were so proud, though they had no princes among them and no part in government . . . replied with insolence: "We are no princes, yet we govern them" (Part iv, Annex p. 48).

¹⁵ The Paris Rothschild is justified in writing in 1819: "Who buys state bonds in Germany? and who has tried to raise the quotation rate, if not our nation . . . " (cited in Corti, Egon Caesar, *Der Aufstieg des Hauses Rothschild 1700–1830* [Leipzig 1927], p. 230).

¹⁶ "[The Jews] seemed very little disturbed about the hostility of the administration of the imperial cities and of the middle-class townsmen. Glückel von Hameln thinks that the situation in Hamburg will always be like that, as long as the burghers will run the town. The Jews knew they were protected by the emperor and the princes. . . . The townsmen complained all the time about their insolent talk, that they felt they were just as independent as the imperial

cities, that they did not care what the town-council decided . . . and said that only the emperor was their master and sovereign" (Priebatsch, *op. cit.*, pp. 598–99).

[17] Stern, Selma, *Jud Suess* (Berlin 1929), pp. 18–19.

[18] Schudt, *op. cit.*, vol. i, p. 19.

[19] It is reported that Frederick II of Prussia, when hearing of a possible conversion of his Jews to Christianity, exclaimed: "I hope they are not possessed by the devil!" See *Kleines Jahrbuch des Nützlichen und Angenehmen für Israeliten*, 1847.

[20] Christian Friedrich Rühs gives a characteristic definition of the whole Jewish people as a "caste of businessmen." "Über die Ansprüche der Juden an das deutsche Bürgerrecht," in *Zeitschrift für die neueste Geschichte* (1815).

[21] Herder, J. G., *Werke,* ed. by B. Suphan, vol. xxiv (1886), p. 73.

[22] *Ibid.*, p. 63.

[23] *Ibid.*, p. 71.

[24] *Ibid.*, pp. 74–75.

[25] Mendelssohn, Moses, Letter to Lavater (1770), in *Gesammelte Schriften*, vol. vii (Berlin 1930).

[26] Priebatsch, *op cit.*, p. 646.

[27] In his preface to his translation of Menasseh Ben Israel, in *Gesammelte Schriften,* vol. iii (Leipzig 1843–45).

[28] Adam Müller expressed the general opinion of the educated Jews of Berlin when he wrote in 1815 to Metternich: "Every legal or political measure for the emancipation of the Jews must necessarily lead to a deterioration of their civic and social situation." See his *Ausgewählte Abhandlungen,* ed. by J. Baxa, (Jena 1921), p. 215. A similar report is given by Jost, *op. cit.*, vol. x, pp. 44ff., when he writes about the "weak defense on the part of the Jews" during the attacks at the time immediately after the Congress of Vienna.

[29] Cited from a letter to Pauline César (Wiesel) in the summer of 1816. *See* my *Rahel Varnhagen, The Life of a Jewess* (London 1957).

[30] *See* Corti, *op. cit.,* ch. iv.

[31] The history of the engagement of Rahel Levin to Count Finckenstein is an excellent instance of the homogeneousness of such personal problems. After a conflict which lasted several years, Rahel broke the engagement because her noble fiancé finally returned to his family's lap.

[32] *See* Hehn, Victor, *Gedanken über Goethe* (1888), p. 260.

[33] Her husband, Karl August Varnhagen, who was particularly careful to eliminate the Jewish question from his edition of Rahel's letters and diaries, published the following sentences from her death bed: "What a story! . . . I, a refugee from Egypt and Palestine, find here such help, love and care! With what sublime delight I think of this my origin and of the whole network of fate. . . . Such a long time in my life it was my greatest shame, my bitterest sorrow and misfortune to know that I was born a Jewess, now I would not miss

this feeling for all the world. . . ." *Rahel, Ein Buch des Andenkens* (1834), vol. 1, p. 43.

[34] Riesser, Gabriel, "Betrachtungen über die Verhältnisse der jüdischen Unter- tanen der Preussichen Monarchie" (1834), in *Gesammelte Schriften,* vol. iii: "By far the largest part of those Jews who in accordance with the law of 1812 . . . devoted themselves to science . . . have adopted Christianity. . . . Only a few were in such a situation that they could afford to serve science and art in independent leisure. . . . Hardly a tenth part of all scholars coming from Jewish families since 1812 could be saved for Judaism in this way."

[35] *Briefe aus Paris,* 74th Letter, February 1832.

[36] *Ibid.,* 72nd Letter.

[37] Unfortunately statistics cover up rather than reveal this fact. They describe as mixed marriages all unions between converted and nonconverted Jewish partners.

[38] Friedrich Schleiermacher protested as early as 1799 against "the practice adopted heretofore," fearing that "single individuals and whole families will more and more frequently go this common way to Christianity. In all serious- ness I consider this as the worst that could ever happen." (*See* his "Briefe bei Gelegenheit der politisch-theologischen Aufgabe und des Sendschreibens jüdischer Hausväter," in *Werke,* Part i, vol. v (1846), p. 19.

[39] The expression was originally used by Herder in his *Adrastea (op. cit.),* but only antisemites continued to use it in the 19th century.

[40] For instance in Wilhelm von Humboldt's "Expert Opinion . . ." (*op. cit.*) we find: "The state should not exactly teach respect for the Jews, but it should abolish an inhuman and prejudiced way of thinking, etc. . . ."

[41] In 1803, the Prussian "Ausnahmekollektiv," that is the *Schutzjuden,* who lived in Prussia proper, amounted to only 19.3 percent of the total number of Jews, while 80.7 percent lived in the territories that were ceded by Prussia after 1808. In 1811, one year before the promulgation of the emancipation decree and after the loss of the provinces with the largest Jewish population, 89.4 percent of all Jews were *Schutzjuden* and only 10.58 percent "foreign Jews." At the same time, the proportion of Jews among the total population of Prussia was reduced from 2.3 percent to 0.72 percent, an even smaller percentage than of the *Schutzjuden* in the country's total population in 1803, viz. 0.94 percent. In 1816, after Prussia had partly recovered her old, formerly Polish, provinces, the percentage of former *Schutzjuden* registered at the time as "Preussiche Staatsbürger jüdischen Glaubens" (Prussian citizens of Jewish faith) sank to 52.8 percent of the total Jewish population, while the percentage of Jews with- out citizen's rights amounted to 42.7 percent. The figures are taken from Heinrich Silbergleit's *Die Bevölkerungs- und Berufsverhältnisse der Juden im Deutschen Reich,* vol. i (Berlin 1930).

[42] Varnhagen reports a remark made by Frederick William IV. "The King was asked what he intended to do with the Jews. He replied: 'I wish them well

in every respect, but I want them to feel that they are Jews.' These words provide a key to many things," *Tagebücher* (Leipzig 1861), vol. ii, p. 113.

[43] Raphael Strauss in "The Jews in the Economic Evolution of Central Europe," in *Jewish Social Studies,* vol. iii, no. 1 (January, 1941), pp. 15 ff., makes a correct assertion, when he says: "Down to the complete political collapse of 1933, there was no period in Central European history in which the rulers did not support the Jews and protect them against the shortsighted pressure of special interests and nationalist prejudice." Whether this opposition against Jewish notables was shortsighted at all times is an open question. In any case, it did not always stem from "nationalist prejudice" and was often vigorously supported by Jewish revolutionists.

[44] Carl Wilhelm Friedrich Grattenauer, as far back as 1791, wrote a pamphlet, *Über die physische und moralische Verfassung der heutigen Juden,* in which he pointed out the growing influence of the Jews in Berlin. Although the pamphlet was reviewed in the *Allgemeine Deutsche Bibliothek,* vol. cxii (1792), pp. 292–96, almost nobody ever read it.

[45] *Wider die Juden* (2nd ed. 1803), Supplement III.

[46] *E.g.,* in the review of Rühs' pamphlet (footnote 20), by Jacob Friedrich Fries in *Heidelberger Jahrbuch* (1816). Fries reproached Rühs with "confounding the Jews with Jewry and with Judaism," adding, "we declare war not on our Jewish brothers, but on Jewry."

The Jew in the Literature of the Enlightenment

The role of the Enlightenment in preparing the intellectual justification for Jewish Emancipation has fostered the belief that the philosophes and other spokesmen had emancipated themselves from the prevailing prejudices against Judaism and the Jews. Professor Barzilay's examination of the voluminous literature of the Enlightenment, however, reveals that the philosophes not only retained the usual negative notions and stereotypes, but also gave birth to new ones in the spirit of the Enlightenment itself. Just as Christian theology condemned the Jews for their obstinate refusal to accept its new teachings, the philosophes abused the Jews for clinging to their faith, which they considered in conflict with the message of the new age. The Talmud continued to be viewed in the light of earlier prejudices as an immoral and inhumane work. The philosophes also had access to Eisenmenger's *Entdecktes Judentum,* a scurrilous and ponderous work typical of the era's scholarship. Many other works about Jews, though better intentioned, repeated accepted misconceptions and introduced new misinterpretations. Talmudic scholarship was not appreciated. The rabbis were even abused for their presumed lack of ordinary common sense. Jewish customs were ridiculed, and Yiddish was viewed as an ugly crypto-dialect.

In their attacks on traditional religion, the philosophes found it safer to address themselves to Judaism rather than to Christianity. Criticism of Mosaic law and the Bible was the weapon, and the Jews constituted the immediate target. A people that obstinately continued to believe in such immoral and unethical works was assumed to be superstitious, prejudiced, and an enemy of mankind, undeserving of humane treatment. Religious tolerance was generally advocated for dissident Christians only. Barzilay views the avoidance of the mention of the treatment of the Jews by the Inquisition as illustrative of this callous indifference.

The presence of former Marranos, presumably "humanized" because they were acculturated in Christian life, softened such opinions to some extent. In contrast, the less acculturated Ashkenazim faced the customary suspicions and prejudices. Nevertheless, belief in human progress and cosmopolitan humanitarianism led to pleas for toleration. Utilitarianism and the appeal to reasons of state produced more liberal policies towards those Jews who were considered useful. Mass hostility continued, however, as seen in the debates in England in 1753 and in the anti-Jewish demands of the French local assemblies on the eve of the Revolution. Contempt and prejudice were cultivated by the portrayal of negative Jewish stereotypes on the European stage.

A new era in Christian-Jewish relations emerged during the Age of Enlightenment. Prof. Barzilay traces both the positive and negative aspects of these changes. The conflicting views and proposals concerning the Jews and their Emancipation of Diderot, Voltaire, Montesqieu, and many others are also discussed in this significant study.

ISAAC BARZILAY is Professor of Hebrew at Columbia University, and a steady contributor to JEWISH SOCIAL STUDIES. He has written numerous studies of the Haskalah and other subjects, including *Between Reason and Faith: Anti-Rationalism in Italian Jewish Thought 1250–1650* and *Shlomo Yehuda Rapoport . . . and His Contemporaries.*

The Jew in the Literature of the Enlightenment

by Isaac Eisenstein Barzilay

* The period covered by the Enlightenment has been somewhat extended in this article. Though chronologically Herder and Goethe belong to early romanticism, because of the identity of their views on the contemporary Jew with those current in the literature of the Enlightenment, their inclusion in the later period was deemed justifiable.

[For background on the ideas of Jewish national redemption in 1750–1815, *see* the introduction to chap. II in Dinaburg (now Dinur), Ben Zion, *Sefer ha-Tsiyyonut*, vol. i (Tel Aviv 1938), pp. 69–168. ED.]

I. *Introduction*

The interest of the leaders of the Enlightenment in Jews and Judaism of the past far overshadowed their concern with the Jews of their own time. In their zealous struggle against old ways of life and an antiquated *Weltanschauung* the Jew and his culture were singled out as a main target[1]; in their vision of a brighter future, he was ignored.

According to the men of the Enlightenment, the Jew represented the epitome of fanaticism and religious zeal. A good example is Diderot's censure of Moses for the spirit of religious fanaticism in the world. It was because of their obstinate allegiance to the Mosaic Law and because of his belief that this allegiance was incompatible with the new spirit of the age that Diderot condemned the Jews of his time.[2] Voltaire expressed in his own sarcastic manner his readiness "to sit

Reprinted from JEWISH SOCIAL STUDIES, Volume XVIII, 1956

down at one table and share his meal with a Turk, a Chinese, a Hindu and . . . even a Jew, provided the Jew frees himself first of his hateful Jewish superstitions and prejudices."[3] How can the Jew, Johann Gottfried Herder asked, expect tolerance and humanitarian treatment as long as he remains so obstinately loyal to his particular national law?[4] "It is inherent in the essence of God," as conceived by the positive religions, "and in the nature of the principles of religion," d'Holbach declared, "not to be tolerant."[5] Little wonder that the articles of Voltaire, Diderot and others on such subjects as the Inquisition or tolerance contain no mention of Jews. Religious tolerance was undoubtedly one of the leading ideals of the age. With few exceptions, however,[6] its scope was restricted to Christians only.

The allegiance of the Jew to his Torah cannot, however, be considered the sole reason for the attitude of the Enlightenment toward him. More basic reasons must be sought in the conditions of Jewish existence in central and western Europe during the eighteenth century.

The restoration of communities of Jews in England, Prussia and France did not reflect a changed attitude toward them. Thanks to the temporary rule of the Puritans and to prevailing mercantilist policies, a small number of Jews were permitted to settle in England. These policies also explain the admission of a handful of Jews to Prussia, and the semi-official toleration extended to the Portuguese Jews in southern France. Most of the West, however, remained closed to the Jews. This was the situation in France (except in annexed Alsace-Lorraine, where severe admission restrictions remained in full force) and in the Germanies.[7]

The expansion of trade and industry, however, led governments and rulers to look more favorably upon Jews with wealth and financial skill. It is significant, in this connection, that the secularized and worldly Sephardic-Portuguese element predominated in the new Jewish settlements in central and western Europe. Thus, the Jews with whom the standard bearers of the Enlightenment came in contact, directly or indirectly, were economically, socially and culturally upper class. Some also were abreast of current developments in the sciences. The presence in the West of rich, worldly and, to use Herder's expression, "humanized" Jews undoubtedly heightened the urgency of solving the problem of their emancipation. When John Toland advocated Jewish naturalization in England early in the century, he was influenced mainly by the financial achievements and cultural standing of the Sephardi Jews whose participation in civic life he considered to be in the best interests of England.[8]

On the other hand, the concentration of the masses of Jewry in emancipation may have been the result of his direct encounter with German Jews, particularly those of the Frankfurt Ghetto.[10] Consequently, attitudes toward Jewish emancipation during the eighteenth century were largely determined by the geographical location of the Jews to whom attention was directed. Emancipation's apologists pointed to the great role played by Jews in the economic development of Holland, Leghorn, Prussia, etc., but their opponents pointed to the economic straitjacket allegedly imposed by the segregated Jews of eastern Europe upon their homelands, to the detriment of the native population.[11]

II. *Positive Aspects of the Enlightenment*

Three positive aspects of the Enlightenment helped produce a new attitude toward the Jews and ultimately led to their emancipation. These were: (1) The universal-humanitarian mood of the age; (2) the mechanical inorganic theory of the state; and (3) the utilitarian point of view prevalent in the political thought of the time.

eastern Europe became an important factor in shaping the views of 18th-century thinkers. As east-European Jews moved westward in increasingly larger numbers, fear of onrushing waves of these immigrants was reflected in various governmental enactments and in the polemical literature of the time.[9] Thus, at the end of the century, when the problem of Jewish emancipation became a subject of public discussion, its opponents, who were mainly Germans, emphasized the great social, psychological and even racial differences between Jews and non-Jews, which they believed unbridgeable. The Germans, closer to the habitat of the east-European masses, were aware of the unique character of Jewish life and culture. Goethe's fear of Jewish

The social philosophy of this age embraced the welfare of the individual as well as that of society at large. The innate equality of of man was the creed of the time, and the perfectibility and happiness of the individual motivated social changes. Society at large was envisioned as constantly improving and steadily advancing to higher forms. Nations were regarded as a means toward this advancement.[12] "Our hopes as to the future condition of the human species," wrote the Marquis de Condorcet, "may be reduced to three points: the destruction of inequality between different nations, the progress of equality in one and the same nation, and lastly the real improvement of man."[13]

Notwithstanding his role in the formulation of a philosophy of nationalism,[14] the deepest expression of this spirit of universal humanitarianism was given by Johann Gottfried Herder, who believed that it was the outstanding quality of man and the measure by which his progress was to be judged. To him humanitarianism was the development in the course of time of the best innate qualities in man, a process governed by the same natural laws as the whole universe. "One and the same law," he wrote in his *Ideen,* "rules the whole universe, beginning with the various systems of suns and ending with the tiniest actions of man."[15] In the universe as a whole, Herder perceived a tendency toward ever greater harmony·so that destructive elements were gradually subdued. Likewise, he believed that in human history, the innate goodness of man steadily reduced destructive elements so that "according to the laws of their inner nature, the rule of reason among human beings must constantly expand and promote an enduring humanitarianism." He believed the progress of the human race was assured with the mere passage of time.[16]

That the lofty humanism of the age strongly influenced its political thought and directly promoted Jewish emancipation, is indicated by two lesser known works of the period. The first is *A Letter to the Right Honourable Sir Thomas Chitty, Lord Mayor of London,* by an "anonymous merchant of London," written in connection with the heated debate about the Jew Bill of 1753.[17] The second is Abbé Gregoire's prize essay written in 1786–87 on the subject posed by the Academy of Metz: "How to make the Jews more useful and more happy in France."[18] The *Letter* was a plea, chiefly on utilitarian grounds, for a more liberal policy of immigration into England, including the free admission of non-Christians, Mohammedans, and

especially Jews. However, the universal-cosmopolitan point of view
was not overlooked:

> In our conception of man we should always accustom ourselves to
> look on the human race, however scattered and dispersed, as one
> and the same grand republic of which God is the common father,
> amongst which equity, generosity and humanity ought ever to pre-
> vail. Each country should not be considered as independent of
> others, but [as] the human race—as one indivisible one, we should
> not be limited to the love of our countries only, or the love of the
> Protestants only—this is a narrow, selfish and contracted principle.
> The Englishman's heart should be more enlarged by a universal
> friendship and confidence between man and man and between
> nation and nation.[19]

The supernational concept of the state was upheld by Gregoire in
his *Essai*. In reply to Michaelis' assertion that Jews could by no means
acquire patriotic virtues,[20] Gregoire wrote:

> Demagogues have forever extolled the loyalty of subjects to their
> native land and sovereign. Actually, one only needs to observe
> people in various countries to realize that the real motivations for
> their behavior are pleasure and self-interest. As long as they dwell
> in their homes securely and enjoy the fruits of their labor in peace
> without being crushed by taxation or despotism, they are content.
> Beyond these considerations, the government and sovereign are
> none of their concern. True, they may be familiar with the word
> "patriotism" but it connotes nothing to them.[21]

Like Locke and Tindal[22] almost a century earlier, Gregoire did not
put any emphasis on the emotional element in the relations of the
individual to the state, an element that was to come to the foreground
with the rise of nationalism. Hence he was convinced that, once
emancipated, the Jews "will become attached to the state by ties of
pleasure, security, liberty and a life of ease."[23]

With the exception of Rousseau,[24] the state, almost to the eve of
the French Revolution, was thought of as a technical and mechanical

rather than organic unity, resulting chiefly from mutual interests and needs. To Locke, the commonwealth was merely "a society of men constituted for the procuring, preserving and advancing of their own civil interests."[25] With the spiritual interests and needs of the individual the state as such had nothing to do. They were deemed the concern of the individual alone. "The care of everyman's soul belongs unto himself and is to be left unto himself."[26] The state was thus considered a mere instrument its inhabitants maintained to safeguard their natural rights. The logical implication of such a view was primarily to deny the ruler the power of imposing any dogma on the people. The idea of a Christian state, Locke and Tindal asserted, not only contradicts the Gospel but the basic idea of the state itself. In short: "There is absolutely no such thing as a Christian Commonwealth."[27] The practical application of this theory required the separation of church and state, the exercise of tolerance and the grant of civil rights to members of all denominations. "Neither pagan, nor Mohammedan, nor Jew ought to be excluded from the civil rights of the Commonwealth because of his religion."[28]

To the cosmopolitan humanitarianism of the eighteenth century and the prevailing concept of the supernational character of the state, a third factor must be added, namely, the utilitarian point of view. During the Enlightenment the functional nature of truth in science, religion and metaphysics was strongly emphasized.[29] This criterion of utility prevailed also in political thought. Since the state was considered necessary to the individual for the pursuit of his welfare and happiness, its development became a primary aim. Agriculture was held in the highest esteem and believed to constitute the basis for a country's strength and riches[30]; however, the vital role of commerce and industry was gradually understood.

In connection with this more balanced view arose a new principle which emphasized the direct relationship between the welfare of a state and the size of its population. Throughout the literature of the eighteenth century this doctrine repeatedly stressed that the greatest asset of a state was a large population. Every workingman is a real source of riches and power. "We all know," wrote John Toland in 1714, "that numbers of people are the true riches and powers of any country."[31] Hence the plea of the anonymous merchant of London for a more liberal policy of immigration to England. "The real strength, power and riches of all kingdoms of the world," he wrote, "will depend on the number of inhabitants, and on that only . . . all countries thinly populated must and ever will be poor . . . it is the number of inhabitants only that can render a place great and power-ful."[32] This argument was further elaborated in the early eighties of the eighteenth century by Dohm,[33] and later by Gregoire[34] and Mira-beau,[35] for central and western Europe then experienced a manpower shortage. The territorial expansion of England and France on the other side of the Atlantic and in the Indies, and the imperial wars in which they became involved, were a great drain on their populations. Men were needed to man the ships, to fight the wars and to increase agricultural and industrial output. Furthermore, the relative peace that prevailed in the western part of the continent during most of the century, coupled with the progress of science and technology, turned men's minds to economic expansion and growth.

The more liberal policies toward the Jews, which became apparent in Europe at this time, tied in with the current stress upon the vital importance of increasing the population to meet the needs of the ever expanding economy. Hence statesmen and intellectuals urged the removal of all restrictions from the Jewish population and the admis-sion of new Jewish settlers. Jewish settlers, they argued, were in no way inferior to others, in many respects even superior.[36] In support of this argument, they pointed to the important role the Jews had been playing in the economic life of Europe. "They are disseminated," Joseph Addison wrote to them in 1712, "through all the trading parts of the world, that they are become the instruments by which mankind are knit together by a general correspondence. They are the pegs and nails in a great building, which, though they are but little valued in themselves, are absolutely necessary to keep the whole frame to-gether."[37] To Toland they were the "brokers of the world," who "whithersoever they come, create business as well as manage it."[38] Montesquieu reiterated this opinion almost verbatim. "Throughout the world," he wrote, "wherever there is money there are Jews."[39] To the Jews of the Middle Ages Montesquieu credited the invention of the Bill of Exchange as a means of safeguarding their effects in face of the constant threat of expulsion.[40] This great service of the Jews to international trade was also acknowledged by Gregoire, who, with specific reference to France, added that "it is again to the Jews that we are indebted for the establishment of the banks at Bayonne and Bordeaux."[41]

The great importance the French government attached to the economic activities of the Jews in southern France during the first half of the 18th century was well indicated in the reply of Cardinal Fleury to the merchants of Bordeaux, who had requested the abrogation of the privileges of the Jews in that town. "We rather wish," the Cardinal answered them, "they could be indulged with more and larger privileges, that thereby greater numbers might be invited to leave other countries and settle in France with their families and effects."[42] Even Diderot, who was by no means friendly toward the Jews, remarked in his *Voyage de Hollande* (1733), that "the Jewish refugees in Holland, by their example, taught the Dutch to form establishments along the coast of Berbery and the Levant."[43] In this context mention may be made of the warm reception given by government officials in Messina to the group headed by Rabbi Hayyim Ibn 'Attar on their way to Palestine in 1740.[44] In the same year the Jews were officially invited to settle in Naples.[45]

Historical confirmation was abundant that the Jews were an important factor in promoting the prosperity of various countries. The decline of Spain and Portugal followed the expulsion of the Jews, the persecution of the Marranos and the expulsion of the Moors, while the flourishing of "the paltry fisher-town of Leghorn," Holland, England and Prussia seemed, to some extent at least, attributable to an opposite policy. These facts were repeatedly pointed out as clear proof of the high value of the Jew in a country's economic life.[46]

III. *Negative Aspects of the Enlightenment*

The Enlightenment itself was a movement restricted to a small fraction of the European people. Its ideas and aspirations were the possession of the intellectual élite alone. But even among them illwill toward the Jew was far more common than goodwill. The masses of the people in the villages and towns held tenaciously to their deep-seated hostility to the Jews. This was clear from their behavior in the assemblies which followed the passing of the Jew Bill of 1753.[47] Some thirty-five years later in France, during the local assemblies that preceded the convocation of the National Assembly, the masses instructed their delegates to extend the restrictive regulations of 1784 to bar the Jews from gaining power and increasing their numbers; to put an end to their exploitation of the peasants or to expel them from the country.[48]

These urban masses throughout the century filled to capacity the newly established playhouses and acclaimed with enthusiasm any play in which the character of "a stupid . . . avaricious . . . cowardly . . . villainous . . . foppish . . . boastful . . . amorous . . . and licentious" Jew was presented.[49] Rarely did the writers of fiction and drama during the age of Enlightenment present a benevolent and human Jew. The few plays in England that did give favorable portrayals of the Jew met with failure.[50] A similar situation also prevailed in Germany, where Gellert's benevolent Jew[51] remained for a long time a solitary figure, imitated perhaps only by Lessing's traveler in his *Juden* (1749).[52]

Favorable references to Jews before Dohm were of a casual nature, and, with the exception of Toland's treatise of 1714, went no further than to suggest the advisability of tolerance and partial economic emancipation. In one of his "humanitarian" statements on the Jews, Voltaire suggested that they should not be burned.[53] Rousseau demanded toleration for "all religions that tolerate others as long as their dogmas contain nothing contrary to the duties of citizenship."[54] Toleration of the Jews on utilitarian and humanitarian grounds was also urged by Motesquieu, who pointed out the negative economic results of intolerance.[55] Herder also expressed his dissatisfaction with intolerance, which produced degrading and inhuman measures against the Jews.[56] Goethe too prayed for the day when mutual tolerance would prevail and wipe out prejudice and hate.[57] All this, however, was mere lipservice. The idea of emancipation did not occur to any of these writers. Even the anonymous *Letter,* which pleaded for an increased immigration of Jews into England and their naturalization, made it quite explicit that "in all respects relating to trade," they should be put "on the same footing as the old inhabitants," but in no other way. "That none of them be permitted to be of His Majesty's privy council or a member of either house of parliament, or to hold any office or place of trust either civil or military under the government—all these should be reserved for the old inhabitants."[58] The plea of some of the Enlightened for a more liberal attitude toward the Jews reflected, in most cases, a regard for a principle rather than an actual change of heart toward them.

The age of Enlightenment was one in which deep-seated emotions and attitudes were often swept aside in the name of the lofty principles of reason. In its desire to inaugurate a new era in the history of mankind, the Enlightenment could not, without violating its own principles, ignore the Jews completely. The emergence of a new attitude toward them clearly marked a victory of reason over passion and prejudice, but this victory was never complete. In the final analysis, reason and emotions were still irreconcilable. Even devoted friends of the Jews such as Dohm, Mirabeau and Gregoire made it clear that theirs was merely a plea for a new experiment in a new historical setting, an experiment whose success or failure depended on the Jews to an even greater extent than on the Christians. They took this liberal stand in the hope that, as a result, a new type of Jew would emerge, ready to abandon his Jewishness for the sake of becoming integrated in society. As far as the contemporary Jew, however, was concerned, there was no difference of opinion between Gregoire and Goethe or between Dohm and Michaelis and others. They all considered him degraded and his role in society pernicious. Ill will toward him was displayed by all, even by his friends.

IV. *Jewish Uniqueness—the Cause of Enmity*

This almost universal, negative attitude toward the 18th-century Jew needs further scrutiny. Its main source must be sought in the basic fact that the Jews, in spite of their having been Europeans for so many centuries, were still considered, even by themselves, to be utter strangers. "The Jews," wrote Gregoire in his prize essay, "are scattered everywhere, they have struck roots, however, nowhere. . . . In London he is not an Englishman, nor is he Dutch at the Hague, nor French in Metz. They are a state within a state."[59] They were strangers in many ways. Culturally, most of them had been living in utter isolation from the rest of European society; economically, their occupations were generally concentrated in trade and finance. Their religion and national hopes further widened the gulf between them and Christian society.

Cultural Isolation

Jewish culture, generally identified with the Talmud as interpreted by the rabbis, was held in contempt by current writers. The Talmud itself was inaccessible to most Christian theologians and scholars of the age. Their opinions on it were based mainly on Eisenmenger's *Entdecktes Judenthum,* which was largely drawn from the polemics of Jewish converts of Christian Spain. Another source was the history of Basnage from which Diderot copied his article "Les Juifs" for the *Encyclopedia.*[60] Michaelis, though aware of the unreliability of Eisenmenger, praised his book and consulted it frequently.[61] No matter what sources were consulted, the picture of the Jews and Judaism was greatly distorted. They sought a counterpart to Christian theology in Judaism, and made the Aggadah their main source of reference. The uncouth imagery frequently encountered in some of the Aggadoth and Midrashim was taken out of context, and what was only a product of the popular mind, became the foundation on which a "Philosophy of Judaism" was erected. The variety of legends woven around such biblical stories as the Creation, Adam and Eve, Cain and Abel, angels and heroes, was thus turned into a source for the portrayal of Jewish "creeds" which were presented as the essence of the Jew's *Weltanschauung.*[62] Though a monotheism, Judaism was characterized as anthropomorphic in its concept of God,[63] pervaded with belief in demons, spirits,[64] and talismans,[65] and a most fanatic and hate-laden religion. It was chiefly the Talmud and the rabbinical interpretations which these writers believed taught Jews to harbor contempt and hate toward Christians and Christianity:[66] "To steal the goods of Christians, to regard them as savage beasts, to push them in a precipice, . . . to kill them with impunity and to utter every morning the most horrible imprecations against them."[67]

While the voluminousness and inaccessibility of the Talmud at times evoked awe and admiration among Christians,[68] contempt for the rabbis was general and their abuse a common feature in the writings of the age. "One can hardly find two among them," wrote Montesquieu who knew so little of them, "who have the least common sense."[69] In the opinion of Gregoire, they were fanatic, narrow and ignorant, and were to blame for the low cultural and moral state of the Jews. "Instead of expanding the horizons of the human spirit, they have consecrated its errors and declared as dogmas the false offspring of a delirious imagination."[70] He thought it a good idea to present Jewish customs and ceremonies in a ridiculous light in an attempt to weaken the hold of rabbinism.[71] Dohm attributed "the extreme inclination of the people for the abstract, their love for usury, cheating," and many "of their other faults," to the casuistry of the rabbis.[72] Goethe greatly enjoyed the caricature of a rabbi presented by Wilhelm Meister:

Nobody ever portrayed the caricature of a rabbi better than he. The fanatic zeal, the repulsive enthusiasm, the wild gesticulations, the confused murmuring, the piercing outcries, the effeminate movements, the sudden ups and downs of exaltation and the queerness of an ancient nonsense—all these he grasped so acutely that the presentation of his distasteful scene could make happy every man of taste as long as it lasted.[73]

Another aspect of rabbinical Judaism which was sharply censured in Enlightenment literature, as evidence of Jewish separateness, was the use of Yiddish. In the sixth letter of his reply "to some objections" raised by "Jewish correspondents," Voltaire begged them not to reproach him for having little love for them:

I love you so much that I would like you all to be in Jerusalem in place of the Turks who are devastating your country. There, you will cultivate this unfortunate desert as you did before. . . . you will be able to transform your territory as the Provençales have transformed theirs. There you will carry on at ease and repose your detestable chant in your detestable Jargon.[74]

Among the first clauses of the *Toleranz Patent* of Joseph II of Austria of the year 1781, was "the removal of their national language from usage in contracts, bills, commercial books, documents, with the only exception of the prayerbook."[75] A few years later, this example was emulated by Louis XVI in his *Lettres Patentes* of July 10, 1784.[76]

Gregoire also looked forward to the day, when "this kind of dialect, the German-Hebrew-Rabbinical Jargon, which is current among German Jews and understood only by them, will be extirpated. . . . This dialect is used only to spread ignorance or to conceal their knavery."[77] "There is something pathetic in the *Judensprache*," Goethe observed[78]; he described it, however, as *naseweises Nestquäckelchen*[79] and considered it the vehicle of a fanatic and anti-Christian rabbinism.[80] The anti-"Jargon" campaign of the Berlin *Maskilim*[81] may thus be traced, to some extent at least, to the influence of the European Enlightenment.

Views on Economic Pursuits

Even such staunch supporters of the Jews as Toland, Dohm, Gregoire and Mirabeau, though acknowledging their financial abilities and importance, could not altogether ignore the prevalent opinion that Jewish economic dealings were essentially unproductive.

As long as the economic behavior of the Jews remained unchanged, Gregoire contended, a more liberal policy toward Jewish immigration was unjustifiable despite the desperate shortage of manpower in western and central Europe.[82] Herder also believed that it was in the interest of the state concerned to restrain the economic activities of the Jews.[83]

Should the English Naturalization Bill pass, its opponents argued, the Jews "would deluge the country with brokers, usurers and beggars . . . the rich Jews would purchase lands . . . and thus influence the constitution of the Church. . . . They would rob the natives of their birthright . . . disgrace the character of the nation. . . . They would acquire so much wealth and consequently also power . . . that Judaism would become the fashionable religion of the land."[84]

The allegedly pernicious results of the financial dealings of the Jews were also emphasized in the *Cahiers de doléance* from Alsace-Lorraine and in the anti-Jewish campaign launched during the first year of the Revolution.[85] Were the Jews to be emancipated, their opponents in the Germanies objected, they would buy all the land, dispossess the Germans, and in the course of a few generations become the sole masters of the country.[86]

A similar opinion was held by Herder who stated that emancipation of the Jews would result in their gaining full control of German economic life, "with the landowners the Canaanites, serving them as manufacturers."[87] Except for his regard for the Bible as a great cultural monument, Herder's views on the Jews were generally as negative as those of Voltaire. Like Voltaire, he also considered Jewish proclivities to usury and brokerage an innate trait traceable to biblical times. "For thousands of years," he wrote, "since their emergence on the stage of history, the Jews were a parasitic growth on the stem of other nations, a race of cunning brokers all over the earth. They have caused great evil to many ill-organized states, by retarding the free and natural economic development of their indigenous population."[88] The example of Holland, he further argued, should not be followed by such European nations as Poland, Germany, Hungary, Italy and France, since none of these lands is or "can be an Amsterdam."[89]

Goethe regarded the Jews as nomads, constantly at war with sedentary European society and living off the spoils. Though impressed by their agility, mobility, aggressiveness and stubborn persistence, he ascribed these attributes to the Jewish drive "to grab the purse (*Beutel*)" of non-Jews. Their economic dealings were responsible for qualities distinguishing them from other Europeans. Thus, as a people, they were far more vivacious, energetic and dynamic than others.[90]

Similar observations, with a clear racial undertone, are found in preacher Schwager's notes on Dohm's book:

> Their vivaciousness is much greater than ours. . . . Their manners and customs are so different from ours that it is hard to conceive that they could change to such an extent that they would integrate in our society. . . . Their temperament is suitable perhaps for a commercial state; not, however, for an agricultural. . . . A quiet, retired and sedentary life seems hardly suitable for their fiery nature.

Schwager concludes with the following racist note: "By his hair and physiognomy the Jew clearly shows how great the difference is between him and us . . . . No less is also the spiritual distance that separates us."[91]

The Jews' Alleged Immorality

The indictment of the Jews on economic grounds was usually accompanied by a moral indictment. From Basnage to Dohm, in drama, novels and polemical pamphlets, the same charges of cheating, stealing, robbing, extortion, etc., were levelled against them. Eisenmenger in his *Entdecktes Judenthum* and Voltaire were most responsible for spreading these charges. Many other authors of the eighteenth century also displayed a marked tendency to hurl abuse at the Jews. In fiction the Jew was treated as illiberally as in drama. It is sufficient to mention Pope's scathing satire on Edmund Curll, Defoe's odious Israelite in *Roxana,* the licentious Jews in Smollett's early novels, Richardson's Jewish libertine in *Sir Charles Grandison* and Fanny Burney's money lenders in *Cecilia.*[92] The low opinion of the morality of the Jews among all classes in the Germanies can be observed in Lessing's *Juden,*[93] and later in the remarks of Dohm's correspondents.[94]

Incidental references to Jews were less frequent in the drama and fiction of France than in the same forms in England and Germany,[95] but this omission was compensated for in the more serious writings of the Enlightenment. Diderot deserves at least some mention here because of his derogatory allusions to Jews in his *Le neveu de Rameau* and *Voyage de Hollande.*[96] Besides attributing to Jews ruthless usury, greediness for money and hatred for Christians, the writers of the eighteenth century added to the catalogue of vices cowardice and sexual dissoluteness. Not only were they described as designers on the purse of the Gentiles, but also on the virtue and innocence of Christian women.[97]

"Zionist" Tendencies

Another criticism of the Jews during the eighteenth century was based on their national hope of returning to Zion. If we may judge from the references to this subject in the writings of the age, these national aspirations were widely diffused among the Jews of the time and exerted great influence upon them. Such was the observation of Basnage,[98] Toland,[99] David Hartley,[100] Diderot,[101] Voltaire,[102] Herder,[103] and Michaelis.[104] More remarkable, however, is the fact that these hopes were shared by many Christians of the time. This was the case particularly in England, where they originated in a humanitarian and religious mysticism.[105] Among the first to give expression to those hopes was Toland. In a small pamphlet, written in 1718, he praised the Mosaic Law, and asserted that such a law would have made a "government immortal" had it ever been fully implemented. He further noted that "the Jews continue still a distinct people from all other, both as to their race and religion." The conclusion he drew was

> that, as the Jews known at this day, and who are dispersed over Europe, Asia and Africa, with some few in America, are found by good calculation to be more numerous than either the Spaniards (for example) or the French: so if they ever happen to be resettled in Palestine upon their original foundation, which is not at all impossible, they will then, by reason of their excellent constitution be much more populous, rich and powerful than any other nation now in the world. I would have you consider whether it be not both the interest and duty of Christians to assist them in regaining their country.[106]

In support of his belief in the future restoration of the Jews, Hartley cited: the preservation of the Jewish people with their distinct way of life in spite of oppression and persecution; their adherence to Hebrew as "an universal language"; their close inter-communal relations which would enable them to seize the opportune moment in world politics for a return to Zion, their undying hope; and, finally, their possession "of money and jewels" rather than "inheritance of land"—a factor which increased their mobility.[107] To this period also belonged the anonymous *Letter* in which the author affirmed his unflinching belief in the divine origin of the Bible, the election of Israel and its final restoration. "A period of time," he wrote, "will come when this people shall be restored and reestablished in their own land and country, and enjoy a degree of dominion and power, more potent and considerable than any other kingdom or nation in the world."[108]

Those who were ardent believers in the future restoration of the Jews also pleaded for their admission into England as naturalized citizens. Jewish national aspirations did not appear to these Gentiles to conflict with their partial emancipation. A friendlier attitude to Jews was advocated precisely because of this anticipated restoration.[109] The regular principles of secular politics, these writers implied, should not be applied to the Jews in whose past history they perceived the guiding hand of Providence.

On the continent, the attitude toward Jewish national aspirations was different. Even before the Revolution, the concept of the nationalist state was gaining acceptance.[110] When Dohm ventilated the problem of Jewish emancipation in the early eighties, it was on nationalist grounds that opposition developed. How can the Jews, argued Michaelis, demand civil rights when they still cherish and revere their Mosaic Law and hope to return to Palestine?[111] Even Dohm and Gregoire could not ignore this argument; however, they did not attach too much importance to Jewish national hopes. Recalling Mendelssohn's view on this problem,[112] Dohm pointed out that these hopes were rather of a spiritual-mystical nature and basically no different from the Christians belief in the Second Coming.[113] Gregoire reiterated Mendelssohn's view on the expected return to Palestine:

> In times of suffering, when misfortune weighs heavily on the Jew, when trembling he eats his bread of affliction, he sighs perhaps for the Messiah. . . . His coming, however, would be less welcome to our Israelite if the humaneness of the people would allow him to breathe in peace and live happily in his home. . . . Very often do the advantages of the present life make one forget the promises of the future. In this sense, the Jew is not in any way different from us. His hopes would by no means make him give up those comforts that would be within his reach.[114]

Herder seems to have resented Jewish national aspirations, particularly because of his conviction that Jews were essentially

Europeans and must be completely integrated into all aspects of European life and culture. National aspirations were incompatible with the demand for political rights and indicative of Jewish separatism. Palestine, he remarked somewhat facetiously, was too small a country for such an active and energetic people as the Jews. They would be willing to return there only if, along with the country, they received the whole *Mittelhandel* of the old and new world.[115] The destiny of the Jews, he concluded, lay in Christian Europe, and hence but one course was open to them: complete adjustment to it, difficult as the experience might prove for both sides. Herder expressed his thought in a metaphor borrowed from the rabbis: "Weeping, Esau and Israel cling to each other. The kiss is painful to both of them; they cannot, however, tear themselves apart."[116]

V. *Conclusion*

The age of the Enlightenment marks the beginning of a new era in Jewish-Christian relations. Against the background of an emerging belief in the equality of man and the importance of education and environment as forces molding the individual, a new attempt was made to analyze the underlying causes of the centuries-old hatred of the Jew as well as to understand the Jew of the time and his unique way of life.[117]

Social thinkers, for the first time, examined the Christian world to seek an explanation of the genesis of the Jewish problem. It was Christian Europe, in whose soil the Jewish personality had long been nurtured, that was held responsible for negative characteristics attributed to the Jew. Such characteristics were regarded not as innate but as the natural result of historical circumstances. The conviction was expressed that under different circumstances, the Jewish personality would necessarily be altered.[118]

The "liberals," among whom were Dohm, Gregoire and Mirabeau, therefore urged immediate emancipation of the Jews—partial at the minimum—as a result of which a new type of Jew would emerge, culturally and economically integrated with the rest of the population.

The "liberals" were opposed by Michaelis, Schwager and other "correspondents" of Dohm in the Germanies, as well as by the reactionary group in the National Assembly of France. Citing the cultural isolation of the Jew, his adherence to his religion, customs and traditions, in face of many hardships and persecutions, they declared that the Jews were an exception to the rule that human nature was subject to change.[119]

A third view was supported by Voltaire, Herder and Goethe, among others. While opposing the emancipation of the Jew on the ground that it would constitute a grave danger to the *bürgerliche Verfassung*[120] and undermine the national economy,[121] these men expressed their belief in the ultimate integration of the Jew in civil society. They regarded reforms within Jewry, along social, cultural and economic lines, as prerequisites for such an integration. Only then would the Jews become "equal partners . . . in the common culture of humanity."[122] This view, which may be termed conditional emancipation, was for all practical purposes meaningless.

The ideals of reason, humanitarianism and tolerance won. Governments began to institute more liberal policies toward the Jews, and the Jews of western Europe, in turn, began to modify their way of life in harmony with the *Zeitgeist* of the eighteenth century.

NOTES

[1] Cf. mainly, Bayle, Pierre, *Dictionaire historique et critique,* 6 vols. (Paris 1820), vol. i, pp. 44–49, 86–92; vol. v, pp. 400–17; vol. vi, pp. 116–20.

On Voltaire *see* Voltaire, François Arouet or François de, *Oeuvres Complètes de Voltaire* . . . par Condorcet, 52 vols. (Paris 1883–88). The most important of his writings concerning Jews and Judaism are: (1) "Juifs," vol. xix, pp. 511–41; (2) "Dieu et les hommes," vol. xxviii, chaps. xiv–xxxi, (3) "Essai sur les moeurs et l'esprit des nations," vol. xi, pp. 110–45. *See also* Emmerich, Hanna, *Zur Behandlung des Judentums bei Voltaire* (Breslau 1930).

On Diderot, *cf.* Diderot, Denis, *Oeuvres Complètes* . . . par J. Assezat, 20 vols. (Paris 1875–77). *See* mainly "Juifs," in vol. xv, pp. 318–400 and "La Moïsade," vol. iv, pp. 118–27; also Sänger, Herman, *Juden und das alte Testament bei Diderot* (Wertheim 1933).

The Jewish people, its creed and history were also sharply attacked in English writings of the age. *Cf.* Tindal, Matthew, *Christianity as Old as the Creation* . . . (London 1730); Morgan, Thomas, *The Moral Philosopher* (London 1738); Foster, James, *The Usefulness, Truth and Excellency of the Chris-*

tian Revelation (London 1734), pp. 14–16; Bolingbroke, Henry St. John, *The Works of Lord Bolingbroke,* 4 vols. (Philadelphia 1841), vol. ii, pp. 200–10; Shaftesbury, Anthony Ashley Cooper, *Characteristics of Men, Manners, Opinions, Times,* etc., ed. John Robertson (London 1900), *cf.* "Jews," in Index, II, p. 373.

For some of Schiller's views on historical Judaism, *cf.* "Die Sendung Moses," *Schillers sämtliche Schriften,* herausgegeben von Karl Gödeke, vol. ix (Stuttgart 1870), pp. 100–24. For Herder and Goethe *see below.*

2 "Et vous, peuple furieux et insense," he addressed himself to the Jews of his time, "hommes vils et grossiers, dignes esclaves du jong que vous portez . . . allez, reprenez vos livres, et eloignez vous de moi." Diderot, "La Moïsade," *Oeuvres,* vol. iv, p. 126.

3 Voltaire, "Tolérance," *Oeuvres,* vol. xx, pp. 525–26.

4 Herder, Johann Gottfried, "Bekehrung der Juden," *Herders sämtliche Werke,* herausgegeben von Bernhard Suphan, vol. xxiv (Berlin 1883), pp. 61–75.

5 D'Holbach, P. H. Dietrich, baron, *La Contagion Sacrée ou histoire naturelle de la superstition,* Ouvrage traduit de l'anglois, vol. ii (Londres 1768), chap. ix.

6 For some exceptions, *cf.* Locke, John, "A Letter Concerning Toleration," *The Works of John Locke,* vol. vi (London 1823); Montesquieu, Charles Louis de Secondant, baron de la Brede, *L'esprit des Lois,* vol. xxi, chap. xx, English tr. *(The Spirit of the Laws)* by Thomas Nugent, vol. ii (New York 1949), p. 54; Lessing, Gotthold Ephraim, *Nathan der Weise,* Everyman's Library, ed. Ernest Rhys (London and New York 1930), Act. II, Scene 5; Act. III, Scene 7; Act. IV, Scenes 4, 7.

7 Hyamson, Albert H., *A History of the Jews in England* (London 1907), 2nd ed. (1928), chaps. xvii, xix, xxix; Freund, Ismar, *Die Emanzipation der Juden in Preussen,* vol. i (Berlin 1912), chap. i; Tscherikower, E., *Yidn in Frankreich* (New York 1942), pp. 109–52; Anchel, Robert, *Les Juifs de France* (Paris 1946), pp. 213–33; Szajkowski, Zosa, *The Economic Status of the Jews in Alsace, Metz and Lorraine* (New York 1954), pp. 25–30. *See also* Dubnow, S., *Dibrei Yemei 'Am 'Olam,* ed. 4, vol. viii (Tel Aviv 1948), Introduction, pars. 2, 8; Baron, S. W., *A Social and Religious History of the Jews* [= *History*], vol. ii (New York 1937), chap. xi, "Geographic Expansion."

8 *Cf.* Picciotto, James, *Sketches of Anglo-Jewish History* (London 1875), pp. 56 ff.; Baron, *History,* vol. ii, pp. 180 ff. For Toland *see* Toland, *Reasons for Naturalizing the Jews in Great Britain and Ireland on the Same Foot With all Other Nations, Containing also Defense of the Jews Against all Vulgar Prejudices in all Countries* (London 1714).

9 The fear of an influx of Jews was strongly emphasized by the opponents of the "Jew Bill" of 1753 in England and in many clauses of the *Lettres Patentes* (1784). *Cf.* Hyamson, *op. cit.,* pp. 220–21; Anchel, *op. cit.,* chap. viii. "Nous sommes environnés des Juifs," was a common phrase in the *Cahiers* from Alsace. Some even believed "que la province contient plus de cinquante

à soixante mille familles Juives." *Cf.* Liber, M., "Les Juifs et le convocation des états généraux, 1789," *Revue des Etudes Juives* [= *REJ*], vol. lxiv [1912], pp. 92 ff.. *Cf.* also Szajkowski, *op. cit.,* pp. 28–29. Frederick II enacted many laws to restrict the Jewish population of Prussia. *See* Dohm, Christian Wilhelm, *Über die bürgerliche Verbesserung der Juden,* vol. i (Berlin 1781), pp. 9–22; Freund, vol. i, *op. cit.,* chap. ii.

Throughout the 18th century there was a marked tendency to exaggerate the number of Jews. Toland wrote in 1718 "that . . . the Jews . . . at this day are . . . more numerous than either the Spaniards (for instance) or the French." "Appendix Concerning Two Problems," in *Nazarenus* (London 1718). Diderot estimated the number of Jews in Amsterdam in the second half of the 18th century at more than one hundred thousand. *Oeuvres,* vol. xvii, p. 432. At the end of the 17th century J. Basnage believed that "there are still near three millions of people who profess this religion" *(The History of the Jews from Jesus Christ to the Present time* [= *History*], translated by Th. Taylor London 1708, p. 748). Some eighty years later Abbé Henri Gregoire estimated their number at four and a half million. *(Essai sur la regeneration physique, morale et politique des Juifs* [Metz 1789], p. 52). Their high natural increase, he pointed out, created a problem which required immediate attention *(ibid.,* pp. 60–66). Fear of an increased Jewish populafion in Germany was also displayed by some of Dohm's correspondents who emphasized "die schrecklichsten Greuel, die daraus enstehen müssten" (Dohm, *op. cit.,* pp. 145–146).

[10] Describing the humanitarian spirit of the 18th century, Goethe remarked: "Die Duldsamkeit der Religionsparteien gegen einander ward nicht bloss gelehrt sondern ausgeübt, und mit einem noch grösseren Einfluss war *die bürgeliche Verfassung bedroht, als man Duldsamkeit gegen die Juden . . .* der gutmüthigen Zeit anzuempfehlen bemüht war" *(Dichtung und Warheit,* in *Goethe Werke,* 55 vols., vol. xxviii [Weimar 1887–1918], p. 190). On another occasion, Goethe opposed Jewish emancipation on religious grounds: "In diesem Sinne, den man vielleicht pedantisch nennen mag, aber doch als folgerecht anerkennen muss, dulden wir keinen Juden unter uns; denn wie sollten wir ihm den Antheil an der höchsten Kultur vergönnen, deren Ursprung und Herkommen er verleugnet" *(Wilhelm Meisters Wanderjahre,* in *Worke,* vol. xxv, p. 210). About the Frankfurt Ghetto *see* his *Dichtung und Wahrheit, ibid.,* vol. xxviii, pp. 325–26.

[11] *See below,* p. 255 ff.

[12] Diderot, "Humanité," *Oeuvres,* vol. xv, pp. 145–46; Condorcet, Marquis de, *Outlines of an Historical View of the Progress of the Human Mind* (London 1796), pp. 255–56; Herder, *op. cit.,* vol. xiii (Berlin 1887), pp. 340–41; Cassirer, Ernst, *Die Philosophie der Aufklärung* (Tübingen 1932), pp. 5, 29; Smith, Preserved, *A History of Modern Culture,* vol. ii, (New York 1933), chap. xvi, par. 3; Kohn, Hans, *The Idea of Nationalism* (New York 1944), pp. 227–28.

[13] *Op. cit.*, p. 317.

[14] *Cf.* Ergang, Robert Reinhold, *Herder and the Foundation of German Nationalism* (New York 1931), pp. 239–66.

[15] *Ideen zur Philosophie der Geschichte der Menschheit* [=*Ideen*] (Leipzig 1812), p. 248.

[16] *Ibid.*, pp. 246–48.

[17] *A Letter to the Right Honourable Sir Thomas Chitty, Lord Mayor of London* [= *A Letter*] (London 1760).

[18] Gregoire, Henri, *Essai sur la régénération physique, morale et politique des Juifs* (Metz 1789).

[19] *A Letter* . . ., p. 55.

[20] Dohm, *op. cit.*, vol. ii (1783), pp. 33–64.

[21] Gregoire, *op. cit.*, p. 109.

[22] Tindal, Matthew, *An Essay Concerning the Power of the Magistrate and the Rights of Mankind in Matter of Religion* (London 1679). For Locke's concept of the state, *see below.*

[23] Gregoire, *op. cit.*, pp. 111–12.

[24] Rousseau, Jean Jacques, *Considerations on the Government of Poland*, translated from the French by Willmoore Kendall (Minneapolis 1947); *cf.* also Hayes, Carlton, J. H., *The Historical Evolution of Modern Nationalism* (New York 1948), pp. 22–27.

[25] Locke, "A Letter Concerning Toleration," *op. cit.*, vol. vi, p. 9.

[26] *Ibid.*, p. 23.

[27] *Ibid.*, p. 38.

[28] *Ibid.*, p. 52.

[29] Smith, *op. cit.*, pp. 145–47.

[30] *See,* for instance, Dohm, *op. cit.*, vol. ii, p. 155: "Auch ich halte es für eine ausgemachte Wahrheit, dass der Staat nur aus denen bestehe, welche das Eigenthum des Landes, in dem er errichtet ist, besitzen oder Rechte an dasselbe erworben haben. Land ist das sicherste und dauernste Eigenthum, daher erscheinen dessen Besitzer vorzüglich als die wichtigsten, ersten und bleibendsten Bürger." *See also* Weulersse, G., "The Physiocrats," in *Encyclopedia of the Social Sciences*, vol. v (New York 1931), pp. 348–51.

[31] Toland, *Reasons for Naturalizing the Jews in Great Britain and Ireland on the Same Foot With all Other Nations, Containing also Defense of the Jews Against all Vulgar Prejudices in all Countries* (London 1714), p. 6.

[32] *A Letter*, pp. 16–17.

[33] Dohm, *op. cit.*, vol. i, pp. 1–5; vol. ii, p. 159.

[34] Gregoire, *op cit.*, pp. 59–61.

[35] Mirabeau, H. G. R., Comte de, *Sur Moses Mendelssohn et sur la réforme politique des Juifs* (Leipzig 1853), pp. 83–85.

[36] Toland, *op. cit.*, pp. 13–14; Dohm, *op. cit.*, p. 93.

[37] *Spectator*, no. 495, quoted in *A Letter*, Appendix, p. 5.

[38] Toland, *op. cit.*, p. 14.

[39] *Lettres Persanes*, Texte établi et presenté par Élie Carcasonne (Paris 1929), Lettre lx.

[40] Montesquieu, *The Spirit of the Laws, op. cit.*, vol. i, pp. 364–65.

[41] Gregoire, *op. cit.*, p. 83.

[42] *A Letter*, pp. 43–44.

[43] *Oeuvres*, vol. xvii, p. 397.

[44] *Cf.* Mann, Jacob, "Massa'am shel Rabbi Hayyim Ibn 'Attir wa-Havurato le-Erets Yisrael," *Tarbiz*, vol. vii (1935–36), pp. 89–90.

[45] *Ibid.*, p. 79.

[46] Toland, *op. cit.*, pp. 6, 42; *A Letter*, pp. 43, 63–64; also, Appendix, p. 4; Montesquieu, *Lettres Persanes*, Lettre lx.

[47] "Such an abominable spirit is raging against them," wrote Thomas Herring, the Archbishop of Canterbury, in 1753, "that I expect in a little time they will be massacred." Quoted by Van der Veen, H. R. S., in *Jewish Characters in Eighteenth Century English Fiction and Drama* (Grouningen 1935), p. 44. *See also* Lecky, W. H., *The History of England in the Eighteenth Century*, vol. i (London 1878), p. 264.

[48] Liber, M., "Les Juifs et le convocation des états généraux," *loc. cit.*, vol. lxiii (1912), pp. 89–108; vol. lxiv (1912), pp. 244–77.

[49] Van der Veen, *op. cit.*, p. 264.

[50] *Ibid.*, p. 42.

[51] Gellert, Christian Fuerchtegott, *Briefe der schwedischen Gräfin von G.*, in *Sämtliche Schriften*, vol. v (Bern, Walthard 1767–76).

[52] Van der Veen, *op. cit.*, pp. 46–47; Dejob, Ch., "Le Juif dans la Comédie au XVIIIe siècle," *REJ*, vol. xxxix (1899), pp. 119–28.

[53] "Juifs," in *Oeuvres*, vol. xix, p. 521.

[54] *The Social Contract*, Everyman's edition, p. 122. For further references on Rousseau and the Jews, *cf.* Baron, *Modern Nationalism and Religion* (New York 1947), p. 27 and p. 279, note 13.

[55] *The Spirit of the Laws*, vol. ii, pp. 54–56.

[56] *Cf.* Kohut, Adolph, *Johann Gottfried Herder and die Humanitätsbestrebungen der Neuzeit* (Berlin 1870), p. 20; *cf.* also, Herder, *op. cit.*, vol. xvii, p. 273.

[57] Goethe, "Briefe des Pastors," *op. cit.*, vol. xxxvii, p. 162; also, "Epigramme," *ibid.*, vol. liii, p. 11.

[58] *A Letter*, p. 80.

[59] Gregoire, *op. cit.*, p. 110.

[60] Compare, for instance, Diderot's opinion on the Talmud and the rabbis with that of Basnage. *See* "Jugement sur le Talmud," in "Juifs," *Oeuvres*, vol. xv, pp. 362–68 and Basnage, "The Gemarists and Talmudists," *op. cit.*, pp. 170 ff.

[61] Dohm, *op. cit.*, vol. ii, pp. 38–41.

[62] *Cf.* mainly Basnage, *op. cit.*, Books II, III; Diderot, *Oeuvres*, vol. xv, pp. 362 ff.

[63] *Op. cit.*, xv, pp. 378–81.

[64] *Ibid.*, pp. 386 ff.

[65] Montesquieu, *Lettres Persanes*, Lettre cxliii.

[66] Basnage, *op. cit.*, p. 468.

[67] Diderot, *Oeuvres*, vol. xv, p. 365.

[68] *Ibid.*, p. 366.

[69] *Mélanges inedits*, publiés par le baron de Montesquieu (Bordeaux 1892), p. 140.

[70] Gregoire, *op. cit.*, p. 173.

[71] *Ibid.*, p. 187.

[72] Dohm, *op. cit.*, vol. i, p. 97.

[73] Goethe, *Werke*, vol. lii, pp. 267–68.

[74] Voltaire, *Oeuvres*, vol. xix, pp. 528–29.

[75] Pribram, Alfred Francis, *Urkunden zur Geschichte der Juden in Wien*, vol. i (Wien und Leipzig 1918), pp. 440–43. The language referred to in the Patent undoubtedly was Yiddish.

[76] Anchel, Robert, *op. cit.*, p. 214. *See also* Dohm, *op. cit.*, vol. i, p. 117.

[77] Gregoire, *op. cit.*, p. 160.

[78] Goethe, "Lesearten," *Werke*, vol. xl, 2, p. 523.

[79] *Ibid.*, p. 196.

[80] *Ibid.*, vol. xxxvii, pp. 59–60.

[81] *Cf.* Raisin, Zalman, *Fun Mendelssohn biz Mendele* (Warsaw 1923), *passim*.

[82] Gregoire, *op. cit.*, pp. 59–64.

[83] Herder, "Bekehrung der Juden," in *Werke*, vol. xxiv, p. 69.

[84] Hyamson, *op. cit.*, pp. 220–21.

[85] Liber, M., *op. cit.*, pp. 194 ff.; *see also* Dubnow, *op. cit.*, vol. viii, chap. i.

[86] Dohm, *op. cit.*, vol. ii, p. 46; *see also* Schwager's notes to Dohm, *ibid.*, pp. 89–111.

[87] Herder, *Werke*, vol. xxiv, p. 74.

[88] Herder, "Hebräer," in *Ideen*, 2nd ed. (Leipzig 1821), book XII, pp. 67–69; *see also* "Bekehrung," *Werke*, pp. 63–66.

[89] *Ibid.*, vol. xxiv, p. 64.

[90] Goethe, *Werke*, vol. xxv, pp. 183–84. *See also* his impressions of the Ghetto of Frankfurt, *ibid.*, vol. xxviii, pp. 325–26.

[91] Dohm, *op. cit.*, vol. ii, pp. 98–100.

[92] Van der Veen, *op. cit.*, pp. 266–67.

[93] Lessing, Gotthold Ephraim, *Sämtliche Schriften*, ed. Karl Lachmann, vol. i (Berlin 1838–40), pp. 304–40.

[94] *See also* Carrington, Herbert De Witt, *Die Figur des Juden in der dramatischen Literatur des XVIII. Jahrhunderts* (Heidelberg 1897).

[95] *Cf.* Dejob, "Les Juifs dans la Comédie au XVIII Siècle," *loc. cit.*, p. 121.

⁹⁶ "At the last moment," Rameau says, "we are equally rich: Samuel Berard, who by dint of thefts, plunder and bankruptcies leaves 27 millions in gold and Rameau who leaves nothing at all" (*Diderot, Interpreter of Nature, Selected Writings*, translated by Jean Stewart and Jonathan Kemp [New York 1938], p. 254). One finds in *Rameau* two more references to the Jew of the time. In one of them Rameau tells a strange story: how a Jew was cheated of his money by a "renegade of Avignon" and burned by the Inquisition (*ibid.*, p. 296). In the other Diderot introduces a sexually dissolute Jew. In *Voyage De Hollande*, Diderot divides the Jews of Amsterdam into "shaven" and "bearded." About the latter he remarks: "Il faut se tenir sur ses gardes avec les barbus, qui ne sont pas infiniment scrupuleux," *Oeuvres*, vol. xvii, p. 432. In Lessing's *Juden*, the two robbers who attacked the traveller considered it best to disguise their identity by putting on Jewish-looking beards.

⁹⁷ Basnage pointed out that one of the causes of Christian hatred of the Jews was their moral looseness: "They love," he wrote, "fair women though they be Christians. . . . They are as fond of money as beauty" (*History*, Book VI, p. 467). This accusation recurs frequently in the literature of the eighteenth century. *Cf.* Van der Veen, *op. cit., passim.*

⁹⁸ Basnage, *History*, p. 748.

⁹⁹ Toland, *Appendix, Containing Two Problems Concerning the Jewish Nation and Religion* [=*Appendix*] (London 1718), p. 8.

¹⁰⁰ Hartley, David, *Observations on Man, his Frame, his Duty and his Expectations* [=*Observations*], 5th ed. (London 1810), pp. 386–87.

¹⁰¹ Diderot, *Voyage De Hollande, Oeuvres*, vol. xvii, pp. 432–33.

¹⁰² Voltaire, "Juifs," *Oeuvres*, vol. xix, pp. 538–40.

¹⁰³ Herder, *Vom Geiste der Ebräischen Poesie*, vol. i (Dessau 1812), p. 304; *see also* "Bekehrung," *Werke*, vol. xxiv, pp. 66–67.

¹⁰⁴ Dohm, *op. cit.*, vol. ii, pp. 41–42.

¹⁰⁵ *Cf.* Sokolow, Nahum, *History of Zionism*, vol. i (London 1919), pp. 55–57.

¹⁰⁶ Toland, *Appendix*, p. 8.

¹⁰⁷ *Observations*, pp. 386–87.

¹⁰⁸ *A Letter*, Appendix, p. 48.

¹⁰⁹ *Ibid.*, p. 39.

¹¹⁰ *Cf.* Rousseau, *Consideration on the Government of Poland, passim.* In his *Essai*, Gregoire wrote: "Aussi peut-on poser en fait que depuis deux ans le caractère Françoise a acquis plus d'energie, et develope plus de patriotisme que depuis deux siècles" (p. 110). *See also* Kohn, Hans, *op. cit.*, pp. 205 ff.

¹¹¹ Dohm, *op. cit.*, vol. ii, p. 43.

¹¹² *Ibid.*, p. 74; Mendelssohn, Moses, *Gesammelte Schriften*, ed. G. B. Mendelssohn (Leipzig 1843–45), vol. iii, p. 366; vol. v, pp. 493–94.

¹¹³ Dohm, *op. cit.*, vol. ii, pp. 214 ff.

¹¹⁴ Gregoire, *op. cit.*, pp. 111–12.

[115] Herder, *Werke,* vol. xxiv, pp. 66–67.

[116] *Ibid.,* p. 67.

[117] For Germany, *cf.* Katz, Jacob, *Die Entstehung der Judenassimilation in Deutschland und deren Ideologie* (Frankfurt 1935); Friedländer, David, *Akten-Stücke die Reform der jüdischen Kolonien in den preussischen Staaten betreffend* (Berlin 1793), pp. 38–39, note 2. For western Europe, especially northern Italy, France and Holland, *cf.* Azulai, Hayyim Joseph David (Hida), *Sefer Ma'agal Tov ha-Shalem* (Jerusalem 1934); for England, *cf.* Margoliouth, M., *History of the Jews in Great Britain,* vol. ii (1851), pp. 70, 83, 92; *see also* Jost, I. M., *Geschichte der Israeliten seit der Zeit der Maccabäer bis auf unsere Tage,* vol. ix (Berlin 1820–28), p. 24.

[118] *Cf.* mainly Toland, *op. cit.,* pp. 15–18; Dohm, *op. cit.,* vol. i, pp. 28, 36, 39, 109; Gregoire, *op. cit.,* pp. 107–8; Mirabeau, *Sur Moses Mendelssohn, passim;* Friedländer, *op. cit.,* p. 9, note.

[119] *Cf.* Dohm, *op. cit.,* vol. ii, *Introduction. See also* Mahler, Raphael, *Dibre Yeme Yisrael, Doroth Aharonim,* vol. i (Merhabya 1952–56), Bk. I, pp. 130–38, 149–53.

[120] Goethe, *Werke,* vol. xxviii, p. 190.

[121] Herder, *Werke,* vol. xxiv, pp. 69–70.

[122] *Ibid.,* p. 70. *See also* Voltaire, *Oeuvres,* vol. xx, pp. 525–26; Goethe, *Werke,* vol. liii, p. 11.

EDITORS' PREFACE

The Polish Democratic Society and the Jewish Problem, 1832-1846

In the aftermath of World War I, Polish Jewry in the Russian partition finally managed to attain almost complete de jure equality following Poland's restoration in 1918. The Versailles Treaty exacted minority rights from the restored state, thus introducing group emancipation for the national minorities, including the Jews. However, ways of "improving" the Jews had been under discussion in independent Poland since the 1760s and seemed to have had greater urgency in times of crises, partitions, and wars. Even the Holocaust and the latest exodus of the Jews from Poland following the 1967 Six-Day War have not brought an end to the Jewish issue in that country.

Unlike other European countries, Poland had had a large and growing Jewish minority, often about ten percent of the total population. The problem of what to do with the Jews was intimately connected with the disenfranchisement of the peasant and equality of the urban population. Until the 1780s, the discussion centered on ways of increasing taxation and limiting autonomy. The fiscal reforms of 1764 abolished Jewish national and regional autonomous bodies, increased the head tax almost fourfold, and further restricted occupa-

116

tional choice. Later on, the elimination of Jews from the rural areas was accelerated. Additional increases in taxes were voted in 1775 and 1789.

Plans for a more realistic improvement of the position of the Jews began to appear in the 1780s. They were encouraged by the Austrian Toleration Patent of Joseph II (1789) and by the French Revolution. However, the Quadrennial Diet (1789–91), which extended suffrage and undertook other measures to strengthen faltering Poland, excluded the Jews from its projected reforms. "Confessors of the Mosaic faith" were deprived of their due political rights in the satellite Duchy of Warsaw (1807–1815) in the wake of Napoleon's "Infamous Decree." Deliberations, petitions, and agitation in the Kingdom of Poland under Alexander I resulted in proposals for doubtful "reforms," as well as in new restrictions and delays of Emancipation until the Jews would "deserve" it. A Jewish offer of a fighting unit in the November 1830 Insurrection was met with the reply of the Minister of War that "we cannot allow that Jewish blood should mingle with the noble blood of the Poles" on the field of battle. Henceforth, the "Jewish question" (to use the nineteenth century term) was frequently portrayed by the opponents of Jewish Emancipation as a war between two nations, the Poles and the Jews.

Important in the discussions were the members of the "Great Emigration," consisting of the Polish exiles who settled in Western Europe, mainly France, after the ill-fated Insurrection. They planned their country's liberation and future and greatly influenced Polish political thinking and literary creativity at home and abroad for generations. They were particularly aware of the insurrectionary leadership's failure to involve the Jews.

There are comparatively few serious publications in English on Polish-Jewish history, and even fewer on the struggle for Jewish Emancipation in Poland. The article by Professor Duker deals with the pre-1846 discussions of the Jewish problem in the Polish Democratic Society, the emigres' radical wing. The Society's writings during its first decade of exile did not display much interest in the Jews. Although the Society was committed to the principle of universal equality in the Poland of the future, a direct reference to it was included in its platform only under pressure. Its Great Manifesto of 1836 included a statement in favor of religious toleration, the result of discussions in several of the Society's branches. It held the *szlachta* (gentry) responsible for Jewish separatism. A radical antisemite's response aptly compared Poland's historical open-door policy to Jews with the closed gates of other countries. The few books published by émigrés on the Jewish problem in the early 1830s were seldom reviewed in the press, which paid little attention to such subjects as the parallel between the two nations in exile, the Jews and the Poles, or the acculturation of Jews in Western Europe as a possible indicator of the future course of Polish Jewry.

Some émigré writers followed the position of Mochnacki, who, in his attempt to account for the defeat of the Uprising, included the failure to involve the Jews. Others advocated conditional emancipation, sometimes combined with stringent "re-education" measures. Still others were not so friendly. One hinted at the desirability of the forced exile of the Jews, a notion considered shocking by another writer but promoted seriously a century later. A few Catholic radicals of Jewish descent who advocated equality for the Jews in Poland were frequently abused as Jews in the Society's humorous paper, *Pszonka*. In contrast, in the 1840s the official *Demokrata Polski* frequently carried news about Jews, mainly concerning tsarist restrictions and Emancipation's progress in other countries.

The seeming disinterest of the Society in securing the cooperation of the Jews and its placidity when it came to public confrontation with the problem may be contrasted with its leaders' vigor and enterprise in maintaining contact with Europe's radicals and in its activities at home and abroad. Indifference and hesitation may have been due to grave doubts about the possibility of securing the cooperation of Polish Jews or about the usefulness of such cooperation even if it could be secured. Clichés about materialistic Jews and Judaism commonly accepted by the progressives and leftists may have contributed to the Democrats' ambivalence. In addition, the traditional dislike of Jews was enhanced by a new stereotype, that of the Jewish spy and betrayer of the Insurrection. The exiles' empathy for the declassed gentry in the homeland, the contrast between the latter's decline and the growing role of Jews in the country's economic development, distrust of assimilated Jews, together with a fear of their influence on Polish culture, and the exiles' nostalgia for a romanticized bucolic past being spoiled by urbanization constituted other factors. The lingering suspicion of the sincerity of the converted Frankists in view of their continued separatism was extended to most if not all baptized Jews and was intensified by rumors of the multitude and success of converted Jews in Russian officialdom.

While Jews were involved in some of the Democrats' underground operations in Poland, little was done by the Society to gather Jewish support for the events of 1846, an unsuccessful prelude to 1848. This contrasts with the Society's active interest in obtaining Jewish cooperation after 1848, particularly during the so-called "Jewish War" of 1859.

ABRAHAM G. DUKER, for many years an Editor, before that Managing Editor of JEWISH SOCIAL STUDIES, and President of the Conference on Jewish Social Studies, 1972-74, has been active in Jewish scholarship, letters, and education. He was the founding Managing Editor of the *Contemporary Jewish Record* (now *Commentary*), President of the Spertus College of Judaica in Chicago, Director of Libraries and Professor of History and Social Institutions at Yeshiva University, and is now Chairman of the Department of Judaic Studies of Brooklyn College, City University of New York. Professor Duker is the author of many studies in Polish and American Jewish history and social life, including *Jewish Survival in the World Today, Jewish Community Relations,* and *The Polish "Great Emigration" and the Jewish Problem.*

The Polish Democratic Society and the Jewish Problem, 1832-1846

by Abraham G. Duker

Like many other radical or socialistic movements of the 19th century, the Polish Democratic Society (or Association; in Polish, *Towarzystwo Demokratyczne Polskie* [T. D. P.]) showed much ambivalence and a good deal of antisemitism when it came to the Jewish question. The Society was the consistently radical party of the Great Emigration (*Wielka Emigracja*—the movement of political exiles and of Poland-in-Exile after the unsuccessful insurrection of 1830–31).[1] Its leaders were drawn from the ranks of the insurrectionary radical "clubbists," many of whom patterned themselves after the Jacobins and *sans-culottes* of the earlier French Revolution. During the first year of their life in exile, these elements demanded that the radical and aggressive Polish National Committee, headed by Joachim Lelewel,[2] adopt a far-reaching social program, but the Committee preferred to maintain a middle course in order to attract additional followers. The "radicals," therefore, left to organize the Polish Democratic Society on March 16, 1832.

* The present article is based on a chapter in my Columbia University Ph.D. dissertation, "The Polish 'Great Emigration' and the Jews. Studies in Political and Intellectual History" [="Great Emigration"] (Publication 16277, Doctoral Dissertation Series, University Microfilms, Ann Arbor, Michigan).

Reprinted from JEWISH SOCIAL STUDIES, Volume XIX, 1957.

The "Founding Act" of the Society (March 17, 1832) attributed the failure of the insurrection to the *szlachta* (gentry) and called for the emancipation of the peasants. Attracted by a vague cosmopolitan ideology, it advocated collaboration with revolutionary democratic forces of other nations and maintained close contacts with these groups as well as with later socialist elements in western and central Europe. The messianic belief in the mission of Poland—a mainstay of émigré ideologies and the psychological bulwark of the exiles— was reinterpreted to apply to the Polish common people.

Unlike other groups, the T. D. P. emerged as a tightly knit and disciplined organization. There was full freedom of discussion in the branches, and elections to the *Centralizacya* (—Centralization, Central Committee) were democratic, but final authority for the execution of decisions and conduct of policy was vested in that central body of nine professional revolutionaries. Discipline became increasingly strict as the Society's leadership grew more and more doctrinaire. The Society proclaimed a policy of non-cooperation with other émigré groups where such groups conflicted with its own principles. Sections as well as leading members were excluded from membership for failure to adhere to the party line. This control even extended to the homeland through underground emissaries.

The Society became increasingly radical as it further emancipated itself from attempts of the Carbonari, Young Poland, and various roof organizations to control its policy.[3] Its Great Manifesto (December 4, 1836) advocated unconditional redistribution of land to the peasants as the first act of the forthcoming insurrection. While Lelewel proposed raising the peasantry, and thus the entire nation, to the level of the gentry, the Manifesto demanded that the *szlachta* become a part of the common people.[4]

The Society stressed preparation for the insurrection in the homeland by military training in the Emigration as well as extensive underground propaganda and organization in Poland itself, particularly in the Prussian and Austrian portions. T. D. P. was chiefly responsible for the Poznanie and Cracow events of 1846 and attempted to play a leading role in the upheavals of 1848. These events precipitated crises in the Emigration and brought about a continued decline in the strength of the organization.[5]

Early Discussions of the Jewish Problem

Various statements and platforms issued by the Society re-emphasized its principle of equality for all people in Poland, regardless of speech, custom and religious faith. However, such official declarations always failed to refer directly to the Jews.[6]

The earliest known formal expression in T. D. P. circles in favor of the Jews was that of Ludwik Osiasz Lubliner, a Jew.[7] In a speech in Paris before the November 1832 reunion of the exiles (presumably a gathering of members of the Democratic Society), Lubliner noted that had the National Government permitted the enrollment of Jews in the army, all the Jewish soldiers in the tsarist ranks would have deserted to the Polish side, an action which might have assured the success of the insurrection.[8] Lubliner submitted a rewritten text of his speech for publication, and a member was delegated to examine it. At a subsequent meeting, the membership voted against its publication, with the excuse that "the essay about the Jews by member Lubliner, being too specialized and [dealing] exclusively with only one class of the Polish people, cannot be included in the brochures of the Society; which should not prevent from having it printed separately, if sufficient funds will be available for this purpose."[9]

A protest by Lubliner necessitated another meeting and, after discussion, the membership again voted against publication. However, in order to clarify the stand of the Society, a motion was also passed stating that it considered Jews to be fully equal. Moreover, it stated, were the Society really anti-democratic, it would have prevented even the separate publication of the essay.[10] To my knowledge, the speech was never published.

There are no other direct data on the attitude of the Society toward Jews until 1836, although the mention of the names of the bankers Frankel and Epstein, in a protest by the Society against the floating of a Russian loan in Poland,[11] could be interpreted as not without some anti-Jewish intent.

Discussions before the Great Manifesto

It would appear that the problem of the Jews had been on the agenda of some sections of the Society during discussions in preparation for the issuance of the Great Manifesto (December 4, 1836). The Caen Section demanded that the Manifesto include a definite statement on religious tolerance, and, with respect to Jews, it observed: "There are no cases of religious hatred among us about which we read in the text submitted. The persecution of the Jews is not a simple result of religious fanaticism."[12] The same demand was put forth by the Sections of Poitiers, Bayeux, Angoulême, and some individual members of Neveil and Montpellier.[13]

In accord with commonly accepted policy, the comments of the Centralization were confined to the intolerance of gentry and nobility in ancient Poland: "Intolerance was not limited merely to the destruction of non-Catholic or dissident churches in Cracow . . . and to the burning and murder of Jews as well as of people suspected of atheism. More than once there was the threat of driving the Jews out of Poland."[14] The *szlachta* was also accused of forcing the burghers and the Jews to wear distinctive clothes.[15] Czacki was cited: "This is how they created a separate nation within the nation."[16] While refusing to enter upon the "religious question," which was omitted from the draft of the Manifesto, the Centralization did consent to inclusion of a statement about religious tolerance.[17] This would lead us to suspect that the rank-and-file members were more concerned with the Jewish question than was the Centralization which viewed it merely as a religious problem, consistently refusing reference to it in its appeals and statements.

Ostrowski's Attack

These remarks of the Centralization about intolerance aroused the ire of J. B. Ostrowski,[18] one of the founders of the Society, who injected the Jewish issue in one of his many and interminable disputes with the T.D.P. after having left it. He attacked the T.D.P. argument that commerce had been controlled by Jews and Germans, that native Poles had never engaged in it, and that the nobility was responsible for this condition. Writing in his *Nowa Polska* (probably in the middle of 1836), he defended the Polish aristocracy, which "shone with angelic virtues," as contrasted with the "barbarous, wild, predatory" aristocracy of Germany, France, and England, where native commerce did prevail. Ostrowski argued that the lot of the Polish peasant was not very bad until the 16th century. He disputed the contention that foreigners and Jews brought commerce to Poland, the Jews having arrived in Poland only around the 14th century, while commerce must have existed before that. He denied the argument that the Jews had been persecuted; rather, he argued that Jews received virtually the same liberties accorded to Polish citizens, that King Casimir the Great had protected them, calling them "deserving and influential residents." He wondered whether the Centralization would condemn Polish society and its king for such treatment. "Jews have not brought harm for a long time to Polish commerce. The cities restricted them. We must surely identify the Germans as the foreigners who created commerce."[19] There seems to be no record of any T. D. P. reply to this argument.

Allusions to Jews in the Society's press do not occur often until 1841. In 1837 a publication of the Society did contain excerpts from an historical work about the situation of the Jews in Poland.[20] However, we have not come across any T. D. P. reactions to Palatine Ostrowski's and Lubliner's works on the Jews in Poland in 1834 and 1838.[21] In a humorous and patronizing report about an unsuccessful November anniversary meeting in London, a speaker, Bartłomiej Beniowski, a convert from Judaism to Catholicism, was identified as a Jew (starozakonny).[22] This practice of identifying Christian political opponents of Jewish descent as Jews became more popular in the late 1840's.

Dispute on the Identity of Catholicism with Polish Nationality

There is no evidence that the publications of the Society were concerned with the Jewish issue in the debate on the relationship of Polish nationality to membership in the Roman Catholic Church. The Society's leader, Jan Alcyato, failed to refer to Jews in his attack on this type of Catholic exclusivism. However, he stated that "there was no trace of religious fanaticism at the time of the last insurrection."[23]

The Economic Factor

T. D. P. discussions also stressed the economic role of Polish Jews —a common practice among émigré groups. Drastic measures to reform the Jews, as part of the process of preparing them for emancipation, were urged by Erazm Wróblewski in 1841. In an article on industry and commerce in the official *Pismo T. D. P.* he wrote:

The Jews, tied down blindly by their nationality, deprived of the light of learning, but naturally shrewd, beguiled by their religious superstitions, held in low esteem for a long time and persecuted by all nationalities; the Jews, having accepted in social life cheating, shiftlessness as a virtue and the gathering of wealth as a purpose in life, became the bane of society. Almost the entire Polish commerce has been in their hands since time immemorial. The Jewish population fills all our smaller cities, [a factor] in which we can also seek the cause of the decline of commerce; the prejudice of the natives against this useful branch of national economy, finally, the deterioration of the cities and the impossibility of independence on the part of the burghers. The expulsion of the Jews from Poland would constitute barbarism. Their exclusion from the enjoyment of civic laws would be rather an injustice. But to demand reform on their part and even to force them to it is an undeniable necessity. Let military service and public service cleanse them from their superstitions and decadence. Let them cease to be a nation within a nation. In one word, let them become worthy of the name of Polish citizens. We have a right to demand this of them. What [kind of] means we can use for this purpose is a different story and remains to be treated in the same practical way as the freeing of the peasants. However, one thing is certain, namely, that no monarchical or oligarchical government will reform the Jews—only a government of the people, a regime to whom the good of the fatherland is its foremost interest, will be in the position to resist the temptation of gold which is scattered plentifully by Jews on such occasions.[24]

In a similar vein Józef Garnysz discussed the Jewish problem,[25] and his remarks about the usefulness of the Jews in the forthcoming insurrection reveal the influence of Mochnacki.[26] The Jews, claimed Garnysz, had enjoyed the best possible conditions in pre-Jagiellonian Poland, but their situation declined, with all of Poland, under the influence of the foreign Catholic clergy. Repeating Słowaczynski's exaggerated estimate of the Polish Jewish population at three and one-half million,[27] Garnysz saw the main difficulty in the Jews' adherence to "commerce, innkeeping, lighter trades (artisanship), usury and other swindling, harmful to the country and especially to the common people." Depending upon the degree of westernization, Jews were either fanatics or materialists. Brutal treatment by occupying powers, recruiting, taxation and other burdens, only intensified "their sluggish and empty character."

However, Jews could still be useful to the planned revolution, Garnysz declared. Jews have always been friendly to Poland, they had not forgotten the haven they found in that country; this was proven by their patriotic deeds in 1794 and again in 1830–31. He contrasted the Jewish participants in these revolts who voluntarily joined their Polish brothers with the forcibly conscripted Jews in the Russian army. He was convinced that, given proper treatment and incentive, Jews would lose their "fanaticism" and, with the award of citizenship, would become a useful element in the country. Bitter over the fact that after so many experiences people still entertained doubts on this subject, he cited Mochnacki to support his contentions.

Pszonka's *Anti-Jewish Policy*

Pszonka (The Grain Millet), the humorous organ of the T. D. P., was most contemptuous of the Jews. Edited by, among others, Seweryn Goszczyński (later a Towianist) and Leon Zieńkowicz, *Pszonka* viewed Jews in a satirical fashion when attacking political opponents—a form of contempt characteristic of many sections of Christian society and particularly prevalent in central and eastern Europe. More direct, however, were attacks against Czyński and Beniowski. In "A List of Prophecies for 1844" Lelewel was castigated for having appealed to Jews: "Lelewel writes the hundredth appeal to the Gypsies and the Jews, urging them to join the *Zjedno-czenie*."[28] The Towianists were ridiculed by references to their Jewish connections.[29] Anthony Gorecki, the poet, was portrayed as "St. Anthony of Wilno who, fleeing from the *Towiańszczyzna* (Towiański group), found refuge in a Jewish synagogue."[30] Nobles were particularly scorned by comparing their behavior with "funny" habits of Jews.[31] Yet, *szlachta* addiction during the Insurrection to the habit of indiscriminate hanging of Jews on the spurious charge of spying on behalf of the Russians was chided in a criticism of that class.[32]

The Campaign against Czyński

In 1843, Jan Czyński, the foremost defender of the Jews in the Emigration, again embarked on a campaign of defense of the Polish Jews by publishing articles in the French and Jewish press.[33] He also launched the periodical *Echo Miast Polskich* (Echo of the Polish Cities) in which, as a solution to the Jewish problem, he advocated that Jews should constitute the middle class in a liberated Poland. When criticizing the failure of émigrés to react to the promulgation of the drastic tsarist edicts decreeing lengthy military service for Jews,[34] he attacked the T.D.P., whose "*szlachta* democracy" he contrasted with "genuine Polish democracy."

It was very likely under Czyński's influence that seven young Polish Jews, recent arrivals in France, addressed a protest and appeal to the Emigration which was published in the *Echo* and distributed at émigré meetings.[36] Interest in their cause was also shown by French Jews.[37] T.D.P. was singled out for special attack. Concerning the silence of the Society about tsarist recruiting laws, the drafters of the appeal remarked:

Neither was the behavior of the Centralization more correct. Here the young *szlachta* inherited from the old one dullness, superstition and hatred. Its organ did not find a single word of regret. All the other European papers were aroused against the barbarism of Nicholas.

The appeal continued:

On the other hand, the money gathered from the bloody sweat of the peasant was turned by them [the leaders of the Society] to the profit of the *Pszonka*. Ludwik Mierosławski[38] amused the members of the Centralization in rhyme and prose by ridiculing our tears and sufferings as well as the sufferings and tears of the Polish masses.

The temple in which we pray to the Lord of Hosts, our house of prayer, was mentioned with opprobrium as if it were a pagan place of worship, this place of deposit for our tears and sighs as if it were a house of licentiousness or robbery. Jakubowski, Darasz, Alcyato,[39] supplied funds for all these knavish, un-Polish pasquinades. They are solidly responsible for all *Pszonka's* abuses.

We, the undersigned, having called God as a witness of our sorrow, accuse the forementioned countrymen as *false democrats* before the homeland and history. We cite their names in order that our co-religionists and all the people, who in their very hearts love God, the fatherland and the common people, should know that a *democrat* is not one who merely assumes the name of a *democrat*, but only one who deep in his soul has respect for the *Highest* and *love for his fellowmen*. We shall publish this protest in the Hebrew and the German tongues, we shall send it to the homeland and we shall bring forth its expressions to the friends of Poland and to the Polish common people.[40]

Aftermath of Protest

The protest aroused a minor furor in the Emigration, particularly among T. D. P. followers. *Pszonka,* which had earlier greeted the appearance of the *Echo* by announcing that the new publication *Ay Way*[41] was the continuation of *La Russie Pittoresque,*[42] now excoriated Czyński and the Jews. *Echo* was now paraphrased into *Echo Miast Żydowskich* (Echo of the Jewish Cities).[43] *Pszonka* termed Czyński's struggle against anti-Jewish restrictions as the effort of "the Talmudists to liberate the Jews from military conscription, payment of taxes and obedience to the general law, so that the converts and the tramps will be given the opportunity to freely poison, skin and whip the Polish peasants."[44] "Out with the Jews!" were the concluding words of another article in *Pszonka,* addressed to Czyński, ridiculing the protest appeal, which it described as "a piece of demagogy on the part of a Jew."[45] A fable, "The Convert and the Burghers," poked fun at the Jews who, unlike the noble "Lechites," were too afraid to fight. The "baptized dog" was represented as in a quandary about what to do with his *payoth* (earlocks). It concluded with the phrase, "To the lantern!"[46]

News in the Democratic Press

Another indication of the attitude of the T. D. P. toward Jews was its treatment of them in the Society's press. The official *Demokrata Polski* frequently published news about Jews, culled mostly from the general press abroad,[47] with some items taken directly from papers published in Poland.[48] The news was chiefly concerned with the tsarist legislation, recruitment laws occupying a place of prominence.[49] It is interesting to note that, while the *Demokrata* described the cruelties of the tsarist conscription, it favored the extension of the right of Jews to serve in the Prussian army, a right demanded by them in the Poznanie region, because it felt "it would influence them properly,"[50] presumably in the direction of enlightenment.

Next in frequency to news about army service were items concerning the limitation to settlement of Jews to fifty versts from the border.[51] Other types of restrictions were also reported.[52] Interestingly, the efforts of the Russian government to colonize the Jews on the land were described as an attempt by Nicholas "to turn the Jews into husbandmen, even at the cost of humanitarianism."[53] News about Jews outside of Poland dealt largely with the progress of emancipation.

In contrast to the attitude of *Pszonka,* news items in *Demokrata* were handled objectively and with due sympathy for the sufferings of the Jews.

Some T. D. P. Leaders

It is pertinent to inquire into the reason for the anti-Jewish sentiments or indifference towards the Jewish issue evinced from time to time by the leadership of the T. D. P. Obvious is the complex of sentiments, prevalent in Poland, that can be traced to the ancient theological odium so assiduously cultivated there.[54] In addition, the declassed *szlachta* was greatly concerned with the growing power of the assimilated or baptized Jews, in consequence of their Polonization and the country's industrialization. This fear was intensified by the social and economic advancement of the Frankists.[55] Account must also be taken of the influence of the growth of antisemitism among

the radicals of western and central Europe. While there is no evidence
in T. D. P. literature of such influence, it would be unwise to ignore
it. The radical émigrés were profoundly influenced by the writings of
Proudhon, Fourier, Marx and others, all of whom identified Jews with
"gold"; some accused Jews of a plot for world domination.[56] It is also
essential to consider the attitude of the top leaders of the Society.
Unfortunately, data about many of them are rather scarce, if not unavailable; however, an insight into the thinking of some T. D. P.
ideologues and leaders may supply some clues.

Wiktor Heltman, a leading spirit of the Society at that stage, while
a young man in the homeland and one of the editors of the *Dekada
Polska* (Polish Decade), maintained in 1821 that Jews should not
receive equal rights until they would become worthy of them and that
Poland's third estate should be formed from the peasant class.[57]
Goszczyński's *Uwagi* (Remarks), a memorandum sent to the T. D. P.
(December 27, 1837), was "the mine from which the Centralization
obtained materials for planning activities." Goszczyński was so hostile
to the Jews that he retained his anti-Jewish views even after his conversion to Towianism.[58] In his *Uwagi,* he rejected any reliance in
revolutionary calculations on the "burghers" estate, composed of the
Jews who were nationally indifferent, of the unfriendly Germans, and
of the petty artisan class."[59] He preferred to rely on the *szlachta,* the
women, and the estate managers' class. While he viewed the peasants
as poor material, he still believed that they could be prepared by the
szlachta to join the insurrection *en masse.* Such advice was hardly
likely to encourage any specific action among the Jews on the part of
the Society's leaders, even in connection with propaganda among the
peasants, who were very much influenced by Jewish innkeepers and
merchants. Nevertheless, some Jews were involved in underground
activities.[60]

Information is also available on Leon Zieńkowicz, another T. D. P.
leader and after 1837 co-editor of *Pszonka* and author of a number of
other publications. Zieńkowicz did not think much of the Jews. "The
Jew and the Englishman," he stated, "are synonyms. Whatever money
the Englishman collects is only for himself."[61] This, of course, could
have constituted more a critique of the English than a diatribe against
the Jews. However, his outstanding writings expressed the *szlachta*

nostalgia for the old order in Poland, together with the awareness that such would never return. When reminiscing about his boyhood, Zieńkowicz sympathetically portrays the old nobleman of the Lublin region, Marcin Hołota—vociferous, opinionated, master of life and death of Jews in his locality. Hołota opines (to the delight of and admiration of Zieńkowicz, then a young boy) that "anyone who holds with the Jews is with the devil; the one who is against the Jews, God is with him."[62] While admitting that Jews were created by God "in the image and likeness of human beings," he cannot understand "why they live not like man but like cattle and worse than cattle." God created them our brethren, "but what kind of brotherhood is it if they steal the last piece of bread from the mouth of the Poles who once upon a time welcomed them and gave them shelter when they were driven out and chased away from the entire world?"[63] He called them a "pestilential plague," which could "infect, poison and kill all of us, entire Lublin, entire Poland."[64] Whenever he passed a Jew (he uses the insulting term *Żydziak*) on the street, he tried to beat him up.[65] Since, however, Hołota did not "wish the Jews evil," his solution of the Jewish problem in Poland was simple. "Let them keep the money which they took from the peasants and emigrate from Poland."[66]

Later, in propaganda directed at peasants, Zieńkowicz advocated brotherhood between them and the Jews.[67] He also condemned Krasinski's views on Jew and peasant.[68] But the basic view that the Jews were hostile to Poland, expressed in the words of Hołota, was evidently the determining factor in his attitudes toward them during the *Pszonka* stage and most likely also in 1848.

As can be seen, some of the top leaders of the T. D. P. were not inclined by their upbringing and contacts to emphasize special efforts to attract Jews to the insurrection. The role of known liberals and Judaeophiles, such as Jan Niepomucen Janowski,[69] a man of peasant birth, is not known. But it was in this mood that the leaders of the Society approached preparations for the insurrectionary actions in 1846.

NOTES

[1] The best summary of the extensive literature on the Great Emigration is contained in Lewak, Adam, "The Times of the Great Emigration," in *Polska,*

Jej Dzieje i Kultura od Czasów Najdawniejszych do Chwili Obecnej (Poland, Her History and Culture from the Earliest Times until the Present Moment), vol. iii (Warsaw 1931), pp. 195–306 [="Polska"]. Of the many recent publications, the most important is Stefan Kieniewicz, ed., *Wiosna Ludów na Ziemiach Polskich* (The Spring of Nations in the Polish Lands [=*Wiosna*] (Warsaw 1948–53), 5 vol. For a brief summary of the problem in English *see* Coleman, A.P., "The Great Emigration" and Gardner, Monica, "The Great Emigration and Polish Romanticism," in *The Cambridge History of Poland from Augustus II to Pilsudski* (Cambridge 1941), pp. 311–55. A useful new publication is Kukiel, M., *Czartoryski and European Unity 1770–1861* (Princeton 1955).

A good summary of the history of T. D. P. will be found in Lewak, "Polska," pp. 221 ff. and *passim;* Kieniewicz, *Wiosna,* Kukiel, *op. cit.* These works supersede the still useful Limanowski, Boleslaw, *Historya Demokracyi Polskiej w Epoce Porozbiorowej* (History of Polish Democracy in the Post-Partition Period) ed. 2 (Kraków 1922), pp. 93 ff. The Society's ideological and organizational shifts are described in detail in Łuczakówna, Helena, *Wiktor Heltman, 1796–1874* (Poznan 1935), pp. 57 ff. Baczko, Bronisław, ed., *Poglady Społeczno-Polityczne i Filozoficzne Towarzystwa Demokratycznego Polskiego* (The Socio-Political and Philosophical Views of the Polish Democratic Society) (Warsaw 1955), is a collection of excerpts useful for background only.

Relatively much research has been carried out in Poland after World War II on the Great Emigration. The T. D. P., the Emigration's revolutionary wing, has understandably been a popular topic for study.

Most important among the recent publications is the biographical guide: Tyrowicz, Marian, *Towarzystwo Demokratyczne Polskie 1832–1863. Przywódcy i Kadry Członkowskie. Przewodnik Biobibliograficzny* (The Polish Democratic Society 1832-1863. Leaders and Membership Cadres. A Bio-Bibliographic Guide) [*–TDP*] (Warsaw 1964) xxxii, 873 pp. *Cf.* also the reviews by Kalembka, Sławomir, "Leaders and Members of the Polish Democratic Society. Notes and Additions to the Bio-Bibliographic Guide," *Kwartalnik Historyczny* (Historical Quarterly), LXXII (1965), pp. 901–17; and Fajnhauz, Dawid, "Remarks on the Participation of Jews in the Polish National Movement. On the Margins of Marian Tyrowicz's Work 'The Polish Democratic Society'," *Biuletyn Żydowskiego Instytutu Historycznego* (Bulletin of the Jewish Historical Institute) (Warsaw), No. 56 (Oct.–Dec. 1965), pp. 115–20.

Another biographical compendium is Krawiec, Lucjan, *Lista Członków Towarzystwa Demokratycznego Polskiego z Lat 1832–1851. Materjaly o Biobibliografii, Genealogii i Heraldyki Polskiej* (A List of the Members of the Polish Democratic Society of the Years 1832–1851. Materials for the Bio-Bibliography of Polish Genealogy and Heraldry), vol. i (Buenos Aires–Paris, 1963).

The researcher should check the entries in the listed works for further information on persons mentioned in the present article.

Historical studies to be noted are: Baczko, B., *Poglądy Społeczno-Polityczne i Filozoficzne Towarzystwa Demokratycznego Polskiego* (Social-Political and Philosophical Views of the Polish Democratic Society) (Warsaw 1955); Kalembka, Sławomir, *Towarzystwo Demokratyczne Polskie w Latach 1832–1846* (The Polish Democratic Society in the Years 1832–1846 [Toruń 1966]. Neither of these authors was acquainted with my present article.

While the biographic guides and the Fajnhauz's review have brought to light a number of names of Jewish members and some pertinent data, they have added little information on the ideological aspects of the T. D. P. My work, dated though it is in some respects, remains the standard publication in this area.

On the attitudes of 19th-century socialists to the Jewish problem *cf.* Silberner, Edmund, *Ha-Sotsialism ha-Ma'aravi u-She'elath ha-Yehudim . . . (*Western Socialism and the Jewish Question. A Study in the History of Socialist Thought in the 19th Century) (Jerusalem 1955).

Some phases of the relations of the Polish émigrés to the Jewish problem are discussed in my works, including "Mickiewicz and the Jewish Problem," in *Adam Mickiewicz. Poet of Poland. A Symposium,* edited by Manfred Kridl, with a Foreword by Ernest J. Simmons, Columbia Slavic Studies (New York 1951), pp. 108–25; "The Tarniks (Believers in the Coming of the Messiah in 1840)" [="Tarniks"] in *The Joshua Starr Memorial Volume, Studies in History and Philology* (New York 1953), pp. 191–201; "Polish Émigré Christian Socialists on the Jewish Problem" [="CS"], in JEWISH SOCIAL STUDIES, vol. xiv (1952), pp. 317–42; "Leon Hollaenderski's Statement of Resignation. A Document of the Great Polish Emigration" [="HS"], *ibid.,* vol. xv (1953), pp. 293–302; "Jewish Volunteers in the Ottoman-Polish Cossack Units during the Crimean War" [="JVO"], *ibid.,* vol. xvi (1954), pp. 203–18, 351–76; "Hollaenderski's Letter of Inquiry to Lelewel" [="HLI"], *Studies in Bibliography and Booklore,* vol. i (1954), pp. 161–66; "The Polish Political Émigrés and the Jews in 1848," [="1848"] in *Proceedings of the American Academy for Jewish Research,* vol. xxiv (1955), pp. 69–102; "The Lafayette Committee for Jewish Emancipation," in *Essays on Jewish Life and Thought, Presented in Honor of Salo Wittmayer Baron* (New York 1959), pp. 169–182; "The Polish Great Emigration's Appeal to the Jews of October 3, 1832," *Sepher ha-Yovel le-Yitshaq Baer* (I. F. Baer Jubilee Volume) (Jerusalem 1960), pp. 431–448 (Hebrew); "Prince Czartoryski, the Emigré, and the Jewish Problem," *The Joshua Bloch Memorial Volume. Studies in Booklore and History* (New York 1960), pp. 165–179; "The Mystery of the Jews in Mickiewicz's Lectures on Slav Literature," *The Polish Review,* vol. vii (1962), pp. 40–66; "The Catholic Centrists and the Jewish Problem in the Polish 'Great Emigration,'" *Jubilee Volume in Honor of Dr. N. M. Gelber* (Tel Aviv 1963), pp. 300–293; "Polish Frankism's Duration: From Cabbalistic Judaism to Roman Catholicism and from Jewishness to Polishness," JEWISH SOCIAL STUDIES, vol. xxv, no. 4 (October, 1963), pp.

287–333; "Władysław Dzwonkowski, An 'Enlightened' Towianist, on the Jewish Problem, 1862," *Meyer Waxman Jubilee Volume* (Chicago and Jerusalem), 1966, pp. 57–75; "The Polish Insurrection's Missed Opportunity: Mochnacki's Views on the failure to Involve the Jews in the Uprising of 1830/31," JEWISH SOCIAL STUDIES, vol. xxviii (1966), pp. 212–32; "Some Cabbalistic and Frankist Elements in Adam Mickiewicz's 'Dziady,' " in Wandycz, Damian S., ed., *Studies in Polish Civilization. Selected Papers Presented at the First Congress of the Polish Institute of Arts and Sciences in America . . . 1966* (New York 1971), pp. 213–35.

[2] Joachim Lelewel, historian and numismatist, also showed much ambivalence in relation to the Jews. My monograph on him is still to be published. *Cf.* my "HLI" and "CS," p. 319, n. 8.

[3] *Cf.* Stecka, Marja, "The Negotiations of the Democratic Society with Young Poland (1834)," *Przegląd Historyczny* (Historical Review), vol. xx (1919), pp. 160–75.

[4] For the evolution of the Society's views on the peasant problem *cf.* Leśniewski, Czesław, "The Rural Community *(gmina)* according to the Projects of the Democratic Society in the Years 1840–41," *Studja Historyczne ku Czci Stanisława Kutrzeby* (Historical Studies in Honor of Stanislaw Kutrzeba), vol. ii (Kraków 1938), pp. 483–516; and Miller, I., "The Peasant Problem in the Program of the Polish Democratic Society During the 30's to the 40's of the XIX century," *Voprosy Istoryi* (Problems of History), no. 9 (September 1948), pp. 41–62.

[5] *Cf.* my "1846" and "1848."

[6] *Cf.* for instance, the brochure, *Towarzystwo Demokratyczne Polskie* (Paris, March 17, 1832), p. 18; *Manifesto of the Polish Democratic Society* (London 1836); *Ostatnie Słowo Towarzystwa Demokratycznego Polskiego przed Zamierzonem w 1846 Powstaniem* (The Last Word of the Polish Democratic Society before the Insurrection Planned in 1846), p. 436; Platform in *Manifest 18 grudnia 1856* (Manifesto of December 18, 1856).

[7] Lubliner, a participant in the 1831 insurrection, was an assimilationist *maskil* and an important figure in the Emigration, where he was most active in democratic circles. He carried out important assignments in preparation of the 1863 revolution. I have collected enough archival material about him for a monograph.

[8] *Cf.* Lubliner, Louis, *Des Juifs en Pologne. Examen de leur condition sous les points de vue historique, legislatif et politique* (Bruxelles-Leipzig 1838), p. 150.

[9] T. D. P., *Okólnik* (Circular) no. 1 (Paris, May 16, 1833), p. 5.

[10] In a letter, dated June 6, 1833, Lubliner protested against this decision. He disagreed with the opinion that "while the Society's desire is the liberation of all the classes of the Polish people, therefore, one of them, that of the Jews, should not be mentioned." The Society's general meeting restated the earlier

decision, repeating its insistence on complete equality for all, regardless of class. If Lubliner's article was anti-democratic, the Society could have prevented its publication, the decision concluded. *Ibid.*, no. 2 (July 15, 1833), pp. 3–4.

[11] T. D. P., *Do Emigracji Polskiej, Obywatele* (T. D. P. to the Polish Emigration, Citizens!) (Poitiers, July 20, 1835).

[12] *Uwagi Centralizacji przy Dyskusji nad Manifestem T. D. P. 3 Sierpnia 1836* (Remarks of the Centralization at the Discussion of the Manifesto of the T. D. P., Aug. 3, 1836) (Paris), p. 78. Luczakówna *(op. cit.,* p. 88) mentions, without giving details, that some T. D. P. sections criticized the omission of references to the Jews in the Manifesto.

[13] *Cf.* Leśniewski, *Manifest Towarzystwa Polskiego R. 1836* (Manifesto of the Polish Democratic Society of 1836) (Warsaw 1836); *Uwagi . . .* (as in preceeding note), pp. 60–61.

[14] *Ibid.,* p. 17.

[15] *Ibid.,* p. 18.

[16] *Ibid.* Tadeusz Czacki (1765–1813), statesman and educator, wrote the famous *Rozprawa o Żydach i Karaimach* (Essay on the Jews and Karaites) (Wilno 1807).

[17] *Uwagi . . .* (as in note 12), pp. 60–61.

[18] Called "Ibuś" in the Emigration, Józefat Bolesław Ostrowski (not to be confused with several prominent namesakes) is a good example of an anti-semitic radical. He moved from one group to another, always, however, flooding the French police files with reports about émigrés, furnished for good money. Known for his acrid tongue, he was described as "a well known noise-maker and calumniator." *Cf.* Lewak, "Polska," pp. 214, 226, 220. For the verification of his authorship of the articles mentioned here, *cf.* Hollaenderski, Leon, *Les Israélites de Pologne* (Paris 1846), p. 134.

[19] *Nowa Polska* (New Poland), p. 634. I regret my failure to note the date. This outburst was one of the many of Ostrowski's attacks on the pro-Jewish position of some émigré organizations. He attacked his namesake Palatine Antoni Ostrowski for his pro-Jewish work, *Pomysły (cf.* below) in *Nowa Polska,* nos. 11–12 (1834), p. 284. Jan Czyński replied to J. B. Ostrowski in *Północ* (The North) no. 5, March 10, 1835, p. 18, in turn eliciting a counterattack from the latter in *Nowa Polska,* vol. iii, part 2, nos. 26, 27, May 3, 1835, pp. 341–45. Stanislaw (Synaj) Hernisz, a Jewish émigré, also joined the debate in *Północ* no. 9, pp. 34–36. Ostrowski continued his arguments in *Nowa Polska,* vol. iii, part 2, no. 30, June 20, 1835, pp. 357–58; nos. 31–32, July 7, 1835, pp. 362–66. For a fuller description, *cf.* my "Great Emigration," pp. 145–52.

[20] *Przegląd Dziejów Polskich* (A Review of Polish History), vol. i (1837), pp. 39–40. The excerpts were from one of many of W. A. Maciejowski's works (possibly from an article) whose title I was not able to verify. It included the enumeration of the numbers of Jews and their status. The remark was made

that the Slav kings have given more privileges to the Jews than to the Germans. Poland was called a "paradise for the Jews."

[21] Palatine Antoni Ostrowski, called the "Polish Lafayette," was the sage author of the weighty *Pomysły o Potrzebie Reformy Towarzyskiey w Ogólności, a Mianowiciey co do Izraelitów w Polszcze, przez Założyciela Miasta Tomaszowa Mazowieckiego* (Thoughts on the Need of Social Reform in General, and, Particularly Concerning the Israelites in Poland, by the Founder of the City of Tomaszow Mazowiecki) (Paris, November 29, 1834). For Lubliner's work, *cf.* above, n. 8.

[22]*Demokrata Polski* (The Polish Democrat) [=*DP*], vol. iii, December 21, 1840, p. 213. Among other things Beniowski was reported to have stated that "in Poland only the Jews have sense, money and all the riches, and that he, hailing as he does from their stock (of which he is most strongly proud) could not sympathize with the earlier speakers."

On Beniowski, a much neglected radical and defender of the Jews, *see* Stocki, E., "Bartłomiej Beniowski, the Forgotten Physician, Politician and Publicist (on the 125th Anniversary of His Embarking upon His Emigration)," in *Biuletyn Żydowskiego Instytutu Historycznego* (Bulletin of the Jewish Historical Institute) (Warsaw) no. 21, (January-March 1957), pp. 115–17. There is no mention in the article of Beniowski's conversion to Catholicism or of his role in the issuance of the "Lelewel Appeal" to the Jews of October 3, 1832, of which he was the most active initiator and writer. *Cf.* my "Great Emigration," pp. 57 ff. and my unpublished monograph on Joachim Lelewel and the Jews. *Cf.* also Mieses, Mateusz, *Polacy Chrzéscijanie Pochodzenia Żydowskiego* (Christian Poles of Jewish Descent), vol. i (Warsaw 1938), pp. 18–25.

[23] *Pismo T. D. P.* (Writing of the T. D. P.), vol. iii (1841), pp. 277–97. Jan Baptysta Antoni Alcyato (1809–1855) was among the main leaders of the T. D. P. Alcyato also traced Poland's decline to the Jesuits and to the persecutions of the Polish Arians (Protestants) in his classic, *Rzecz o Rozumie Stanu w Polsce* (An Essay on Political Understanding in Poland) (Leipzig 1864), pp. 70 ff., published originally in 1849 in Leipzig.

[24] *Pismo T. D. P.*, vol. ii (1841), pp. 307–08.

[25] *Kilka Myśli dla Polski i o Polsce* (A Few Thoughts About Poland and for Poland) (Poitiers, 1842), pp. 81–85.

[26] Maurycy Mochnacki argued in his history of the insurrection that the revolutionary leaders failed to take advantage of the important positions of the Jews in Russia and in the West. *Cf.* chapter on Mochnacki in my "Great Emigration," pp. 99–109 [or my article on him listed in note 1, above].

[27] The statistics were most likely obtained from Słowaczyński, Jędrzej, *Cinq statistiques générales de la Pologne* (Paris 1838), 4 vols.

[28] *Pszonka*, part VI, no. 2, pp. 6–7. The issues of this periodical were more often numbered than dated, the reason for the incomplete references. It appeared in Strassburg from 1839 to 1842 and was published in Paris since

1842. Groups dominated by Lelewel issued appeals to Jews. *Zjednoczenie* (Unification) was a Lelewel-led body which joined the T. D. P. in 1846. *Cf.* my "Great Emigration," pp. 159–98.

[29] *Pszonka,* no. 12, p. 48. The followers of Andrzej Towiański, a Lithuanian mystic, believed in his teachings about the three chosen nations, the French, the Slavs and the Jews and in the new epoch of redemption of mankind. *Cf.* my "Tarniks." My book on Towianism and the Jewish problem is awaiting publication.

[30] *Ibid.,* no. 8, p. 32. Gorecki was very friendly to the Jews.

[31] *Ibid.,* no. 4, p. 40; No. 6, p. 24; No. 7, p. 28. Another instance is shown in the note: "Place of residence unknown: Prince Adam Czartoryski. The Jew *(starozakonny)* Mosko Byk," *Pszonka,* section IV, no. 10, p. 40.

[32] As in the humorous description of the typical aristocrat Jan Szambelnica: ". . . Henceforth *Pan* Jan until his crossing of the Prussian border shared all the fate of the revolution. He even hanged with his own hand a few Jews on his way: therefore, upon crossing the border, he exclaimed with the pride of a clear conscience: 'If only everyone had carried out this way his obligation on your behalf, oh, precious fatherland!' " *Ibid.,* no. 2, May 15, 1839, p. 6.

[33] A series of his "Letters" on the Jews and the Jewish problem appeared in *Archives Israélites.* A "letter" was also published in *Le Constitutionel,* Paris, no. 134, May 14, 1843, p. 7.

On Czyński (1801–67), a radical of Frankist descent who was an outstanding fighter for Jewish emancipation and defender of the Polish Jews, *see* my "HS," p. 295, n. 7. *Cf.* also J. Danielewicz, "Jan Czyński and His Struggle for the Equality of the Jewish Population," in *Biuletyn Żydowskiego Instytutu Historycznego,* Warsaw, nos. 11–12 (July-December 1954), pp. 96–108.

[34] *EMP,* October 20, 1843.

[35] *Ibid.,* May 9, 1844, p. 53.

[36] Published in *EMP,* August 26, 1844. The appeal was distributed at a joint conference of the Zjednoczenie and T. D. P., *Pszonka,* sec. VII, sheet 2, 1844, p. 7.

[37] The signers of the appeal met at the home of the artist, Adam Solomon. *EMP,* August 26, 1844.

[38] Ludwik Mierosławski (1804–78), participant and historian of the insurrection of 1830–31 and member of the Centralization of the Society, was appointed by it to head the revolt in Poznanie in 1846. He was caught by the police, sentenced first to death and later to lifetime imprisonment, and was liberated by the revolutionaries in 1848. He was active in the 1848–49 events in Poland, Sicily, and Baden, and became dictator during the insurrection of 1863. On his unfriendly attitude to the Jews, *cf.* my "1848," p. 80, and "1846."

[39] Henryk Jakubowski and Darasz were members of the Centralization. On Alcyato, *see* above no. 23. For information on the T. D. P. leaders, *see* Kieniewicz, *Wiosna.* There were two Darasz brothers in the T. D. P. Involved in the

Pszonka was Wojciech Władysław. *Cf.* Tyrowicz, *TDP*, pp. 119–21. His *Pamiętnik Emigranta* (Memoirs of an Emigré) was published by Anna Rynkowska (Wroclaw 1953).

40 I have not been able to locate any of the translations.

41 *Ay Way* is the Yiddish transformation of the German *Oh Weh*—an excla-   •
mation of pain or shock.

42 Czyński was severely criticized by his political opponents for this publishing venture.

43 *Pszonka,* section V, sheet 8, p. 32. Earlier (November 1839; no. 8, p. 47), the *Pszonka* in a lighter moment announced for sale among others the work *About the Means of Introducing Fourierism among the Polish Jews* by Jan Czyński.

44 *Pszonka,* section VI, sheet X, 1844, p. 35. The derogatory terms *wychrzty i łapserdaki* were used.

45 *Ibid.,* section VII, sheet II, 1844, p. 6. The same issue contained a parody of an article in *EMP,* Aug. 8, 1844, p. 78.

46 *Ibid.,* section V, sheet 11, p. 43 (probably the end of 1843).

47 Among the papers figuring more prominently were the *Frankfurter Zeitung, Magdeburger Zeitung, Augsburger Zeitung, The Times* (London) and *Preussische Allgemeine Zeitung.*

48 *Tygodnik Petersburski* (Petersburg Weekly) and *Gazeta Poznańska* (Poznan Gazette) furnished most of the items taken from the Polish press.

49 *DP,* vol. v (1842), pp. 151, 158, 168, 175; vol. vi (1843), pp. 48, 63, 136; vol. vii (1845), p. 7; vol. x (1847), p. 176.

50 *Ibid.,* May 31, 1845, p. 171.

51 *Ibid.,* vol. vi (1843), pp. 3–4, 28, 63, 79, 108, 119, 140; vol. vii (1845), p. 87.

52 *Ibid.,* vol. iii (1842), p. 2; vol. vi (1844), pp. 92, 100, 119, 128, 136, 140, 192; vol. vii (1844) pp. 95, 158; vol. viii (1845), p. 68.

53 *Ibid.,* vol. vi (1844), p. 175.

54 No study of the history of antisemitism in Poland or of attitudes of the Poles towards the Jews is available. Ample illustrative material of the virulence of antisemitic religious propaganda will be found in Bartoszewicz, Kazimierz, *Antysemityzm w Literaturze Polskiej XV–XVII W.* (Antisemitism in Polish Literature in the 15th to 17th Centuries) (Warsaw 1914).

55 *Cf.* my "Polish Frankism's Duration . . .", *op. cit.*

56 *Cf.* Silberner, *op. cit.,* and Spiro, George, *Marxism and the Bolshevik State. Democratic World Government versus National Bureaucratic 'Soviet' and Capitalist Regimes* (New York 1951), pp. 742 ff. The first reference in an émigré publication on this subject is a news item in Czyński's journal (*Le Reveil d'Israél,* April [?] 1848, p. 130), reporting that the Jewish émigré Frankel had circulated a letter to the press in protest against anti-Jewish expressions in *Democratie Pacifique* and *Journal du Peuple.*

⁵⁷ Łuczakówna, *op. cit.*, pp. 30–32, cites Heltman's articles in *Dekada Polska* to this effect.

⁵⁸ *Cf.* Łuczakówna, *op. cit.*, pp. 133–34. Goszczyński, though never a member of the T. D. P., was very close to it until his conversion to Towianism. I fortunately copied or summarized many of his unpublished writings in the *Rapperswyl* Archives in Warsaw which were later destroyed by the nazis. Regrettably, I had no opportunity to work on this very interesting and valuable material.

⁵⁹ Łuczakówna, *loc. cit.*

⁶⁰ *Cf.* Bałaban, Majer, *Dzieje Żydów w Galicyi i w Rzeczypospolitej Krakowskiej 1772–1868* (A History of the Jews in Galicia and in the Cracow Republic 1772–1868) (Lwów 1916), p. 120; Gelber, N. M., "Die Juden und die polnische Revolution im Jahre 1846," in *Aus Zwei Jahrhunderten* (Vienna 1924), pp. 263–64; Wisłocki, Władysław Tadeusz, *Tajne Druki Zakładu Ossolińskich* (Secret Publications of the Ossolinski Foundation) (Lwów 1934), p. 24. Stefan Kieniewicz is not aware of Gelber's publication. *Cf.* his *Konspiracye Galicyjskie* [Galician Conspiracies] (Warsaw 1950). Underground activities by and among Jews are treated in greater detail in my "1846."

⁶¹ Handelsman, Marceli, *Pomiędzy Prusami a Rosją. Studja Historyczne* (Between Prussia and Russia. Historical Studies) Third Series (Warsaw 1922), p. 226. I regret my failure to copy the date of this statement.

⁶² *Wieczory Lacha z Lachów czyli Opowiadania przy Kominku Starego Literata Polskiego* (The Evenings of a Lechite of the Lechites or Tales at the Fireplace of an old Polish Literateur) (Leipzig 1864), p. 196.

⁶³ *Ibid.*, p. 222.

⁶⁴ *Ibid.*, p. 223.

⁶⁵ *Ibid.*, p. 197.

⁶⁶ *Ibid.*, p. 223.

⁶⁷ *Ibid. Cf.* our chapter on "1846."

⁶⁸ In his lectures on Polish literature in 1860, Zieńkowicz criticized Zygmunt Krasiński for viewing the peasant and the Jew as "an ox or a horse . . . who from generation to generation can be only an ignoramus or a slave, a faker or a reprobate." He called Krasiński's *Undivine Comedy* the "perpetuum stabile of racism," reminding that the aristocracy obtained its riches by exploitation and bad deeds. "That prefect shot at old women in the trees and roasted Jews alive . . . Another falsified and bribed." *Wizerunki Polityczne Literatury Polskiej* (Political Portraits of Polish Literature), vol. i (Leipzig 1867), pp. 149–51. Zieńkowicz also criticized the Vatican for its attitude to Poland and for siding with Russia (*ibid.*, vol. i, p. 136; vol. ii, p. 140). On the other hand, Zieńkowicz reprinted K. A. Hoffman's *Cztery Powstania* (Four Revolutions), which contained passages accusing the Jews of having betrayed the insurrection, without any comments concerning them.

⁶⁹ For instance, there is no indication of his attitude toward the Jews in his

biography by Maria Pawlicowa, "Jan Niepomucen Janowski (1803–1868)," *Przegląd Historyczny,* vol. xl (1949), pp. 277–95. An unpublished letter by him is cited in my unpublished monograph on Joachim Lelewel, n. 27. His friendship to Jews remains unquestioned. He translated into Polish Moses Mendelssohn's *Ritualgesetze der Juden (Obrzędowe Ustawy Żydów* . . . Ritual Laws of the Jews) (Warsaw 1830). His archives are preserved at the Jagiellonian University Library in Krakow. His memoirs were published by Marian Tyrowicz, *Notatki Autobiograficzne 1803–1853* (Autobiographical Notes 1803–1853) (Wroclaw 1950). They contain stray information on some Frankists and some remarks on the interest in the Jewish problem in consequence of Father Luigi Chiarini's activities.   Pertinent is also Rzadkowska, H., *Polemiki Ideologiczne J. N. Janowskiego* (Ideological Polemics of J. N. Janowski) (Warsaw 1960), which I had no opportunity to examine.

EDITORS' PREFACE

The Impact of the Revolution of 1848
on Jewish Emancipation

From the vantage of a multi-discipline approach and his long-range historical view, Professor Baron presents a well-rounded account of the dynamics of Emancipation during the "Spring of Nations," its impact on the Jewish people, and their response during a period of expanding democracy. Clearly, equality had to be granted to the Jews. As industrialization advanced, the feudal corporate structure no longer served the purposes of the state, and inequality had to end. Nevertheless, considerable opposition to Jewish Emancipation remained, and the revolutionaries of 1848 betrayed more than a tinge of antisemitism. To the standard objections of Emancipation's earlier opponents, a powerful new weapon was added: the racial. Attacks on Jews were not limited to street-corner and parliamentary oratory or to the printing press; pogroms were no rarity. Jews preferred to view them as temporary aberrations. Yet, the principles of equality could not be excluded from the new constitutions and laws. Neither were they withdrawn everywhere after the revolutions' failures. The march of Emancipation continued in Central Europe under the auspices of the established governments.

There were also significant changes in the Jewish response to the rapid revolutionary shifts. As Baron points out, the eighteenth-century revolutions affected only a small number of Jews, most of whom remained insulated from the mainstream of ideological developments; however, the 1848 events affected nearly 1,500,000 Jews. Their occupational composition was more variegated. They included sizeable numbers of persons who were important in economic life and who were increasingly assimilated to the environing cultures. Even the orthodox voiced no objections to political emancipation. These developments help to explain a new phenomenon: the European Jew as political man. Jews participated actively in the revolutionary events, from the barricades to the parliamentary podia. Two Jews became members of the French cabinet. Jews occupied high positions in other legislative bodies and were active in the liberal`and radical press. The high visibility of the new type, the politically engaged Jew, produced a backlash that strengthened the notion of the close relationship of Jewish equality to radicalism and revolution, despite the stereotype of the Jew as the symbol of materialism and capitalism, taken over by xenophobic leftists. Significantly, in the battle for Emancipation, Jewish leaders emphasized the interests of democracy in general rather than their own welfare. Jewish defense policies in many countries were to follow suit for a long time to come.

Conditional Emancipation continued to be taken for granted, with demands for baptism and intermarriage as the prerequisites for equality and with Jewish emancipationists declaring their disbelief in the coming of the Messiah. Economic emancipation brought to the fore the need for occupational restratification, while the economic dislocations of the times precipitated the "On to America" movement as an immediate solution for the crisis and resulted in the emigration of the forty-eighters, a group that was to have an important influence on the Jewish community in the United States. Cultural emancipation and the acceptance of the notion of conditional emancipation by many Jews were also evident in attitudes to the organized Jewish communities. A number of them went bankrupt because of the refusal of Jews to pay their taxes to the *kehillot*. Demands were voiced for radical religious reform. Youth was deserting the community en masse. On the other hand, there was evidence that the Jewish communities would survive even rapid emancipation.

Of great importance are Baron's indications of the emergence of harbingers of issues that were to become international in scope during the twentieth century. They included the dilemma inherent in the position of the Jews in the nationality struggle in multi-national states. Thus, in Prussian Poznanie and Austrian Czechia, Jews generally sided with the Germans against the Poles and Czechs because of their identification with German culture, which they viewed as the superior one. In Galicia, the Jews espoused the cause of the Poles. In Hungary, Jews opted for the Magyar side, and brought upon themselves the wrath of the Austrian authorities. Jews also joined the Hungarians against the Slavs (Slovaks, Serbo-Croats) and the Rumanians. The collaboration of the Jews with the ruling nationalities resulted in attacks, tame by comparison with the Ukrainian massacres following the Bolshevik Revolution, but not without some parallels in motivation. In the long run, pro-Slav activities among Jews were generally forgotten. Their anti-Slav actions were remembered by the Slavs and overlooked by the Germans.

The events of 1848, as Baron points out, also brought out indications of subsequent solutions to important problems, including pluralism as a cure for instability in multi-national states. Such were the belated attempts to reorganize Austria-Hungary as a state of multiple nationalities rather than a partnership of several ruling nations over disadvantaged national groupings. The refusal of outstanding socialists to include national recognition for Jews in the proposed reorganization stems from the same source as the original Leninist policy, namely Marx's and his followers' antipathy to Jewish survival. Baron suggests that the national struggles of the Central European minorities during and after the 1848 uprisings gave encouragement to Jewish revivalist ideologies, including Zionism. These, as well as many other ideas in this extensive monograph, bring 1848 closer to 1974.

SALO W. BARON was a founder of the Conference on Jewish Social Studies, served as its President, and is now Honorary President of the Conference. He has been an Editor of JEWISH SOCIAL STUDIES since its inception and is Emeritus Professor of Jewish History, Literature, and Institutions at Columbia University. Baron was a founder and President of Jewish Cultural Reconstruction and is now also President of the American Academy of Jewish Research. Among his numerous works on many aspects of Jewish history are: *The Jewish Community* (3 volumes); *History and Jewish Historians; The Russian Jew under Tsars and Soviets; Ancient and Medieval Jewish History; Bibliography of Jewish Social Studies;* and, of course, his monumental *A Social and Religious History of the Jews* (Second Edition, Revised and Enlarged, 15 volumes; further volumes in preparation). A volume of studies by his students, *Essays on Jewish Life and Thought Presented in Honor of Salo Wittmayer Baron,* appeared in 1959. Another jubilee volume in his honor is scheduled for early publication.

The Impact of the Revolution of 1848 on Jewish Emancipation

by Salo W. Baron

The year 1848 looms very large in the historiography of Jewish emancipation. Despite the ephemerality of many legislative changes brought about by the revolutionary upsurge, Jewish and non-Jewish historians of the Jewish question have assigned a place of honor to the emancipatory developments set in motion by the February uprisings in France and the subsequent revolutionary movements in southern Germany, Austria, Prussia, Italy, and other countries.

This was more than the customary myopic exaggeration of events occurring in one's own time or country. In our case the long-established German leadership had in effect produced an irresistibly Germanocentric view in the entire Jewish historical literature of the 19th and early 20th centuries. Objectively, too, these revolutionary transformations made a lasting impression insofar as they had come after a long period of inner and external preparation and occurred in a vast area inhabited by thousands of Jewish communities. Through the subsequent emigration of Jewish and other liberals, they also intensified the struggle for Jewish emancipation all over the world, a struggle whose most dramatic chapters have been written by nazi extermination squads and Israeli pioneers.

Reprinted from JEWISH SOCIAL STUDIES, Volume XI, 1949

Revolutionary vs. Religious Principles

Essentially the ideas of 1848 were but an extension of those enunciated by the French Revolution. The basic approach was still that of 18th-century "enlightened" liberalism and of the "Rights of Man." The general principle of equality, rather than the peculiar situation of the Jews, was consistently invoked by the protagonists of emancipation. Even Rabbi Isak Noa Mannheimer of Vienna, representing at the Austrian National Assembly the Galician community of Brody, where the Jewish population outnumbered the Christian at least three to one, explained, in his address of October 5, 1848, the urgency of abolishing special Jewish taxes by saying:

> The urgency does not rest with the Jew. The Jew can stand a great deal, he has stood a great deal. The Jew is of very tough fibre! . . . If necessary, the Jew will carry that tax for another year. . . . The urgency rests with you, with your mission, your calling, the dignity of this House . . . whether at this first enactment [of a budget] you would wish to sanction such an abnormal, inhuman tax.[1]

Benjamin Disraeli represented a small minority when he insisted that Jews should be given equality of rights not because of general egalitarian principles, but because of the greatness of the Jewish race as such. He believed that, on the contrary, the Jews were "a living and a most striking evidence of the falsity of that pernicious doctrine of modern times—the natural equality of man."[2] Ironically, this position was usually taken by antisemites, especially of the leftist variety, who wished to point out that the Jewish case was exceptional and should not be treated within the framework of general equality. The editor of the *Jewish Chronicle* voiced the prevailing pro-Jewish as well as Jewish public opinion when, in August 1850, he attacked Disraeli's "eccentric fictions" and demanded equal treatment for Jews precisely because, in his opinion, they were no longer a peculiar race or tribe.[3]

There were, however, also striking differences between 1789 and 1848. In the intervening six decades Europe had traveled very far on the road toward a uniform, democratic society. The irresistible march of the Industrial Revolution through the European continent undermined the very foundations of its traditional corporate structure which alone had made possible the segregation of a Jewish corporate body endowed with special rights and special duties. With the progressive disintegration of the feudal order, the maintenance of a special status for Jews became increasingly anachronistic. A Jewish publicist, discussing (in the Leipzig *Orient*) Jewish emancipation in Saxony, emphasized that "he who believes that a country can be free while legally withholding human rights from a single resident knows nothing of the essence of liberty." The hero of one of Berthold Auerbach's novels written as early as 1840 observed, not implausibly, that "the position of Jews has always been the barometer of humanity."[4]

The intervening period had also furnished a considerable amount of experience with the effects of Jewish emancipation in several countries. The United States, France and the Netherlands had so evidently suffered none of the evil consequences predicted by its opponents during the revolutionary era that now Moritz Mohl, the spokesman of restrictive legislation at the Frankfurt National Assembly, had to resort to strained explanations of the alleged differences between Germany and these western countries. If England, the "mother of the parliaments," was still heatedly debating the problem of so changing the prescribed formula of the oath as to enable conscientious Jews to accept election to the House of Commons, this was but a relatively minor, though conspicuous, flaw in an otherwise almost wholly egalitarian structure. Lord George Bentinck, for example, admitted that he had given little attention to the Jewish question which involved but a small minority of the British population. In his letter of January 9, 1848 to Jacob Franklin, editor of the *Voice of Jacob*, he also argued that "a Jew can, by the Laws as they stand, be *'Privy Councillor,'* a *'Secretary of State,' 'Keeper of the Great Seal,'* and, for anything I know to the contrary *'Prime Minister'* were it not for the *incidental necessity* of the Prime Minister being in Parliament."[5]

Of course, no more than any other generation, that of 1848 was particularly eager to learn from experiences in neighboring lands. In fact, the arguments voiced against Jewish emancipation in Germany and Austria were in part almost verbatim, if unconscious, repetitions of similar contentions heard in 1789–91, although in France proper they had almost entirely lost their validity. But the champions of emancipation spoke up with greater confidence and authority, since they now could invoke the practical lessons of history, in lieu of sheer theory. These lessons, moreover, had been borne out within Germany itself by the experience of those western states and Prussian provinces which, in accordance with Art. XVI of the Confederate Act of 1815, had maintained the basic legal equality established under their previous revolutionary regimes.

Equally significant was the difference in religious attitudes. In 1789 Jewish emancipation was intertwined with a revolutionary movement which, becoming ever more radical, led to the denial of all established religions, including Judaism, and their replacement by the "Religion of Reason." Along with Catholicism, Judaism suffered from severe persecution on the part of the very champions of Jewish equality. In Jean Mendès, French Jewry produced a modern religious martyr. Now the revolutionaries, even if belonging to the extreme Left and personally agnostic or atheistic, refrained from sharp attacks on existing religious bodies. The very manifesto of the Communist Party in Germany, signed on April 1, by Marx, Engels and others, asked for no more than "complete separation of state and church. The clergy of all denominations shall be supported only by their respective voluntary communities."[6]

One of the most remarkable features of the Second French Republic was the fact that it was established as if by unanimity. From the beginning, the churches collaborated with the new regime, in fact claimed that all the revolutionary ideals had been derived from Scripture. Typical of the general fraternization during the first revolutionary honeymoon was the reception given by the Provisional Government to a Jewish delegation headed by the Chief Rabbi of France, Marchand Ennery, and the President of the Central Consistory, Col. Max Cerfberr:

The two principles [Cerfberr declared] which the Republic had inscribed on its flag, equality and fraternity of all men, have emerged from our holy Scriptures. It was the voice of our prophets which proclaimed them for the first time. Transferred by our immortal Revolution from the religious to the political sphere, they

have lent strength to liberty. . . . For this reason our faith combines
with our patriotism in making us cherish this new era of our history.

In his reply, Armand Marrast assured the delegation that the Provisional Government considered protection of all cults its first order of
business and added:

We wish that equality become a serious matter; that liberty be
assailed by none; and that fraternity, rooted in mores, unite all
hearts and spread among the various social groups that necessary
pervasive feeling of unity which love and devotion alone can en-
gender. It is particularly up to ministers of the various denominations to assist us in this endeavor.

The Republic continued, in fact, its financial support of all denominations and later (May 1850) raised the annual Jewish quota to 160,000
francs or almost two francs *per capita*.[7]

In a number of German states, on the other hand, Jewish and non-
Jewish liberals often combined forces with clerical deputies in advocating full religious freedom, discontinuation of state control over
religious bodies, and, sometimes, complete separation of state and
church. Unprecedented calls to interdenominational reconciliation
and good will appealed strongly to some Jewish theologians. While
there seem to have been no Jewish followers of Robert Haas's German
national church, which was to embrace all Germans regardless of
their previous creed, a leading Jewish preacher, Adolf Jellinek, joined
the Kirchlicher Verein für alle Religionsbekenntnisse, organized in
Leipzig by Pastor Moritz Alexander Zille. This association in many
ways adumbrated our modern societies of Jews and Christians. Similar groups, addressing themselves chiefly to Protestants, sprang up
in Darmstadt and Dresden.[8]

Not that the Jewish community was unaware of the dangers resulting from such removal of governmental props. Having long enjoyed
official standing as an organ of public law and, on the whole, suffering
little from direct governmental interference, it stood to lose much more
than to gain from the new forms of purely voluntary allegiance. Whatever benefits might ultimately accrue to it from being forced to rely on

its own spiritual resources, organizationally it faced tremendous difficulties in a generation whose Jewish loyalties had been undermined
by boundless admiration of German *Kultur*. Israel Hildesheimer, a
well-known leader of German-Jewish Orthodoxy, was not grossly
overstating his recollection of conditions in the 1830's and 1840's.
"At least nine-tenths of youth," he wrote in 1867, "belonged at that
time in part to the deprecators of religion, in part to religious traitors
or at best to the indifferent. They were ashamed to display their
descent or their Jewish faith either through religious observance or be
it in name only." Not incongruously, therefore, with this state of mind
among progressive Jews, a liberal member of the Baden Diet, Zentner,
now renewed a demand, long considered desirable by the Diet, that
the Jews, in return for equality which he had consistently championed,
abandon their talmudic observances. He revealed a profound misunderstanding of the activist, rather than dogmatic, essence of Judaism
when he tried to explain, "I have not said that I expect the Jews to
give up their dogmas. I was referring to many talmudic doctrines.
These they must give up, otherwise they do not fit into the organism
of our state."[9]

It is small wonder that even Prussia's new Jewish community law
promulgated on the eve of the revolution (July 23, 1847) could not
fortify the community against the inroads of political liberalism. Since
numerous Jewish taxpayers now refused to pay their communal dues,
many a communal organization was brought to the verge of bankruptcy. Berlin itself had to cut salaries of officials earning more than
300 or 500 thalers by ten to twenty percent, respectively. The Breslau community, long rocked by inner dissension between the Orthodox
and Reform groups, disintegrated completely not to be rebuilt until
several years later. In October 1848 the comunal leaders informed
their distinguished rabbi, Abraham Geiger, that they could no longer
pay his salary. In Austria Jewish leaders, including Rabbi Mannheimer, successfully fought for the abolition of special Jewish taxes,
although they eliminated thereby a major source of income from their
own institutions. Before long the Jewish hospital in Vienna ran into
serious financial difficulties. In Galicia some Jewish farmers of this
governmental as well as communal revenue actually joined forces with

the archconservatives in trying to perpetuate such discriminatory taxation.[10]

All these communal difficulties were largely of Jewish making, however, and hence did not alienate the bulk of Jewry from the emancipation movement as such. There certainly was nothing akin to the Orthodox opposition to emancipation evinced by the Amsterdam Jews in 1796, forewarned as the latter had been by the excess of the French religion of reason. The Orthodox rabbis of Bavaria who, early in 1848, allegedly submitted to the Bavarian government a petition against Jewish equality were silenced by the success of the revolution. Even the Orthodox of Galicia and Hungary, though generally less active than their more "progressive" co-religionists, did not actually combat the idea of Jewish participation in public life on the basis of equality. At least one Orthodox rabbi, Berush Meisels of Cracow, was one of its outspoken champions. Elected deputy to the Austrian National Assembly he never took the floor, but was very active behind the scenes, especially among the Poles, who greatly appreciated his ardent Polish patriotism.[11]

One of the revolution's major permanent results, shortlived as it otherwise proved to be, was not only the ever-widening area of Jewish equality, but also the practical demonstration that Jewish emancipation need not be detrimental to Jewish religious and communal aspirations. It was shown that just as the establishment of an egalitarian and democratic society was not necessarily contingent on separation of state and church, the Jewish community, too, could survive as an active force, even as an organ of public law, provided the Jews themselves were interested in its preservation. Sanguine Samuel Cahen, editor of the *Archives israélites,* claimed in an early editorial that "far from having anything to fear from the new order established in France on February 24, true religion can only profit from it." In November 1848 the editor of the *Jewish Chronicle* of London, surveying the "Results of Jewish Emancipation on the Continent," referred to the numerous reconversions of baptized Jews in Prussia and declared that these "results are not (as is yet suspected by some fanatics) tending to diminish the religious fervor of the Jewish people, but to increase and strengthen it."[12] Whether or not sharing this enthusiasm, most Jews readily recognized that a substantial measure of their long-cherished religious and cultural autonomy could be salvaged under the new system of equality and that the former's vitality would, in the long run, depend far more on the strength of their own convictions than on its external legal framework.

Centers of Jewish Life

Such reconciliation of equality with a modicum of autonomy became doubly significant as the social and political unrest spread into areas of Jewish mass settlement. The French Revolution had at first affected only French Jewry, which in 1789 numbered no more than 40,000. Some three-quarters of that number lived in Alsace-Lorraine under medieval conditions and, like most of their Christian compatriots, were hardly touched by the great intellectual upsurge of Enlightenment. Apart from falling prey to antisemitic riots, they were affected by the revolution, too, as passive bystanders rather than as active participants. Only two or three of their leaders took part in the literary debate over Jewish rights.

Even two decades later the Central Consistory in Paris still complained that less than one-tenth of Alsatian-Jewish school children were able to attend public schools. The few thousand Sephardi and Avignonese Jews at the other end of France, in themselves a heterogeneous group, had long been isolated from the mainstream of Jewish life in central and eastern Europe. Only the 700–800 Jews residing in Paris, the focal point of the revolutionary movement, were in a position to play a more active role. If in its later triumphant march through the Netherlands, Italy and western Germany the revolution swept away the disabilities of many older and larger Jewish communities, it accomplished this feat, too, with little direct Jewish co-operation. Many Jews were actually antagonized by certain coercive measures of the conquering armies. Certainly a threat like that, recorded in Worms, where the Jewish leaders were told to renounce their ancient privileges at once or else be sentenced to the confiscation of their property and to work on barricades in exposed positions —a threat partially carried into effect—was not likely to convince them, or their average constituents, of the redemptive qualities of emancipation.[13]

The revolution of 1848, on the other hand, within a few weeks set on fire the whole structure of Jewish minority life in countries extending from the Atlantic to the Black Sea. In France herself, again the matrix of the revolution, the Jewish population had more than doubled in the intervening six decades. The community of Paris, particularly, had grown from 6,000 in 1821 to 12,000 in 1842 and to nearly 17,000 in 1845 and become a significant center of Jewish culture. Here and in the Netherlands, whose 60,000 Jews had enjoyed equal treatment since 1796, the new revolutionary legislation added but little to formal Jewish emancipation. But it marked a complete reversal of previous trends in the Germanic Confederation, the Austrian Empire, Italy, and Rumania. The Germanies alone embraced more than 200,000 Jews in Prussia (including Posen-Poznan) and the other non-Austrian states, and more than 100,000 in Austria's "hereditary" provinces. The emperor's non-Germanic possessions, including Galicia, Hungary and Lombardo-Venetia, had an even larger Jewish population. Some Galician and Posen communities constituted majorities on the local level. Together with their co-religionists in the rest of Italy, including the Papal States, and of Denmark and Rumania, some 1,400,000 Jews, or approximately one-third of world Jewry living in thousands of old communities, were drawn into the revolutionary vortex within a few weeks after the Paris outbreaks of February 24.[14]

From the economic standpoint these large Jewish communities were much further along the road toward integration in European society than had been most of their co-religionists in France before 1789. German Jewry, in particular, had made rapid economic progress and included among its members such leaders of European capitalism as the house of Rothschild which, originating in Frankfurt, had now spread to Vienna as well as to London, Paris and Naples. On the whole, the house of Rothschild and its great influence in public affairs were more of a liability than an aid to the Jewish people. Typical of a vast pamphlet literature of the age is G. M. Matthieu-Dernvaell's *Histoire édifiante et curieuse de Rothschild Ier, Roi des Juifs*. This pamphlet, which appeared in at least nineteen editions in 1846 under the appropriate pseudonym of "Satan," contended not only that "the kingdom of Rothschild I is today officially recognized," but concluded with the expostulation: "It is not the creed of the Jews to which this pamphlet addresses itself, but to their sharpness, their insolence of slaves of yesterday who had become free and rich today, to their thirst for gold and their irrepressible drive for wealth and power."[15]

On the other hand, rumor had it that the Rothschilds were consistently refusing loans to governments oppressing their co-religionists. Even in 1849 they allegedly hesitated to lend money to Pope Pius IX because he had reversed himself and restored the Jews to the Roman ghetto. Tsar Nicholas I who, after helping suppress the Hungarian revolt, turned to the London market for a loan was said to have encountered there the opposition not only of such liberals as Richard Cobden but also that of the house of Rothschild.[16]

The revolution, to be sure, greatly undermined the financial power of the continental branches of that firm. According to the Paris police commissioner, Marc Caussidière, the senior partner of the French firm pleaded: "My fortune and my ready money are all converted into shares which at the present moment are valueless." Wild rumors spread through the city that he was shipping funds abroad in preparation for a declaration of bankruptcy. Even in the more distant British capital, Disraeli, a keen, though temperamental, observer, commented in the first flush (March 20, 1848): "It seems to be impossible for the Rothschilds even to stand the storm. They must lose everything everywhere except here [London]. Austria has tumbled to pieces, Naples has lost Sicily and France must be bankrupt, and these are their three principal debtors."[17] Together with other factors, the revolutionary changes accelerated the relative decline of private banking and stimulated the growth of banking corporations which gradually reduced the financial pre-eminence of the house of Rothschild in the latter part of the century. Yet, especially in its heyday, this preeminence could but underscore the incongruence between the economic and political status of Jews.

No less obvious, though less spectacular, was the contrast between the desire of various governments to attract, for financial reasons, Jewish businessmen and tourists, and their efforts to maintain intact all Jewish disabilities inherited from the pre-capitalistic age. Papal Rome jealously guarded the gates of the ghetto, lest any Jews escape from its overcrowded and unsanitary confines, but it permitted foreign

Jewish visitors to reside in any section of the city. Staunchly Protestant Erlangen gloried in its age-old exclusion of Jewish settlers, but extended a hearty welcome to Jews owning 20,000 florins and wishing to acquire a house of their own. Imperial Austria artificially held down the number of "tolerated" Jews in Vienna by requiring them to secure from the police special, periodically renewable permits. Yet as early as 1820 the Vienna leaders petitioning for liberalization of Jewish status pointed out with pride the numerous honors bestowed by the government upon individual members (the 50-odd resident families embraced at that time no less than eleven raised by the emperor to the rank of nobility). Conversely, large-scale Jewish emigration at times affected a state's financial standing. In 1850 the prices of Bavarian bonds were steadily to decline at the Frankfurt Stock Exchange "owing to the determination of the principal influential Jewish houses to emigrate from the kingdom of Bavaria and at the same time to withdraw their invested capital, they having resolved not to remain unless civil and religious liberty be granted them."[18]

Socially and culturally, too, the Jews had begun to play a significant role. Ever since the Napoleonic era Jewish salons in Berlin, Vienna and other capitals were major centers of attraction to both "socialites" and men of letters. Despite manifold legal obstacles, intermarriage became an increasing factor in drawing closer the upper classes of both groups. As soon as the legal impediments were removed, some Reform rabbis, such as Bernhard Wechsler of Oldenburg, began officiating at weddings where the non-Jewish partner continued to adhere to his or her Christian faith. Many an impoverished German nobleman, in particular, replenished his family fortunes by marrying into a wealthy Jewish family. Even conservatives often welcomed, as did later Bismark with his accustomed crudity, such mating of German stallions with Jewish mares as an accession to national strength. An anonymous writer (Christian Reinhold Köstlin?) in an essay on the civil conditions of the Jews in Germany strongly advocated intermarriage as a means of eliminating "an alien, hostile nationality in the midst of German society." Another, hiding behind the initials, E. K., harked back to Napoleon's pet idea and demanded that intermarriage be made a "condition" for Jewish emancipation.

Some Jew-baiters, on the other hand, already began complaining of the success of Jewish suitors.[19]

Writers like Heine or Börne enjoyed international reputations. That they combined their literary work with the espousal of radical liberalism made them even better known, though not necessarily more heartily appreciated. Although ultimately both these men were converted to Christianity, they did not hesitate to play up anti-Jewish discrimination as one of the major vices of the existing German political systems. Börne's oft-cited *Letters from Paris* emphasized the nexus between the oppression of Jews and Germany's national liberal movement: "Yes, because I was born a slave," he exclaimed, "I love freedom more than you. Yes, because I have experienced slavery, I understand freedom better than you. Yes, because I was born without a fatherland, I yearn for a fatherland more passionately than you." He predicted that when the spring of freedom comes, the Jewish plants will be greener than the Christian. It had also become quite commonplace for Jewish magazines to enumerate the names of Jewish artists among the exhibitors in the art galleries of Paris and elsewhere.[20] Jewish promoters of arts and sciences were no less prominent. Apart from the numerous art patrons among the Jewish bankers, there were such distinguished Jewish publishers and booksellers as Calmann Lévy in Paris (regular publisher of George Sand, Balzac, Lamartine, Flaubert, later of Renan, Anatole France and others) or Moritz Veit in Berlin. Lévy and Veit, who at the same time were loyal Jews, served as a living repudiation of most anti-Jewish arguments current in the literary world.

Jewish participation in modern science was still greatly hampered by the exclusion of Jews from teaching and research posts in central-European universities. While the generally liberal student bodies appreciated their more brilliant Jewish colleagues and in 1848 spearheaded both the revolution and Jewish emancipation, their professors were often found in the reactionary camp. When on September 28, 1847 the Prussian Ministry of Cults asked the various university faculties both to describe the existing statutory limitations on the admission of Jews to the academic profession and to express their opinions concerning the desirability of amending these laws, it received for the most part pleas for the retention of the existing practices. Among the professors of law at the University of Berlin only one (Heffter) unrestrictedly favored the appointment of Jews. The majority of the Breslau medical faculty gave such a sharply negative answer that all practicing Jewish physicians in the city resigned in a body from the local medical club. Even in liberal Königsberg, two members of the faculty of philosophy (Druman and Voigt) were said to have argued with typical sophistry that, if Jews were Orthodox, they could not enter into the spirit of the existing (*i.e.*, Christian) state; if they were not, they would help to undermine it. Only after the outbreak of the revolution did a preliminary assembly of some German professors at Leipzig vote by a large majority in favor of abolishing all religious tests in academic appointments, as suggested by Julius Fürst, one of the few Jewish scholars then allowed to lecture at the University of Leipzig.[21]

No less abrupt was the reversal in the traditional attitude of churches to Jewish rights. Pope Pius IX, on his own initiative, had begun gradually liberalizing the status of Roman Jewry when he was scared away by the radicalism of the revolution. Early in 1848 a petition in behalf of Jewish equality circulating in Bologna bore the signatures of four bishops. In the early stages of the Vienna uprisings the university chaplain, Father Füster, played a noteworthy role in promoting interdenominational good-will. While traditional anti-Judaism was not devoid of spokesmen in both the Catholic and Protestant camps, the aforementioned agitation for an all-embracing German national church, as well as the formation of interdenominational religious groups, opened up new vistas for genuine good-will.[22]

In short, economic and cultural emancipation, which generally preceded and paved the way for legal and political emancipation, had been far advanced before 1848. [Opposition thereto now had to resort to ever more devious reasonings.] Even the pseudo-scientific biological-racial arguments of purported Jewish natural inferiority now made their appearance in a fairly respectable journal. Discussing Jewish emancipation, "from the standpoint of natural science," A. Cscherich argued that both the biological history of the Jewish people and the anatomical structure of each Jew proved that the relationship of Jews to all other races, including primitives, resembled that of weeds to other plants. Hence their ubiquity and indestructibility![23]

Political Debut

No greater transformation had taken place in the six decades since 1789 than the newly acquired active participation of Jews—both professing and converted—in domestic and international politics. During the American Revolution the Jewish question was hardly discussed. The few incidental steps taken by Jewish leaders, for instance, their congratulatory letters to George Washington on his election to the presidency and his well-sounding but noncommittal replies, had little bearing on Jewish equality which in essence was secured by the general constitutional safeguards for religious liberty and the growth of an egalitarian society. Nor were there many Jewish champions of emancipation in revolutionary France. The few active pleaders belonged to a small upper crust in the Jewish population. They were restricted to some form of "lobbying" at the National Assembly or the Paris popular sections and clubs, rather than direct political action.

In 1848, on the contrary, Jews played from the outset a most active political role. They belonged, often in leading positions, to various political parties and were influential in the general press. Their youth actively participated in the uprisings and mass demonstrations. Even in France, where legal discrimination had long been abandoned, the new opportunities brought to the fore Jewish leaders of considerable eminence. The first cabinet formed after the February revolt included two Jewish ministers, Adolphe Crémieux as Minister of Justice, and Michel Goudchaux as Minister of Finance. Universally admired as "one of the most brilliant lawyers of the Paris bar" and long influential in parliament, Crémieux was given the portfolio of justice, although his appointment necessitated the transfer of the Bureau of Cults to the Ministry of Public Instruction. Otherwise it would have been incumbent upon the Jewish minister to appoint Catholic bishops. Goudchaux, "one of the heroes of finance," was persuaded to accept office only when he was told that his country needed him to reassure the Paris *haute finance*. The great bankers and industrialists, including the Rothschilds, had been so frightened by the socialist implications of the revolution, that they allegedly were on the point of leaving the country. That Goudchaux, "whose calm eloquence reminds one of a spring of warm water," and, even more, Crémieux were also loyal Jews, the latter for many decades before and after 1848 a leading champion of Jewish rights throughout the world, helped dramatize the new political position of the Jewish people.[24]

Among the other candidates to the National Assembly was the Jewish scholar, Adolphe Franck, then vice-president of the Central Consistory in Paris. It was characteristic of the new age that the *Archives israélites* advocated Franck's election by pointing out that he had been born in poverty and had never forgotten the difficulties confronting the poor man. Although insisting that religious groups as such should not be represented in political assemblies, this progressive organ of French Jewry exhorted the rabbis to "set an example of their zeal for the republic by exerting all their influence in favor of the election of proven patriots and tolerant men."[25]

Much greater was Jewish participation in the central European uprisings. In Vienna the chain of events initiated by the students' assembly of March 12, and the revolutionary attacks of March 13, brought forth to positions of leadership the young Jewish doctors, Adolf Fischhof and Joseph Goldmark. Less than a year previously the administration of Lower Austria had considered itself liberal when it allowed Jewish physicians employed by the General Hospital to secure a residence permit for two years, rather than one. But it also reminded the Hospital that Jews should be employed only "in case of their definite superiority over Christian physicians."[26] Now as head of the Committee on Security, which maintained public order in Vienna during the breakdown of all governmental authority, Fischhof became practically the uncrowned emperor of Austria. Needless to say that he thereby aroused the resentment of all unregenerated Jew-baiters. They spread, for example, the rumor that he had taken the emperor's traditional place at the head of the church procession on Corpus Christi day, although he had in fact tactfully abstained. Many Jewish publicists and writers likewise achieved sudden fame and influence. At least eight of them joined about a score of their non-Jewish confrères in signing the "Manifesto of Vienna's Writers," issued on March 15, 1848. Ludwig August Frankl, secretary of the Vienna

Jewish community, became overnight one of Austria's most popular poets. His poem, *Die Universität*, glorifying the role of the students during the March uprisings, eventually reached a circulation of more than 500,000 copies and was set to music twenty-seven times.[27]

It was obvious that Fischhof and his intimate friends, Goldmark and Joseph Unger (later one of Austria's famous jurists), could not tolerate the perpetuation of Jewish disabilities. At the Austrian National Assembly the Jews had even more direct spokesmen in such deputies as Rabbis Mannheimer of Vienna and Meisels of Cracow. The fact that Jewish youngsters in hundreds manned the Vienna barricades, that at least one of them was killed and buried in the same grave with his Christian compatriots, that Mannheimer officiated together with the Catholic and Protestant clergy at the funeral—all clearly demonstrated the new role played by Jewry in the political struggles of the day.[28]

In Prussia, too, Jews played a leading role in the March events. It seems that they suffered no less than 21 casualties during the street fights in Berlin, a high percentage indeed considering the general ratio of less than 2.5 percent for the Jewish population in the Prussian capital.[29] Here, too, their burial, along with their non-Jewish comrades, turned into a large public demonstration of the new feeling of brotherhood, the Jewish faith being represented by such eloquent spokesmen as Michael Sachs and Leopold Zunz.

The Jewish deputies to the Prussian Assembly included such influential politicians as the physicians, Johann Jacoby and Raphael Kosch, both of Königsberg. If in an unguarded moment Jacoby, as a member of a delegation sent to the king, warned Frederick William IV that "kings who do not wish to hear the truth may be ruined," his much-publicized "tactlessness" served to accentuate the new position of Jewry before friend and foe. So did his great personal popularity in Königsberg where his birthdays were publicly celebrated with the participation of delegations from various cities. The parliaments of lesser German states likewise included prominent Jewish members.[30]

Ironically, the outstanding exponent of the "Christian" state and, hence, leader of the new Prussian conservative party, Friedrich Julius Stahl, was a scion of an Orthodox Jewish family in Munich. Con-

verted to Christianity at the age of seventeen under the impact of the
anti-Jewish *Hep-Hep* movement of 1819 and long an exponent of a
"Christian" philosophy of law, he now headed the small faction of
thirteen deputies at the extreme Right. It must have been quite a
sight to watch this little "Jewish" professor serve as the mouthpiece
of Junkerdom at the new Prussian Diet on all issues including Jewish
emancipation.[31]

Above all, the Jews played a considerable role at the Frankfurt
National Assembly. Gabriel Riesser, particularly, for many years the
leading protagonist in the struggle for Jewish emancipation, was held
in general esteem, often being compared to Nathan of Lessing's
drama. In October 1848 he was elected second vice-president of the
assembly. He courageously upheld the cause of Jewish equality on all
occasions. Other Jewish members included Moritz Veit, the publisher,
Ignatz Kuranda, Austrian editor of the Leipzig *Grenzboten,* a leading
organ of German liberalism, and the Bohemian writer, Moritz Hartmann. In announcing his candidacy to the chairman of the Constitutional Society of Leitmeritz, Hartmann did not even bother to
mention his Jewish affiliation as a possible obstacle. He received,
indeed, 81 of the 89 electoral votes cast. If, on the other hand, at a
dramatic moment the Assembly despatched a delegation to the Prussian king offering him the imperial crown of united Germany it was
headed by its then president, Martin Eduard Simson of Königsberg,
a converted Jew who, after 1871 as first president of the new German
Reichsgericht, was to play in the German judiciary a role similar to
that of John Marshall in that of the United States. This fact caused
much chagrin not only to the Jew-baiters of his time but also to the
nazi writers of the 1930's.[32]

Most of these Jewish deputies belonged to the moderates in the
Center or Left Center (Veit alone had joined the Right), but many
Jews also joined the revolutionary ranks further to the Left. The so-
called democratic congresses, especially, included many Jews or
converts. The best known figure among them was Karl Marx who, a
few months before, had prepared, jointly with Friedrich Engels, the
Communist Manifesto and now returned from Paris to take part in
the rebuilding of Germany. Ferdinand Lassalle's active participation
was limited to a few months between two periods of imprisonment

which, however, spared him the necessity of forcible expatriation and enabled him to work for the realization of a socialist program inside Germany. Among the well-known political leaders of a later age were also Eduard Lasker and Ludwig Bamberger, outstanding parliamentarians of the Bismarckian era. Lasker, born in the typical ghetto of Jaroczyn (province of Posen), joined, at the age of eighteen, the revolutionary forces, edited a socialist magazine in Breslau, and fought with Robert Blum in the tragic October days of Vienna's subjugation by Prince Windischgrätz. Forced to flee to London, he returned in 1856 and, soon thereafter organized the National-Liberal Party. He was joined by Bamberger, six years his senior who, at the outbreak of the revolution, had been writing fulminating editorials in the *Mainzer Zeitung.* "Red" Bamberger's essay, "Intolerant Tolerance" of September 30, 1848 was fairly typical of the entire Left. "We admit," he declared, "we are political fanatics and respect even the consistent religious fanatic more than the watery, 'tolerant,' half-enlightened person." After the victory of the reaction Bamberger fought the last-ditch battle of the revolutionary legion in the Palatinate (May-June, 1849) and escaped to England. Although condemned to death *in absentia,* he was allowed to return in 1866 and resume his political activities, now in a more moderate camp.[33]

Another radical publicist, Moses Hess, known for many years before the revolution as the "socialist rabbi," escaped condemnation because he had continued serving the cause only through his writings from Paris and Zurich. Despite frequent quarrels with other socialist leaders, particularly Marx, he staunchly adhered to his radical convictions. Less lucky was Hermann Jellinek, brother of the well-known preacher, Adolf Jellinek, who in a number of philosophic writings (including a "Critical History of the Vienna Revolution") espoused the cause of a liberalism more extreme than the "weak-kneed liberalism of the *Grenzboten.*" Caught during the Windischgrätz conquest of Vienna, he was court-martialed together with Robert Blum and other revolutionary "martyrs."[34] Even Berthold Auerbach, then on a visit to Vienna, became somehow involved. In a letter dated Breslau, November 1848, he described his deep despondency over the loss of his young wife at childbirth several months before and declared:

"Were it not for the child, I would surely have fallen on the Vienna barricades."[35]

Jewish participation in the Italian uprisings was no less pronounced. Among the victims of the so-called Five Days of Milan (March 18–22) was Ciro Finzi, a Jewish lad of fifteen. Mazzini's old-time associate, Giuseppe Revere, edited the *Italia del Popolo* during the former's short-lived regime. He and two other Jews (Abraham Pesaro and Salvatore Anau) were also elected to the National Assembly. Daniele Manin, leader of the Venetian uprising, was not a professing Jew. He was, as Disraeli said, "a Jew who professes the whole of the Jewish religion, and believes in Calvary as well as Sinai,—'a converted Jew', as the Lombards styled him, quite forgetting, in the confusion of their ideas, that it is the Lombards who are the converts—not Manin."[36] But his Cabinet included two professing Jews, Leone Pincherle, Minister of Agriculture and Commerce, and Isaac Pesaro Maurogonato, Minister of Finance. Jews were also found in considerable numbers in the Italian armies of liberation, served in various National Guards, etc. For example, a Jewish major, Karl Lamm, was on the staff of the Piedmontese General Durando, living later in Rome from which he was expelled in 1851. Jewish soldiers in the French army later helped restore the Papal regime in Rome, unwittingly paving the way for the anti-Jewish reaction. But according to reports in foreign journals, they secured from their officers permission to memorialize the Papal administration not only for the right to attend services in the local synagogue, but also for the amelioration of the status of Roman Jewry.[37]

Even in far-off Rumania the new revolutionary movement, though impeded by Russian intervention, made temporary headway. At least two prominent Jews are known to have actively co-operated with the revolution. One of them, Davicion Bally, allegedly saved the lives of such revolutionary leaders as his intimate friend, Ion M. Manu. Another Jew, Constantin Daniil Rosenthal, seems to have served the cause primarily through his talent as an historical painter.[38]

Only Russia, under the autocratic regime of Nicholas I, still remained quiescent; in fact, the tower of strength for all counter-revolutionary currents. The Russian Jews could do little about their country's military intervention against the Hungarians or about the aid it extended to the Rumanian reactionaries which enabled the latter to include a number of anti-Jewish provisions in the reform laws of 1850 for Moldavia and Wallachia. Some Jews serving in the Russian army must have resented the disservice they were doing to their own people by helping suppress the revolution. Only their co-religionists in more distant areas, like England, could vent their ire at the Russian atrocities. Speaking at a mass meeting in London to protest against a projected Russian loan, Mitchel, the proprietor of the *Jewish Chronicle,* assured the audience that Jewish capitalists had washed their hands of this affair. "He could, as a Jew, take his stand upon peace principles in this matter; for did not God prevent David from building a Temple to Him because he had shed much blood?"[39]

In this struggle for emancipation Jewish leaders rarely spoke up as representatives of specific Jewish interests. As a rule they merely invoked the general principle of equality as the sole justification. Jacoby was fairly typical in denying that his liberalism stemmed from his interests as a Jew, although conceding their intrinsic nexus. "Being simultaneously a Jew and a German," he declared in a letter, "the Jew in me can never be free without the German, nor the German without the Jew." Even Rabbi Mannheimer declared, in his sermon of March 18, 1848:

What shall be done for us now? Nothing! Everything for the people and the Fatherland, as you have done it the last few days . . . No word about Jewish emancipation unless others speak up for us . . . No petitions, no requests, implorations or complaints in behalf of our rights . . . First the right to live as men, to breath, think, speak, first the right of a citizen, of a noble, free citizen in his legitimate aspirations in his dignified position—afterwards comes the Jew. They should not reproach us that we always think first about ourselves!

Similar views had been expounded a short time before by Salvatore Anau, the prominent Italian revolutionary leader. In three letters on Jewish emancipation published in *Patria* of Florence he argued that the Jews should patiently await the progress of liberal ideas which would of itself secure Jewish equality. He was controverted by Leone

Carpi, a young economist of growing distinction, who pointed out that even the French National Assembly of 1791 required two years of prodding by Jewish petitions before it applied to the Jew the principles proclaimed in 1789.[40]

Before long it became evident, however, that the Jews had to marshal all their resources for the impending struggle. Mannheimer himself was overwhelmed by the flood of anti-Jewish pamphlets and placards which appeared in the first weeks of the revolution. In his "Declaration" of March 24, he blamed it in part on the rash action of Jewish students who had circulated a petition for Jewish equality among patrons of coffee houses. But he had to admit that the communal leaders had been working on a similar petition which, after its approval by the full membership, was to be submitted quietly to the Austrian "Estates."[41] This was essentially but the old difference in tactics between the "democratic" appeal to public opinion through the press and street harangues and the more "diplomatic" behind-the-scene negotiations with responsible authorities. But no one doubted any longer that a tremendous effort was necessary to secure not only the adoption of the general principle of equality, but also the removal of specific disabilities which might have remained on the statute books in defiance of that principle. When the decisive deliberations on Austria's fundamental laws were drawing closer, representatives of many Jewish communities assembled in the Moravian city of Kremsier in which the Austrian parliament was meeting since November 1848, to exert pressure for the inclusion of unequivocal safeguards for Jewish equality.

They could not altogether rely on the vote of even outspoken liberals. Although the Reichstag's Committee on Constitutional Affairs had already submitted a draft which included provisions for the civil equality of all denominations, Fischhof and Goldmark felt it necessary to invite a number of influential deputies to a dinner arranged at the expense of the Vienna community. Despite the great esteem in which both hosts were held, it appears that a toast in behalf of Jewish equality was received with considerable reserve. Ultimately, one need not doubt, parliament would have adopted the pertinent constitutional provisions if it had not been forcibly dissolved a few days before its debate reached that point. But the fact that, once peasant emancipation had been secured, many rural deputies had lost all zeal for general liberal legislation augured badly for the revolutionary cause, including Jewish rights. When four Austrian battalions paraded through Kremsier a rumor, probably instigated by the government itself, found widespread acceptance that this force had to be marshalled to forestall an attack on parliament by neighboring farmers seeking to prevent the enactment of Jewish emancipation.[42]

It was a profound irony, indeed, that what the democratic parliament was unable to accomplish in several months of endless debates —Fischhof, not the most vocal of its deputies, spoke fifty times in the Committee on Constitutional Affairs alone[43]—was granted by a stroke of the pen in the imperial constitution of March 4, 1849, autocratically enacted by the government after its forcible dissolution. Although most Jewish leaders perforce acquiesced, they dimly realized that, together with the liberal cause, their own would unavoidably suffer. Their instincts were right. Two years later the increasingly reactionary Austrian regime revoked the constitution, replacing it by another which revived many discriminatory provisions. Only the reestablishment of a constitutional regime in 1867 granted the Jewish masses of the Dual Monarchy permanent equality of rights. True, anti-Jewish reaction was less pronounced in other German states. Prussia and several others never revoked the equality promulgated in 1848. Nevertheless the majority of Prussian Jewry doubtless shared the early forebodings of the *Orient's* Berlin correspondent who wrote, "Emancipation is with us a legacy of the revolution. With the latter emancipation, too, will be vanquished."[44]

The Jewish people thus took the management of its political affairs into its own hands. In this respect 1848 proved a hard but successful school. Whether as spokesmen for the Jewish community or as individuals belonging to various parties and representing conflicting interests and points of view, Jewish politicians from that time on began to play a great, often disproportionately great, role in the domestic as well as international affairs of various countries. Of course, they often displayed considerable political immaturity and unwittingly caused much harm to Jewish interests. As is usual in the case of minorities, opponents were more prone to blame their blunders on their people than were friends to credit it with their achievements. But once having entered the political arena the Jewish people, no matter how high the price, was never able nor willing to abandon its new role and return to its political quietism of the ghetto era.

Before very long, various Jewish organizations undertook to conduct the struggle for worldwide Jewish equality in a systematic fashion. The most important of these, the *Alliance Israélite Universelle,* was founded in 1860 by leaders like Crémieux who had gone through the school of the revolution. The *Alliance* was seconded in this endeavor by the Board of Delegates of American Israelites which antedated it by one year; the Anglo-Jewish Association, established in 1871, fourteen years after the removal of Jewish parliamentary disabilities in England; the Vienna *Allianz* and other bodies. These in turn paved the way for still more powerful and effective Jewish political and defense organizations functioning on national and international scenes during the 20th century.

Leftist Reorientation

Active participation of Jews in the revolutionary movements gradually changed the attitude of radical groups to Jewish emancipation. In the 1840's most socialists had identified Jews with the spirit of capitalism. Not only outright Jew-baiters, like "Satan," but also leading champions of the "fourth estate" saw in the house of Rothschild a symbol of Jewish capitalist domination which revolutionary socialism must destroy. Recent studies have revealed how deeply anti-Jewish generalizations of this kind had permeated both the Fourierist and the Saint Simonian circles, although the latter included influential Jewish members. The Fourierist, A. Toussenel's *Les Juifs roi de l'èpoque. Histoire de la féodalité financière,* first published in 1845, was in many respects the fountainhead of "Satan's" and other virulent outpourings.[45]

German socialists shared this prejudice, since most Jews with whom they personally came in contact belonged to the capitalist class. Forgetful of the masses of Jewish workers in eastern Europe, they saw in the Jewish people but the embodiment of the economic drive for power characteristic of the Industrial Revolution. Philosophically they followed Ludwig Feuerbach's lead. In his critique of Christianity

the materialistic reinterpreter of Hegel's sweeping generalizations
deprecated its Jewish antecedents, for the Jewish "God is the most
practical principle of the world—egotism, that is the egotism in the
shape of religion." In his widely read "Song of a Cosmopolitan Night-
watchman," Franz Dingelstedt started from another point and declaimed in 1841,

> Wisst Ihr, wie tief sein [the Jew's] Zauber schon gedrungen?
> Schaut um, die Ihr von Menschenrechten träumt,
> Sie reden drein mit den metall'nen Zungen
> Wo scheu der Christ verstummt und zagt und säumt.
>
> Was kann dem Stamm Emanzipiren frommen,
> Der nie vom Schacher sich emanzipirt?
> Was Ihr ihm schenken wollt, hat er genommen,
> Die weil Ihr um Prinzipien disputirt!
>
> Wohin Ihr fasst, Ihr werdet Juden fassen,
> Allüberall das Lieblingsvolk des Herrn!
> Geht sperrt sie wieder in die alten Gassen,
> Eh sie Euch in ein Christenviertel sperren!

Similar reasonings in many variations reappeared in numerous later
polemics. They were picked up in 1844 by Karl Marx himself when,
in his two essays on the Jewish question, he openly identified Judaism
with the spirit of what he called "civil society." Hence the main need
of the age, declared this baptized scion of a long line of rabbis and
Jewish scholars, was not the emancipation of the Jew but the emancipation of society from the Jew, i. e., from the shackles of capitalism.[46]

At the outbreak of the revolution many anti-Jewish movements
seemed to underscore this popular opposition to Jewish emancipation.
Even in French Alsace, where the Jews had enjoyed equality of rights
for several decades, a large-scale pogrom movement was set in motion
by peasant leaders within three days after the successful uprising in
Paris. Unlike the peasant revolts in southern France, these movements
in Alsace had religious as well as social facets. Crémieux's former
secretary, Schöngrun, rightly pointed out in his report from Colmar
to the Minister of Justice: "In Oberdorf they attacked the Jews,

although they were almost all indigent. Everywhere they started by attacking the synagogues, although the synagogues engage in neither trade nor usury." Ironically, in a city like Durmenach, whose bourgeoisie had not hesitated before the revolution to elect a Jewish mayor, the populace disarmed and beat up twenty-five Jewish members of the National Guard. Only the intervention of the local Catholic curate and rabbi who had retained their composure prevented an outright massacre of the whole Jewish population. In some localities *(e. g.,* Hegenheim) a quickly improvised Jewish self-defense repulsed the peasants "with such vigor that the miserable wretches were forced to retire." To add insult to injury some Alsatian courts, impressed by sharply anti-Jewish harangues of defense attorneys, discharged all accused.[47]

Anti-Jewish riots spread through many parts of revolutionary Europe. Three hundred Jewish refugees from Germany's southern states escaped to Basel eliciting the Prussian minister, Siegismund von Arnim's caustic remark, "The mob celebrates Jewish emancipation in its own fashion by—destroying Jerusalem." A radical leaflet set up four major revolutionary aims: (1) the destruction of nobility; (2) the expulsion of the Jews from Germany; (3) the removal of all princes and establishment of a German republic along American patterns; and (4) the assassination of all officials. In Posen, Bohemia and Hungary, the Jews became such a target for attack that, for example, in Pesth and Pressburg, the local revolutionary administration had to suspend the Jewish members of the National Guard. In Vienna, where early in March the popular journal *Der constitutionelle Hans Jörgel* had bitterly blamed the Jewish Stock Exchange jobbers and moneybags for the economic depression, the guild of shoemakers petitioned against the extension of Jewish rights. In fact, a vast pamphlet literature appeared, reproducing all pre-revolutionary arguments against Jewish equality at the very time when the people followed Fischhof and Goldmark's leadership in wresting from the government concessions to popular liberties. In Bavaria some 600 petitions opposing Jewish emancipation were received by the Chamber in 1849 largely from rural communities, as against only four petitions in its favor. Among the petitions submitted to the Chamber of Deputies in Turin was one asking that the populace be given free reign to pillage the ghetto for four hours. While four battalions of the National Guard in Rome freely admitted Jewish members, four others (including one recruited from the Trastevere which embraced the Jewish quarter) threatened to disband if forced to serve with Jews.[48]

Optimistic Jews and liberals were ready to dismiss these outbreaks as temporary aberrations. Berthold Auerbach's comments on the events in Heidelberg are fairly typical. "Occasional stupidities of the German *Michel* against the Jews," he wrote to his father-in-law, on March 5, "must be regarded from broader vistas. These ugly outbursts have been quickly suppressed, particularly by liberals, whereas the upheaval in general remains exalted and exalting." Even the writer in the *Österreichisches Central-Organ* who pointed out the unprecedented extension and ferocity of these attacks for more than a century—he might have added in all centuries of modern west-European history—the very *Hep-Hep* movement of 1819 having been in comparison with them but "a minor and unimportant street commotion," comforted his readers with the thought that the proletarians now fighting for their freedom would evince a sense of kinship for their Jewish fellow-sufferers. Rather than believing that all Jews were "moneybags" and harsh exploiters, they could observe, at first hand, the evidence of Jewish misery and degradation.[49]

At the same time, a correspondent of the *Jewish Intelligence*, the organ of the London Society for the Promoting of Christianity Amongst the Jews, commented:

In several of my letters, I expressed my opinion that the Jewish people are hastening very fast toward a fearful persecution. In this opinion I have been much corroborated by late events and daily occurrences. Scarcely a day's paper appears without the news of some new excess against the Jews, in some part of the civilized world. And, moreover, I have come to the full persuasion, after having for years past closely watched the movement, that the more the Jews wedge themselves into Christian affairs and legislature, the more they fraternize and make common cause with Deists, Atheists, and Republicans of the day, the more do they expose themselves to the hatred of those very persons.[50]

S. Cahen, editor of the *Archives Israélites,* was not altogether wrong when, in a letter sent on March 3 to many Paris papers, he spoke of the "evil passions [which] assumed the mask of republicanism as they had previously covered themselves with the mantle of religion." As a curiosity one might mention a toast raised at a republican celebration in the provincial city of Tonnère against "the Jews, monarchists and Jesuits, these eternal enemies of the Republic."[51]

It is not surprising, therefore, that the only deputy of the Frankfurt National Assembly who ventured to suggest continued anti-Jewish discrimination was Moritz Mohl of Stuttgart, himself a Leftist. Curiously, his amendment (of August 28) ran counter to all previous trends in the struggle against emancipation. While earlier legislators *(e. g.,* in Prussia of 1812) were prepared to grant Jews civil equality, but hesitated to extend to them political franchise, Mohl's motion was designed to invest them with all political, but withhold from them a number of civil rights. Protesting vigorously, as did most Jew-baiters of that day, that he nurtured no religious prejudices, Mohl argued that granting the Jews complete civil equality would only lead to their greater exploitation of the peasantry. He also denied, that, after a period of transition, the progress of Jewish assimilation would of itself obliterate all economic distinctions between the Jewish and non-Jewish citizens. "The Hebrew population," he exclaimed, "will forever and ever swim like a drop of oil upon the waters of the German nationality."[52]

Liberal spokesman, particularly Gabriel Riesser himself, replied that laws administered uniformly toward all denominations would prove more successful in combating such evils than discriminatory provisions. Riesser pointedly referred to a previous experience in Mohl's home state of Württemberg which, in 1828, had forbidden Jews from trading in rural real estate. Eight years later speakers in the Württemberg Diet had to admit that in the intervening period such trade had been "practised by Christians in a far more ruthless and abominable fashion."[53] Riesser's effective address, supported by other spokesmen of liberalism, as well as by members of the clerical party interested in the autonomy of churches, carried the day. Mohl's amendment did not even marshal the support necessary for further deliberation and voting.

The zest with which young Jews threw themselves into the espousal of liberal and even radical ideas slowly turned the tide. The first to recognize it were their enemies. The London *Standard,* long an opponent of Jewish emancipation, explained to its readers, shocked by the extremism of the revolutionary outburst, that "all the mischief now brooding on the Continent is done by Jews." In vain did the *Jewish Chronicle* point out in its reply that the most prominent Jewish politicians belonged to moderate liberal parties. In vain did the *Archives israélites* exhort all writers to favor the return to order and the service of an "honest Republic based upon the three great principles of morality, family and property." Neither the examples set by the Jewish press, nor declarations like those of the Königsberg rabbi, Joseph L. Saalschütz, that politically Jews were not Jews but "good Germans and law-abiding Prussians," nor even outright attacks on communism by Adolphe Franck, succeeded in stemming the growing penchant of identifying Jews with continental radicalism. A few years later Disraeli tried to convince his Conversative colleagues that, left to themselves, the Jews represented a most conservatory force. Since "their bias is to religion, property and natural aristocracy," he insisted, it ought to be "the interest of statesmen that this bias of a great race should be encouraged, and their energies and creative power enlisted in the cause of existing society." Even he admitted, however, that as a result of the short-sighted policies of European governments the Jews had been driven in large numbers into the radical camp. Pointing particularly to the experiences of the revolution of 1848, he declaimed:

An insurrection takes place against tradition and aristocracy, against religion and property. Destruction of the Semitic principle, extirpation of the Jewish religion, whether in the Mosaic or in the Christian form, the natural equality of man, and the abrogation of property, are proclaimed by the secret societies who form provisional governments, and men of Jewish race are found at the head of every one of them. The people of God co-operate with atheists; the most skillful accumulators of property ally themselves with communists; the peculiar and chosen race touch the hand of all the scum and low castes of Europe! And all this because they wish to destroy that ungrateful Christendom which owes to them even its name, and whose tyranny they can no longer endure.[54]

In this respect 1848 marks, indeed, an important turning point. Jewish emancipation became so intimately identified in the public mind with the revolution that, to steal its thunder, the Austrian government itself, as we recall, granted full Jewish equality in the constitution of March 4, 1849, only to revoke it as soon as it regained its composure under Prince Schwarzenberg's vigorous leadership (December 31, 1851). On the other hand, socialists now increasingly became confirmed opponents of every form of anti-Jewish discrimination. The German Social Democratic Party, in particular, at least in all such formal pronouncements as the resolution of the Cologne Congress of 1893, sharply condemned every form of antisemitism as an abettment of counter-revolution. The victorious communist revolution in Russia for the first time in history outlawed all antisemitic activities, counting them among major counter-revolutionary crimes. Whatever antisemitic trends persisted within the socialist parties—and there were many even within the French and German parties—had to take recourse to all sorts of subterfuges. At times, for example, they rationalized their prejudices by accepting the antisemitic premise of a widespread peculiar Jewish usury and exploitation, but placing the entire blame on some foreign Jews.[55] One must remember, however, that in this particular variant of xenophobia socialists were often surpassed by French and German Jews themselves.

At the same time, the intensified debate on the merits of a capitalist versus a socialist economy highlighted the "lopsidedness" of the Jewish economic structure. For about a century Jewish communities as well as governments had made more or less consistent efforts to "normalize" Jewish participation in economic life by stimulating the transfer of Jews from mercantile occupations to such "useful" pursuits as agriculture, crafts and liberal professions. These efforts were crowned with success wherever, as in the case of professions, they were favored by the general economic trends. As soon as legal disabilities were removed, the Jews rushed into the fields of medicine, law and journalism and, by 1848, one already heard frequent complaints of excessive Jewish control over the press. Less successful was

the promotion of Jewish crafts and agriculture, since the progress of
the Industrial Revolution was simultaneously undermining the status
of established artisans and converting multitudes of farmers into an
urban proletariat. Nevertheless 1848 added impetus to the work of
older and newer societies for the promotion of crafts and agriculture
among Jews. A Silesian Jewish landowner, Berliner, offered to convert his estate, Kirchbert, in the district of Falkenberg, into an agricultural colony, accommodating some sixty Jewish families. Were this
colony, which he wished to name Mendelssohn, to prove successful, he
proposed to establish a second colony under the name of Jakobsohn.
A similar proposal by a wealthy Jew of Brody, who offered to donate
the first 5,000 florins, stirred Fischhof's imagination and induced him
to prepare a memorandum on the tasks of the projected society.[56]

Many leaders realized, however, that such a far-reaching restratification would be practically impossible in the crowded areas of central
Europe and turned their eyes toward the younger countries. Together
with the other German residents, the Jews had been leaving in ever
increasing numbers for America and other lands. The economic pres-
sures, in their case aggravated by existing legal disabilities, had set in
motion their long inert masses at an ever self-accelerating speed. The
events of 1848 helped further dramatize this trend by adding a considerable number of political expatriates. While the German emigration in general, however, had reached a peak of some 110,000 in the
depression year of 1847 and declined somewhat in 1848–50, Jewish
emigration seems to have continued to gain ground immediately after
the revolution. *Via* Posen and Bohemia it soon extended to eastern
Europe as well, where it was more intensively combined with ideological efforts at social restratification by large-scale colonization. As
early as July 1848 the *Archives Israélites* commented on the activities
of the numerous societies formed in Pesth, Prague, Pressburg, Vienna
and other localities to aid prospective emigrants to America. "Since
the latter propose, following the example of those who had preceded
them in that country, to exchange commerce for rural labor, they find
it necessary to acquaint themselves with work enabling them to build
houses or bungalows. An appeal was addressed to all charitable persons to aid Hebrew youth in acquiring familiarity with masonry, car-
pentry, the locksmith's trade, etc." Isidor Busch's *Österreichisches*

Central-Organ, in particular, was filled with eloquent pleas in behalf of the "On to America" movement and with equally emotional exhortations to stay home and fight it out with the Jew-baiters.[57] Within a generation there sprang up those movements which, known in their early stages as *Am-Olam* and *BILU,* intiated those manifold Zionist and socialist, sometimes combined Zionist-socialist, attempts at solving the economic as well as the political aspects of the Jewish question.

Minority Rights

In other respects, too, the revolution of 1848 unwittingly laid the foundation for the rise of modern Jewish nationalism and, ultimately, for the Jewish struggle for national minority rights. At first the opposite was true. Like the French revolution, that of 1848 insisted upon Jewish assimilation as an integral part of Jewish emancipation. Only Jew-baiters claimed that the Jews were unassimilable and, hence, should not be granted equal treatment. In his address before the Frankfurt National Assembly, Moritz Mohl, as we recall, reinforced the alleged threat of greater Jewish exploitation of peasants through the nationalist argument that, by maintaining their segregated mode of living and refusing to intermarry, the Jews would always resist amalgamation with the mass of the German nation. "There certainly exists no greater misfortune," he contended, "than to have lost one's fatherland. This misfortune has befallen the Hebrews dispersed over the whole world. . . . The Jews are an alien element. They stick together throughout the world but do not consider themselves part and parcel of the people among whom they live." Whether or not he realized it, Mohl merely reiterated the economic pleadings of the Alsatian Jew-baiter, Reubell, together with Abbé Maury's nationalist reasonings during the debates of the French National Assembly in 1790–91.[58]

Neither was Riesser's aforementioned reply to the economic argument strikingly novel. In regard to the problem of assimilation, however, Riesser could refer to the Assembly's previous vote to abolish all discriminatory laws against the various ethnic and linguistic groups in Germany.

Shall history report about you [he exclaimed] that you have tried, by granting full equality, to appease powerful nationalities which may destructively interfere with the future of Germany and which stand before you fully armed and equipped; that you have opposed mild words to threatening force? But that you have maltreated and maintained the discriminatory laws against a weak, religious denomination which, with respect to civil relations, wishes nothing else but to be absorbed by Germany; a group of people who do not wish to have national existence of their own such as had formerly been imposed upon them by their enemies, but who think and feel as Germans?

In the same vein argued the clerical deputy, Von Linde. "To the essence of nationality," he contended, "belong not only a people which continues speaking its own language, but also a number of other prerequisites, such as territory, one's own country. The Jewish people has none, and hence it represents within the German people not a nationality but a sect." A simple act of conversion suffices, therefore, for any Jew immediately to overcome the barrier separating him from the Christian Germans.[59]

Jewish deputies of the Austrian Constitutional Assembly took a similar stand. During the debate on Article XIX of the constitution concerning the emperor's appointment of government officials, one deputy, Kautschitsch, argued that only Protestants were reliable civil servants, while Catholics, Greek-Orthodox and Jews possessed central ecclesiastical authorities outside their own country and hence were dangerous to the state. But Goldmark countered: "With respect to the Jewish religion the deputy is in error. That the independence of the Jewish church is not dangerous to the state may be readily deduced from the fact that, as such, it possesses no property. If it be true that we are awaiting the coming of a messiah, he must be coming in 1849. If we are no longer oppressed, we need no messiah. We shall gladly offer our hierarchy on the altar of the fatherland."[60]

The realities of the revolution of 1848, however, showed that both sides tried to oversimplify a complex and in some respects unique situation. It was easy enough for the champions of Jewish emancipation in 1789–91 to demand complete national assimilation from the Jews.

Count Clermont-Tonnère's exclamation that the Jews should give up their separate laws and self-governing institutions or otherwise "let them be banished," encountered little opposition among the protagonists of Jewish equality at the National Assembly.[61]

One could still take the same unequivocal position in France, the Netherlands or the lesser German states in 1848, but not quite so easily in Prussia, where Jews of the eastern, formerly Polish, provinces found themselves ground between the millstones of competing Polish and German national aspirations. Samuel Holdheim, himself a native of that section of the country, was right in saying that the 50,000 Jews of Posen were "in the worst possible plight" in deciding which party to support. Their majority, however, was not only loyal to the crown and hence opposed to Polish insurrectionary forces, but felt great affinity to German culture. Some of its liberals, like other German progressives of that time, wishfully dreamed of the reconciliation of these national antagonisms by securing for the Poles perfect economic and cultural equality. They thought that Jews could perform useful services as intermediaries. Their hopes were heightened when the radical parties at the Frankfurt Assembly submitted the following resolution: "The National Assembly declares the partitions of Poland a shameful injustice. It recognizes the sacred duty of the German people to collaborate in the reconstruction of an independent Poland." When submitted to a vote, however, on July 28, the resolution was defeated. Of the Jewish deputies only Hartmann joined 100 others in voting in the affirmative, Kuranda was absent, while Riesser was among the 458 to vote in the negative. Together with a great many others he merely salved his conscience by signing an expostulatory declaration that "it is not the task of the Constitutional Assembly to issue a judgement on past historic events nor to utter vague promises for the future."[62]

At the same time, the National Assembly itself had to divide the eastern provinces through a "demarcation line" between the predominantly German and predominantly Polish districts, a measure denounced by Polish patriots as another partition of Poland. It also had to recognize Prussia's military measures in suppressing the Polish revolt. Most Jews, not only in the rest of Prussia, but also in the Polish areas, sided with the German authorities. At first many were found wearing ribbons of both nationalities, but when the uprisings assumed an overt anti-German character, the Jews of Lissa in an excess of patriotism began tearing down the Polish colors. In the much-debated case of Krotoschin a local German official surrendered the city hall to the Polish rebels, but a patriotic Jewish merchant L. Benas almost single-handedly restored governmental authority. The result was a growing estrangement between Jews and Poles, nurtured by the revival of the ever-present Judeophobia. Wild and unsubstantiated rumors found general credence that Jews instigated the Prussian military to commit atrocities on the Polish rebels. Polish mobs retaliated by acts of pillage and murder, attacking their more defenseless Jewish neighbors rather than the Prussian soldiers. Of course, Jewish shopkeepers also were a more remunerative target. News of outrages, readily exaggerated, led to mutual recrimination and growing hostility. The newly formed Polish League, modeled after the English Anti-Corn-Laws League, proclaimed a strict commercial boycott of Jews. The boycott failed because Jews still were an indispensable element in Posen's mercantile class, but it put in bold relief the untenable position of Jews in that exposed area.[63]

It is small wonder that the Jewish masses, long knocking at the exit gates kept shut by Prussia's restrictive legislation of 1816, now availed themselves of the newly gained freedom of movement. In ever-increasing numbers they began leaving the eastern provinces for both western Germany and overseas countries. Despite their general biological fertility during that period, their total population in the two administrative districts of Posen and Bromberg declined from 76,757 in 1849 to 61,437 in 1871 and to 35,327 in 1900. The proportionate decrease was, of course, even more glaring.[64]

The equivocal position of the Jewish people was underscored in this case by the new fraternization between Poles and Jews in both western Europe and Galicia. The great poet, Adam Mickiewicz, the mystic Towianski, and other leaders of the Polish emigration in Paris, had preached for several years the brotherhood of the two suffering messianic peoples of Israel and Poland. Supported by such Jewish emigré publicists as Léon Hollendaerski, who in 1848 again issued an enthusiastic appeal to his co-religionists to fight for Poland's independence, these teachings struck a responsive chord. In the first flush of revolution Polish noblemen in Brody were reported by the *Deutsche Allgemeine Zeitung* to have jubilantly marched arm in arm with Orthodox Jews clad in their long robes and fur hats chanting: "We share the same fate and hence have the same goal." Jewish emigrés in western Europe enlisted in large numbers in a legion which was to fight for Polish independence on the Italian battlefields. Sixty such Jewish legionnaires were feted by the community of Strasbourg after the great celebration of planting the tree of liberty in the presence of the Catholic bishop, Protestant pastor and chief rabbi.[65]

Such deep cleavage among Jews on the Polish issue was further demonstrated by the appeal of Galician Jewish leaders, headed by Rabbi Meisels, to their co-religionists in Posen, urging them to support the Polish national cause. At the same time, a Leipzig society for the defense of the German character of the eastern provinces, organized in part by outstanding Jewish leaders, invoked the aid of Posen Jewry in that task. In fact, some of the latter's spokesmen, in a flush of over-patriotism, sharply repudiated the Jewish appeal from Cracow.[66]

In the multi-national Austrian empire, this conflict of loyalties was obviously even more intense. Most Hungarian Jews enthusiastically responded to the liberal appeals of Louis Kossuth and his fellow revolutionaries. On one occasion, Kossuth appeared in the synagogue of Grosswardein and delivered an address asking pardon of the people of Israel for past persecutions and solemnly pledging himself to work for absolute equality of all citizens. Despite constant delays in the formal enactment of such constitutional safeguards—the revolutionary government's explanation that it had "no time" to attend to this matter was downright insulting—more than 20,000 Jews enlisted in the Hungarian national army and fought bitterly to the end. By thus furnishing one-ninth of all combatants they allegedly trebled their expected numerical contribution. Exaggerating rumors raised the figure to 50,000, wholly impossible in a population of but 250,000. Some of the extremely Orthodox felt justified in desecrating the Sabbath for the sake of their country's war of liberation. Outstanding leaders like Rabbi Loeb Schwab and his son-in-law Leopold Löw joined the revolutionary cause. Löw served as chaplain in the Hungarian army, while Schwab was imprisoned for six months by the

Austrians for having delivered insurrectional sermons. Other Jews suffered similar retribution when the Austro-Russian armies squashed the rebellion. The anti-Jewish atrocities committed particularly by the soldiers of General Haynau (renamed Hyena in popular parlance), and the imposition of severe indemnities upon the Hungarian-Jewish communities, created a stir in the entire Jewish world. The Jewish press in all countries regularly reported these events and, in accordance with the prevailing temper in each country, used sharper or more moderate terms in condemning the Austrians. "I must ask you," ultimately inquired an Hungarian correspondent to the *Jewish Chronicle,* "how it is that the philanthropic Jews of England do not memorialize Lord Palmerston to intercede in our behalf?"[67]

More decisively, by thus allying themselves with the Hungarians the Jews became the natural antagonists of the Slavonic peoples. A young Budapest rabbi, J. Einhorn, thus rationalized the Jews' affection for the Magyar cause, for which he had severely suffered after the downfall of the revolutionary regime:

> Common Asiatic origins, the great similarity in the destinies of the Jewish and the Magyar peoples, the conspicuous lexicographic and grammatical affinities of the Magyar and Hebrew languages, etc., may have contributed their share to that affection . . . Purely material considerations may have added their weight: The Jew lived off nobility, from which he purchased for resale grain, wine, wool and other agricultural produce, while selling to it in turn industrial products which he imported from abroad . . . In contrast thereto the poor Slav could not be a lucrative customer, whereas the German burgher was an outright competitor.

For decades thereafter the Jews found themselves in the equivocal position of being the exponents of Magyar culture among the Slovaks, Serbo-Croats and Rumanians who, between them, outnumbered the Magyar-speaking population of Hungary.[68]

No less awkward was the position of the Jews in Austria's Czech provinces. While a few younger Jews evinced strong sympathies for the Czech national cause, the majority joined the German side, provoking the ire of Czech nationalists. To appease their conscience

many of them doubtless thought along the lines of Berthold Auerbach's strange rationalization. "Freedom and nationality are insep-
arable," the celebrated writer stated in an address at a stormy session
of the Breslau Democratic Society, "but the Czech movement springs
from a nationalist affectation and has nothing in common with the
spirit of genuine democracy." In that heyday of their "heroic" nationalism the Czechs of Bohemia, Moravia and Silesia resented, in particular, the widespread Jewish resistance to the revival of the Czech
language. All but two churches in Prague adopted in 1848 Czech
sermons, but Jewish preachers long continued to address their audiences in German. Hence Jews became not only the victims of popular
riots in Prague and many provincial cities (in Prerau, Moravia, the
government had to proclaim in 1850 martial law before restoring
order), but also tempered the zest for Jewish equality on the part of
the important Czech delegation at the Austrian Constitutional Assembly.[69]

Indeed, while the Bohemian Jewish deputies to Frankfurt, Kuranda
and Hartmann, were enthusiastic exponents of German unity, the
Czech leaders in Vienna and Kremsier, Palacky and Rieger, saw in
such unity the greatest menace to their own national survival. It is
not surprising that the latter played a rather equivocal role in the
discussions on Jewish emancipation. During the debates on Art.
XVII in the Committee on Constitutional Affairs, Palacky, on December 16, 1848, warned that it was "in the Jewish interest" not to ask
for sudden emancipation which might produce a violent reaction particularly in Prague's "highly intolerant populace." Although he
refrained from suggesting any restrictive amendments, another Czech
deputy, Brauner, actually defended the existing discriminatory taxation at least to the extent of suggesting that the pre-payments already
made by the Bohemian Jewish communities (some had paid up to
1852) be considered forfeited to the state. When in March 1849 the
hour of decision drew near, most Czechs were prepared to vote for
the article safeguarding Jewish equality. Nevertheless, the Jews of
Austria, mindful of Rieger's declaration, "We Slavs are in the majority
and the preservation of the monarchy depends on us," realized the
difficulties of their position. "With whomever they side," complained
a Vienna journalist, "they find a powerful party opposing them."[70]

In Lombardo-Venetia, on the other hand, only few Jews were staunch Habsburg patriots. The majority, long Italian-speaking, joined their non-Jewish compatriots in trying to throw off the yoke of the oppressive Austrian regime.[71]

Before long it became clear even to German Jewish patriots that simple identification with German nationalism would not do. Berthold Auerbach was as loyal a German as any. As a writer of the *Schwäbische Dorfgeschichten* he articulated the sentiments of the German peasant masses like no one else in his time. During the revolution of 1848 he unsuccessfully ran for parliament against a long list of candidates which included Moritz Mohl and, we recall, might have fallen victim on the barricades of Vienna. By 1869, however, even before the rise of the new racial antisemitism of the 1870's, he began to realize the peculiarities of the Jewish position. At that time Adolphe Crémieux was visiting Berlin in behalf of the *Alliance* in order to co-ordinate the assistance to Jewish emigrants from western Russia. Stirred by this evidence of interterritorial Jewish community of interests, Auerbach, perhaps unaware of what he was saying, spoke at the reception for Crémieux

> about the mission of the Jews who are to become full-fledged Frenchmen in France, full-fledged Germans in Germany, and so forth. It was their mission to help establish the life of state and nationality on a superior plane, not on the basis of blood descent but on that of the spirit. I concluded with a simile that the Jews are like the Bible which, translated into all national languages, nevertheless retains the same immutable content.

This reasoning reminds one of the equally strained explanation, later offered by Aristide Briand, for the peculiarities of the allegiance of Catholics of all lands to the papacy. Rather than being the head of a foreign state creating conflicting loyalties, Briand argued, the pope may be considered a *souverain intérieur* in every country embracing a large Catholic population.[72]

The very complexity of the Austrian situation, however, pointed to a new way out. The mixture of nationalities and languages was so great, their separation along purely geographic lines so clearly impossible, that the need of some new constitutional formulas to reconcile the interests of the varying local majorities and minorities was universally felt. Even the government recognized that Austria's survival depended on a new meaningful alliance between the various provinces and ethnic groups. In its program of November 27, 1848 it merely argued that, despite ethnic diversity, "Austria's continued existence in political unity is of importance to both Germany and Europe." Ultimately, the draft constitution submitted by the Committee on Constitutional Affairs stated in Article XXI that

all ethnic groups in the empire enjoy equality of rights. Every ethnic group has the inviolable right to cultivate its nationality and particularly its language. The equality of rights of all languages used in a particular area, in school, office and public life is guaranteed by the state.

Although disbanded before it could adopt this article, the Constitutional Assembly so deeply impressed the government that it included similar provisions in its constitution of March 4. In his reply to the Jewish community of Vienna, dated April 3, 1849, Francis Joseph I emphasized that the newly granted constitutional "equality of rights for all peoples and all tribes . . . will, I firmly believe, establish the lasting welfare and happiness of the whole country and of each individual." The Kremsier parliament thus left for Austria, and indirectly for Europe, a memorable bequest which, with reference to the fundamental laws of 1867, Jacques Fouques-Duparc justifiably compared with that of the Rights of Man of 1791.[73]

Among the protagonists of national reconciliation were the Jewish politicians, Fischhof and Goldmark. Already in his famous address of March 13, 1848, which sounded the clarion call to the revolution, Fischhof stated: "Ill-advised statesmanship has hitherto kept apart Austria's nationalities. They now must find their brotherly way to one another and increase their strength by unity." All through his life he remained a staunch supporter of all efforts at harmonizing the conflicting national interests on the basis of justice. Although as president of the Committee on Safety he once violently reacted to the overbearing behavior of some delegates of the nationalistic Czech

Swornost, he never relinquished his hopes of ultimate national reconciliation. His volume, in particular, *Österreich und die Bürgschaften
seines Bestandes,* published in 1869, advocated a federal reorganization of the Austrian empire which, it now appears, might have salvaged the unity of the Dual Monarchy.[74]

Although preaching to an unresponsive generation, Fischhof found
many disciples in the following decades. Particularly among the
Austrian socialists there arose leaders of the rank of Karl Renner and
Otto Bauer who rethought the entire national problem in terms of the
Austrian realities. At the turn of the century the socialist opposition
in Austria began to advocate a consistent program of national minority rights based on the subjective criteria of group sentiment of "community of destiny and culture," rather than those derived from sharing
the same territory or language. These new theories altered the entire
picture of the struggle of nationalities in Austria-Hungary, the Balkans and the Russian empire. They ultimately laid the foundation
for the adoption of the national minority safeguards by the Peace
Conference of 1919 and the inclusion of such provisions in the suc-
cessive Soviet constitutions.[75]

The new emphases upon subjective, rather than objective, criteria
of nationality enabled Jewish thinkers and publicists, too, to find new
solutions for the perplexing difficulties of their people in the midst of
that nationalist turmoil of eastern Europe. If neither territory nor
language were essential ingredients of nationality, why should not
Jews, too, claim national existence of their own and thus avoid the
pitfalls of identification with one or another of the many warring
nationalities from the Baltic to the Aegean? Without quite realizing
the implications of his reasoning why Bohemian Jews side with the
Germans, Adolf Jellinek had stated in July 1848: "Neither descent
nor language alone, but sentiment accounts for the essence of nationality." Combined with other positive forces, which need not be elaborated here, the new situation, arising from the national conflicts since
1848, created the new ideology of Jewish nationalism and Jewish
minority rights, espoused ever since 1892 by the socialist, Chaim
Zhitlovsky, the middle-class "Diaspora nationalist," Simon Dubnow,
and many others. By a curious concatenation of circumstances
spokesmen of east-European Jewry, obeying a need even more press-

ing after the dissolution of the great multinational empires during the
First World War, became the most influential protagonists of minority
rights at the Paris Peace Conference. Aided by western coreligionists,
even by such who rejected national rights for Jews in their own
countries, the Committee of Jewish Delegations in Paris was most
instrumental in persuading the Allied powers to insert into the treaties
with the new or newly enlarged countries of eastern Europe, safeguards for legal equality and cultural autonomy of all national minorities including Jews.[76]

Whatever one thinks about the success or failure of these minority
provisions, one cannot deny the impact of the revolution of 1848 on
the national movements in Europe, including that of the Jews. It
was inherent in the liberal program of Frankfurt and Kremsier, though
not yet fully formulated then, that equality of rights must not be
predicated upon national self-abnegation. The same revolutionary
organs which had consciously proclaimed Jewish emancipation on the
basis of national assimilation, paradoxically, laid the ground for Jewish national revival under which equality was to be combined with
the retention of Jewish ethnic identity.

More recently nazi expansion, extermination of millions of Jews,
and general political and demographic changes brought about by the
Second World War, have greatly reduced the importance of minority
rights to Jews, at least outside the Soviet orbit. But by the stimulus
they gave to the rise of the State of Israel they brought to fruition
certain other trends in the historic evolution of the Jewish people
which, though temporarily obscured, had come to the fore also during
the revolutionary debates of 1848. Despite verbal and on the whole
doubtless sincere, protestations of such Jewish champions of emancipation as Riesser, there were many Jews even then who agreed with
Moritz Mohl about the unfortunate position of a people which had
lost its fatherland. In his editorials, written in 1848–49 in the more
remote and calmer atmosphere of the United States, the Rev. Isaac
Leeser of Philadelphia commented:

And if ancient Germany again becomes a nation—if Poland throws
off successfully the chains of mighty oppressors—if fair Italy takes

a rank as one people . . . why should not the patriotic Hebrew also look forward to the time . . . when he may again proudly boast of his own country. . . . Where is the heart that would not swell with a mighty sensation, could he once more see our fair land restored to its former beauty, when . . . the waste cities be built up again, and the son of David rule in righteousness among his equals?[77]

To be sure, some European Jewish leaders resented such "indiscretions." Referring, in particular, to Major Noah's well-known *Discourse on the Restoration of the Jews* of 1845 and the polemics against it in the *Jewish Chronicle,* S. Cahen asked rhetorically: "Will not such tacit acceptance of Jewish nationality entitle the inflexible defenders of outdated institutions to claim that Palestine has always been the true and only fatherland of the Jews?" However, the very struggle for emancipation appeared to some sensitive souls as the expression of a newly awakened tiredness of the "Wandering Jew" with his perennial homelessness. Moritz Hartmann beautifully caught the spirit of the Hungarian Jew who, in fighting for his country's liberation, really sought a refuge from this despair:

> Jetzt steh ich da der Güter baar
> Kein Jude mehr, doch ein Magyar . . .
> Gib eine Muskete mir in die Hand,
> Auf dass ich fühle, dass endlich ich fand
> Was lange mir fehlte, ein Vaterland,
> Und wenn ich's auch fühle in blutigem Sand.

Jewish yearning for a return to Palestine, on the other hand, was so much taken for granted that many papers repeated the canard of Louis Napoleon's agents soliciting the votes of Alsatian peasants by promising them the removal of all Jews from Alsace to the Holy Land. In Vienna, Mose Ehrenreich, a Galician-born Italian rabbi, warned that "in our quest for proving ourselves as citizens of the country which we call our fatherland, . . . we must not forget the interests of our nationality" and urged the cultivation of the Hebrew national language. Another Jewish educator, Simon Szanto, already suggested the adoption of blue and white as Jewish national colors. Before very long, Moses Hess, one of the leading Jewish revolutionary fighters, issued his memorable call for the "solution of the last national question" through the restoration of the Jews to their ancient land. His *Rome und Jerusalem,* published in Leipzig, 1862, rightly belongs to the classics of modern Zionist literature. It showed, and subsequent history confirmed it, that rather than being antagonistic principles, as then generally believed, emancipation and Zionism really complemented one another.[78]

NOTES

[1] *Verhandlungen des österreichischen Reichstages nach der stenographischen Aufnahme,* 5 vols., Vienna (1848–49), 51st Session. *See also* Rosenmann, M., *Isak Noa Mannheimer, Sein Leben und Wirken* (Vienna 1922), p. 172. The tax was abolished by a vote of 243 to 20, the main plea of the opposition being that the treasury could not afford the ensuing loss. This was true in 1848, as it had been in 1818, when three cabinet ministers explained to the Emperor that "in view of its size, this revenue could not be dispensed with. The Court Chamber [Treasury] would find its replacement greatly embarrassing if—as we ought to desire it—the majority of Jews would suddenly embrace any of the three Christian denominations." *Cf.* Pribram, A. F., *Urkunden und Akten zur Geschichte der Juden in Wien,* 2 vols. (Vienna 1918), vol. ii, p. 298. This interdependence of Jewish and general historical forces raised in Abraham Geiger's penetrating mind the question as to whether the Jews in modern times were altogether masters of their own destiny. *Cf.* the brief summary of his lectures on "Jüdische Geschichte von 1830 bis zur Gegenwart," delivered in 1848–49 and published in his *Nachgelassene Schriften,* 5 vols. (Berlin 1875–78), vol. ii, p. 247.

To avoid frequent repetition the reader is herewith referred generally to various related problems discussed in my essays, "The Revolution of 1848 and Jewish Scholarship," Parts I-II, *Proceedings of the American Academy for Jewish Research,* vol. xviii (1949), pp. 1–66; vol. xx (1950), pp. 1–100; "Aspects of the Jewish Communal Crisis in 1848," *Jewish Social Studies,* vol. xiv (1952), pp. 99–144; "Church and State Debates in the Jewish Community of 1848," *Mordecai M. Kaplan Jubilee Volume* (New York 1953), pp. 49–72; and "Samuel David Luzzatto and the Revolution of 1848" (Hebrew), *Sefer Assaf* (Jerusalem 1953), pp. 40–63.

[2] *Lord George Bentinck: A Political Biography,* 8th ed. (London 1872), p. 356. Although written several years after the revolution and, in part, intended to counteract the revulsion to the socialist doctrines of 1848 in Britain's conservative circles, this statement reflects Disraeli's long-cherished convictions on race.

[3] *Jewish Chronicle,* vol. vi (1849–50), p. 345.

[4] *Orient,* vol. ix (1848), p. 213; Auerbach, B., *Dichter und Kaufmann,* vol. ii, p. 38. The original title of that novel, *Der jüdishe Dichter. Ein Tableau aus der Zeit Friedrich des Grossen,* is somewhat more descriptive. *Cf.* also M. I. Zwick's analysis of *Berthold Auerbachs sozial-politischer und ethischer Liberalismus* (Stuttgart 1933), p. 13 ff., 99 ff. The Vienna correspondent of the *Orient* (vol. ix, p. 366) uses the simile of Jews serving as a "barometer of freedom" to describe the overcharged atmosphere in Vienna during the last days of October 1848.

[5] Meyers, Maurice, "Some Ms. Sidelights on Anglo-Jewish Emancipation," in *Transactions of the Jewish Historical Society of England,* vol. vi (1912), p. 241.

[6] Art. 13. This demand was repeated verbatim in the "Program of the Commission for the Solution of the Social Question" of the radical Second Democratic Congress which met in Berlin during October 1848. *Cf.* the texts reprinted in Gustav Lüders's *Die demokratische Bewegung in Berlin im Oktober 1848* (Berlin 1909), pp. 159, 162.

[7] *Archives israélites,* vol. ix (1848), pp. 212 f.; *Jewish Chronicle,* vol. vi, pp. 239, 271. *See also* de Lanessan, J. L., *L'état et les églises en France* (Paris 1906), pp. 159 f. Although divided on many issues, including the separation of state and church, at that time advocated by Hugues de Lamenais and Pierre Leroux, most Jews must have felt relieved by this state aid to their religious bodies. Even the *Archives israélites,* which opposed denominational representation in Parliament, pointed out how greatly total separation would have hurt the Jewish Reform movement (vol. ix, pp. 197, 205, 207)! Only as taxpayers some Jews, too, must have resented the growing burden on the treasury since, according to the radical *Liberté,* the budget for cults had more than doubled in the years 1806–44. *Cf.* the remarks of the Paris correspondent of the *Orient,* vol. ix, p. 174. Needless to say that Jewish shopkeepers and artisans rejoiced in the National Assembly's chilly reception of an amendment suggested by Abbé Sibour which would have forced them to close their shops on Sunday. *Cf. Archives israélites,* vol. ix, p. 483, and, more generally, Frydman, Szajko (Z. Szajkowski), "Internal Conflicts in French Jewry at the Time of the Revolution in 1848," in *Yivo Annual of Jewish Social Science,* vols. ii-iii (1947–48), pp. 100–17.

[8] *Orient,* vol. ix, pp. 105, 122, 151, 201, 214, 283, 301, 310 ff.; Teller, M., "Keine Staatsreligion im konstitutionellen Österreich," in *Österreichisches Central-Organ für Glaubensfreiheit* (1848), pp. 173 f.; Lempp, Richard, *Die Frage der Trennung von Kirche und Staat im Frankfurter Parlament* (Tübingen 1913); Strauss, Herbert Arthur, *Staat, Bürger, Mensch, Die Debatten der deutschen Nationalversammlung 1848/1849 über die Grundrechte* (Aarau 1947), pp. 79 ff. It should be noted that even a conservative rabbi like Zacharias Frankel of Dresden actively participated in the formation of an interdenominational religious association. *Cf. Der Israelit des neunzehnten Jahrhunderts,* vol. ix (1848), p. 175.

[9] Hildesheimer, *Drei Vorträge* (Vienna 1867), p. 16; *Orient*, vol. ix, p. 156 (summarizing the debate of March 2, 1848 in the second Baden Chamber). *Cf.* also Lewin, Adolf, *Geschichte der badischen Juden seit der Regierung Karl Friedrichs (1738–1909)* (Karlsruhe 1909), pp. 275 ff. and Stern-Täubler, Selma, "Die Emanzipation der Juden in Baden," in *Gedenkbuch zum hundertfünfundzwanzigjährigen Bestehen des Oberrats der Israeliten Badens* (Frankfurt 1934), pp. 7–104, particularly pp. 98 f., 102.

[10] *Archives israélites*, vol. ix, p. 545; Geiger, Ludwig, *Abraham Geiger: Leben und Lebenswerk* (Berlin 1910), p. 109; *Jewish Chronicle*, vol. vi, p. 230; *Orient*, vol. ix, pp. 240, 254, 265; *Österreichisches Central-Organ für Glaubensfreiheit* (1848), p. 190. *Cf.* Friedmann, Filip, *Die galizischen Juden im Kampfe um ihre Gleichberechtigung (1848–1868)* (Frankfurt 1929), pp. 69 ff. The Jewish community benefited, however, from the abrogation of existing laws prohibiting conversion or reconversion of Christians to Judaism. When the Prussian minister of public instruction on Sept. 22, 1848, answered in the affirmative a Jewish teacher's inquiry concerning the permissibility of his return to Judaism, his reply made the rounds of the Jewish press in Germany and elsewhere. *Cf. Orient*, vol. ix, 311.

[11] *Allgemeine Zeitung des Judentums*, vol. vii (1848), p. 127 (communication dated February 10, 1848); Friedmann, *op. cit.*, pp. 55 f., 67 n. 1. It should be noted, however, that Joseph Saul Nathansohn, Meisels' Lwów colleague, was somewhat disturbed by Meisels' political activity. Meisels expostulated to him by pointing out how much his intervention had helped save Jewish lives during the Polish uprising in Cracow in 1846. *Cf.* Frankl-Grün, Adolf, *Geschichte der Juden in Kremsier,* 3 vols. (Breslau and Frankfurt 1896–1901), vol. i, p. 180 n. 2. *Cf.* also the Lwów correspondence dated July 16, 1848, in *Orient*, vol. ix, p. 254; and the ungracious remark concerning the "wholly irresponsible" Polish-Jewish deputy, *ibid.*, p. 406.

[12] *Archives israélites*, vol. ix, p. 205; *Jewish Chronicle*, vol. v. p. 45, referring to some 40 Jewish families which were said to have found their way back to Judaism since the Prussian minister's aforementioned decision of Sept. 22, 1848.

[13] Posener, S., "The Immediate Economic and Social Effects of the Emancipation of the Jews in France," in JEWISH SOCIAL STUDIES, vol. i, no. 3 (July 1939), p. 310; Kober, Adolf, "The French Revolution and the Jews in Germany," *ibid.*, vol. vii (1945), p. 306; Hansen, Joseph, *Quellen zur Geschichte des Rheinlandes im Zeitalter der französischen Revolution, 1780–1801,* 4 vols. (Bonn 1931–38), vol. ii, p. 760.

[14] The estimates of Jewish population in 1848, particularly in Russia and the Ottoman Empire, are very unreliable. *Cf.* my observations in *Social and Religious History of the Jews,* 3 vols. (New York 1937), vol. iii, pp. 129 f., 153 f.; and the literature listed there. Contemporary "guestimates" are illustrated by Isaac [Samuel] Reggio's "Zur Statistik der Juden, in *Österreichisches Central-Organ für Glaubensfreiheit* (1848), pp. 117 f. (on the world Jewish population);

by the study of Jewish population in Austria which appeared in the *Orient,* vol. x, p. 26; and was extracted in the Philadelphia *Occident,* vol. vii (1849–50), pp. 280 f.; and in *Jewish Chronicle,* vol. v, p. 410; and shorter notices on that of Germany in *Archives israélites,* vol. x, p. 554; and *Jewish Chronicle,* vol. vi, p. 55. Somewhat more reliable are the data assembled by specialists like Eugene Huhn. *Cf.* his "Zur Religionsstatistik Deutschlands," in *Zeitschrift des Vereins für deutsche Statistik,* vol. i (1847), pp. 764–65. *Cf.* also *Orient,* vol. ix, pp. 49 f., 91, etc. On France *cf.* Kahn, L., "Histoire des écoles consistoriales et communales de Paris (1809–1883)," in *Annuaire de la Société des études juives,* vol. iii (1884), p. 125 n. 3; *L'Univers israélite,* vol. v (1849–50), p. 40; Szajkowski, "The Growth of the Jewish Population of France," in JEWISH SOCIAL STUDIES, vol. viii, no. 3 (July 1946), pp. 179–96, 297–318 (particularly p. 300, Table v). In any case, these western and central-European communities played a leading role in world Jewish affairs far beyond their numerical strength.

[15] *Histoire édifiante,* 4th ed. (Paris 1846), pp. 5, 36. These denunciations were not limited to antisemites, however. Two years earlier Alexandre Weill, the same Alsatian Jew who was to play a certain role in French revolutionary circles, had likewise attacked the Rothschilds' excessive power in international affairs. *Cf.* his *Rothschild und die europäischen Staaten* (Stuttgart 1844). Since this pamphlet is not available in New York, the identity of its author cannot be fully ascertained, but *cf.* the reference thereto in Karl Gutzkow's letter to Weill of Oct. 1, 1843, published in *Briefe hervorragender verstorbener Männer Deutschlands on Alexander Weill* (Zürich 1889), p. 37. During the Revolution Isidor Busch denounced with particular bitterness the Rothschilds' responsibility for Austria's financial plight. *Cf.* his "Die Geldaristokratie und die Juden," in *Österreichisches Central-Organ für Glaubensfreiheit,* pp. 33 f.

[16] *Jewish Chronicle,* vol. vi, pp. 119 (reprinting also a letter from Richard Cobden against the Russian loan), 125 f., 183. In his comment on Rothschild's refusal to conclude the negotiations with the Papal government "until certain political concessions are made to our brethren residing at Rome" the editor of the *Chronicle* added the cautious remarks: "If the above be founded in truth we shall indeed be rejoiced. It will be an additional evidence of that increasing moral influence which will, we trust, ere long make money the supporter of liberal opinions, instead of being, as it had too generally been made, the abettor of oppression and tyranny." Cobden's appeal elicited, on the other hand, the London *Standard's* caustic observation that after all the Jews had been the *agents provocateurs* of all wars. *Cf.* *Archives israélites,* vol. x, pp. 531 f. *Cf.* also the *Orient's* reiterated criticisms of the Rothschilds' often misplaced benefactions, vol. ix (1848), pp. 3, 6, 118, 240, etc.

[17] *Memoirs of Citizen Caussidière,* English transl., 2 vols. (Paris 1848), vol. i, pp. 208 f.; Lord Beaconsfield (Disraeli), *Correspondence with his Sister, 1832–52,* 2d ed., (London 1886), p. 214. Financial losses were indeed sustained by a great many Jewish as well as non-Jewish businessmen. An echo of the

financial crisis is found also in the controversy over Jewish emancipation. The anonymous Viennese author (possibly J. B. Weis, editor of the popular magazine, *Hans Jörgel*) of a pamphlet *Nur keine Judenemancipation,* rapidly distributed in 25,000 copies, alleged that the Jews were undermining public credit. In his "Erklärung bezüglich auf die Judenfrage" of March 24, 1848, Rabbi Mannheimer replied that the wealthy Jews—not to mention the overwhelming majority of poor Jews—were, as a creditor class, interested in the stability of public finance. "The Jews were indeed the faithful, public credit their gospel. As in many other matters they have become martyrs for their faith." Reprinted in Rosenmann's *Mannheimer,* p. 157. There also is a melancholy touch in Berthold Auerbach's letter of March 5, 1848, to his much-esteemed father-in-law, Moritz Schreiber in Breslau. "He who trusts the Stock Exchange too much," declared the novelist, "will suffer. I beg you, dear father, to let me know whether you are sustaining serious losses; I hardly believe it and am sure that you will take it with equanimity." Cited by Anton Bettelheim in his biography of Berthold Auerbach (Stuttgart 1907), p. 211.

[18] Loevinson, Ermanno, "Gli israeliti dello Stato Pontificio e la loro evoluzione politicosociale nel periodo del Risorgimento italiano fino al 1849," in *Rassegna storica del Risorgimento,* vol. xvi (1929), pp. 768–803; *idem,* "Ausländische Juden im Kirchenstaat während der Revolution 1848/49," in *Zeitschrift für Geschichte der Juden in Deutschland,* vol. ii (1930), pp. 247 f.; *Orient,* vol. ix, pp. 248; Husserl, Sigmund, *Gründungsgeschichte des Stadt-Tempels der israel. Kultusgemeinde Wien* (Vienna 1906), pp. 45 f.; *Jewish Chronicle,* vol. vi, p. 239. By 1848 some Jewish writers already spoke of the "humiliating" elevation to the nobility of a Trieste coreligionist at a time when nothing but complete equality would do. *Cf. Archives israélites,* vol. ix, p. 243.

[19] *Ibid.,* vol. x, p. 157; [Köstlin], "Die bürgerlichen Verhältnisse der Juden in Deutschland," in *Die Gegenwart,* vol. i (1848), pp. 305–407 (particularly, p. 406; this essay was greatly influenced by David Friedrich Strauss, whose biography immediately precedes it); E. K. *Die Bedingung zur Emanzipation der Juden* (Vienna 1848) (unavailable, but *cf.* the polemical review thereof in *Österreichisches Central-Organ für Glaubensfreiheit,* p. 178); Brand, Theodor, *Die Judensucht christlicher Frauen und Jungfrauen verhindert christliche Heirathen,* 2d ed. (Breslau 1840 [?]). Although this pamphlet could not be consulted, its title seems quite expressive. To foster social and cultural rapprochement the Jews, on their part, stressed increasingly the use of pure German. Typical of such organized communal efforts are the ordinances of the Oberrat, the central Jewish agency in Baden, of April 4, 1834 and Feb. 24, 1848, eliminating the Yiddish (or, as they called it, the Judeo-German) dialect and script as a subject of instruction from the Jewish schools under its jurisdiction. *Cf. Orient,* vol. ix, p. 333.

[20] *Briefe aus Paris* (Offenbach 1833), vol. iii, pp. 140 f. (letter of February 7, 1832); *Archives israélites,* vol. x, p. 354. *Cf.* also Kober, Adolf, "Jews in the

Revolution of 1848 in Germany," in JEWISH SOCIAL STUDIES, vol. x, no. 2 (April 1948), p. 137; and Ras, Gerard, *Börne und Heine als politische Schriftsteller* (Groningen 1926).

21 *Orient,* vol. ix, pp. 35, 292, and Kalish, M., *Die Judenfrage in ihrer modernen Bedeutung für Preussen* (Leipzig 1860), where most of the votes of the Prussian faculties and their individual members are given in full. The attitude of the academic profession of Jewish emancipation in various countries, in both theory and practice, would merit monographic treatment.

22 It must be borne in mind, however, that religious liberalism did not necessarily go hand in hand with political liberalism or friendliness toward Jews. Just as in 1843 Bruno Bauer had created a stir through his anti-Jewish pamphlet on the Jewish question, David Friedrich Strauss, author of the well-known radical life of Jesus, created a mild sensation, at least among Jews, through his essay, "Judenverfolgungen und Emancipation," in *Jahrbücher der Gegenwart,* vol. vi (1848), pp. 117 ff. (reprinted in full in *Literaturblatt des Orients,* 1848, cols. 426–28, 443–48) in which he marshaled extenuating circumstances for the contemporary anti-Jewish outbreaks. He advocated legal encouragement of intermarriage as a means of breaking down the Jewish "state within the state" and amelioration of Jewish social ethics, but otherwise was opposed to any precipitate moves toward Jewish equality. *Cf.* also *Orient,* vol. ix, p. 384. Strauss himself may have regretted this outburst, however. This essay was neither included in his *Gesammelte Schriften,* ed. "according to the author's testamentary dispositions" by Edward Zeller, 12 vols. (Bonn 1876–77), nor mentioned by his admiring biographer, Theobald Ziegler, in his *David Friedrich Strauss,* 2 vols. (Strassburg 1908). On his simultaneous advocacy of Jewish equality, cf. Kohut, Adolph, *David Strauss als Denker und Erzieher* (Leipzig 1908), pp. 133 f. *Cf.* also above n. 19.

23 Cscherich, "Die Judenemansipationsfrage vom naturhistorischen Standpunkte," in *Deutsche Vierteljahrs-Schrift* (1848), no. 4, pp. 97–118. We encounter here already the usual pseudo-scientific reasonings from physical measurements, such as had been presented by G. Schulz of the Anatomical Museum in St. Petersburg, the greater fertility and longevity of Jews according to Bernouilli's population statistics, etc.

24 *Cf. Archives israélites,* vol. ix, pp. 189 f.; Posener, S., *Adolphe Crémieux,* English transl. (Philadelphia 1940), pp. 148, 151; Caussidière, *op. cit.,* vol. ii, p. 222. *Cf.* also Crémieux's *En 1848. Discours et lettres* (Paris 1883); Crémieux, Albert, *La Révolution de Février. Étude critique sur les journées de 21, 22, 23 et 24 Février 1848* (Paris 1912); Lazare, Raymond, *Michel Goudchaux (1797–1862), son oeuvre et sa vie politique* (Paris 1907).

25 *Archives israélites,* vol. ix, pp. 191, 197, 207, 352, 374, 395 f.; Frydman in *Yivo Annual, l. c.* Of course, Jews had been active in French politics long before 1848. Several years earlier the election of Achille Fould to the French chamber in a non-Jewish district of the Pyrenees filled Heinrich Heine with

particular satisfaction. Only if a Jew, he believed, like anyone else, can be elected without special merits of his own, can one speak of genuine tolerance. *Cf.* his *Confessio Judaica*, ed. by Hugo Bieber (Berlin 1925), pp. 170 f. During the revolution, even non-politicians had an opportunity of contributing their share. According to Caussidière *(op. cit.,* vol. i, p. 184), "the song of the Marseillaise repeated night after night by the energetic talent of Mademoiselle Rachel" excited the holy enthusiasm for the revolutionary cause among the numerous workers who attended as guests the performances of the Théâtre National.

[26] *Cf.* its decrees of June 2, and October 30, 1847, in Pribram's *Urkunden,* vol. ii, p. 529.

[27] *Cf.* Charmatz, Richard, *Adolf Fischhof* (Stuttgart 1910), p. 65; von Helfert, Joseph Alexander, "Die konfessionelle Frage in Österreich 1848," in *Österreichisches Jahrbuch,* vol. vi (1882), p. 138; Frank, L. A., *Erinnernungen,* ed. by Stefan Hock (Prague 1910); Wolbe, E., *Ludwig August Frankl, der Dichter und Menschenfreund* (Frankfurt 1910), pp. 67 f. "Fischhof's position in [Austria's] political world," comments Heinrich Friedjung, "is insofar especially remarkable as he occupied a parliamentary seat only in 1848–49, but later served neither as deputy nor as member of the administration. Yet, because of the weight of his personality, his voice was always listened to attentively." *Cf.* his *Historische Aufsätze* (Stuttgart 1919), pp. 363 f.

[28]Mannheimer's address was particularly impressive "because of its precision and clarity," according to one of the "Geheimberichte aus den Märztagen," in *Österreichische Rundschau,* vol. xiv (1908), p. 464. It is still uncertain whether Fischhof in his famous keynote speech of March 13 actually demanded full equality for all denominations. He certainly intended to do so, even if the transcript seems to have omitted this passage. *Cf.* his letter to the *Wiener Zeitung,* the latter's editorial comment and that by Saphir in his *Humorist* reported in *Orient,* vol. ix, p. 111; and Charmatz, *Fischhof,* p. 277.

[29] According to Heinrich Silbergleit, there were 9,595 Jews among the 412,154 inhabitants of Berlin in 1849 or 2.33 percent. *Cf.* his *Die Bevölkerungs- und Berufsverhältnisse der Juden im Deutschen Reich,* vol. i (Berlin 1930), p. 25. It may be noted that the success of the revolution and the consequent freedom of movement did not produce an immediate sudden increase in this small ratio.

[30] Although Jacoby did not continue with his public espousal of Jewish emancipation begun in 1833–34 with his *Zur Kenntniss der jüdischen Verhältnisse* (Halle 1834) (which included a reply to Karl Streckfuss's much-debated pamphlet, *Über das Verhältniss der Juden zu den christlichen Staaten*), his stand in this matter was unequivocal. *Cf.* his *Gesammelte Schriften und Reden,* 2 vols. (Hamburg 1872–77), vol. i, pp. 4 ff.; and Adam, R., "Johann Jacoby's politischer Werdegang, 1805–40," in *Historische Zeitschrift,* vol. cxliii (1931), pp. 48–76 (including an unpublished letter to Riesser of Sept. 29, 1832). Kosch,

who in 1848 allegedly failed to become Prussian minister of cults only because of his Jewish faith, likewise defended Jewish rights as a part of his liberal program. He was later particularly influential in removing the special Jewish oath, a frequent residuum of pre-emancipatory discrimination. *Cf. Orient,* vol. ix, pp. 243 f. and J. Bamberg's obituary *Rede bei dem Trauergottesdienst für Dr. Raphael Kosch am 4. April 1872* (Königsberg 1872), p. 8. *Cf.* also Schay, R., *Juden in der deutschen Politik* (Berlin 1929), p. 140 ff., 145 n. 1. If we may trust the report in *Archives israélites,* vol. x, p. 159, though neither source nor method of computation is indicated, the Jews numbered one-seventeenth among Prussia's electors, as against but one-fortieth in the population. While such disproportion may largely be accounted for by their higher ratio in the urban and taxpaying population, it would nevertheless illustrate their active participation in the elections. Among Jewish parliamentarians in other German states one need refer only to the lawyers Fischel Arnheim and David Morgenstern elected in 1848 to the Bavarian Diet. Contrary to Jewish expectations, the former was constantly reelected by his almost wholly non-Jewish constituency until his death in 1864. *Cf. Der Israelit,* vol. ix (1848), p. 160; Eckstein, A., *Beiträge zur Geschichte der Juden in Bayern,* vol. i: *Die bayerischen Parlamentarier jüdischen Glaubens* (Bamberg 1902).

[31] Schay, *op. cit.,* pp. 171 ff. Stahl had just published, with reference to the extensive debates on the Jewish question at Prussia's "Vereinigter Landtag," a study of *Der christliche Staat und sein Verhältniss zu Deismus and Judenthum* (Berlin 1847). Here he contended that the Jewish people was so wrapped up in its religious mission that it was devoid of such "ethical impulses springing from man independently of God as honor, self-assertion, manly defiance in behalf of one's rights and beauty of manner which, particularly honor, are the natural foundation of the Germanic tribe." *Cf.* the debate thereon in the contemporary press mentioned in *Der Israelit,* vol. viii (1847), p. 391; Samuel Holdheim's later attack, *Stahls christliche Toleranz beleuchtet* (Berlin 1856) and, more generally, Margarete Dierks's *Die preussischen Altkonservativen und die Judenfrage 1810–1847* (Rostock 1939), pp. 133 ff., 156 ff.

[32] *Cf.* Hartmann's letter to Dr. Thomas Landa of May 1, 1848, in his *Briefe,* selected by Rudolf Wolkan (Vienna 1921), pp. 29 f.; Koppen, W., *1848 das Jahr der Warnung und grossdeutschen Mahnung* (Leipzig 1939), p. 37; Gabriel Riesser's *Gesammelte Schriften,* ed. by M. Isler, 4 vols. (Frankfurt 1867–68) includes a full-length biography by the editor; Friedländer, F., *Das Leben Gabriel Riessers* (Berlin 1926). *Cf.* also M. Veit's "Dem Andenken G. Riessers," in *Preussische Jahrbücher,* vol. xi (1863), pp 516–32; *Orient,* vol. x, p. 70 (listing the Jewish members of the German, Prussian and Austrian parliamentary bodies and their party allegiance), and, more generally, Rosenbaum, L., *Beruf und Herkunft der Abgeordneten zu den deutschen und preussischen Parlamenten von 1847–1919* (Frankfurt 1923).

[33] Bamberger, *Gesammelte Schriften,* 5 vols. (Berlin 1894–98), vol. iii, p. 44.

Nine of Bamberger's twenty-seven editorials are here reprinted; also his reminiscences of the uprising in the Palatinate. *Cf.* also the comment on the "arch-revolutionary" Bamberger quoted from the *Deutsche Allgemeine Zeitung* by A. Jellinek in *Orient*, vol. ix, p. 185. On Lasker, *cf.* L. Bamberger's obituary address, *Eduard Lasker* (Leipzig 1884) and Paul Wentzke's "Aus Eduard Laskers sozialistischen Anfängen," in *Archiv für Geschichte des Sozialismus*, vol. xi (1925), pp. 207–14. *Cf.* also the large number of Jewish names listed among the participants at the two Democratic Congresses by Lüders, *op. cit.*, pp. 137 ff., 164 ff.

[34] Among H. Jellinek's writings the following are of particular interest to our subject: *Uriel Acosta* (Zerbst 1847); *Die religiösen, socialen und literarischen Zustände der Gegenwart. In ihren praktischen Folgen untersucht* (Zerbst 1847); *Die Täuschungen der aufgeklärten Juden und ihre Fähigkeit zur Emancipation* (Zerbst 1847); *Kritische Geschichte der Wiener Revolution vom 13. März bis zum constituirenden Reichstag* (Vienna 1848); *Kritischer Sprechsaal für die Hauptfragen der österreichischen Politik*, 3 pts. (Vienna 1848). A critical analysis of the views of this forgotten radical pioneer and particularly of his agitation for a "democratic," rather than "constitutional," monarchy would still seem meritorious today. *Cf.* the interesting description of one of his campaign speeches and replies to a heckler quoted from the *Democrat* in *Orient*, vol. ix, p. 231. His execution on Nov. 23, 1848, shortly before his twenty-sixth birthday, as well as some earlier events are extensively reported *ibid.*, p. 389, 398 ff. *Cf.* also Moritz Hartmann's moving description in *Reimchronik des Pfaffen Maurizius* (Frankfurt 1849), p. 26 ff.; *idem., Revolutionäre Erinnerungen*, ed. by H. H. Hauben (Leipzig 1919), p. 71 f.; and Maximilian Bach's *Geschichte der Wiener Revolution im Jahre 1848* (Vienna 1898), pp. 854 f. On Hess, *cf.* especially Theodor Zlocisti's biography, *Moses Hess, der Vorkämpfer des Sozialismus und Zionismus, 1812–1875*, 2nd ed. (Berlin 1921), p. 244 ff.; and Irma Goitein's *Probleme der Gesellschaft und des Staates bei Moses Hess* (Leipzig 1931).

[35] *Cf.* Auerbach's *Briefe an seinen Freund Jakob Auerbach*, ed. by the latter (Frankfurt 1884), p. 66; and Eduard Lasker's memorial address, *Berthold Auerbach* (Berlin 1882), p. 18. Of course, like every other mass movement, the revolution attracted also less idealistic elements. Among the Vienna radicals there appeared an influential, though unscrupulous agitator, Avrum Chaizes *alias* Dr. Adolf Chaises or Chassé, exaggeratedly called the "Marat of the Vienna Revolution" in Heinrich Ritter von Srbik's highly colored description of these events in "Die Wiener Revolution des Jahres 1848 in sozialgeschichtlicher Beleuchtung," in *Schmollers Jahrbuch für Gesetzgebung*, vol. xliii (1919), pp. 54 f.

[36] *Lord George Bentinck*, p. 358. *Cf.*, e. g., Mazzini's introduction of Revere as a representative of the Assoziazione nazionale italiana, dated Aug. 3, 1848 in his *Scritti editi ed inediti*, Edizione nazionale, vol. xxxv (Imola 1922), pp.

267 f.; and Revere's own *Opere complete* with a preface by Alberto Rondani, 4 vols. (Rome 1896–98). *Cf.* also Levi, A., "Amici israeliti di Giuseppe Mazzini," in *Rassegna mensile di Israel,* vol. v. (1930–31), pp. 587–612.

[37] *Jewish Chronicle,* vol. vi, pp. 230, 271. *Cf.* also such contemporary news items as appeared in *Orient,* vol. ix, pp. 85 f., 144, 204 f.; *Archives israélites,* vol. ix, p. 626, etc.; Loevinson in *Rassegna storica del Risorgimento,* vol. xvi, pp. 801 f. (naming various Jews serving in Rome's armed forces); and *idem,* "Gli Ebrei dello Stato della Chiesa nel periodo del Risorgimento politico d'Italia," in *Rassegna mensile di Israel,* vols. viii–xii.

[38] *Cf.* Schwarzfeld, M., Rumanian essays on "The Revolutionary Leaders of 1848 Saved from Death by a Jew," in *Annuar pentru Israeliti,* vol. viii (1885–86), pp. 155–57; "Constantin Daniil Rosenthal," *ibid.,* pp. 157–59; and "Davicion Bally," *ibid.,* vol. ix (1886–87), pp. 1–29. I. Massoff's *Davicion Bally —Revolutionarol dela 48* (Davicion Bally, a Revolutionary of 1848) (Bucharest 1938) was not available to me.

[39] *Jewish Chronicle,* vol. vi, pp. 125 f. (Jan. 25, 1850).

[40] Jacoby's letter to Alexander Küntzel of May 12, 1837, published by Gustav Mayer in his "Liberales Judentum im Vormärz," *Der Jude,* vol. i (1916–17), p. 676, reprinted in Franz Kobler's *Jüdische Geschichte in Briefen aus drei Jahrhunderten* (Vienna 1938), p. 39; *Österreichisches Central-Organ für Glaubensfreiheit,* no. 1, Appendix; Rosenmann, *Mannheimer,* pp. 143 f.; Anau, *Della emancipazione degli Ebrei* (Florence 1847), reprinting the letters in *Patria; idem, Schiarimenti sulle sue lettere per la emancipazione degli Ebrei* (Florence 1848), a reply to Carpi; and Carpi, *Alcune parole sugli Israeliti, in occasione d'un decreto pontificio d'interdizione* (Florence 1847).

[41] Rosenmann, *Mannheimer,* pp. 146 ff. *Cf. Österreichisches Central-Organ für Glaubensfreiheit,* pp. 1 f., 14. According to a secret report of March 20, the mass petition found considerable support among all non-Catholics, but failed to attract the interest of the Catholic majority. *Cf. Österreichische Rundschau,* vol. xiv, p. 467. Soon Mannheimer himself appeared too radical to the Vienna elders, for as member of parliament he joined the moderate Left. They entrusted, therefore, to their secretary, L. A. Frankl, the unwelcome task of "advising" their rabbi to the point of drafting his speeches. *Cf.* Frankl's letter to A. Frankl-Grün of April 4, 1892, published by the latter in *Allgemeine Zeitung des Judentums,* vol. lxxiv (1910), pp. 57 f.

[42] Wolf, G., *Joseph Wertheimer* (Vienna 1868), pp. 71 f.; Frankl-Grün, *Kremsier,* vol. i, pp. 124 f., 184 f. The latter's doubts about the ultimate outcome, in the face of Fischhof's positive assurances in a private letter, seem little justified by general considerations.

[43] Charmatz, *Fischhof,* p. 95.

[44] *Orient,* vol. ix, p. 374 (dated November 16, 1948). Three days earlier an editorial writer in that journal stated no less succinctly, "The Jew stands and falls with democracy." *Ibid.,* pp. 374 f.

⁴⁵ In its critique of Louis Napoleon, Proudhon's *Le Peuple*, referring to the Rothschild influence under Louis Philippe and that of Fould under the new regime, acidly commented that France had merely changed its Jews. *Cf. Archives israélites*, vol. x, p. 180. *Cf.* also Silberner, E., "Proudhon's Judeophobia," in *Historia Judaica*, vol. x (1948), pp. 61–80; *idem*, "Charles Fourier and the Jewish Question," in JEWISH SOCIAL STUDIES, vol. viii (1946), pp. 245–66; *idem*, "The Attitude of the Fourierist School towards the Jews," *ibid.*, vol. ix (1947), 339–62; and Szajkowski, "The Jewish Saint-Simonians and Socialist Antisemites in France," *ibid.*, pp. 33–60.

⁴⁶ Feuerbach, *Das Wesen des Christentums*, 2d ed. (Leipzig 1848), p. 169; Dingelstedt, *Lieder eines kosmopolitischen Nachtwächters*, vol. i (Hamburg 1842), pp. 59 f. (or in *Sämmtliche Werke*, 12 vols., Berlin, 1877, vol. viii, p. 51). Curiously, Dingelstedt intended to dedicate this poem to Heinrich Heine, to whose poetry he was deeply indebted. *Cf.* Sperling, H., *Franz Dingelstedt's Lyrik auf ihre Quellen und Vorbilder untersucht* (Münster 1927), pp. 34 ff. *See also* Marx, "On the Jewish Question," in *Selected Essays*, English transl. (London 1926), pp. 40–97; Hoyer, K., "Beitrag zur Judenfrage in Deutschland, II (1830–1848)," in *Deutschlands Erneuerung*, vol. xvii (1933), pp. 257–65. If a year before his attack on Bruno Bauer's *Judenfrage* Marx had promised a Jewish elder of Cologne to submit a petition to the diet in behalf of Jewish rights, he immediately expostulated (in a letter to Arnold Ruge of March 13, 1843) that he did it only because "every petition rejected increases the bitterness" of the public. *Cf.* his and Engels' works, *Historisch-kritische Gesammtausgabe*, ed. by D. Rjazanov (Berlin 1929 ff.), vol. i, pt. 2, p. 308. The revived *Neue Rheinische Zeitung*, which appeared under Marx's editorship in 1848–49, likewise carried many unfriendly news items and editorials. *Cf.* the attacks thereon in *Orient*, vol. x, pp. 1 f., and, more generally, Mayer, C., "Early German Socialism and Jewish Emancipation," in JEWISH SOCIAL STUDIES, vol. i (1939), pp. 409–22; Bloom, Solomon F., "Karl Marx and the Jews," *ibid.*, vol. iv (1942), pp. 3–16; and Silberner, Edmund, "Was Marx an Antisemite?", in *Historia Judaica*, vol. xi (1949), pp. 3–52. Ruge himself, before and after his controversy with Marx, shared some such anti-Jewish sentiments. Early in 1848 he did not hesitate to attack publicly the *"Knoblauchfresser"* (garlic-eater) Kuranda. *Cf. Orient*, vol. ix, p. 91.

⁴⁷ Saboul, Albert, "La Question paysanne en 1848," in *La Pensée*, n. s. pt. 19 (July-Aug. 1948) 33; *Jewish Intelligence*, vol. xiv (1848), pp. 243 ff.; Vidal, A., "Encore sur l'acquittement des accusés dans les troubles de l'Alsace," in *Archives israélites*, vol. ix, p. 466. These outbreaks were extensively reported in the press, Jewish and non-Jewish. Some additional documents were published by M. Ginsburger in "Les troubles contres les Juifs d'Alsace en 1848," in *Revue des études juives*, vol. lxiv (1912), pp. 109–17; Pouteil, F., *L'opposition politique à Strasbourg sous la Monarchie du Juillet 1830–48* (Paris 1932), pp. 899 ff. *Cf.* also, in general, Paul Muller's *La Révolution de 1848 en Alsace*

(Paris 1912) for the political aspects, and on the economic background, Marie-Madeleine Kahan-Rabecq's *La classe ouvrière en Alsace pendant la Monarchie de Juillet* (Paris 1939), especially, pp. 78 f., 390.

⁴⁸ Valentin, V., *Geschichte der deutschen Revolution von 1848–49*, 2 vols. (Berlin 1930–31), vol. i, pp. 344 f., 592; Wolf, *Wertheimer*, p. 69; Von Helfert, *Geschichte der österreichischen Revolution*, 2 vols. (Freiburg 1907–1909) vol. i, pp. 313 f., 442; *idem*, in *Österreichisches Jahrbuch*, vol. vi, pp. 106 ff.; Charmatz, *Fischhof*, p. 278; Bach, *Wiener Revolution*, p. 126; Eckstein, *Beiträge*, vol. i, p. 10; *Archives israélites*, vol. x, p. 679; *Orient*, vol. ix, p. 167 (citing the Rome correspondence to the *Deutsche Allgemeine Zeitung* dated April 29, 1848). Needless to say that some representatives of the traditionally anti-Jewish feudal classes joined the parade. In the Hungarian upper house, Count Berengi suggested that the diet cancel all past and future debts owed by Christians to Jews and that the latter be taxed in addition 10,000,000 florins needed for road building. According to the Pressburg correspondent of the *Orient* (vol. ix, p. 143), the Count himself was indebted to Jewish firms to the tune of 70,000 thalers. In the arch-Catholic province of the Vendée the appointment of Isidore Cahen as teacher of philosophy at a local lyceum had to be cancelled at the insistence of the Catholic bishop and press. *Cf. Archives israélites*, vol. x, pp. 557 f., 621 ff. More farsighted citizens, on the other hand, soon realized the dangers inherent in the uncontrolled fury of popular fanaticism. "Do you believe," the mayor of Prague asked the leading townsmen, "that, once having finished with the Jews, the excited populace would not covet also the money bags of burghers and nobles?" Reported by Amalie Taubels in a letter to her sister in Kobler's *Jüdische Geschichte*, p. 67. The more lackadaisical Pressburg municipal authorities were sharply called to account by the Minister of Interior. *Cf. Orient*, vol. ix, p. 159.

⁴⁹ Bettelheim, *Auerbach*, p. 212; "Die Judenverfolgung und die Judensache," in *Österreichisches Central-Organ für Glaubensfreiheit*, pp. 78 ff.

⁵⁰ Vol. xiv (1848), pp. 217 f. Referring to the Swiss expulsion of Jews another writer in the same journal pointed out that, although more humane than the neighboring Alsatians, "the Swiss government have added their mite towards the fulfillment of the prophecies fortelling Israel's outcast state among the nations, despised and contemned, a proverb and a byword to all men." *Ibid.*, p. 244.

⁵¹ *Archives israélites*, vol. ix, pp. 185 f.; x, 181 f. In its appeal to the burghers for toleration the new *Österreichische Konstitutionelle Deutsche Zeitung* declared, "Not the Christian is intolerant now, but the cobbler, tailor or glovemaker. This intolerance of cobblers, tailors and glovemakers has called forth scenes, before which the constitutionally-minded citizen must hide his face in shame." This appeal was reprinted in *Orient*, vol. ix, p. 135.

⁵² *Stenographischer Bericht über die Verhandlungen der deutschen constituirenden Nationalversammlung zu Frankfurt am Main*, ed. by Franz Wigard, vol. iii, pp. 1754 ff. No such anti-Jewish amendment seems to have been

submitted to the Committee on Constitutional Affairs. In the course of its lengthy deliberations Rev. Karl Jürgens once raised the question of Jewish national rather than religious disparity and generally warned against overhasty emancipation, but he did not suggest any constitutional remedy. *Cf.* Droysen, J. G., *Die Verhandlungen des Verfassungsausschusses der deutschen National-versammlung* (Leipzig 1849), pp. 8 f.

53 Wigard's *Stenogr. Bericht*, vol. iii, pp. 1755 ff. *Cf.* also Riesser's *Gesammelte Schriften*, vol. i, pp. 418 ff.; vol. iv, pp. 403 ff.; Strauss, H. A., *op. cit.*, pp. 112 ff.

54 *Archives israélites*, vol. ix, pp. 341, 345, 535 f. (includes extracts from Franck's "Le communisme et l'histoire," published in *Liberté de Penser;* it was subsequently reprinted in an enlarged 2d ed., entitled *Le communisme jugé par l'histoire*, Paris, 1849); *Orient*, vol. ix, pp. 361 f. (reprinting Saalschütz's essay, "Die Republik und die Juden," from the Königsberg *Staats-, Kriegs- und Friedenszeitung);* Disraeli, *Lord Bentinck*, p. 357. *Cf.* also Kaulla, R., *Der Liberalismus and die Juden. Das Judentum als konservatives Element* (Munich 1928).

55 In his essay "Über Emanzipation der Juden" in the *Leipziger Tageblatt* of May 12, 1848 (reproduced in *Orient*, vol. ix, pp. 169 f.) A. Fecht had already occasion to argue against such invidious distinctions with respect to immigration. Some Saxon friends of emancipation were ready to grant equality to the few Jewish natives of Saxony, but to discriminate against "alien" Jews, including such as came from other German states. On socialist attitudes *cf.* e. g., R. F. Byrnes, "Edouard Drumont and *La France Juive*," in JEWISH SOCIAL STUDIES, vol. x (1948), pp. 181 f.; *idem*, "Antisemitism in France before the Dreyfus Affair," *ibid.*, vol. xi (1949), 49–68; Szajkowski, "Socialists and Radicals in the Development of Antisemitism in Algeria (1884–1900)," *ibid.*, pp. 257–80; and above n. 46.

56 Berliner's appeal of July 1848 was published in *Orient*, vol. ix, p. 246. *Cf. ibid.*, p. 283. On the Brody society and Fischhof's memorandum of 1851, *cf. Jewish Chronicle*, vol. vi, p. 382 and Charmatz, *Fischhof*, pp. 79 ff. *Cf.* also the data assembled by R. in "L'agriculture parmi les israélites," in *Archives israélites*, vol. x, pp. 469–73.

57 *Archives israélites*, vol. ix, p. 386; *Österreichisches Central-Organ für Glaubensfreiheit*, nos. 6–8, 10–12, 15–16, etc. Many of the latter articles have been reprinted with an explanatory introduction by Guido Kisch in "The Revolution of 1848 and the Jewish 'On to America' Movement," in *Publications of the American Jewish Historical Society*, vol. xxxviii (1948–49), pp. 185–234. Unfortunately we possess reliable information on neither the number of Jews who left Germany and Austria, nor that of Jewish arrivals in the United States in each of the years from 1816 to 1870. *Cf.* the meagre data assembled by Max J. Kohler in "The German Jewish Migration to America," *ibid.*, vol. ix (1901), pp. 87–105; and by Rudolf Glanz in "The Immigration of German Jews up to 1880," in *Yivo Annual*, vols. ii–iii (1947–48), pp. 81–99. The difficulties are

further aggravated by the unreliability of even the official statistics concerning the general emigration from Germany, as is rightly stressed, *e. g.,* by Alexis Markow in *Das Wachstum der Bevölkerung und die Entwickelung der Aus- und Einwanderungen . . . in Preussen* (Tübingen 1889), pp. 137 f., 149 ff. It would seem, however, that Jewish emigration increased, rather than decreased, in the immediate post-revolutionary years, particularly on account of the new tensions in the province of Posen. Very likely, too, fewer Jewish than non-Jewish emigrés returned to Germany in later years. Joseph Goldmark, for one example, was so attached to his home country that, in 1868, he went back to stand trial, in order to clear his name from the 1849 condemnation for high treason. But he speedily returned to America where his family was to play a very significant role. *Cf.* Goldmark, *Pilgrims of '48,* pp. 272 ff. The entire problem of Jewish migrations and restratification in 1848–49, for which only brief hints could be given here, would deserve monographic treatment.

[58] Wigard's *Stenographischer Bericht,* vol. iii, pp. 1754 f. Mohl must have been aware, however, that he was merely echoing the much-debated arguments voiced by such Prussian arch-conservatives as the Ministers Von Thile and Von Bodelschwingh during the protracted debates at the Prussian Diet in 1847.

[59] *Ibid.,* pp. 1755 ff., 1758. On the earlier developments *cf.,* especially, Offenburg, B., *Das Erwachen des deutschen Nationalbewusstseins in der preussichen Judenheit (von Moses Mendelssohn bis zum Beginn der Reaktion)* (Hamburg 1933).

[60] Frankl-Grün, *Kremsier,* vol. i, p. 183. Similar views were often expressed by the liberal Jewish press. The *Reform-Zeitung,* for instance, contrasted the attitudes of Poles and Jews, the two groups which were to be lumped together by Prussian conservatives as mainly responsible for the March "disorders." Unlike the Poles, the paper declared, the majority of whom worked hard for the reestablishment of an independent Poland, not even ten percent of the Jewish people dreamed of Zion as their fatherland, and hardly an arm would be raised for the restoration of the Jewish state. *Cf.* the summary in *Archives israélites,* vol. ix, pp. 114 f. (this issue of the *Reform-Zeitung* could not be consulted by me.)

[61] Address of December 23, 1789 reproduced in *Revue des grandes journées parlementaires,* ed. by Gaston Lèbre and G. Lebouchère, vol. i (1897), p. 10.

[62] Holdheim, "Die Revolution von 1848," in *Der Israelit,* vol. ix (1848), p. 123 (*cf.* also *ibid.,* p. 142); Wigard, *Stenographischer Bericht,* vol. iv, pp. 1242 ff.; Appens, W., *Die Nationalversammlung zu Frankfurt a/M, 1848–49* (Jena 1920), pp. 88 f., 112, 114; *Archives israélites,* vol. ix, p. 115. *Cf.* also von Voigt-Rhetz, C., *Aktenmässige Darstellung der polnischen Insurrektion 1848* (Posen 1848) (not available to me); Schmidt, H., *Die polnische Revolution des Jahres 1848 im Grossherzogtum Posen* (Weimer 1912); and more generally, Buzek, J., *Historia polityki narodowościowej rządu pruskiego wobec Polaków* (A History of the Prussian Government's National Policies toward the Poles,

1816–1908) (Lwów 1909) and Perdelwitz, E. R., *Die Posener Polen 1815–1914. Ein Jahrhundert grosspolnischer Ideengeschichte* (Schneidemühl 1936), pp. 23 ff., 42 ff.

[63] These events, reported with much exaggeration and bias in the contemporary press, would merit monographic treatment. Their memory continued to envenom Polish-Jewish relations in Posen and elsewhere, particularly as the Germanizing efforts of the Prussian administration grew more intensive and systematic. Even the extremely nationalistic and essentially antisemitic organizers of the notorious H-K-T Society (named after the initials of its three founders) at the end of the century realized that promotion of German culture depended far more on the attitude of native Jews than on the ever-fluctuating German bureaucracy and army. On Jan. 9, 1895, Christoph von Tiedemann informed a high Prussian official, Hesekiel, that his society did not refuse admission to Jewish applicants for "by joining us the Jew of our province declared himself a German and exposes himself to the danger of the Polish commercial boycott. To reject him would be injurious to the German cause." *Cf.* the letter published by F. S. Krysiak in his *Hinter den Kulissen des Ostmarken-Vereins* (Posen 1913), p. 54 f.; Tims, R. W., *Germanizing Prussian Poland: The H-K-T Society and the Struggle for the Eastern Provinces, 1894–1910* (New York 1941) *passim*. It is not surprising that in the tense anti-Jewish atmosphere of independent Poland after 1918 an official commission appointed by the city of Posen to prepare a jubilee volume on the tenth anniversary of the liberated municipal administration could make the wholly unsubstantiated claim that in 1848 the Jews had "persecuted the Polish revolutionaries with far greater violence that the German soldiery and, through their instigations, greatly contributed to the exacerbation of Polish-German relations." *Cf. Księga pamiatkowa miasta Poznania*, ed. by Sylwester Pazderski, *et al.* (Posen 1929), p. 81 f.

[64] Von Bergmann, E., *Zur Geschichte der Entwicklung deutscher, polnischer und jüdischer Bevölkerung in der Provinz Posen seit 1824* (Tübingen 1883), pp. 27 f.; Heppner, A., and Herzberg, J., *Aus Vergangenheit und Gegenwart der Juden und der jüd. Germeinden in den Posener Landen* (Koschmin-Bromberg 1909), pp. 5, 267 and *passim*. *Cf.* the more detailed figures for each decade from 1825–1925 given by Silbergleit, *op. cit.*, pp. 18x–19x. In the city of Posen itself the Jewish ratio dropped from 20.5 percent in 1832 to 15 percent in 1867 and to only 4 percent in 1905, according to Moritz Jaffe in *Die Stadt Posen unter preussischer Herrschaft* (Berlin 1909), pp. 150 n. 2, 411 n. 1. *Cf.* also the memorandum submitted, in behalf of the "Verband der deutschen Juden," by Bernhard Breslauer, *Die Abwanderung der Juden aus der Provinz Posen* (Berlin 1909).

[65] *Archives israélites*, vol. ix, pp. 288 f., 385; Friedmann, *Die galizischen Juden*, pp. 58 f.; Oberländer, L., "Jewish Aspects of Adam Mickiewicz' Thought" (Polish) in *Miesiecznik żydowski*, vol. ii, pt. 1 (1932), pp. 467–74.

Cf. also, with respect to a somewhat later episode Roman Brandstätter's well-documented study of "Adam Mickiewicz's Jewish Legion" (Polish), *ibid.*, pp. 20–45, 112–32, 225–48. The Polish publicist, Jean Czyński, started in 1848 his short-lived magazine dedicated to *Le Reveil d'Israël. Cf.* also his "Les Israélites français et polonais," in *Archives israélites*, vol. ix, pp. 355–61; Cahen's open letter to Czyński, "Les Israélites de Pologne," *ibid.*, pp. 301 ff.; the imaginary "Dialogue between a Polish Jew and a Christian in England," in *Jewish Chronicle*, vol. v, pp. 366 f., 383; vol. vi, pp. 19, 26 f., and, especially the comprehensive study of *The Polish Emigration and the Jews, 1831–1863*, now being prepared by Abraham G. Duker.

[66] *Orient*, vol. ix, pp. 172 f., 181, etc. According to the Lwów correspondence of June 9, 1848 to the *Österreichisches Central-Organ für Glaubensfreiheit* (pp. 182 f.), the Polish National Council requested from the local rabbi a letter to Posen asking Jews to abstain from attacking the Poles. The rabbi promised to do so, but implored the Council in turn to use its good offices in reducing the hostility of the Posen Poles toward their Jewish compatriots. The Posen Jews, on their part, were said to have expressed doubts about the possibility of such reconciliation, but blamed all the existing tensions on the violence of Polish insurgents.

[67] Einhorn, J., *Die Revolution und die Juden in Ungarn* (Leipzig 1851), p. 116; *Jewish Chronicle*, vol. vi, pp. 15 f. *Cf. ibid.*, vol. v, p. 340; vol. vi, pp. 23, 39, 62, 77 f., 122 f., 239, 263, 297 f., 341 f., 345 f. Pathetic "Gefühle eines jüdischen Freiwilligen," written Sept. 21, 1848, appeared in *Orient*, vol. ix, p. 341. What comfort, he asked, were his parents to derive were he to fall in the field of battle? "He died for the fatherland!—but not for his fatherland, but for a country in which he was a slave!" *Cf.* also "Pressburger Briefe eines Rabbinatskandidaten [Salomon Pollak] aus dem Jahre 1848," ed. by Bernhard Wachstein in *B'nai B'rith Mitteilungen für Österreich*, vol. xxx (1930), pp. 1–9, 109–21. *Cf.* also *Orient*, vol. ix, pp. 119, 172, 215 f.

[68] Einhorn, *Revolution*, p. 35. A Vienna correspondence to the *Orient* (vol. ix, p. 365) dated Oct. 20, 1848, well illustrates the prevailing political myopia of central-European Jewry. Four weeks before, the readers of the Leipzig weekly were informed, 600 volunteers, including many liberty-loving Jewish young men, left Vienna "in order to fight for Hungary, for its liberty and against the Slavs."

[69] *Österreichisches Central-Organ für Glaubensfreiheit*, p. 196. *Cf.* also the text of an interesting Easter message of the Prague archbishop (dated April 23, 1848), *ibid.*, p. 72. In warning all faithful Catholics against participating in any anti-Jewish riots the archbishop wished doubly to emphasize the fact that these outrages had not been the effect of *religious* fanaticism.

[70] Russian and Slavophil influences on the Czech national movement increased Czech resentment against the pro-German and pro-Magyar attitude of most Jewish subjects of the Habsburg monarchy. Combined with the economic

crisis it added stimulus to Jewish emigration from Bohemia and Moravia which now assumed mass proportions. *Cf.* Alfred Fischel's edition of the *Protokolle des Verfassungsausschusses über die Grundrechte. Ein Beitrag zur Geschichte des österreichischen Reichstages vom Jahre 1848* (Vienna 1912), pp. 126 f.; M. Hartmann's graphic description of the early attacks on the Jews in Prague in his *Revolutionäre Erinnerungen*, p. 24 ff.; *Orient*, vol. ix, pp. 221, 314 f., 337, 344, 345, 366, 387, 409, etc.; and, more generally, Arnost Klima's *Rok 1848 v Čechach* (The Year 1848 in Bohemia) (Prague 1948), not available; and Guido Kisch's *In Search of Freedom: A History of American Jews from Czechoslovakia* (London 1949).

71 *Cf.* above notes 36–37.

72 *Briefe an Jakob Auerbach*, vol. i, p. 407; my *Modern Nationalism and Religion* (New York 1947), pp. 92, 294, n. 6.

73 Bach, *Wiener Revolution*, p. 880; Hugelmann, K. G., ed., *Das Nationalitätenrecht des alten Österreich* (Vienna 1934), pp. 40 f.; Pribram, *Urkunden*, vol. ii, p. 549; *Orient*, vol. x, p. 81; Fouques-Duparc, *La protection des minorités de race, de langue et de religion* (Paris 1922), p. 44. *Cf.* Geist-Lanyi, P., *Das Nationalitätenproblem auf dem Reichstag zu Kremsier 1848 bis 1849* (Munich 1920), pp. 153 ff.

74 Charmatz, *Fischhof*, p. 19; Friedjung, *Historische Aufsätze*, pp. 363 ff.; and, particularly, Redlich, J., *Das österreichische Staats- und Reichsproblem*, 2 vols. (Leipzig 1920–26), vol. i, pp. 221 ff.

75 *Cf.*, in particular Kann, Robert, *The Multinational Empire: Nationalism and National Reform in the Habsburg Monarchy*, 1848–1918 (New York 1950 [1964]), vol. 2, *Empire Reform*.

76 *Orient*, vol. ix, p. 209. *Cf.* my *Social and Religious History*, vol. ii, p. 262 ff.; vol. iii, p. 153 ff.; and *Modern Nationalism and Religion*, pp. 213 ff., 335 ff.; as well as the extensive literature cited there.

77 *Occident*, vol. vi (1848–49), pp. 61 ff., 71 f.; *Archives israélites*, vol. x, 150 f., 293, 430.

78 Hartmann, *Reimchronik des Pfaffen Maurizius*, c. IV, pp. 198 f.; *Orient* vol. x, p. 5; Ehrenreich, M., "Ein Wort über das hebräische Sprachstudium," in *Österreichisches Central-Organ für Glaubensfreiheit*, p. 149–51; Szanto, "Wappen und Farben," *ibid.*, p. 408; Hess, *Rom und Jerusalem, die letzte Nationalitätenfrage* (Leipzig 1862) (also in English transl., New York, 1918, etc.). *Cf.* also such poetic utterances as Ludwig Wihl's *West-östliche Schwalben* (Mannheim 1847), whose main theme, to cite a contemporary reviewer, was concerned with the basic question raised at the Prussian Diet, "How far can an Israelite go in praising Palestine as his original homeland and cherishing his ancient national memories, without denying his new fatherland and betraying the state whose citizen he is?" *Cf.* Heinrich Bihr's review in *Der Israelit*, vol. viii (1847), p. 337. *Cf.* also *ibid.*, pp. 236 f.; vol. ix (1848), p. 167. Two years before Hess's appeal, Napoleon III allegedly conceived the fantastic plan

of crowning Rothschild king of Jerusalem. *Cf.* Isaac M. Wise's caustic comment in the *American Israelite* of Aug. 31, 1860. Less concerned with the implications of Jewish restoration to Palestine for the struggle for Jewish emancipation, the Christian world of the 1840's could view far more calmly the Palestine problem. *Cf.* the extensive materials assembled in Nahum Sokolow's *History of Zionism,* 2 vols. (London 1918); N. M. Gelber's *Zur Vorgeschichte des Zionismus* (to 1845) (Vienna 1927).

EDITORS' PREFACE

Emancipation of the Jews of Italy

The ups and downs of Jewish equality in Italy can serve as fairly convincing illustrations in support of the cyclical theories of Jewish Emancipation, namely, that it advances with the progress of democracy and recedes with reaction's return, leading to what became virtually an act of faith in the inevitable and non-too-distant victory of equality and freedom. The simple formula and assumptions, generally accepted in the nineteenth century and during the earlier decades of the twentieth, appeared to be plausible until antisemitism's ultimate racist stage when Jew-hatred became the most appealing and ruling ideology in much of Europe. Counter-Emancipation was then the policy of state in many countries. Alas, most European Jews did not live to reap any benefit from Emancipation's seemingly solid restoration after the victory over nazism in 1945.

The Jewish people continues to be the scapegoat in power politics in the 1970s. Anti-Jewish propaganda has become state policy of some "socialist" countries, masked by a drive ostensibly aimed against Zionism and Israel only. Obvious is the substitution of the alleged leftist anti-capitalist Jewish plot for world domination of the Elders of Zion by the libel of a world-wide Jewish anti-communist conspiracy for the restoration of capitalism and the spread of colonialism and imperialism. Promoters of both versions, atheists, Moslems, and Christians, are pressing the war against the survival of the Jewish people, the latest phase of post-war Counter-Emancipation, with the State of Israel, the center of Jewish continuity, as their main target.

Viewed in this light, the history of Emancipation and Counter-Emancipation in Italy is a minor theme. However, Rossi's article is a splendid case record for the study of the political and legal aspects of this historical conflict in modern times. Jewish Emancipation was introduced in Italy by the French revolutionary army during its victorious march across the peninsula that began in 1796. In many cities entered by the French troops, the "barbarous and meaningless name of Ghetto" was replaced by that of Via Libra. Soon after, the principles of religious equality were entered into the local constitutions. Just as the contraction of the feudal order brought with it the extension of Jewish Emancipation, reaction's return resulted in the almost automatic restoration of restrictions. In Italy, equality was soon after abolished by the Austro-Russian invasion of 1797, a process accompanied by bloody pogroms. Twelve Jews were burned alive in Sienna and thirteen were killed in Sinigaglia. The cycle was repeated with the re-entry of the French in 1800 and the victory of the anti-Napoleonic coalition in 1814, and again in 1831 and 1848 with the victories and defeats of the popular uprisings. However, with each repetition of the cycle, the reduction of Jewish rights became less drastic.

Jewish equality was achieved by the democratic forces, and as such was a result of a concatenation of world-wide and local trends in which Jews played a rather minor role. Nevertheless, having tasted relative freedom under the French, and later under the insurrectionist regimes and the new constitutional governments, the Jews knew that they would be free only after the elimination of feudalism's remnants, foremost among them the Church's temporal power. Thus, the interests of the small Jewish populations of the Italies and of the advocates of liberal nationalism, constitutionalism, and unification were identical. Jews, therefore, participated actively in the revolutions. They joined the Carbonari and Young Italy. Jewish Emancipation became the concern even of Catholic patriots. The unification of Italy in 1870 spelled the end of disabilities in the last stronghold of feudalism, the Papal State. In 1889, Italy's Criminal Code extended equality to Judaism as a religion by declaring the equal protection of the state for all "freely admitted cults."

The historical cycle was repeated fifty years later when, in 1938, Italy, then a junior partner and later a satellite of Nazi Germany, introduced racist legislation against the Jews. Counter-Emancipation in the second quarter of the twentieth century almost inevitably led to Auschwitz. Rossi's study ends in the nineteenth century. We must search the histories of the Holocaust and the post-war era for the continuity of the cycle of Emancipation and Counter-Emancipation in Italy.

MARIO ROSSI, Ph.D. has been United Nations correspondent of *The Christian Science Monitor* and the *St. Louis Post-Dispatch*. He has also contributed articles to major magazines, such as the *Atlantic Monthly, Nouvelle Observateur, The New Republic, The Virginia Quarterly*. He is author of *The Third World: the Developing Countries and the World Revolution* (1964). His book on North Africa will appear this year. He is currently engaged in a project on the United Nations and Crisis Diplomacy.

Dr. Rossi's article was abstracted from his doctoral dissertation on the emancipation of religious minorities in Italy at *the New School for Social Research*.

Emancipation of the Jews of Italy

by Mario Rossi

I

According to the painstaking researches of Riccardo Bachi,[1] the number of Jews in Italy rose from 31,385 in 1800 to 33,873 in 1840, a few years before their emancipation. "The Jews," Bachi points out, "had already acquired at that time the character of a prevalently urban population, and contrary to what is happening today, they were concentrated in small towns rather than in large urban centers, while not a negligible proportion of Jews lived in rural centers."[2]

French rule, which promoted religious tolerance everywhere, was favorable to the Jews in Italy. The first Italian constitution of March 27, 1797, modelled on the French constitution of 1795, was that of the Cispadane Republic (Central Italy). Its Article 4 stated that:

> The Cispadane Republic preserves the religion of the Catholic Apostolic Roman Church. It does not permit the public exercise of any other religion. Only the Jews are permitted to continue the free and public exercise of their religion throughout this territory. It does not wish, however, that any citizen or inhabitant of this territory, so long as he is obedient to the laws, shall be molested on account of religious opinions.[3]

Reprinted from JEWISH SOCIAL STUDIES, Volume XV, 1953

The Cisalpine Republic (Northern Italy) also guaranteed religious freedom. Article 455 of the Constitution of July 9, 1797, read:

No one can be impeded in the exercise of the religion he has chosen so long as he conforms to the laws. The executive power watches over the carrying out of the laws and prevents those ministers of any religion who prove to be unworthy of the confidence of the Government from exercising their functions. No one can be compelled to contribute to the support of any religion.[4]

The second paragraph of this article was directed against the Catholic clergy. It caused such a stir that in the revised Constitution of September 1, 1798, it was abridged as follows in Article 349:

To everyone is guaranteed the free exercise of the religion which he has chosen so long as he conforms to the laws. No one can be forced to contribute to the support of a religion.[5]

The French occupation brought freedom also to the Jews of Rome.[6] Measures in favor of the Jews and other non-Catholics were welcomed by liberal Italians, but were viewed with suspicion and at times with hostility by the large masses of the population. The Jews, of course, had embraced the cause of the revolution that brought them liberty and equality, and this made them even more hated by the supporters of the *ancien régime*. When during Napoleon's Egyptian campaign Austrian and Russian armies invaded Northern Italy in August 1799, pogroms took place in the Marches, Tuscany and Piedmont. The Sinigaglia ghetto was sacked by mobs, who demolished houses and stores and murdered thirteen Jews. Pitigliano was also sacked but only one Jew was killed there. In Siena, twelve Jews were burned alive and the synagogue was desecrated. Near Florence, Salomone Fiorentino, the celebrated poet, was thrown in jail. In Verona, the Austrian government had to issue a proclamation threatening severe penalties for molesting or insulting the Jews. Ancona was spared a pogrom thanks to the French General Monnier, who insisted before the city's surrender that all those who supported the

Republic, especially the Jews, should not be molested.[7] Early in 1800, the French army drove the Austrians and the Russians from the peninsula and restored religious liberty. When, in 1806, Napoleon convoked the Sanhedrin, the Jews of Italy sent over twenty delegates to Paris.[8] Following Napoleon's final defeat, the Jews made efforts to retain the rights that they had won under the French. The Jews of Piedmont attempted to dispatch a commission to Lord Bentinck to plead for his protection; but time was too short. They then hoped to enlist the help of one of the ministers of King Victor Emanuel I who upon the payment of a considerable sum of money promised to fight for their rights. The community of Turin, unwilling to assume the entire responsibility, delayed the negotiations until they eventually fizzled out.[9]

The Jews of the Papal State also submitted in September 1815 two petitions to Count Lebzeltern, Austrian Envoy Extraordinary and Minister Plenipotentiary. Lebzeltern transmitted this petition with his recommendation to Secretary of State Consalvi. There was no reply to these petitions. On November 17, 1815, Lebzeltern forwarded another petition to the Secretary of State who answered in a friendly way that he had brought these petitions to the attention of the Pontiff [Pius VII] who, without deviating in any way from the norm set by his predecessors, would do everything possible to ensure peace and quiet for the Jews within his domain.[10]

The restoration of the dethroned princes marked the beginning of a wave of reaction in which the Pope played a leading part.[11] One of the Pope's first acts upon returning to his throne was the issuance of the Bull of August 7, 1814, re-establishing the Jesuit Order, the champion of blind reaction and religious intolerance. Piedmont was a citadel of loyalty to the Holy See. After Napoleon's downfall, the former order was swiftly restored and the Jesuits again regained their influence. The position of the Jews became virtually intolerable, despite the fact that there were no more than 6,752 of them in the state or only three out of every 2,000 inhabitants.[12] Most of them were wretchedly poor, and they were kept alive by the Jewish relief committees.[13] The Royal Decrees of March 1, 1816 and February 15, 1822 were uncompromisingly harsh.[14]

Conditions were much better for the Jews of the ancient Duchy of Genoa, incorporated into Piedmont after the Congress of Vienna, where the French laws were not abrogated.[15] However, the Jewish population of Liguria counted only about 170 persons.[16] The Kingdom of Lombardo-Venetia which was given back to Austria was always more independent of the Church's political influence and its 6,900 Jews found conditions there rather tolerable. The Patent of Toleration of Joseph II (May 30, 1782) also applied to Lombardo-Venetia. While the Jews were excluded from government administration, they were admitted to the General Assembly of Taxpayers and the city councils. They were allowed to enter the militia, to occupy certain public offices and to practice law.[17] Conditions in the Duchy of Parma, where the influence of the Church was never very strong were also quite good. Jews were admitted to all public and municipal offices. They could own real property and practice law and medicine. There were only 630 Jews in the state, and this small number may have accounted for their toleration.[18]

On the other hand, the Church enjoyed tremendous prestige in the Duchy of Modena where the situation of its 2,654 Jews was deplorable.[19] The privileges granted them by the French were revoked, and the laws of March 31, 1831 stripped them of many of their civil rights, forced them to live in ghettos, to wear a yellow band and to pay annual tribute for the privilege of residence.

In the Grand Duchy of Tuscany, which was independent of the Church's political influences, 7,066 Jews enjoyed especially good conditions. The reaction of 1814 failed to stamp out all the reforms. Although never admitted to citizenship, the privileges granted to the Jews virtually gave them equality. As early as June 10, 1593, Grand Duke Ferdinand I, in order to foster trade, had granted the franchise to the Jews of Pisa and Leghorn. It remained in force until Tuscany's annexation to Piedmont and was very liberally interpreted and applied by jurists and magistrates.[20] After the Restoration, Grand Duke Ferdinand II conferred on the Jews all civil rights by the Law of December 17, 1814 and, in addition, recognized the previously granted privileges.

The plight of the Jews was particularly bad in the Papal State with its Jewish population of 9,200. Upon his return to the throne on April 12, 1814 the Pope ordered the Jews back to the horrible ghetto that was so vividly described by the revolutionist Massimo d'Azeglio.[21] The Jews of Rome were not allowed to own real estate and to practice any of the liberal professions. Nor were they allowed to be blacksmiths and stonecutters. By some strange execption they were permitted to become carpenters, cotton weavers and cabinet makers. They also suffered from many other disabilities.[22] On his death, Pius VII was succeeded by Leo XII (1823–29) who restored many of the most brutal laws of the Middle Ages.[23] His successor, Pius VIII (1829–30), added to the bitter plight of the Jews the prohibition against any contacts with Christians. Conditions were not very different for the Jews of the small communities within the Papal State, namely, Ancona, Senigallia, Pesaro, Urbino, Ferrara, Cento and Lugo.[24]

At the time of the Restoration there were no Jews in the Kingdom of the Two Sicilies which included Southern Italy and Sicily. The last decree of expulsion was signed by Charles of Bourbon on September 18, 1746 and was put into effect on July 30, 1747. It was only after 1830 that Jews began to return sporadically to the Naples region.[25]

II

In view of this situation and because of the failure of the negotiations with the restored princes, the Jews could find no way of obtaining civil equality and political rights other than by participation in the revolutionary movements for Italy's unity. This wholehearted participation brought them full citizenship and equality. It was also an important factor in Italy's relative freedom from antisemitism, as subsequent events were to prove.

The first important revolutionary movement, the Carbonari, emerged immediately after the Restoration.[26] Many Jews joined it and were especially active in the distribution of clandestine publications. Such illegal activities were facilitated by business connections in other states and the ease of concealing such items in shipments of secondhand merchandise. A police report of 1817 listed 44 Jewish members of the Carbonari in Leghorn alone. In 1820, other Jews were involved in this movement in the Duchy of Parma; several were arrested and condemned to one to seven years of imprisonment. Among the many Jewish Carbonaris in 1831 were the brothers Angelo and Emilio Usiglio, well-known figures in the history of the Risorgimento.[27]

The Jews played also an active role in the revolutionary upheavals in the Duchies of Este and Modena and in the Papal State in the year 1831 which witnessed revolutions in France, Belgium and Poland. In Rome, to cite Vogelstein:

> At the very beginning of the movement the people removed the gates of the ghetto and proclaimed the equal rights of the Jews (February 10, 1831). Austrian intervention restored papal rule, to be sure, but the representatives of the powers in a collective note pointed to the pressing need for reform within the Papal State. But in the meanwhile everything remained as it had been. . . . It was only due to the house of Rothschild's satisfying the papal government's requirements for a large loan that the Jews were spared further limitations.[28]

Many Jews joined Young Italy (*Giovane Italia*), which was founded by Giuseppe Mazzini in 1831 and soon supplanted the Carbonari.[29] The distribution center for Mazzini's publications in Piedmont was Salvador Levi's bookshop in Vercelli, whence they were shipped out in baskets of *paté de foie gras* for which Lazzaro Levy was famous. Another Vercelli Jew, Giuseppe Vitalevi, served as the liaison person between the Mazzinians of Marseilles and Lugano. His house was ransacked by the police but he was able to escape in the disguise of a priest. Mazzini's expedition to Savoy in 1833 was financed in part by a member of the banking firm of Todros of Turin. Two Leghorn Jews were the leaders of Tuscany's *Società dei Veri Italiani* (Society of True Italians). In 1834, the poet David Levi of Chieri distinguished himself as the intermediary between the Young Italy committees of Piedmont, Tuscany and Romagne. During the Bandiera brothers' expedition to Southern Calabria in 1844, Levi was entrusted with Young Italy's important missions to London and Paris. The Florentine printer, Alessandro Paggi, founder of the still-existing Bemporad publishing firm, printed clandestine Mazzinian propaganda. Jewish writers contributed to many patriotic reviews, among which *L'Antologia* of Florence was the most noteworthy. A number of Jews were arrested as the authors of manifestos and brochures protesting its suppression by the police in March 1833.[30]

The patriotism of the Jews won for them soon the friendship of the great liberals and served to popularize among them the cause of Jewish emancipation. Gabriello Pepe published an article in favor of the Jews in *L'Antologia* of January 1830. Later, in 1834, Count Camillo Cavour began a campaign in favor of Jewish emancipation in the newspaper *Il Risorgimento*.[31] A similar campaign was undertaken by Giuseppe Mazzini. In *Jeune Suisse* of November 4, 1835 he stated: "We claim that the best way of making good citizens of the Jews, whenever they may not meet the standard, is to make brothers of them, equal to everybody else under the law; we claim that wherever this has been done, the religious sect that has given Europe men of such intelligence as Spinoza and Mendelssohn, has rapidly improved." On November 9 he wrote to his mother: "During the 19th century exceptional laws for the Jews can be nothing more than a blunder and an absurdity."[32]

Foremost in promoting the cause of Jewish emancipation was Carlo Cattaneo's celebrated study *Ricerche economiche sulle interdizioni imposte dalla legge civile agli Israeliti* (Economic Studies on the Restrictions Imposed by Civil Law Against the Jews), published in Milan in 1836. Cattaneo, one of the Risorgimento's greatest intellects, argued that with equality, "there would be diffused among them [the Jews] as among the others love . . . of honors, of study, of country, of public esteem, in short, it would aid their complete assimilation into the social unit. The love for petty gain that is hateful to the multitude would vanish; the natural inclination to rest and to economic well-being would send back to the earth the savings amassed over the years."[33]

Other liberal newspapers published articles favoring emancipation.

Among the most important were Brofferio's *Messaggero Torinese,* Pomba's *Mondo Illustrato,* and Valerio's *Letture di Famiglia.*[34]

When Mazzini went in exile to London in January 1837, he was accompanied by the Ruffini brothers and Angelo Usiglio. During his long years abroad he found friendship and support among many Jews. He became closely attached to the Rosselli family in London in whose house he spent long evenings, talking politics and playing music. There he met Sara Levi Nathan, called by him "an angel of goodness." She was an Italian Jewess married to a German merchant. The Nathans established an enduring friendship with Mazzini. They dedicated their energies and a substantial fortune to the cause of Italy's independence. Their London home became the center of the Italian patriots in exile. When Sara moved to Switzerland, Mazzini and Carlo Cattaneo were there, too, among her frequent visitors. Giuseppe Garibaldi visited her home in Milan.[35]

Soon Catholic patriots began to join the liberals in advocating Jewish equality. The philosopher Vincenzo Gioberti, an influential person in the Risorgimento and later prime minister, often wrote in defense of the Jews. The following eloquent passage appeared in his book *Del primato civile e morale degli Italiani,* published in 1842:

> [We] hope that the day is not far distant when the claims of humanity and of religion will be completely realized and the Italian Jews will be able to share civil rights together with all other citizens. . . . The best way to bring the strayed Israelites back to the fold is to extend to them that fine, merciful benevolence which is the mark of our laws. And whoever acts to the contrary . . . such a man can be considered a Christian or a Catholic in name only; in truth he belongs in the ranks of the heathen.[36]

The election in 1846 of Pius IX, a man of liberal sentiments which he later abandoned, stirred the hope of the patriotic Catholics that he would become the leading figure both in the country's unification and in the attainment of Jewish emancipation. In fact, one of the Pope's first measures was to appoint a commission to examine the condition of the Jews in Rome. He rescinded some of the restrictions imposed on them and even allowed some of them to reside outside the ghetto.

Most active among the Catholic proponents of Jewish emancipation were the brothers Massimo and Roberto d'Azeglio, scions of a noble and very devout Piedmontese family. Massimo, a well-known writer who was later to become prime minister, wrote a pamphlet entitled *Dell'emancipazione civile degli Israeliti* (On the Civil Emancipation of the Jews). In it he accused Christianity of inconsistency in its attitude toward the Jews[37] and urged their treatment as brothers in line with Christian tenets. He defended the Jews against the usual accusations, arguing that

> intolerance and the persecutions that arise from it are not only unjust, contrary to reason, to the commandments of the Gospel and the example of Jesus Christ and his Apostles, not only are they ineffectual in reaching their objective, but they are contrary to it, and lead to diametrically opposite ends.[38]

After praising Pope Pius IX, the "man of God," for having taken the initial steps toward emancipating the Jews and thus having put "into effect the teachings of the Gospel," d'Azeglio concluded with the statement that

> the cause of Jewish regeneration is closely bound up with that of Italian regeneration; because there is only one justice and it is the same for all. Moreover, it is strong and invincible only when it is both requested impartially from whoever is in power above us, and dispensed impartially to whoever is dependent on us.

D'Azeglio's booklet produced a deep impression throughout Italy and gave impetus to his brother Roberto's pro-emancipation campaign. The latter had declared to King Carlo Alberto that he viewed such activities as his sacred duty;[39] but the King failed to appreciate his efforts, and in a letter to Minister Borelli, he referred to Roberto as a "meneur."[40] Taking advantage of some reforms granted by the King on October 30, 1847, Roberto d'Azeglio appealed on November 16, in a letter to the bishops of the Kingdom, for their help. However, the bishops protested against d'Azeglio's efforts and declared their opposition to emancipation in a petition to the King.[41] This stand greatly angered Roberto.[42] However, the bishops could not have taken a stand against the *Corpus iuris canonici* without papal permission, and the Pope had no intention of advocating the emancipation of the religious minorities.[43]

On December 23, 1847 Roberto submitted to the King another petition, signed by 600 citizens of Piedmont, including distinguished persons such as Cavour, the historian Cesare Balbo (soon after prime minister), Admiral Carlo Pellion di Persano, G. A. Reynieri, and Goffredo Casalis.[44] D'Azeglio also received the support of Vincenzo Gioberti. In a letter from his exile in Paris, dated December 14, 1847, Gioberti wrote: "Divine indeed is the work of achieving for the Jews and Protestants of our country a better status of civil equality, and I don't know of any other effort that is more certain to merit the benedictions of both men and heaven."[45] On January 7, 1848 Gioberti wrote with reference to priest Bertetti's pamphlet against emancipation:

I have held the emancipation of the Jews and of the Waldenses to be not only a just cause but a holy one. I made a public profession of that faith when I wrote the *Primato*. Today I have read the paper of Father Bertetti. What do you think of it? I laughed over it so much that my head, still feeling the effects of a migraine, began to spin.[46]

III

The eventful year 1848 hastened the wave of reform. Early in January an uprising broke out in Sicily, the first of many revolutions that were to shake Europe with the coming of the Spring of Nations. To pacify his subjects, King Ferdinand II issued an edict on January 29 announcing the forthcoming constitution which was enacted on February 11. While it contained no liberal provisions with regards to religious freedom, it nevertheless forced the other Italian states to take action.[47]

Anxious to lead the unification movement, Piedmont was preparing to liberate Austria's Italian regions at the cost of war. In need of help from the liberals, Carlo Alberto reluctantly consented to grant a constitution to his people. The announcement of February 8 outlined its main features of the new constitution. Its first Article read: "The Apostolic Roman Catholic religion is the only religion of the State. The other cults now existing are tolerated according to the laws."[48] The news spread joy throughout the Kingdom.

A week later (February 15), the Grand Duke of Tuscany likewise granted a liberal constitution which assured religious freedom as follows: "The Apostolic Roman Catholic religion is the only religion of the State. The other cults now existing are permitted in conformity with the laws."[49] The Pope was little pleased with the usage of the word "permitted" instead of "tolerated."[50] The limited constitution granted by him on March 15 contained not a word about religious freedom.[51]

Under the pressure of the liberals, Carlo Alberto conferred upon the Waldenses all civil and political rights by the decree of February 17.[52] However, he failed to emancipate the Jews because the Crown Council, influenced by the bishops' opposition, remained adamant against it.[53] The constitution (*Statuto*) was signed by the King and his minister on March 4. It became effective on the following day, thus changing Piedmont's absolute regime into constitutional monarchy. However, this very devout king insisted that the position of the Catholic Church remain unchallenged, even in this liberal constitution.[54] The first Article therefore proclaimed a state religion, thus violating not only the principle of the separation between state and church, but also that of the equality of all religions. Non-Catholics were merely tolerated as an unavoidable nuisance. Tolerance was extended only to the Waldensian and the Jewish religions whose followers lived in Piedmont at the time of the constitution's enactment. Finally, toleration was to be carried out according to the existing laws. These were most intolerant and discriminatory.[55] To cite the authority on this question: "The king and the authors of the Constitution were insistent that the condition of inferiority imposed by the existing laws on the non-Catholic cults remain intact while agreeing to diminish or to annul the restrictions imposed on the faithful."[56] Most revealing in this connection is the conference of the Crown Council of February 10 that preceded the emancipation of the Waldenses, during which the king resisted any clear demarcations between church and state and the granting of equality to Protestants and directed that the limitations on the exercise of the Waldensian cult be not modified. The debate ended with the decision that the regulations regarding the Protestant cult remain unchanged.[57]

The term "tolerated cults" was first employed in Piedmont in the Civil Code of 1836. Because of its obscurity, the minister of justice gave the following definition at the meeting of the State Council of January 5, 1836: "Cults that are not admitted, not approved, but also not excluded, that is, tolerated."[58] The first Article of the constitution failed to satisfy the liberals. For instance, Count Cavour expressed his hope in *Il Risorgimento* of March 10, 1848 that the Article would be revised by the future Constituent Assembly of united Italy. Meanwhile, he hoped that the discriminatory laws would be amended.[59]

On March 15, 1848 Piedmont declared war on Austria, and a few days later revolts against Austrian rule broke out in Milan and Venice, where the Jews enjoyed more freedom than in Piedmont. This anomalous situation was made known to the king by a Jewish delegation headed by David Levi, who told him:

> Sire, you are about to enter Lombardy as liberator. The Jews already enjoy there all civil rights under Austrian rule, they constitute a most influential class in Milan, Verona and Venice. The Liberator King, I am sure, would not wish to grant them a status worse than the one they have enjoyed under foreign rule.[60]

The king promised the delegation that he would give the matter careful consideration. Strong pressure was also brought by his own Minister of the Interior, Marchese Vincenzo Ricci, who sent the king a memorandum on March 22, in which human and practical considerations were intermingled.[61] He also submitted to the king the following draft of a partial emancipation decree:

At the suggestion of Our Minister Secretary of State for the Interior, we have ordered and are ordering:

The Jews of the Kingdom will enjoy, as of the date of this decree, all civil rights and the possibility of pursuing academic degrees. Nothing is changed regarding their cult and the schools run by them. All laws contrary to the present one are abrogated.[62]

The new democratic cabinet was liberally inclined towards the non-Catholic religions. This is shown in Article 16 of the Edict of March 28 on the freedom of the press, which ordered punishment against "whoever [through the press] . . . derides or offends any of the religions permitted in the State."[63] On March 29, on the battlefield of Voghera in Lombardy, Carlo Alberto signed the Decree submitted by Marchese Ricci. Shortly afterwards, on April 15, a subsequent decree admitted the Jews to the armed forces. However, even before that many Jews volunteered in their desire to liberate Italian territories. *"Les Juifs qui se sont enrolés se conduisent à merveille,"* wrote Costanza d'Azeglio to her son Emanuele.[64] As the majority of the Jewish volunteers were assigned to the Seventh Bersaglieri Company, that unit was called the "Jewish Company."[65]

The problem of completing the emancipation of the Jews was repeatedly discussed during the parliamentary debates of May 28 and 30 and of June 5. On June 6, the chamber of deputies expressed to the king the wish that "the proclaimed equality of the citizens before the civil and political law be a right, a self evident truth for everyone, without distinction of cults."[66] Doubts concerning the status of the Jews arose at first in the interpretation of the electoral law of March 17. It is important to examine its background in detail since it led to significant developments.

Article 1 of the constitution proclaimed the toleration of the non-Catholic cults. Article 24 recognized the equality of all the citizens before the law, but it included the following qualifying clause: "except for the exclusions established by the laws." Furthermore, it was admitted that the edict which emancipated the Waldensians could be interpreted as valid only in their case and that therefore the constitution did not proclaim the perfect equality of all citizens. This interpretation was strengthened by the edict of Jewish emancipation of

March 29, which granted to the Jews only *civil* rights.

All citizens could be candidates for election, irrespectively of "the regulations regarding the civil rights of which someone may be limited because of his religion." But as to the right to vote, the law (Article 97) referred to Article 40 of the constitution, which required as a condition for voting the full enjoyment of all political and civil rights.[67] Therefore, in view of the dispute concerning the political status of the Jews, the question of their right to vote was hotly debated.

In his desire to settle the problem, Deputy Riccardo Sineo presented to Parliament on June 7 the following bill:

In view of the doubts caused by . . . the electoral law: We [the King] have declared and are declaring that as to the right to vote as well as to the exercise of any other political rights, there is perfect equality among all citizens, without distinction of cults.

During the debate on the bill in the chamber of deputies on the following day, Deputy Pietro Albini argued against the distinction between civil and political rights. He stated: "We believe that all doubts should be dispelled, especially now that the Jews are now being subject to all the duties of citizens, it is only that there should be no difference between them and the others as to rights and advantages."[68]

The Sineo Bill was presented to the chamber in the following modified form:

Wishing to dispell any doubt concerning the political and civil capacity of the citizens who do not profess the Catholic religion, the Senate and the Chamber of Deputies have adopted: We [the King] have ordered and are ordering what follows:

Single Article. Difference of cult does not constitute an exception to the enjoyment of the civil and political rights and to the admissibility to civil and military positions.[69]

After a brief debate, the bill was passed on the same day by the vote of 102 to 17.[70] On June 15 it was sent to the senate, where the debate in which Massimo d'Azeglio participated, opened on June 17. The bill was approved by 32 senators out of 35 present. Two days later, the king issued the decree giving the Jews the right to hold public and administrative offices in the kingdom. The Sineo Act was enacted by the king on July 8, 1848 and became one of the fundamental laws of the state. It not only conferred equal rights on all citizens regardless of their religious beliefs and on religions other than those existing at that time in Piedmont, but also cancelled out the exclusionary implications in the first Article of the constitution. Italian liberalism had won a great victory!

Meanwhile, the revolution triumphed in Venice. The Austrians were expelled and the republic was proclaimed. One of the first acts of its provisional government, under the leadership of Daniele Manin (whose grandparents were converted Jews) was to proclaim in the decree of March 29, 1848 that "the citizens of the united provinces of the republic, irrespective of creed, and without exception, will enjoy complete equality of civil and political rights."[71] In a circular of April 5, 1848, "Citizen Rabbi" Abraham Lattes urged the Jews to join the civil guards and to make financial contributions to the republic. The response was generous, and on September 7, 1848 Daniele Manin, in answer to a letter from the chief rabbi, wrote:

The needs of the government are both great and urgent. They must be met more than ever before by the generosity of the citizenry. And to arouse this generosity the work of priests is needed. Your Reverence, acquaint your co-religionists with the country's need of help. Never again must our great motherland fall under the heel of a foreign ruler. Any funds you may collect should be turned in to the public treasury on Thursday. Your Reverence, the government entrusts the Levite with the task of teaching his people the Holy Book of the Nation![72]

Rabbi Lattes won great popularity and was elected deputy to the Venetian Assembly both in 1848 and 1849. Another Jew, Baron Giacomo Treves, was elected deputy to the Assembly with the widest margin of votes next to Manin and to the great writer and patriot Nicolo' Tommaseo.[73] Other Jewish deputies included Isacco Pesaro Maurogonato, Rabbi Samuele Salomon Olper, Angelo Levi, Abramo Errera, Leone Pincherle and Dr. Benedetto Del Vecchio. Maurogonato became minister of finance, while Pincherle held the portfolio of minister of agriculture and commerce in the provisional government.[74]

After the flight of Pius IX to Gaeta near Naples in the autumn of 1848, the republic was proclaimed in the Campidoglio on February 9, 1849. Rome was governed by an assembly and a triumvirate, with Giuseppe Mazzini an one of the triumvirs. Article 7 of its constitution guaranteed religious freedom as follows: "The exercise of the political and civil rights is independent from religious beliefs."[75] The Jews, Salvatore Anau of Ferrara and Leone Carpi of Cento, were elected to the constituent assembly. They were entrusted with delicate missions and after the unification of Italy were elected deputies to parliament. Emanuele Foligno, a Jew, became minister of finance, and the Jews Davide Almagia and Abramo Ascoli were members of the committee for the defense of the city.[76]

IV

The year 1849 was a tragic one for Italian unification. The Austrians defeated the Piedmont troops at Novara in March. Carlo Alberto abdicated, and Victor Emanuel II was proclaimed King. Several Lombard cities tried in vain to rise against Austria. The Roman Republic was then attacked at the behest of the Pope by France, Austria and Naples. Many Jews fought to save the republic[77] in the epic battle for the Eternal City's defense under Garibaldi's leadership.

Rome was forced to surrender on June 30, 1849. Venice, starved, besieged, bombarded and a prey to cholera, fell to the Austrians on August 24. The cause of Italian independence and democracy seemed to have reached an unprecedented low. Except for Piedmont, Italy remained for the next decade under the absolute domination of foreign princes. The insurrections which broke out here and there were drowned in blood.

The return of Pius IX to Rome marked the resumption of a new reactionary policy against the Jews who were thrown back into the ghetto. The medieval laws were restored. In addition, the Jews suffered from arrests and from the depredations of the French soldiers. Efforts at mollification were unsuccessful.[78] The economic situation of the Jews continued to deteriorate, to the extent that it "was never so desperate as in the last decade of the papal rule."[79] . . .

This last decade of papal rule became also characterized by incidents of compulsory baptisms. The most notorious of these was the Mortara Affair. Edgardo Mortara, eleven months old, the son of Girolamo Mortara Levi of Bologna, was christened with tap water during his illness by his nurse, Anna Marisi. This fact was brought six years later to the attention of the Dominican Father Feletti, Inquisitor of the Curia. On June 24, 1858 he ordered the child to be forcibly taken away from his desperate parents and to be placed in the foundling home for Catechumens. The unremitting efforts of the Jews who pledged enormous sums for the child's restoration to his family, the parents' negotiations with various bodies, including the Vatican, and the expressions of sympathy for the family sent to the Pope by England, France, Prussia and Piedmont, were all in vain. Mortara saw his family again thirty years later. He was then an ordained priest.[80]

V

Cavour who had taken a deep interest in the Mortara affair, when he was prime minister of Piedmont,[81] was assisted by many Jews in his campaign for Italy's unification.[82] The most influential interpreter of his policy in the press was Giacomo Dina whose writings appeared especially in the *Risorgimento's* successor *Opinione*, Cavour's official mouthpiece, of which he became co-owner in 1856. Even closer to Cavour was his confidential secretary, Isacco Artom, who succeeeded Costantino Nigra in this capacity, after the latter became ambassador to Paris in 1859. Artom's appointment was criticized by the clerical faction. A particularly violent attack against it appeared in *L'Armonia,* a Catholic journal. Cavour defended Artom and his appointment.[83]

Well known are Cavour's connections with the great Jewish banks, Todros in Turin, Avigdor in Nice, and Rothschild in Paris. The latter granted a loan for the digging of the Frejus tunnel in 1856; but the money was instead used to prepare another war against Austria.[84]

The war was declared in 1859, with Garibaldi taking an active part in the campaign. Lombardy was freed, and on July 4 the new Governor General issued a decree that all citizens were equal before the law irrespective of their religion.[85] Meanwhile, the Duchies of Tuscany, Parma and Modena and Romagna rebelled and set up their own provisional governments. The discriminatory laws were once more abolished. The pertinent decrees were issued for Tuscany on April 30, for Modena on June 14, and for Romagna on August 10.[86]

Jews again participated in the military campaigns as volunteers or in the regular army. The name of Tullio Massarani deserves to be remembered. Among the *Garibaldini* who distinguished themselves in 1859 were David Funaro, Giuseppe Archivolli, Moise' and Angelo Calo' of Leghorn, and Giacomo Bassi of Venice.[87] Jews held important positions in the provisional governments which were formed in the old states. Giuseppe Finzi became Cavour's personal representative in Mantua. In Florence, Sansone d'Ancona was appointed to the finance commission. His brother Alessandro was editor of the noted magazine *La Nazione.* In Modena, Giacomo Sacerdote and Cesare Castelli were elected to the Assembly. Fortunato Modena of Reggio served on the National Committee. In Bologna, B. Osimo was appointed to the council on finance. Four other Jews were named to the provisional government's working committee in Ferrara.[88]

In 1860, many Jews fought gallantly with Garibaldi's One Thousand volunteers who landed at Marsala, Sicily, initiating the campaign that was to culminate in the liberation of Southern Italy. They also fought with the royal army that was advancing from the north to join with Garibaldi's forces. We need only mention the name of Lieutenant Giuseppe Ottolenghi, later minister of war, who received the silver medal for valor.[89]

The Royal Decree of February 12, 1861, ordered that non-Catholics living in Sicily were to enjoy all political and civil rights. On February 17, a decree of the Lieutenant General of the Neapolitan Provinces annulled the concordat between the Bourbons and the Holy See (February 16, 1818) and declared that differences in religion would no longer represent an obstacle to the perfect equality of all the citizens.[90] Except for Rome and Venice, Italy was now free and united under the House of Savoy. On March 17, 1861 the proclamation of the Kingdom of Italy was greeted with joy and celebrations by all Italian Jews. But only a few months later were they saddened when their staunch friend Count Cavour died on June 6. Services were held in all Italian synagogues, and a moving tribute to his memory was paid by the Alliance Israélite Universelle in Paris.[91]

There were many Jews in Garibaldi's ill-fated expedition to free Rome in 1862. Included among these volunteers were Colonel Enrico Gustalla and Cesare Parenzo.[97]

Embittered by the loss of all his state, except for the city of Rome, and in the hope of stemming the wave of liberalism in Italy, Pius IX issued in 1864 the *Syllabus of Errors,* which G. A. Borgese rightly defined as "the official inauguration of the second Counter-Reformation."[73] It re-emphasized that Catholicism was the only religion of the state and voiced its objection to public worship by non-Catholics.[94]

Jews participated in the 1866 campaign for the liberation of Venice from Austria's rule. Almost two hundred Jews fought as volunteers, and not a few lost their lives on the battlefield. When Venice was turned over to Italy, the laws conferring equality of political and civil rights upon the Jews were extended to this region by the Decree of August 4, 1866.[95]

Again Garibaldi tried to liberate Rome in 1867, but he was routed by superior French forces. Among the Jewish volunteers in his forces were Alberto Fiorentino, who was killed in action not far from Bagnorea, and Leopoldo Rava, who was seriously wounded. Transferred to a hospital in Rome, he was subjected to intense proselytizing efforts to convert him to Catholicism. He was not allowed to leave the hospital despite the intervention by the Alliance Israélite Universelle and the French Embassy.[96] Jews also contributed large sums of money to the Italian struggle for independence. A number of titles of nobility were bestowed by the king on Jewish families between 1860 and 1866 in recognition of these services.[97]

On September 20, 1870 Italian troops entered Rome. The temporal power of the pope was suspended. On October 13, King Victor Emmanuel II signed a royal decree extending to the city of Rome the benefits of the Law of March 29, 1848, thus equalizing the status of the Jews with that of all the other citizens of the capital of United Italy.[98] This act threw down the last ghetto walls on the peninsula.

There remained the task of interpreting the laws on religious minorities. As we have seen, the Sineo Act of 1848 practically set up the equality of all the creeds in Savoy. Count Cavour, in his celebrated article in *Il Risorgimento* (March 10, 1848) expressed the hope that by recognizing the Catholic religion of the state, the latter merely meant to pay its respect to the majority faith. In 1851, Deputy Tecchio proposed that the first Article of the constitution should be interpreted to mean that whenever the state held official ceremonies, the rite followed should be that of the Catholic Church.[99] Nothing could have been further from the intention of the authors of the constitution, but this interpretation became accepted and undisputed. It was reaffirmed by Minister of the Interior Chiaves in his speech before the chamber of deputies on March 24, 1866.[100] Minister Lanza once more confirmed this interpretation in 1872.[101]

As to the "tolerance" extended by the constitution to religious minorities, it came to be interpreted after Italy's unification as a "protection" and a "quasi privilege" granted by the law to all cults and their ministers. This is how it was expressed in the judgment of the Supreme Court [*Corte di Cassazione*] of Turin on September 6, 1871.[102]

Eventually, the expression "tolerated cults" was abandoned in Italian legislation. The Criminal Court *(Codice Zanardelli)* of 1889 made no distinction whatever between Catholic and non-Catholic cults and extended the protection of the state equally to all religious faiths. Henceforth, all religions were described as "freely admitted cults."[103] This code brought about the separation between church and state, the aim of the tradition of the *Risorgimento*. It made real Cavour's definition of a "free church in a free state" *(Libera chiesa in libero stato)*.

NOTES

* JEWISH SOCIAL STUDIES, vol. xv, no. 2 (April 1953), pp. 113–34.

[1] During this period almost one third of the Jews lived in the lowland communities of Mantua, Venetia, Emilia and Romagna. The others were segregated in eleven communities, with more than 2,500 each in the communities of Leghorn, Rome and Trieste and between 1,000 and 2,500 inhabitants in each of the remaining eight. The rest were scattered among 27 communities numbering fewer than 100 inhabitants each; 30 communities had between 100 and 500 inhabitants and four between 500 and 1,000 each. There were no Jews in Southern Italy, in Sardinia, in most of Liguria and Lombardy and in the Papal States, except in Rome and in several scattered centers in the Marches and Romagna. *Cf.* Bachi, Riccardo, "La demografia dell'ebraismo italiano prima dell'emancipazione," in *Israel,* vol. xii (1938), pp. 256–320.

[2] *Ibid.,* p. 258.

[3] "From the most ancient times there had been Jews in Bologna, Ferrara, Modena, and Reggio, by special permission of the Holy See, and it was natural that they should be granted every liberty. But there were absolutely no other non-Catholics, and especially no Protestants and, therefore, equally natural was the general dislike [of them] . . . Hence those restrictions which, tacitly but none the less directly, are aimed at the Protestants." Ruffini, Francesco, *Religious Liberty* (New York 1912), p. 450.

[4] *Ibid.,* pp. 450–451.

[5] *Ibid.,* p. 452.

[6] An edict by the French military commander declared that "the Jews, who possess all the conditions required to be Roman Citizens, will be subject only to the laws common to all Citizens of the Roman Republic." It abolished all laws and special "consuetudes concerning the Jews." The Edict was supplemented by a pertinent law. *Cf.* Milano, Attilio, "Ricerche sulle condizioni economiche degli ebrei a Roma (1555–1848)," in *Israel,* vol. v (1931), pp. 554–555.

[7] Servi, Flaminio, *Gli Israeliti d'Europa nella civiltà* (Torino 1871), p. 24.

[8] Roth, Cecil, *The History of the Jews of Italy* (Philadelphia 1946), pp. 442 ff.

[9] Foà, Salvatore, "Israeliti," in *Dizionario del risorgimento nazionale* (Milano 1931), p. 524.

[10] The first petition requested the continuation of the rights obtained under the French and, in particular, freedom to engage in all trades; the revocation of the obligation to wear discriminatory insignia; the right to own real estate; freedom of residence; the right to practice medicine and surgery; and the right to engage in arts and crafts having no connection with Christianity. *Cf.* Loevinson, Ermanno, "Gli ebrei dello stato pontificio e la loro evoluzione politico sociale nel periodo del risorgimento italiano fino al 1849," in *Rassegna storica del risorgimento,* vol. xvi (1929), pp. 768–803.

[11] Della Torre, Arnaldo, *Il Cristianesimo in Italia dai filosofisti ai modernisti* (Palermo s.a.), p. 58.

[12] Vigna, L. and Aliberti, V., *Della condizione attuale degli ebrei in Piemonte* (Torino 1848), *passim.* For population statistics, *see* p. 58.

[13] Dina, Giacomo, Introduction to Eotvos, Giuseppe, *Sull'emancipazione degli israeliti* (Torino 1848), p. 9, note 2.

[14] The Jews were shut up in ghettos to which they had to return before 9 p. m., requiring special permission to leave. Jewish students were expelled from universities and schools. Jews were forbidden to hold civic, government or military offices, and were obliged to earn their living in the lowliest trades and petty businesses. The poor were excluded from public welfare. Property owners were obliged to liquidate within five years any real estate or holdings acquired during the French domination. *Cf. Raccolta degli atti del governo dal 1814 al 1822,* for 1816, First Semester, p. 283. A deferment was granted by Royal Decree of February 15, 1822.

[15] Vigna and Aliberti, *op. cit.,* pp. 23 ff.

[16] Cantoni, Lelio, *Nuovo ordinamento del culto israelitico nei regi stati* (Torino 1848), p. 8.

[17] As the expression "religious toleration" occurs frequently in this work, it may be interesting to know what it meant to Joseph II. In the letter of July 20, 1777 to his mother Maria Theresa he wrote: "I would give all that I possess in order that all the Protestants of your states should pass over to Catholicism. For me the word *toleration* only means that I, in all purely temporal affairs, would employ anyone without any regard to religion, and permit him to possess property, to exercise a profession, to become a citizen of the State, so long as he was suitable and might assist the State and its industry" (Ruffini, *op. cit.,* p. 401).

[18] Serristori, L., *Statistica dell'Italia* (Firenze 1839), p. 30.

[19] "Costituzione del ducato di Modena," in *Collezione dei moderni codici d'Italia,* edited by Vaccarino, pp. 848, 854.

[20] It provided that Jews establishing residence at Leghorn or Pisa could not be molested either for debts incurred or for crimes committed, before having benefited from the privilege of domicile which could be obtained by registering on a special list at the toll house. Jews, like Christians, could trade in all goods and enjoy abroad protection equal to that enjoyed at home by the other citizens of the Duchy. They were admitted to give testimony, exempted from wearing discriminatory insignia, and protected from physical injury and from all forms of popular insult. Jews could take degrees in medicine or surgery and practice among Christians. They were allowed to have Christian nurses and servants. They could also own real estate and dispose of it in their wills as they saw fit. *Cf.* Rignano, I. E., *Sulla attuale posizione giuridica degli israeliti in Toscana* (Firenze 1874), *passim.*

[21] In his *Dell'emancipazione civile degli israeliti* (Firenze 1848), pp. 24–26.

[22] D'Azeglio furnishes a long list of abuses to which Jews were subjected. They had to pay 73.60 scudi to the Secretary of the Vicariate for the required attendance at a Christian sermon to which they were escorted by carabinieri. The guard at the ghetto gates was paid 163.60 scudi. The parish priests of the surrounding districts were paid 123 scudi monthly as indemnity for the loss of Christian parishioners who might have dwelt in the area. Jews were not eligible for public relief or works. To cite d'Azeglio: "There are over two thousand completely destitute individuals among them, whose maintenance when they are well and whose care when they are afflicted by illness or old age must perforce be supplied by the more prosperous Jews. . . . One-third of the Jews are obliged to provide for the remaining two-thirds!" *Ibid.,* p. 27.

[23] Farini, Luigi Carlo, *Lo Stato romano dell'anno 1815 al 1850* (Firenze 1853), *passim.*

[24] Roth, *op. cit.,* p. 448. Also Loevinson, *op. cit., passim.*

[25] Ferrorelli, Nicola, *Gli ebrei nell'Italia meridionale* (Torino 1915), *passim.*

[26] For Jewish participation in the Carbonari *see* Foà, *op. cit.,* p. 525.

[27] Levi, Alessandro, "Amici israeliti di Giuseppe Mazzini," in *Israel,* vol. v (1931), p. 588.

[28] Vogelstein, Herman, *Rome* (Philadelphia 1940), p. 335.

[29] On Jewish participation in Young Italy *see* Foà, *op. cit.,* p. 526.

[30] Roth, *op. cit.,* p. 458.

[31] *Ibid.*

[32] Levi, *op. cit., passim.*

[33] Citation from later edition, Rome, 1932, p. 135.

[34] Foà, *op. cit.,* p. 528.

[35] Levi, *op. cit.,* p. 599.

[36] Cited by Grilli, Marcel, "The Role of the Jews in Modern Italy," (Second Part) in *The Menorah Journal,* vol. xxviii (1940), p. 63, from the Torino edition, vol. ii (1925), pp. 84–85.

[37] To quote from p. 6 of this work which appeared in Florence in 1848: "Christian civilization has been guilty of a strange syllogism in regard to the Jews. Christianity orders me to love all men without distinction. The Jews are men. Therefore, I hate them, I persecute them and torment them. The object of this small book which I offer to the public is to co-operate, in so far as my feeble efforts will permit me, in the correction of the above-mentioned syllogism; and to restore the terms of the syllogism to their true and rational relation."

[38] *Ibid.*, p. 41.

[39] D'Azeglio, Emanuele, *Carteggi e documenti diplomatici inediti,* vol. i (Torino 1920), p. 14, note 3.

[40] Crosa, Emilio, "La libertà religiosa nello statuto albertino," in *Archivio giuridico,* Fourth Series, vol. ix (Modena 1925), p. 88.

[41] Only Monsignor Lovana, Bishop of Biella, was in favor of emancipation. The texts of the bishop's replies appear in Bert, Amedeo, *I valdesi* (Torino 1849).

[42] "I received a letter from Roberto who is angry at our bishops and their petition [to the King] against the Jews," wrote Massimo d'Azeglio on January 25, 1848 to L. C. Farini. Rava, Luigi, *Epistolario di L. C. Farini,* vol. ii (Bologna 1911–1914), pp. 62–63.

[43] Jemolo, Arturo Carlo, *Chiesa a stato in Italia negli ultimi cento anni* (Torino 1948), p. 74.

[44] In a letter to her son Emanuele, Costanza d'Azeglio wrote: "Il a entrepris à lui seul l'émancipation des israélites et des protestants; ce qui lui donne une besogne énorme. Il lui a fallu écrire à tous les évêques, interroger tous les théologiens, explorer toutes les notabilités pour connaitre l'opinion; enfin écrire sa requête motivée, des articles de journaux, mais il a amené son affaire à bien, et cette adresse appuyé de toutes signatures qui pouvait la faire valoir à été présentée et très bien acceuillié par le Ministre Désambrois. Voilà donc une enterprise finie. Elle aura son effet en temps et lieu, s'il plait a Dieu." *Cf.* d'Azeglio, Costance, *Souvenirs historiques* (Torino 1844), p. 175.

[45] Gioberti, Vincenzo, *Epistolario,* vol. vii (Firenze 1934), p. 141.

[46] *Ibid.*, pp. 214–15.

[47] Article III provided that "the only religion of the State shall forever be the Christian Apostolic Roman Catholic and the profession of any other religion will never be permitted." *Cf. Raccolta di costituzioni italiane* (Torino 1852), p. 14.

[48] Jahier, Davide, *Il I° articolo dello statuto e la libertà religiosa in Italia* (Torino-Genova 1925), p. 7.

[49] *Raccolta di costituzioni italiane,* p. 30.

[50] Jemolo, *op. cit.*, p. 74.

[51] *Raccolta di costituzioni italiane,* p. 59.

[52] For the emancipation of the Waldenses, *cf.* Bert, *op. cit., passim.*

[53] Foà, *op. cit.,* p. 528.

[54] Ruffini, Francesco, *Diritti di libertà* (Torino 1926), pp. 68 ff.

[55] Jahier, *op. cit.,* p. 7.

[56] Crosa, *op. cit.,* p. 83.

[57] *Ibid.,* p. 82.

[58] *Ibid.,* p. 83.

[59] Shortly before the enactment of the constitution, Cavour wrote to his cousin, Matilde De La Rive: "J'espère que notre charte consacrera le principe de la liberté religieuse . . . S'il en était autrement, je ne renierais pas ce principe que j'ai professé toute ma vie." *Cf.* Jahier, *op. cit.,* p. 81.

[60] Foà, *op. cit.,* p. 528.

[61] Rignano, I., *Della uguaglianza civile e della libertà dei culti secondo il diritto pubblico del regno d'Italia* (Livorno 1868), p. 9.

[62] *Ibid.,* pp. 10–11.

[63] Ruffini, *Diritti di libertà,* p. 66.

[64] D'Azeglio, Constance, *op., cit.,* p. 175.

[65] Foà, *op. cit.,* p. 529.

[66] Perreau, Pietro, *Per la storia delle comunità israelitiche in Italia e la loro emancipazione* (Trieste 1887), p. 5.

[67] Crosa, *op. cit.,* pp. 88–89.

[68] *Atti del parlamento subalpino. Sessione del 1848* (Torino 1855), p. 64.

[69] *Ibid.*

[70] *Ibid.,* pp. 64 ff.

[71] Ottolenghi, Adolfo, "Abraham Lattes nei suoi rapporti con la repubblica di Daniele Manin," in *Israel,* vol. v (1930), p. 27.

[72] *Ibid.,* pp. 25 ff.

[73] In January 1848 Tommaseo wrote an article in favor of Jewish emancipation, but the Austrian censor forbade its publication. Only on November 25 did it appear in *Il Telegrafo della Sera* of Trieste. The text was reprinted in *Israel,* vol. x (1935), p. 163.

[74] Ottolenghi, *op. cit.,* p. 33.

[75] Jemolo, *op. cit.,* pp. 64–65.

[76] Grilli, *op. cit.,* third part, p. 177.

[77] Foà, *op. cit.,* p. 530. Among these volunteers were Giacomo Veneziani, a national hero; David Almagià; Giuseppe Coen Cagli, who fought with the Death Brigade; Mosè Esdra and Salomon Vitali, who distinguished themselves at the battle of the Janiculum; Ciro Finzi, who lost his life on June 16, 1849, after having fought in the Five Days of Milan. Many Leghorn Jews followed Garibaldi to Rome. Worthy of note was Raffaele Telio, who was wounded at Villa Pamfili, promoted to the rank of an officer for distinguished service, and fought at Velletri, Ponte Molle, and Vascello.

[78] "The prohibition against keeping Christian servants was renewed, the tribute to the House of Catechumens and to the pastorate of St. Angelo was again demanded, and other violent regulations against the Jews followed. In October the French soldiery occupied the ghetto for some paltry pretext, and for three days searched houses for stolen church property, which was naturally not found. On the other hand, silverware, linens, carpets, materials, even brocades from the synagogues and cash were carried off, and many Jews were arrested. A deputation of the Jewish community which called on Cardinal Savelli was told that Jews were responsible for the long duration of the revolutionary government. Even the attempts of Rothschild, whose financial assistance was indispensable to the government, to obtain concessions for the Jews of the Papal State were entirely without result." Vogelstein, *op. cit.*, p. 342.

[79] "There was scarcely a profession or a calling that was open to the Jews. Arts and sciences were closed to them, and they were refused access to trades or to any form of manufacture by machinery. Even trade in old clothes required a special license. Shops which they had in the city had to be closed at twilight." *Ibid.*, p. 344.

[80] *Ibid.*, p. 343. On the Mortara case *see* also Gotthard Deutsch's article in the *Jewish Encyclopedia,* vol. ix (1905), pp. 35–36 and literature listed therein.

[81] On December 15, 1858, Cavour wrote to Count della Minerva, charge d'affaires at the Vatican: "The Holy See is gravely in error in assuming an attitude of complacency about the Mortara affair. This inaction has served the purposes of the Emperor [Napoleon III]. But the consequences will be felt when a crisis will break out in Italy." *Cf. Lettere edite ed inedite di Camillo Cavour,* vol. vi (Torino 1887), p. 353.

[82] Loevinson, Ermanno, "Cavour e gli israeliti," in *Nuova Antologia,* Fifth Series, vol. cxlviii (1910), pp. 453–64.

[83] To cite: "There is nothing in all my political life that pleases me more than to have been able to choose as my most intimate and efficient collaborators men like Costantino Nigra and Isacco Artom; the latter, though of a faith different from ours, is a young man endowed with singular ability, with untiring zeal, and irreproachable character. . . . Public opinion will justly condemn the ignoble attacks on the part of those persons who still bewail the passing of an era when religious differences were enough to keep out of public office young men of training and ability." *Ibid.*, p. 457, note 1.

[84] Grilli, *op. cit.*, third part, p. 181.

[85] Perreau, *op. cit.*, p. 6.

[86] *Ibid.*

[87] Foà, *op. cit.*, p. 532.

[88] *Ibid.*

[89] *Ibid.*, p. 533.

[90] Perreau, *op. cit.,* p. 6. He also mentions two other decrees for Umbria (September 27, 1860) and Marche (September 25, 1860). *Ibid.*

[91] Foà, *op. cit.,* p. 534.

[92] *Ibid.*

[93] Borgese, G. A., *Common Cause* (New York 1943), p. 274.

[94] Article 77 declared that it is expedient that "the Catholic religion shall be held as the only religion of the State, to the exclusion of all other modes of worship." Article 78 stated that it is unwise and subject to anathema "that it has been provided by law, in some countries called Catholic, that persons coming to reside therein shall enjoy the public exercise of their worship." Cited by Borgese, *ibid.*

[95] Perreau, *op. cit.,* p. 7.

[96] Foà, *op. cit.,* p. 535.

[97] *Ibid.,* p. 532.

[98] Perreau, *op. cit.,* p. 7.

[99] Crosa, *op. cit.,* p. 100.

[100] To cite: "What does the first Article of the constitution mean when it says that the Catholic religion is the only religion of the state? Simply (and this has been so often repeated in and out of Parliament that it is above dispute) that whenever a religious ceremony is or will be required, it must follow the Catholic rite. This and no other is the meaning of this Article of the constitution." *Cf.* Perreau, *op. cit.,* p. 8.

[101] Crosa, *op. cit.,* p. 100.

[102] Perreau, *op. cit.,* p. 9.

[103] This was expressed in Articles 140–144. *Cf.* Ruffini, *Diritti di libertà,* p. 74; Peyrot, Giorgio, *La libertà di coscienza e di culto di fronte alla costituente italiana,* ed. 2 (Rome 1946), pp. 10–11.

EDITORS' PREFACE

Friedrich Engels and the Jews

Marx, Kautsky, Luxemburg, Lenin, Trotsky, Stalin, Mao, and other socialist and communist ideologues have generally spoken with one voice on the Jewish problem in modern society. It is a voice which is reluctant to or even refuses to recognize the Jews as a nationality or ethnic-national group with the right to its own collective survival under socialism. Religion was ignored or shelved as of little or no consequence in the socialist order. Moreover, Judaism was generally viewed as a function of capitalist society, and the Jews an economic caste doomed to disappear in the proletarian society of the future. Territory was the indispensable determinant of nationality. With occasional exceptions, the existence of cultural, psychological, and ethnic and national aspects that enter into the making of a nation or nationality is not deemed to be valid in the case of the Jewish people. The existence of the State of Israel has not been accepted by many Marxist thinkers as supplying the territorial ingredient which would justify the recognition of a Jewish nation.

This approach was sanctified by Karl Marx, a man of Jewish birth and Polish rabbinical stock whose father was baptized mainly for economic reasons, when, after Napoleon's defeat, Jews in Westphalia

236

were deprived of their civil equality. Baptism seemed then a practical solution for certain types of culturally emancipated Jews well on the road to assimilation, especially when threatened by the danger of loss of income and status.

Silberner holds that it is difficult to separate the individual contributions of Marx and Engels to socialist thought and direction because of their long and close collaboration, with one important exception: the vital differences in their approaches to Jews and the Jewish problem. The author traces some of these distinctions to the fact that Engels outlived Marx by some twelve years and had the opportunity to observe both the growing appeal of political antisemitism and the rise of the Jewish labor movement. Silberner concludes that Engels, the Gentile who learned to read Yiddish and possibly Hebrew as well, faced the Jewish problem more objectively than Marx, the convert to Christianity, who spent a lifetime in constant fear of being reminded of his ancestry.

In the 1830s, Engels' references to Jews were unbiased. In the forties, he did no more than follow Marx's hostile opinions in the latter's classical 1844 essay, *Zur Judenfrage*. Thereafter, Engels, like his partner, employed the terms "Jew" and "Jewish" in a derogatory manner, stereotyped Jews in publications and in private letters, and shared the prevailing prejudices against individual Jews.

But in 1878 a change took place, a consequence of Dühring's racist attack on Marx. In 1890, Engels strongly denounced antisemitism and extolled the Jewish contribution to socialism. Silberner suggests an additional reason for the change in Engels' attitude, namely, the influence of Eleanor Marx Aveling, Marx's daughter, who identified herself as a Jewess. Like his classical essay on Marx's antisemitism, published in *Historia Judaica*, and many of Silberner's other writings, the present study is essential for an understanding of the Marxist positions on the Jewish problem.

EDMUND SILBERNER, a Professor at the Hebrew University in Jerusalem, has written extensively on the socialist movement and the Jewish question. He is the author of *Ha-sotsialism ha-maaravi u-sheelat ha-yehudim* (Western Socialism and the Jewish Question; German version, *Sozialisten zur Judenfrage*). He is also an authority on Moses Hess. Silberner wrote Hess' biography, *Moses Hess, Geschichte seines Lebens*, and edited his letters, *Briefwechsel*. He also edited Hess' works and compiled *Moses Hess: An Annotated Bibliography*.

Friedrich Engels and the Jews

by Edmund Silberner

In the history of socialism the names of Friedrich Engels and Karl Marx are linked together so closely and so justly that in most cases it does not seem very important to distinguish the contribution of each to the common work. From our particular point of view, however, a separate analysis is indispensable because of certain vital differences between them. The fact that Marx was of Jewish origin while Engels was not is important inasmuch as Marx, just because of his origin, was emotionally blocked on the Jewish question,[1] while Engels never was. Marx held during his whole lifetime more or less the same ideas on the Jews while Engels' view on the subject underwent an interesting change. This change is partly due to the fact that Engels outlived Marx by over a decade (1883–1895), during which time he witnessed not only a rising wave of political antisemitism, but also a rapid development of the Jewish labor movement, in England as well as in the United States.

Abraham Cahan, a leading figure in the American Jewish labor movement who in 1892 was introduced to Engels by Eleanor Marx, recounts how his host read to him a few lines in Yiddish (from the New York *Arbeter Tseitung*) and then remarked: "Do you think that I cannot read *lashon hakodesh?* . . . The capitalist newspapers had some reason in saying that I, myself, am a Jew."[2]

Reprinted from JEWISH SOCIAL STUDIES, Volume XI, 1949

Among Engels' writings of particular significance for our subject are, apart from his correspondence with Marx, Sorge, Bernstein and others, his articles in a variety of newspapers and magazines such as *Telegraph für Deutschland* (1839), *The Northern Star* (1846–47), *Deutsche Brüsseler Zeitung* (1847–48), *Neue Rheinische Zeitung* (1848–49), *New York Tribune* (1851–52), *Volksstaat* (1872), *Arbeiterzeitung* (1890), *Vorwärts* (1893), and *Neue Zeit* (1894–95). Of his books, *Herrn Eugen Dühring's Umwälzung der Wissenschaft* (1881) includes a relevant passage, and one must add to this *Die deutsche Ideologie* (1845–46), which was written by Engels and Marx in such a way that the recognition of their individual shares seems impossible. The Marx-Engels Institute, which has published thus far only a small part—though an important one—of the manuscripts of Engels, suspended the publication of his collected works in 1935. There is little doubt that some of the currently inaccessible manuscripts would be of interest for the present study. Thus Gustav Mayer points out the existence of a manuscript note by Engels "on the Jew in Germany," but does not say a word about its content.[3] None the less, enough material is available on Engels' attitude toward the Jews. As yet the subject has not been examined in a monograph nor analyzed in general works. Even Gustav Mayer's fine biography of Engels neglects to examine this subject.

I

The very first casual remarks that Engels made about the Jews are of interest only insofar as they reflect his rather unbiased attitude towards them. Evaluating the work of certain contemporary writers, he indicates in passing the Jewish origin of some of them.[4] He was particularly impressed by Karl Isidor Beck, "a man of genius," and the fine picture of Jewish misery that he painted in his *Nächte, gepanzerte Lieder* (1838).[5] Soon, however, his new poems disappointed Engels.[6] A few years later he ridiculed his appeal to his coreligionist, Rothschild, to improve the world.[7] His *Trödeljude*,[8] says Engels, includes some "naive and nice" verses,[9] but his description of economic discrimination against the Jews is devoid of all poetry and is nothing but "liberal-Young-German Jewish drivel *(Judensabbel)*."[10]

II

From the middle forties, Engels' ideas on the Jews moved in the same direction as those of Marx. In 1844, Marx published his *Zur Judenfrage*. That Engels was fascinated by Marx's views of the Jewish problem is clearly visible, not only from some of his later pronouncements, but also from his letter to Marx about their first joint work, *Die heilige Familie* (1845). The latter includes three sections on the Jewish question written by Marx, in which he briefly summarized what he had said on the subject in *Zur Judenfrage*. Engels was delighted with these sections. "Your discussion of the Jewish question," he wrote to Marx, is "brilliant" and will produce an "excellent effect."[11] It is clear that almost from the beginning of his literary career, Engels' opinions on the Jews were to a large extent determined by those of Marx.[12]

Typically enough, the word "Jew" is used by Engels as an equivalent of "speculator" or "financier." This is done first indirectly by way of translation or quotation of texts in which the word appears with this connotation. In fact, Engels included in his translation of Fourier three pages from the latter's *Théorie des quatre mouvements,* where the Jews are identified with fraudulent defaulters.[13] True, in his introductory note, Engels himself does not make use of antisemitic terminology; but neither does he find fault with the language of Fourier, which he certainly would have done if he had any objection to make. The same procedure is followed by Engels when he reproduces a passage from an anonymous article in *La Réforme*—a leftist organ to which he himself contributed—where the words "these Jews, these poison-mongers," are used in reference to different kinds of tyrants and exploiters.[14]

Engels also defends, by implication at least, a well-known antisemitic pamphlet brought out in 1846.[15] In an article in *The Northern Star,* a Chartist newspaper, he points out that the contemporary social system in France is attacked in different ways by different sections of the French people. He writes:

But there has been started in Paris, a short time ago, a new mode of attack which deserves to be mentioned. A working man has written a pamphlet against the head of the system, not against Louis-Philippe, but against "Rothschild I. King of the Jews." The success of this pamphlet (it has now gone through some twenty editions) shows how much this was an attack in the right direction. King Rothschild has been obliged to publish two defenses against these attacks of a man whom nobody knows, and the whole of whose property consists in the suit of clothes he wears.[16]

Whether the attack was in the right direction simply because the pamphlet was a best-seller is a question which does not fall within the scope of this study. It is, however, necessary to recall that the anonymous pamphlet was not at all socialist in character but rather what the authors of the *Communist Manifesto* were accustomed to call petty bourgeois. It was a kind of forerunner of the modern antisemitic pamphlets which appeared in great numbers at the end of the 19th century and later. Its vocabulary is reminiscent of the language of many instigators of pogroms. Its anonymous author ("Satan"), known as a specialist in the *chronique scandaleuse,* was not as poor as Engels depicted him. He was Georges-Marie Mathieu-Dairnvaell, a democratic writer and bookseller in Paris. None of his opuscules shows the slightest trend towards communism. In view of these facts, Engels' praise is the more significant.

The Jew as reflected in the writings of Engels at this time is either a merchant or money-lender. The Jews have monopolized the exchange of manufactured commodities against agricultural produce in Poland and Bohemia. "This," he writes, "has been, though in a lesser degree, the case in all the east of Europe. The handicraftsman, the small shopkeeper, the petty manufacturer, is a German up to this day in Petersburg, Pesth, Jassy, and even Constantinople; while the money-lender, the publican, the hawker—a very important man in these thinly populated countries—is very generally a Jew, whose native tongue is a horribly corrupted German."[17]

On the other hand, he notes that there are, in the west, wealthy Jews. Speaking of recent social changes in Prussia, Engels points out that the rapid development of industry and especially of the stock-exchange swindling has dragged all ruling classes into the whirlpool of speculation. The corruption imported from France is growing with an unheard of rapidity. "Strousberg [a German-Jewish financier] and Péreire [a French-Jewish banker]" says Engels, "take off their hats to each other. Ministers, generals, princes and counts deal in stocks in spite of the most cunning bourse-Jews, and the state recognizes their equality by making the bourse-Jews barons in large numbers."[18] The singling out of Jewish speculators is the more strange as Engels saw in the stock-exchange an institution which does not directly affect the workers: the bourse changes only the distribution of the surplus value already stolen from the workers. But it also accelerates the concentration of capital and therefore is as revolutionary as the steam-engine. Hence he was opposed to the introduction of taxes on stock-exchange dealings.[19]

The Jew is a subject of ridicule in more than one article written by Engels in 1848. Since he sympathized with the Polish cause, it is obvious that he was opposed to those Germans and Jews of Posen who wanted to Germanize this province.[20] In his polemics, however, he went far beyond what was necessary for the elucidation of a political problem. In order to show that the Jews of Posen are not Germans— as the German bourgeoisie then asserted—he simply mocks at the way they speak German.[21] And he also points to what all antisemites consider as specifically Jewish characteristics. In his controversy with Prince Felix Lichnowski, who advocated a policy of Germanizing the Poles, and alluding to the well-known lines of Ernst Moritz Arndt, Engels wrote that the fatherland of the Prine extends

> *So weit ein polnischer Jude deutsch kauderwelscht,*
> *Auf Wucher leiht, Münz und Gewicht verfälscht.*[22]

Curiously enough, Engels himself, in an article written for Marx, asserted only a few years later that in western Slavic countries (Poland, Bohemia) the Jews, "if they belong to any nationality, are in these countries certainly rather Germans than Slavonians."[23] And speaking of Hungary, where, according to him, the Germans are in all respects except language true Magyars, he noted that only "the Jews and Saxons in Transylvania make an exception and insist upon the preservation of an absurd nationality within an alien country."[24] It is not clear from the context what the real nationality of these Jews is supposed to be; their "absurd nationality," according to Engels, seems however, to be German.

Evidence of Engels' contemptuous attitude towards the Jews is particularly abundant in his correspondence with Marx. To designate a Jew, he used, apart from the regular German word *Jude,* the slang terms *Jud* and *Jid.*[25] Alexander Weill, in Engels' opinion, "is too much of a Jew" to write articles without being paid for it.[26] The Jewish parentage of Leo Fränkel, a well-known revolutionary, is expressed in an untranslatable way: *"Das Fränkelche ist das richtige Jidche."*[27] Leibel Choras, a man about whom biographical data do not seem to be available, is called "the old damned Jew," because of the unsolicited visits he paid to Engels.[28] In order to ridicule someone, Engels simply called him a Jew or compared him with a Jew. "To cheer you up," he wrote to Marx, "I am sending you a pamphlet on banks by Professor Geffcken of Strassburg, which belongs to Utin. How clever these people are! And they quote always only their own lousy gang, authorities like Augspurg (who ever heard of the Jew [*Jud*]?) and the great [Adolf] Wagner, of whom it is said:

> *Gilt nichts mehr der Tausves-Jontof,*
> *Was soll gelten? Zeter! Zeter!*[29]

Occasionally Engels also mocked at Jewish names. Once he called Moses Hess "Mauses";[30] at another time he wrote to Marx: "There appeared in Paris a naturalist who calls himself *Chmoulevitch* (Schmulsohn!). This beats even Ephraim Gescheit [Lassalle]."[31]

A particularly spiteful vocabulary is used in connection with Lassalle. Engels called him by turns "the silly Yid," "Judel Braun," "Ephraim," "Ephraim Gescheit," "pure Ephraim Gescheit," "Jacob Wieseltier" (weasel beast), "Itzig," "the great Itzig," and posthumously: "Itzig selig" and "Baron Itzig."[32]

It would be erroneous to attribute these epithets only to personal animosity of Engels to Lassalle. This animosity undoubtedly sharpened the tongue of Engels, but it is indisputable that, for him, Lassalle typified the Jew and particularly the eastern, Polish Jew, whom he deeply disliked. Lassalle, Engels agreed, certainly had great talent, yet "as a genuine Jew from the Slavic border, he always was ready, under the pretext of party interests, to exploit everyone for his private ends. His mania for forcing his way into high society, for succeeding, even if only in semblance, in whitewashing with all kinds of pomade and make up [the fact that he is] a greasy Jew (*Jud*) from Breslau, has always been repulsive."[33] Lassalle is also characterized by "Jewish impudence"[34] as well as by "Jewish reverence for momentary success."[35] In spite of his being one of the most notable political figures in Germany,[36] Lassalle was called "the Polish Schmuhl,"[37] a nickname which in Engels' mouth was the less flattering as even much later, in 1890, he still considered "the Polish Jew as the caricature of the Jews."[38] Let us also recall that Lassalle's Jewishness is held as partly responsible for his tragic end in a duel. "Such a thing could only happen to Lassalle, with that singular mixture of frivolity and sentimentality, Judaism and knight errantry which was peculiar to him."[39] After all that has been said, it is rather surprising that Engels himself points to the fact that Eugen Dühring, the well-known antisemite, referred to Lassalle as "our Jewish hero."[40]

Little attention was paid by Engels to Jewish sufferings. In 1848 he noted in passing that, in Russia, Jews are persecuted in the interest of the indigenous bourgeoisie whose business is spoiled by hawkers.[41] Twenty years later, he interviewed the above-mentioned Leibel Choras about the persecution of Jews in Moldavia and arrived at the conclusion that the situation there did not seem to be "too bad."[42]

This is virtually all that can be found on the Jews in the writings of Engels up to 1878. Up to this date, his pronouncements are chiefly contemptuous and, to our knowledge, contain no reference to any positive aspects of Jewish history. Even "the so-called sacred writings of the Jews are nothing more than the record of the old Arabian religious and tribal tradition, modified by the early separation of the Jews from their tribally related but nomadic neighbors."[43] Once, he refers, by implication only, to a heroic event in Jewish history. He quotes the following passage from Gneisenau's memorial of 1811: "The clergy of all denominations are to be ordered, as soon as the war [of liberation against Napoleon] breaks out, to preach insurrection, to paint French oppression in the blackest colours, to remind the people of the Jews under the Maccabees, and to call upon them to follow their example. . . ."[44]

III

From 1878 on, one can perceive a gradual change in the attitude of Engels towards the Jews. In that year, he published his famous *Anti-Dühring*, which contains an important, though casual comment on antisemitism. Dühring is attacked there, among other things, for his rabid Judeophobia:

His hatred of the Jews, [writes Engels] which he carries to ridiculous extremes and exhibits on every possible occasion, is a feature which, if not specifically Prussian, is yet specific to the region east of the Elbe. That same philosopher of reality who has a sovereign contempt for all prejudices and superstitions is himself so deeply imbued with personal crotchets that he calls the popular prejudice against the Jews, inherited from the bigotry of the Middle Ages, a "natural judgement" based on "natural grounds," and he rises to the pyramidal heights of the assertion that "socialism is the only power which can oppose population conditions with a strong Jewish admixture." (Conditions with a Jewish admixture! What 'natural' German language!)[45]

Why did Engels denounce antisemitism in his *Anti-Dühring?* To understand his motivation it is sufficient to recollect that Dühring considered Marx as a "member of the same race" as Lassalle and attacked him not only on theoretical but also racial grounds. In the struggle between Marx and Bakunin he saw a manifestation of a "racial contradiction in the International" and a warning that "the emancipation of labor cannot be accomplished in the manner of an Alliance Israélite." He also pointed out that Bakunin's repugnance to Marx's "Jewish blood and German ballast of erudition" is "understandable." Furthermore, he noted that one cannot "dismiss the suspicion that obstinate Judaism may still have preserved some residues in his [Marx], despite his own ridicule of certain Jewish authors."[46] None of these "charges" against Marx is quoted by Engels, for the obvious reason that he did not want to give them any indirect publicity, realizing well that they would remain unknown to the average reader of *Anti-Dühring*. None the less, to pass them over in complete silence would have been for Engels too great a concession to Dühring's aggressiveness. Hence his summary denunciation of antisemitism. The "charges" against Marx were disposed of by a general confutation of Judeophobia. This was the more sufficient as he accused Dühring of mental incompetence due to megalomania.[47]

Three years after the publication of *Anti-Dühring,* some anti-Jewish riots occurred in Pomerania (July 1881), and elections to the Reichstag were to be held in October 1881. To keep Engels informed about events, Eduard Bernstein dispatched to him some unspecified antisemitic pamphlets. Engels found them more silly and childish than anything he had ever read. The German antisemitic movement, Engels observed, was initiated by the government to obtain a conservative vote and would collapse, on higher orders, as soon as the elections were over, or even sooner if, as had just happened in Pomerania, it overshot the mark set by the authorities. Such government-fostered movements, added Engels, cannot be treated scornfully enough, and the *Sozialdemokrat* did well to treat them so. It is obvious that Engels did not see any great threat in the antisemitism of those days. As if to justify his point of view, he quoted Carl Hirsch, a well-known Social-Democratic publicist, who had reported to him from Berlin that, though "the Germans have a natural aversion to the Jews," German workers and progressive petty bourgeois hate the government "more energetically."[48]

The strongest denunciation of antisemitism was made by Engels in a letter to an unknown correspondent, on April 19, 1890. It was published, in part, with the consent of both but without mentioning the name of the addressee, in the Vienna *Arbeiterzeitung* of May 9, 1890. Relatively little publicity was given to it by socialists and its first reprint appeared, to our knowledge, only after the First World War.[49] The addressee, some important Austrian Social-Democratic leader, Engelbert Pernerstorfer perhaps,[50] must have been antisemitically minded, otherwise Engels would not have warned him personally of the dangers of political antisemitism, as he in effect did. "I must leave it to your consideration," he stated emphatically, "whether with antisemitism you will not cause more misfortune than good."[51] After this introductory remark, Engels observed: "Antisemitism is the distinctive sign of a backward civilization and is, therefore, only found in Prussia and Austria or in Russia."[52] If pursued in England or the United States, anti-Jewish propaganda would simply be laughed at. In France, Drumont's writings—though incomparably superior to those of the German Judeophobes—provoke only an ineffective one-day sensation. Moreover, Engels thought that Drumont, who was then coming forward as a candidate for the City Council, would himself have to declare that he was as much against Christian as Jewish capital.[53]

Who is fomenting antisemitism in Prussia? The *junkers,* who with an income of 10,000 marks spend 20,000 and, therefore, fall into the hands of usurers. Who forms the chorus and screams in unison with them? Both in Prussia and Austria it is the petty bourgeois, the artisan, the small shopkeeper, sinking into ruin because of the competition of large-scale capitalism. Yet if capital destroys these reactionary classes, it is accomplishing its historical function, and whether it is Semitic or Aryan, circumcised or baptized, it is doing good work: it is helping the backward Prussians and Austrians to reach a stage of development in which all the old social differences are resolved into the one great contradiction between capitalists and wage-workers.

> Only where this is not yet the case, where there is as yet no strong capitalist class and hence no strong wage-earning class, where capital, being still too weak to get hold of the whole national production, has thus the Stock Exchange as the main scene of its activity, and where, consequently, production is still in the hands of peasants, landowners, artisans, and similar classes surviving from the Middle Ages—only there is capital predominantly Jewish and only there is antisemitism to be found.[54]

Engels does not furnish any substantial evidence to prove the correctness of his "historico-materialist" analysis of modern antisemitism. He simply says that, among the millionaires of the whole of North America, there is not a single Jew, and that, compared with these Americans, the Rothschilds are real beggars. Even in England, Rothschild is a man of modest means compared, for instance, with the Duke of Westminster. And even in western Germany, on the Rhine, where are the Jews? asks Engels.

Antisemitism is thus nothing but a reaction of the medieval, per-
ishing strata of society against modern society, which essentially
consists of capitalists and wage-earners; under the cloak of apparent socialism it, therefore, only serves reactionary ends; it is a
variety of feudal socialism, and with that we can have nothing to
do.[55]

It seems to be an axiom for Engels that antisemitism is a product
of capitalistically undeveloped countries and that it hinders the development of capitalism.[56] Some socialists considered that, after all,
antisemitism is an anti-capitalist manifestation, and hence favorable
to socialism in the long run. Engels tried to show that antisemitism
does not favor the socialist cause, because, as long as conditions are
not ripe for social revolution, it is not in the interest of socialism to
impede the development of capitalism.

Added to this [remarks Engels in a revealing passage] antisemitism
falsifies the whole state of affairs. It does not even know the Jews
it cries down. Otherwise, it would know that here in England, and
in America, thanks to the eastern-European antisemites, and in
Turkey, thanks to the Spanish inquisition, there are thousands and
thousands of *Jewish proletarians;* and, what is more, these Jewish
workers are the worst exploited and most wretched of all. Here
in England we had *three* strikes of Jewish workers within the last
twelve months, and then are we expected to carry antisemitism as
a fight against capital?[57]

For the first time, Engels draws attention here to the existence of a
Jewish working class. Inasmuch as he lived in London, it is obvious
that he refers in the first place, to Jewish workers in Anglo-Saxon
countries. Why, however, he mentions the Jewish workers in Turkey
rather than those, more numerous, in eastern Europe, is not clear.
However this may be, one easily discerns the sympathetic tone in
which he speaks of Jewish workers.

His sympathy is not limited to Jewish proletarians exclusively.
Quite apart from Jewish workers, concludes Engels, in a more personal way,

we owe much too much to the Jews. To say nothing of Heine and Börne, Marx was of purest Jewish blood;[58] Lassalle was a Jew. Many of our best people are Jews. My friend, Victor Adler, who is now sitting in jail in Vienna for his devotion to the cause of the proletariat, Eduard Bernstein,[59] editor of the London *Sozialdemokrat,* Paul Singer, one of our best men in the Reichstag—people of whose friendship I am proud, are all—Jews! Have I not been turned into a Jew myself by the *Gartenlaube?*[60] And indeed if I had to choose, then rather a Jew than "Herr von . . ."[61]

Whatever he wrote on the Jews after 1890 is only casual but none the less permeated with a new spirit. He no longer singles out *Jewish* bourse-wolves. "Rothschilds and Vanderbilts"[62] are treated alike. He still sees in the Polish Jew "the representative in Europe of commerce in its lowest stages"—but envisages his "pettifogging business tricks" as a characteristic of capitalist production in its early stages rather than a peculiarity of the Jews as such.[63] He was favourably impressed by the American-Jewish labor leader, Abraham Cahan, or "the Jewish apostle,"[64] as he called him. At the request of Cahan, who then intended to prepare a Yiddish translation of the Communist Manifesto, Engels promised to write a preface for it.[65] He not only does not tolerate antisemitism any longer, but censures it even if it manifests itself among workers. In a letter to Sorge, he does not feel happy about the opposition of the English dockers to the immigration of what they called "foreign paupers," meaning, in fact, Russian Jews.[66] At the end of 1894 he warned the French comrades not to make untenable promises to peasants and handicraftsmen, such as guaranteeing to them the ownership of their land or small shops; such promises are worthy of antisemitic demagogues but not of consistent socialists. To make such pledges would mean "to degrade the party to the level of rowdy antisemitism."[67] If peasants and artisans do want such pledges, let them go where they belong, namely to the antisemites. There they may learn of how much consequence are the "splendid phrases" of the antisemites and "what tunes are played by the fiddles of which the antisemitic heaven is full."[68]

Even in his last years, when he showed a greater interest in Jews than ever before, Engels did not examine their ethnic or national

character. Of the bulk of the Jewish people, then concentrated in
Russia, he only says, in another connection, that the tsarist government had turned them also into deadly enemies of the regime.[69] Yet
from a casual pronouncement made in 1892, one may infer that,
contrary to what he had thought of the Jews in 1852,[70] he now considered them as a distinct nationality. In fact, dealing with the
position of the native workers in the United States, Engels noted, in a
letter to Herman Schlüter, that the American "bourgeoisie knows
much better than the Austrian government how to play off one
nationality against the other: *Jews,* Italians, Czechs, etc., against
Germans and Irish . . ."[71] This clearly involves the recognition of
the Jews as a nationality apart.

There is no record left to show what, if anything, Engels thought
of the national aspirations of the Jews. Even Hess' *Rom und Jerusalem* (1862) is not mentioned by Engels. The two friends had parted
many years before the book was published, and they did not see each
other after May 1848.[72] Yet Engels showed so little understanding
and sympathy for small nations that there can be no doubt that he
would have considered Hess' Zionist ideas, at best, as the fantastic
utopia of a dreamer.

IV

From the preceding pages, it is clear that during the latter part of
his life—from 1878 on—Engels gradually turned from an antisemite
into a staunch enemy of antisemitism. Four main factors of personal
as well as of an objective nature seem to explain this about-face:

(1) As a close friend of Marx, who was attacked by Dühring on
theoretical and racial grounds, Engels—in his polemic against the
German philosopher and antisemite—could not limit himself to doc-
trinal issues only. He also had to take into account the racial
"charges" against the author of *Das Kapital,* which, incidentally, had
also been made a few years earlier by Bakunin. This was the more
necessary as Dühring was very popular in German Social-Democratic
circles, particularly in the years 1875 to 1877.[73] The easiest and the
most logical procedure for Engels was to condemn antisemitism *in
toto,* and thus to get rid of the necessity to refute antisemitic "charges"

in detail. This was done by Engels in 1878.

(2) From what is known about Marx's daughter, Eleanor Marx-Aveling ("Tussy"), whom Engels treated as if she were his own child, one may infer that she very probably contributed to his reorientation. Both Engels and "Tussy" lived in London, at that time an important center of Jewish immigration with a lively Jewish labor movement. How she got in touch with that movement cannot be ascertained. It is, however, known that in 1887 Engels encouraged a small group of his followers, including "Tussy," to start a campaign in the East End of London, with a view to establishing trade unions for the great mass of poor, unskilled workers.[74] She agitated in the radical clubs, and her work was successful.[75] Here in the East End, "that immense haunt of misery," "Tussy" must have met, perhaps for the first time, Jewish workers. She was frequently seen at the Jewish Socialist Club in Berner Street, in the late eighties, and, even more frequently, in the early nineties, after the Club, having separated itself from the Anarchists, moved to Christian Street.[76] She is reported to have learned Yiddish in order to take an active part in the Jewish labor movement.[77] Abraham Cahan, Morris Winchevsky, and Eduard Bernstein, all of whom knew her personally, were all struck by her definite consciousness of being a Jewess. Cahan reported that in 1891 she told him: "We Jews have a special duty to work for the working class."[78] He also adds that she liked to speak of herself as being a Jewess,[79] though in fact she was only half-Jewish. During the International Socialist Congress at Zurich (1893) she said—though half-jokingly—to Winchevsky, delegate of Jewish trade unions in London: "We Jews must stick together."[80] When he observed that many a socialist cannot imagine that Jewish workers do exist, she was glad to draw the attention of the congress to the fact that he was there representing just such workers.[81] Bernstein reported, after her death, that she used to start her speeches to the workers with the words: "I am a Jewess."[82] He also pointed out that her sympathy was not limited to Jewish proletarians, but extended to persecuted Jews of all social classes.[83]

Under these circumstances, one can hardly escape the conclusion that "Tussy," by frequent insistence on her own Jewish origin and by reporting to Engels on her experience with the Jewish labor movement, drew his attention to the Jews and thus contributed, directly or indirectly, to his reorientation in the Jewish question.

(3) The rising wave of antisemitism in Germany, and even more in Austria, could not escape Engels' attention. Since the antisemites fought also against the socialists, the latter had to think about measures of self-protection, so much the more as some of their outstanding leaders, Marx, Lassalle, Bernstein, Singer, Victor Adler were of Jewish origin. By 1890, if not earlier, Engels must have realized that antisemitism is, to some extent at least, a dangerous rival of social-democracy, and that to denounce it means also to defend socialism.

(4) The emergence of a Jewish labor movement was another important factor responsible for Engels' reorientation. London, where he resided, harbored tens of thousands of Jewish workers. They immigrated in increasing numbers from Russia and Poland after the pogroms of 1881. So miserable was the condition of their life under the "sweating system," that an English magazine in 1884 drew attention to the extreme poverty of some 30,000 Russo-Polish Jews huddled together in the overcrowded districts of London.[84] Ten years later the number of Jews in London was officially estimated at 80,000, most of them being workers.[85] They were organized in several trade unions and had their own organs in Yiddish as well as a well-known club in Berner Street, already referred to. They struck not infrequently for higher wages or better working conditions.[86] There can be no doubt that Engels was aware of these facts. His reading of Yiddish must have made it easier for him to keep informed about the Jewish labor movement in England as well as in the United States. The existence of such a movement obviously could not fail to affect his position towards the Jews. It is true that he had no particular connections with Jewish labor groups.[87] None the less, he could not, as he had done in the past, continue to identify Jews with exploiters.

These were the reasons why Engels reversed his stand on the Jews. Once freed from many, if not all, prejudices against them, he fought antisemitism more consistently and courageously than many a socialist, Jew or Gentile. This is evident especially in view of the events at the Second International Socialist congress at Brussels in 1891. While Engels had unconditionally condemned antisemitism in 1890, the congress did it only half-heartedly and in a very diluted form, since it was afraid of being accused of favoring the Jews. Abraham Cahan made a motion that antisemitism be condemned outright. Because of this, Victor Adler, supported by Paul Singer, reproached him with "tactlessness,"[88] and the congress, after hearing two French socialists, Regnard and Argyriadès, voted a hybrid resolution condemning both "antisemitic and philosemitic incitement."[89] Engels' criticism of antisemitism was also more far-seeing, because he did not seem to have thought, as did the German Social-Democrats at their congress at Cologne (1893), that antisemitism, in spite of its reactionary character, plays "after all" a "revolutionary" role.[90] In contradistinction to many of his comrades, he thus avoided making a virtue of necessity.

NOTES

[1] On Marx and the Jewish problem *see* my "Was Marx an Antisemite?" in *Historia Judaica*, vol. xi (1949), pp. 3–52; Mayer, G., "Early German Socialism and Jewish Emancipation," in JEWISH SOCIAL STUDIES, vol. i, no. 4 (October 1939), pp. 409–22; Bloom, Solomon, "Karl Marx and the Jews," *ibid.*, vol. iv, no. 1 (January 1942), pp. 3–16.

[2] Cahan, A., *Bleter fun mein leben*, vol. iii (New York 1926), p. 264. Words written in Hebrew already occur in a letter by Engels to Friedrich Gräber of February 22, 1841. (Marx-Engels *Gesamtausgabe*, ed. by the Marx-Engels Institute, pt. i, vol. ii, p. 562). *Cf.* also *Neue Zeit*, vol. xiii (1894), p. 40.

[3] Mayer, *Friedrich Engels, Eine Biographie* (The Hague 1934), vol. ii, p. 455.

[4] Engels to Friedrich Gräber (January 1839), *Gesamtausgabe*, vol. ii, p. 497. *Cf.* also p. 539.

[5] Engels to Wilhelm Gräber (July 1839), *ibid*, p. 536.

[6] *Ibid.*, vol. ii, pp. 57–61.

[7] *Ibid.*, vol. vi, pp. 35–47.

[8] In Karl Beck, *Lieder vom armen Mann* (Leipzig 1846), pp. 53–59.

[9] *Ibid.*, p. 40.

[10] *Ibid.*, p. 41.

[11] Engels to Marx, March 17, 1845, in Marx-Engels, *Briefwechsel,* 4 vols. (Berlin 1929–31), vol. i, p. 19.

[12] For a few disparaging remarks on the Jews in their joint work *Die deutsche Ideologie,* cf. *Gesamtausgabe,* vol. v, pp. 162, 386.

[13] Engels, "Ein Fragment Fouriers über den Handel," in *Gesamtausgabe*, vol. iv, pp. 409–53. On Fourierist antisemitism *see* my "Charles Fourier on the Jewish Question," in JEWISH SOCIAL STUDIES, vol. viii, no. 4 (October 1940), pp. 245–66, and "The Attitude of the Fourierist School towards the Jews," *ibid.*, vol. ix, no. 4 (October 1947), pp. 339–62.

[14] *Gesamtausgabe,* vol. vi, p. 341.

[15] Mathieu-Dairnvaell, George-Marie, *Histoire édifiante et curieuse de Rothschild Ier, Roi des Juifs, par Satan, pseud.,* 5th ed. (Paris 1846).

[16] *Gesamtausgabe* vol. vi, p. 30. Engels himself rarely points out the Jewish origin of Rothschild. It was but a joke when Engels, alluding to the English-French financial interests in Egypt, wrote to Bebel (September 23, 1882), a few days after the British had defeated the Egyptians at Tell-el-Kebir: "Die ganze ägyptische Geschichte war die Rache der Juden (Rothschild, Erlanger, etc.) für die alte Austreibung aus Ägypten unter Pharao." Marx-Engels, *Briefe an A. Bebel* . . . (Moscow 1933), vol. i, p. 274.

[17] Engels, "Germany, VIII. Revolution and Counter-Revolution," in *New York Tribune,* March 5, 1852, p. 7. For other short references to Jewish peddlers or merchants *see Neue Rheinische Zeitung,* June 9; August 9, 1848, *Gesamtausgabe,* vol. vii, pp. 41–42, 228.

[18] *Volksstaat* (January 4, 1873), p. 2.

[19] *Die Briefe von F. Engels an E. Bernstein* (Berlin 1925), pp. 110, 112, 116.

[20] *Gesamtausgabe,* vol. vii, pp. 165, 176.

[21] *Ibid.,* vol. vii, pp. 41–42, 291, 297, 331. Some 40 years later, in a letter to Sorge (April 29, 1886), Engels gives the following example of the Jewish way of constructing sentences in German: "Als der Bismarck ist gekommen vor die Zwangswahl, hat er lieber den Papst geküsst auf den Hintern als die Revolution auf den Mund." *Briefe . . . an Sorge* (Stuttgart 1906), p. 218.

[22] "Die Polendebatte in Frankfurt," in *Neue Rheinische Zeitung,* September 1, 1848, *Gesamtausgabe,* vol. vii, p. 331.

[23] "Germany . . . ," in *New York Tribune,* March 5, 1852. Engels says nothing about the nationality of the Jews in the non-Polish provinces of Russia. He notes, however, that Russia—in contradistinction to Poland—knows thoroughly how to assimilate ("nationalize") foreign elements such as Germans and Jews (Engels to Marx, May 23, 1851, *Briefwechsel,* vol. i, p. 206).

[24] Engels, "Ungarn," in *Neue Rheinische Zeitung,* January 13, 1849, in *Aus dem literarischen Nachlass von Karl Marx,* vol. iii, p. 239.

[25] *Briefwechsel,* vol. iii, p. 128; vol. ii, pp. 121, 210, vol. iii, p. 433; vol. iv, p. 137. About a few Austrian writers "of very indifferent ability, but gifted with that peculiar industrialism [*sic*] proper to the Jewish race," *cf.* Engels, "Germany. IV. Revolution and Counter-Revolution," *New York Tribune,* November 7, 1851. *Cf.* also Engels' letter to Marx, February 11, 1868 (vol. iv, p. 21): "Wiener Literaten, lauter in allen Wassern gewaschene Juden."

[26] *Briefwechsel,* vol. i, p. 28.

[27] *Ibid.,* vol. iv, p. 305.

[28] *Ibid.,* vol. iii, p. 432.

[29] *Ibid.,* vol. iv, p. 410 (December 5, 1873). The verse is from Heine's "Disputation" *(Romancero,* Pt. III) and refers to Rabbi Yom Tov Lipmann Heller's *Tosfoth Yom Tov,* additions or glosses to the six orders of the Mishnah.

I could not establish whether the economist Dietrich W. A. Augspurg was of Jewish origin.

[30] *Ibid*, vol. iii, p. 269 (May 12, 1865).

[31] *Ibid*., vol. iv, p. 3 (January 6, 1868). The catalog of the Bibliothèque Nationale, Paris, mentions a certain Dr. Ia. M. Chmoulevitch, translator into Russian of several veterinary treatises.

[32] *Briefwechsel*, vol. ii, pp. 191, 323, 371, 401, 458; vol. iii, p. 47; vol. ii, pp. 494, 507; vol. iii, pp. 85, 138, 141, 219, 235.

[33] *Ibid*., vol. ii, p. 122.

[34] *Ibid*., vol. ii, p. 494.

[35] Engels to Weydemeyer, November 24, 1864, in Marx-Engels, *Sochineniia*, vol. xxv, p. 423.

[36] *Briefwechsel*, vol. iii, p. 188.

[37] From an undisclosed MS. of Engels, according to Mayer, *op. cit.*, vol. ii, p. 80.

[38] Engels to Paul Ernst, June 5, 1890, Marx-Engels, *Sochineniia*, vol. xxviii, p. 221.

[39] *Briefwechsel*, vol. iii, p. 188.

[40] Engels, *Herrn Eugen Dührings Umwälzung der Wissenschaft* (Leipzig 1878), p. 15.

[41] *Gesamtausgabe*, vol. vi, p. 396.

[42] "Gestern kam der unvermeidliche Leibel Choras und verhinderte mich am Schreiben. Ich fragte ihn nach den Judenverfolgungen in der Moldau; er jammerte etwas, aber so arg scheint es nicht zu sein: mir missen's halt dulden, mir Jiden haben nit die Macht; er wäre gern russisch oder östreichisch, aber fällt ihm nicht ein fortzugehn. Der Hohenzoller sei ein dummer Junge und die Regierung in der Hand der 'Schreiber' (heruntergekommene Bojaren, die Bureaukratie spielen), und die zwacke die Juden so." Engels to Marx, May 6, 1868, *Briefwechsel, vol. iv, p. 52*.

[43] *Briefwechsel*, vol. i, p. 471 (May 18, 1853). Engels reached this conclusion after having read Charles Forster's *The Historical Geography of Arabia* (London 1844). About Engels' later views on the Jewish contribution to early Christianity—which I do not intend to discuss here—*see* his "Zur Geschichte des Urchristenthums," in *Neue Zeit*, vol. xiii (1894–95).

[44] Gneisenau as translated by Engels in his "Prussian Franc-Tireurs," in *Pall Mall Gazette*, December 9, 1870, reproduced in Engels, *Notes on War* (Vienna 1923), p. 107.

[45] Dühring, *Kritische Geschichte der Nationaloekonomie und des Sozialismus*, 2nd ed. (Berlin 1875). *Cf.* also pp. 119–20.

[46] *Ibid*., pp. 529, 572–75.

[47] Engels, *Herrn Eugen Dührings . . . in fine*.

[48] Engels to Bernstein, August 17, 1881, in *Briefe von F. Engels an E. Bernstein*, pp. 24–25.

[49] Engels, letter to an unknown correspondent, April 19, 1890, in Adler, Victor, *Aufsätze, Reden und Briefe* (Vienna 1822), vol. i, pp. 6–8.

[50] As suggested by Max Ermers, *Victor Adler* (Vienna 1932), p. 230.

[51] Adler, *op. cit.*, p. 6.

[52] *Ibid.*, p. 6.

[53] *Ibid.*

[54] *Ibid*, p. 7.

[55] *Ibid.*

[56] *Ibid*, pp. 7–8.

[57] *Ibid.*, p. 8.

[58] This seems to be the only exception to the otherwise correct statement of I. Berlin *(Karl Marx* [London 1939], p. 236): "The fact that he [Marx] was a Jew neither he nor Engels ever mention." Even as late as 1884 Engels, commenting on Lawrence Gronlund's *The Cooperative Commonwealth* (Boston 1884, p. 50), wrote to Bernstein: "Marx is not quoted, but it is only said: 'such noble Jews as Marx and Lassalle.' Au weih!" *Briefe von F. Engels an E. Bernstein*, p. 154.

[59] Some of his qualities are explained by his Jewish origin: Engels to Bebel, January 20, 1886, in Marx-Engels, *Briefe an A. Bebel* (Moscow 1933), vol. i, p. 427.

[60] A popular German antisemitic magazine.

[61] Engels, in Adler, *op. cit.*, p. 8.

[62] Engels, Preface (1892), to his *Condition of the Working-Class in England in 1844* (London 1892), p. viii. *Cf.* also his letter to Sorge, December 31, 1892, full text in Marx-Engels, *Correspondence 1846–1895* (New York 1934), p. 503; abridged in view of censorship in *Briefe . . . an Sorge* p. 387 (for an explanation of the word "Löwe-Judenflinten" used by Engels *cf. Universal Jewish Encyclopedia*, I, p. 366; VII, p. 162).

[63] Engels Preface (1892) to his *Condition of the Working-Class*, pp. v-vi. *Cf.* also his letter to Florence K. Wischnewetzky, March 12, 1886, in Marx-Engels, *Sochineniia*, vol. xxvii, p. 544.

[64] Engels to Sorge, September 14, 1891, in *Briefe . . . an Sorge*, p. 368. On the other hand, Georg Adler, author of an anti-Marxian book *(Die Grundlagen der Karl Marxschen Kritik . . . ,* Tübingen 1887), is described by Engels as a "miserable Jewish apostate" (Engels to Danielson, January 5, 1888, in *Die Briefe von Marx und Engels an Danielson* [Leipzig 1929] p. 44).

[65] Cahan, *Bleter,* vol. iii, p. 265.

[66] *Briefe . . . an Sorge,* p. 365 (August 9, 1891).

[67] Engels, "Die Bauernfrage in Frankreich und Deutschland," in *Neue Zeit,* vol. xiii (1894–1895), p. 303.

[68] *Ibid.*, p. 301.

[69] Engels, *Kann Europa abrüsten?* (Separatabdruck aus dem *Vorwärts* 1893) (Leipzig 1929), p. 20.

[70] See *supra,* footnote, 23.

[71] Engels to Schlüter, March 30, 1892, *Briefe . . . an Sorge,* p. 281. Italics mine.

[72] Engels to Kautsky, December 2, 1885, in Marx-Engels, *Briefe an A. Bebel . . .* (Moscow 1933), vol. i, p. 420.

[73] Riazanov, D. B., "Fünfzig Jahre Anti-Dühring," in *Unter dem Banner des Marxismus,* vol. ii (1928), pp. 466–74. Dühring was also popular among Russian socialists; *ibid.,* pp. 476–80.

[74] Mayer, *op. cit.,* vol. ii, p. 406.

[75] *Briefe von F. Engels an E. Bernstein,* p. 192 (May 5, 1887); Engels to Sorge, December 7, 1889, June 10, August 9, 1891, in *Briefe . . . an Sorge,* pp. 324, 363, 366.

[76] Winchevsky, Morris, "Eleanor Marx," in his *Gezamelte Verk,* vol. viii (New York 1927), pp. 194–95.

[77] Winogradasgaia, P., *Jenny Marx (von Westphalen) (in Russian) (Moscow 1933),* p. 126.

[78] Cahan, *Bleter,* vol. iii, p. 119.

[79] *Ibid.*

[80] Winchevsky, *op. cit.,* p. 200.

[81] *Ibid.,* p. 199. She also volunteered to furnish Winchevsky with materials on her father that only she possessed *(ibid.).* It is a great loss, perhaps an irreparable one, that he did not take advantage of this unique opportunity and did not inquire at all about her father's attitude toward the Jews.

[82] Bernstein, "Eleanor Marx," in *Neue Zeit,* vol. xvi, Pt. ii (1898), p. 122.

[83] *Ibid.*

[84] "Report . . . on the Polish Colony of Jew Tailors," in *The Lancet* (May 3, 1884), pp. 817–18.

[85] Soloweitschik, L., *Un prolétariat inconnu. Étude sur la situation sociale et économique des ouvriers juifs* (Brussels 1898), p. 29. *Cf.* also Halperin, G., *Die jüdischen Arbeiter in London* (Stuttgart 1903).

[86] Burgin, H., *Di geshikhte fun der yidisher arbeterbavegung* (New York 1915), pp. 41, 46, 54, 251, 254.

[87] An appeal made to Engels (1893) by an otherwise unknown "Association of Jewish Socialists" in Russia had nothing to do with matters Jewish; *cf.* Tscherikower, A., in Yivo *Historishe Shriften,* vol. iii (1939), pp. 798–800.

[88] Cahan, *op. cit.,* p. 162.

[89] *Congrès International Ouvrier Socialiste tenu à Bruxelles du 16 au 23 aôut 1891.* (Brussels 1893), p. 44: "tout en condamnant les excitations antisémitiques et philosémitiques . . ."

[90] *Cf.* the Cologne resolution on antisemitism, in Schröder, W., ed., *Handbuch der sozialdemokratischen Parteitage von 1863–1909* (Munich 1910), pp. 35–36.

EDITORS' PREFACE

Antisemitism in France
Before the Dreyfus Affair

Professor Byrnes' article is a guide through the labyrinth of French politics during the decade that preceded the Dreyfus Affair. The thread was antisemitism. By the 1880s, earlier tendencies had transformed antisemitism into a seemingly viable political movement which even had hopes of enlisting the Left. The aim of the antisemites was to take over the government of France, with Jew-hatred as the chief instrument of public persuasion.

The leading theoretician of antisemitism in France was Edouard Drumont, an activist and the author of the best-seller *La France Juive* (1886). Until the Dreyfus Affair, a drama of which Drumont was one of the playwrights, Jew-hatred appeared to be the wrong approach to power. The chances for its success improved with the anti-Dreyfus campaign, but were greatly diminished following the exoneration of the accused Jew. Later, there were other agitators. Most notorious among these in the inter-war period was Celine. But it was not until 1940 that Drumont's racist antisemitism became the none-too-reluctant policy of the Vichy regime which transformed the Third Republic into a Nazi protectorate. Byrnes' article provides a case study in the training of antisemites for the take-over of government

259

and, as such, can serve as a valuable lesson in the history of the Counter-Emancipation.

Convinced of antisemitism's popularity among the conservative elements, Drumont directed his propaganda to the working class. He was encouraged by the socialist leaders' empathy with antisemitism. Byrnes traces Drumont's failure to his incorrect assumptions and tactics. He was unsuccessful in uniting the antisemites of the Right and Left, the hoped-for basis for an effective political movement. Convinced of the popularity and usefulness of stigmatizing capitalism as a Jewish trait and stratagem, he urged in 1888 collectivism plus the "confiscation of all wealth won in the Jewish system," thus drawing the distinction between alleged evil Jewish capital and beneficial Christian wealth. His radicalism frightened the conservatives, who feared that antisemitism might lead to socialism. Resentful, Drumont for a time shifted his attack to the bourgeoisie rather than the Jews, and in 1892 ran for the Chamber of Deputies as a socialist. Hitherto, many socialist leaders had been convinced that the workers, attracted by the tactic of singling out the Jewish capitalists as the proletarians' enemies, would turn against all capitalists. However, Drumont's electoral competition posed the danger that the invocation of Jew-hatred as an anti-capitalist stratagem was likely to backfire in favor of reaction. This fear helped to put an end to the flirtation between the socialists and the antisemites, for the time being.

Drumont also tried to organize antisemitism on an international scale. He was elected in 1886 to the presidency of the short-lived *Alliance Antisemitique Universelle*. But the leadership of the antisemitic movements in the different European countries did not feel too keenly the need for an international organization. Drumont then attempted to work with the Boulangists, many of whom were antisemites. This turn alarmed both conservatives and socialists. It ended with Drumont's condemnation of Boulanger.

A more promising idea was the launching of the rabid antisemitic daily, *Le Libre Parole*, in 1882. It specialized in exposés, with frequent attacks against Jews in the Army. These sometimes resulted in duels, intended as circulation-builders. One notorious duel led to the deliberate murder of a Jewish officer. Such sensationalism, particularly the exposé of the Panama Scandal, raised the paper's circulation to 200,000 copies in 1893.

Again Drumont's success was short-lived. The fickle Paris public soon tired of a steady diet of minor scandals and duels. More tactical errors followed. Drumont's anti-Church tactics and his defense of anarchists, despite their bombings and assassinations, weakened his position and with it also that of organized antisemitism. The *Parole*'s circulation dropped to only several thousand by the summer of 1894. Again, Drumont appeared to have lost the battle. The Dreyfus Affair came just in time to offer the antisemites a fresh opportunity to appeal for public support both on the Right and on the Left.

ROBERT F. BYRNES, a specialist in Russian and East European History and first Director of Indiana University's International Affairs Center, has been Distinguished Professor of History at that University since 1967. A graduate of Amherst College and Harvard University, he was Director of the Mid-European Studies Center in New York, as well as head of the Inter-University Committee on Travel Grants. A recipient of several honorary degrees, he is the author and editor of a number of books, including *Anti-Semitism in Modern France,* and a contributor of articles to JEWISH SOCIAL STUDIES. Professor Byrnes was President of the American Catholic Historical Association in 1961.

Antisemitism in France Before the Dreyfus Affair

by Robert F. Byrnes

Antisemitism was a dying movement in France by the summer of 1894 for a great number of reasons, but the most important and indeed the decisive reason was the failure of Edouard Drumont or of any other antisemitic leader to develop an economic and social program which was both radical and conservative so as to keep the major wings of the movement united. Some antisemites were stumbling vaguely towards a national socialism, which might have provided them a sure foundation, but no one succeeded in developing a binding program. As a consequence, all French Socialists by 1890 had left the movement, many French Catholics by 1892 discovered that any "radical" movement, even one directed against "the enemies of the Church" might be dangerous for all Catholics, and those still anti-semitic in 1894 were confused and embittered by the maneuvers of Drumont, who became violently anti-clerical as his Catholic supporters deserted him. Thus, one of the unfortunate consequences of the antisemitic movement in France was its contribution to the division of the French Catholics during the last decade of the 19th century, which led to the failure of *railliement* and to the perpetuation of *les deux Frances*.

Probably because of the influence his republican parents had exercised upon him, Drumont did not discover the heart of the Jewish

Reprinted from JEWISH SOCIAL STUDIES, Volume XI, 1949

question in the principles of the Revolution, which were the foundation of the Third Republic, but in the misuse of the republic by the Jews and opportunists. His 1879 volume on French national celebrations had praised the Revolution's early burst of fraternity and then had only mildly criticized the violence of 1793. At that time, the Third Republic itself was immune from criticism, and he appeared to hope that the French people would obtain the ideal republic his father had wanted.[1]

The account of French history since 1870 in *La France juive* assigned major responsibility for the failure to re-establish the monarchy to Chambord. Though Drumont declared he wept during Chambord's illness, he ridiculed the Pretender for his timidity and the Count of Paris for his American materialism. Moreover, a good share of the second volume was devoted to a blistering impeachment of the immorality and stupidity of the decadent French nobility and upper bourgeoisie, and the very important preface to the entire work was a vigorous denunciation of these natural supporters of monarchy as "a finished generation."[2]

Since Drumont believed that the failure of the royalists during the first decade of the republic and the death of Chambord in 1883 had destroyed the possibility of the restoration of the monarchy, he had of necessity to accept the republic or to advocate some new type of polity. However, one of the most remarkable facts concerning the political theory of the French antisemites was their failure to suggest serious constitutional reforms for the republican system or to endorse another form of government. In his most precise statement, Drumont left the ultimate decision to the revolutionary workers' government, which was to select "the regime most fitting for all." Throughout his career, he flirted with the royalists, especially during crises when the republic was shaken. However, his general position was that action be taken against the Jews within the framework of a republican form of government and that a modified type of that form of government be retained after his "revision of the Revolution."[3]

Until the Dreyfus Affair roused most French Socialists to the defense of the republic, Drumont's antisemitic movement masqueraded as a kind of socialism. This position was a very clever disguise, for it won to antisemitism many Christians who could not accept orthodox continental socialism and who sought some party of opposition for voicing their discontent with the contemporary social system or their rank in that system. The disguise was so clever and Drumont's ranting about social injustices and the necessity for drastic changes was so constant that even some genuine Socialists were deceived for a few years.[4]

Drumont in *La France juive* stated that the regime he attacked weighed most upon "the revolutionary worker and the conservative Christian." His second book, written hastily and published late in 1886, made an important advance towards the sentimental socialism which soon became typical of him and the movement. In the chapter devoted to an attack upon Rothschild, Drumont attempted to establish a distinction between capitalism, which was Jewish and was based upon usury, and property. Moreover, he warned the conservatives that the workers would not forever tolerate the contemporary social system and that revolution and liquidation of their wealth and position would surely come if the workers' grievances were not soon redressed.[5]

Believing that the "conservative Christian" had been converted to antisemitism, Drumont in 1888 made several other attempts to persuade the "revolutionary worker" to join his crusade. The most important of these was *La Fin d'un monde,* which resembles *La France juive* more closely than any other of his works. Paris society received another severe scourging for its decadence and for the opportunities its materialism gave the ambitious Jews. Even more important, however, was Drumont's declaration that he had lost all hope of reform from either the Right or the Left, equally corrupt and equally heedless of the general welfare. His criticism of the Count of Paris and of the royalists was even more stinging than that of the opportunists and radicals. Asserting frankly that the return of the monarchy would bring no change, he devoted the major part of this book to a discussion of 19th-century French socialism.[6]

Drumont not only described socialism as simply the natural reaction to the flagrant injustices of the contemporary social system, but he also interpreted modern history in a manner frightening for his conservative readers. The Revolution, for example, was described as a conservative bourgeois maneuver against the monarchy *against* the will of the people. After the bourgeoisie alone had profited from this great upheaval, they had simply distorted history to ensure their position. Thus, they had endorsed the legend that the Revolution had been made by the people in order to make their privileged status defensible. Then they had tried to enshrine property, which Drumont described this time as merely another way of organizing society for the benefit of a privileged few.

Socialism represented the invincible uprising of the people against bourgeois exploitation. Drumont declared that what he termed "the revision of the Revolution" was near because the line between the enemy forces was becoming increasingly clear as the petty bourgeoisie lost their grip and joined the proletariat. The Commune, according to Drumont, had been an attempt by sagacious and ruthless conservatives to forestall this revision by destroying a whole generation of workers for crimes which they had never committed. Collectivism then received a most idealistic description, and Drumont even lashed Brousse for leaving Guesde's militant movement in 1881.[7]

Socialism as it was then known, however, was not the remedy for society because it lacked capable leaders and was so divided into squabbling groups. Neither were the Catholic Workers' Clubs of Count Albert de Mun and the marquis de La Tour du Pin, because the workers had irrevocably left the church earlier in the century when it failed to show any interest in their vital problems. Moreover, Drumont declared that no movement accepting the contemporary social system could provide a solution, even though it did try to sweeten that method of organizing society with the balm of charity. Salvation lay, of course, with the antisemites, for Drumont proposed "the confiscation of all wealth won in the Jewish system" and a collectivist "revision of the Revolution" by a workers' chamber. This proposal was defined not as an attack upon property, but only as an attack upon wealth gained through speculation.[8]

From the conservative point of view, La Fin d'un monde advanced an extremely dangerous program. However, there is far more evidence than this single book to explain why careful observers confused the movement against the Jews with socialism and why many conservatives became wary of antisemitism. In his next book, for instance, Drumont denounced the conservatives for supporting the Jews because of their blind fear of socialism. The bourgeoisie in this volume shared with the Jews and Masons the responsibility for the republic and its many faults, and Drumont gravely asserted in an interview that he was "dropping the Jews to attack the bourgeois world." Moreover, he ran for the Paris municipal council in the spring of 1890 as "a real Socialist in every sense of the word" and campaigned for a seat in the Chamber of Deputies in 1893 as a Socialist.[9]

The declaration that the antisemites were Socialists became an important part of their propaganda after 1888. Thus, Jacques de Biez, Drumont's first disciple and the vice-president of the French National Antisemitic League, told a reporter late in 1889, "We are Socialists, for we demand an accounting with the financial feudality. We are National Socialists, because we attack international finance so that we may have France for the French. We are for the workers against the exploiters." The League's first meeting, held on January 18, 1890 to support the candidacy of Francis Laur for the Chamber of Deputies, voted a resolution endorsing "the citizen Laur, the enemy of Rothschild, the Republican and the Socialist."[10]

It required only the emergence of antisemitism as an organized movement to enlighten the genuine Socialists upon the real intentions of the movement against the Jews. The *Revue Socialiste,* which had been antisemitic before 1886 and which had become increasingly so after Drumont's success, never followed the antisemitic leader blindly. As its editors saw the dangers in a campaign including clerical and anti-republican elements, they became increasingly cautious and circumspect. Henri Tubiana, for example, demonstrated how mistaken and foolish the Algerian radical republicans were in being antisemitic. Rouanet's book reviews began to suggest that antisemitism could be turned against the republic, and his review of Drumont's long discussion of socialism warned all sincere republicans to beware the use the monarchists would make of the book. Still another article condemned the *Union générale's* Serbian policy and urged Drumont to remember its wild speculation before denouncing the Jews for its failure.[11]

The first organized meeting of the French National Antisemitic League resulted in the journal's adopting a clearly hostile attitude towards antisemitism. Arranged by the marquis de Morès to support the candidacy of the Boulangist, Francis Laur, and to form a united movement of workers and members of the aristocratic clubs, this meeting led Rouanet to write a brilliant and conclusive article in the February 1890 issue. Declaring no ethnic line could be drawn between groups of capitalists, Rouanet urged all Socialists to remain aloof from antisemitism, which this assembly had revealed to be allied to the Right in an attack upon the republic. Questioning the sincerity of any conservative attack upon capitalism, Rouanet asserted there could be no compromise between socialism, which sought racial equality and the suppression of economic inequality, and the contrary aims of antisemitism.[12]

After the Rouanet definition, the *Revue Socialiste* betrayed no trace of antisemitism. Regnard, the author of a long series of articles on the dangerous semitic religious spirit, immediately resigned in protest. The studies of credit and banking by Chirac and Malon differed completely from their earlier ones, while Malon's new statement of policy, published in December, 1891, emphasized the need for tolerance within the republic. A series of articles by Adrian Veber in 1892 reveals that anticlericalism had replaced antisemitism, which was denounced categorically as "a born enemy of socialist progress." Moreover, the journal's attitude during the Panama scandal was a strong defense of the republic, explaining that corruption existed under every form of government and that Drumont's Jewish microbe was no more deadly than the others.[13]

Socialist leaders of all shades by 1892 had discovered the real power behind antisemitism. Paul Brousse fought and defeated Morès in the Paris municipal elections in April, 1890, and the most severe and thorough attacks upon this doctrine of hate were made by Guesde and Lafargue in a debate with Morès and Jules Guérin in July, 1892. The antisemites revealed their lack of a clear program when they devoted most of their talks to autobiography. Their Socialist rivals then riddled the puerile plan of Morès for 5,000 francs of credit for every worker and Guérin's proposal of financial decentralization as a panacea. Guesde demonstrated that many leading French bankers and industrialists were Catholics and declared that "in spite of its Socialist mask" antisemitism was "an economic and social reaction."[14]

The opposition to antisemitism demonstrated after 1890 by Socialist leaders and by the organized Socialist groups was naturally a disappointment to Drumont, but it must always be remembered that he was advocating a kind of sentimental socialism and was interested primarily in establishing a movement directed against the Jews, not against capitalism. Shortly after the publication of *La France juive* in 1886, he wrote hopefully of a new organization, the *Alliance antisémitique universelle,* as a weapon against the Jews. In the late summer of that year Jacques de Biez journeyed to Bucharest to represent France at a congress for the founding of the *Alliance anti-israélite universelle.* Biez was disappointed by the small attendance, but he joined seventeen Roumanians and Hungarians in preparing the constitution. Drumont was unanimously elected president of the new organization, and the constitution was very elaborate and detailed. However, the only measure ever undertaken by this vainglorious league was the publication of two pacifist pamphlets during the Schnaebele crisis in 1887.[15]

After the early disappearance of this premature international federation, the antisemites did not endeavor to organize again until shortly before the important elections of September, 1889, when the French National Antisemitic League was founded. This attempt of the antisemites to organize in 1889 and 1890 resulted in the formation of a close, but valueless, tie between antisemitism and ebbing Boulangism. The antisemites acquired permanently a few Boulangists of authority, but the privilege of associating with a cause already defeated was a costly one.

Antisemitism had had little influence in Boulangism until late in 1888, primarily because Naquet and Eugène Mayer, two of the leading Boulangists, and Hirsch, a heavy contributor to the Boulangist treasury, were Jews. However, when the Left became alarmed and Mayer retired from the movement, hatred of the Jews began to infiltrate. Some Boulangists were irritated by Joseph Reinach's helping lead the opposition, and a few, particularly provincial conservatives, had been both Boulangists and antisemites since 1886. Drumont himself had hailed Boulangism joyfully in 1888 as a symbol of "the universal disgust we all have for parliamentarians," though he had refrained from visiting the general because his entourage was "unattractive."[16]

The two movements against the republic began to ally forces openly in January, 1890, when the French National Antisemitic League decided to use its first public meeting to support Francis Laur, an antisemite who was a member of the National Republican Committee, in his campaign for re-election to the Chamber of Deputies. Arranged by the marquis de Morès, the demonstration was designed both to blend the two movements and to help build a new party of young aristocrats and workers. An audience which included five deputies and several noted aristocrats heard violent antisemitic speeches by Morès, Drumont, Laur, and Paul Déroulède.[17]

This first venture into politics had disastrous results for the cause of the campaign against the Jews, although Laur was ultimately re-elected. Rabid Boulangist papers such as *Le Pilori* and Catholic papers such as *Univers* were vociferous in their praise, but the meeting alarmed both the conservatives and the Socialists. Several Paris dailies, including *Figaro* and *Temps*, censured the first public act of the movement, and the letter of indignation written by Grand Rabbi Zadoc Kahn was given a warm reception by all of the republican press. Moreover, this Neuilly meeting resulted in the complete break from antisemitism of the *Revue Socialiste*, which had been an important, if critical, disseminator of antisemitic propaganda since 1885.[18]

Laur was disavowed by the National Republic Committee, but feeling against the Jews had grown so strong within the Boulangist movement that only Naquet's threat of resignation prevented a complete alliance with the antisemites in the winter of 1890. When Morès sought Boulangist cooperation in the Paris municipal elections in April in return for his financial support, the Committee decided to leave the final decision to the general himself. Since Boulanger had swung to the extreme left as his defeats continued, it seems quite possible that an agreement could have been reached through stressing the "socialism" of Drumont and Morès and temporarily omitting any open reference to the Jews.[19]

However, in March, 1890, while this important issue was being considered, Drumont intervened by publishing *La Dernière Bataille*. This book not only denounced Boulanger as a coward and a servile instrument of the Jews, but it also heaped ridicule upon his parents. Moreover, it was fulsomely dedicated to Morès and was supported by Drumont's statement to the press denying the antisemites had allied with the Boulangists at Neuilly or planned to in the future.[20]

La Dernière Bataille enraged Boulanger and led to the decision of the National Republican Committee to oppose the antisemites in the spring elections. Paul Déroulède and Gabriel Terrail thus found themselves denouncing the antisemites only a few months after they had allied with them. Both campaigned actively against Drumont and Morès, and Terrail even described Drumont as "a vile pamphleteer and wretched calumniator."

The French National Antisemitic League's second and last meeting, in April, 1890, was a distinct failure. Members of the Jockey Club, former Boulangists, a few Blanquists, and even some anarchists attended, and again Drumont, Biez, and Morès harangued the crowd, advocating their "socialism." This time, however, the meeting was broken up "by Jews and anarchists," and the antisemites were forced to flee in confusion. The 1890 elections were, therefore, crushing defeats for the antisemites. Morès received 950 votes in losing to Paul Brousse, while Drumont obtained only 613 votes in a district which had had an average conservative vote of 1500. The League collapsed completely during the summer of 1890 and was formally dissolved on October 20, 1890.[21]

The French National Antisemitic League and the electoral campaigns of 1890 had both failed so miserably that the antisemites themselves confessed the movement's weakness and their discouragement. In a letter to his supporters after the election, Drumont declared that his defeat had been "as complete as possible" and that antisemitism had failed utterly to convert the people of Paris. The first book he wrote after these reverses not only had a significant title, *Le Testament d'un antisémite,* but it also acknowledged that antisemitism had encountered complete apathy. His next book, written in 1891, revealed that there had been no renaissance, for Drumont continued bitterly to denounce French indifference to his teachings.[22]

However, this decline in the strength of antisemitism proved to be only temporary, for on April 20, 1892, the first issue of Drumont's daily newspaper appeared. It was during the last decade of the nineteenth century that the newspaper business all over the world underwent a revolution. The new press capitalized upon the tremendous improvements made in printing and communications to flaunt a gigantic appeal to the vulgar tastes of the masses. The *Libre Parole* thus appeared at a time when a full-scale assault upon the standards and position of the dignified and conservative older newspapers was being launched.

Drumont's was not the first important attempt to found an anti-semitic newspaper in France. Several brief efforts had appeared in 1882 and 1883. Boulangism had brought into existence *Le Pilori,* a violent anti-republican paper with strong traces of antisemitism, and in 1887 another short-lived paper had appeared in Paris. As the antisemites attempted to organize more formally and to enter politics in 1889 and 1890, a flurry of ephemeral papers appeared. Although most of these publications produced little permanent effect upon the movement because each was the work of a small isolated group, the titles they bore do reveal a great deal concerning their aims and the aims of antisemitism. The most impressive of the Paris weeklies, for instance, was *La Croisade française,* founded "to defend Catholic and French ideas."[23]

During the decade after 1892, Drumont's *Libre Parole* was one of the most important daily newspapers in France. There were occasions during the Panama scandal and the Dreyfus Affair when the *Libre Parole* was the most widely read and feared newspaper in Paris. The primary reason for its success, of course, was the great fame of Drumont, who alone held the allegiance of all antisemites in France. In addition, however, the newspaper had sound financial backing and an extremely able staff.

Most of the predecessors of the *Libre Parole* had had scant hopes of lasting success because they had been attempts of individuals or small groups without any careful preparation or program. Each of them failed at its first crisis because of its weak financial foundation. Drumont, however, succeeded in founding a company with an authorized capital of 1,600,000 francs. Although perhaps not even half of this sum was ever actually paid up, the paper had ample resources to advertise its appearance fully, to publish its first numbers as a complete Paris daily, and to withstand the financial shock which delayed success might have caused.

The major contributor to the financial power of the *Libre Parole* was J. B. Gérin, the editor of the *Semaine financière,* "one of the most important economic and financial journals in France, an authority

consulted by the outstanding leaders in banking and investment."
Gérin contributed 300,000 francs towards financing the *Libre Parole,*
although only a year earlier his journal had campaigned actively in
defense of the French Jews, particularly the bankers. It seems clear
that he financed Drumont largely so that a printing firm which owed
him a considerable amount of money might be able to sell its equip-
ment to the *Libre Parole.* He retained financial control of the paper
and named the business manager for the first few years to ensure his
new investment. This arrangement was of great benefit to the antisemites, for the paper was remarkably well managed.[24]

As the new focus of the entire movement, the *Libre Parole* attracted
the support of all French antisemites. Country priests traveled to
Paris solely to give their blessing to their defenders, and all of the
antisemitic writers, known and unknown, volunteered their services.
Drumont was thus able to collect a remarkably zealous and active
staff and to obtain free contributions from such talented writers as the
Countess Martel de Janville, a popular novelist who wrote under the
pseudonym of Gyp, and of Madame Guebhard, or Séverine.

The regular staff was composed of six journalists whose average
age in 1892 was thirty-one. These young men not only showed
considerable skill and versatility, but they also labored for Drumont
at some financial sacrifice. Talented Raphaël Viau thus spent seventeen years on the *Libre Parole* at 150 francs a month. Writing for
such a newspaper required some physical courage, too, for *Libre
Parole* policy demanded articles which frequently were the cause of
duels. Viau, for example, fought twelve duels before 1900 and was
wounded in four of them.[25]

The *Libre Parole* aimed to be as sensational and provocative as
possible. Its methods did not differ from those of the earlier antisemitic papers, for it concentrated upon individuals such as Rothschild and Arton, referred constantly to all Jewish villains from Judas
forward, and sought always to rouse a lawsuit or a duel by its attacks.
These tactics naturally drew attention to the new publication, but the
first two publicity ventures almost destroyed the infant paper.

One was an anonymous series of articles denouncing the growing
number and the special privileges of Jewish officers in the French
army. This group resulted in three duels. In the third duel, on June

23, 1892, the marquis de Morès, the special protector of the paper, killed a Jewish officer, Captain Armand Mayer.

The reaction to this unhappy incident was so tremendous that the *Libre Parole* was severely shaken, although its circulation did increase. Grand Rabbi Zadoc Kahn's vigorous denunciation of the paper and of Morès was acclaimed by almost all of the Paris press, and the Mayer funeral procession attracted thousands of sympathetic Frenchmen. Moreover, the affair led to an interpellation of the Minister of War in the Chamber of Deputies. Freycinet's declaration that "the army does not distinguish between Jews, Protestants, and Catholics" was applauded by the entire chamber, and his assertion that it was a crime against the nation to sow division in the army was voted a unanimous order of the day. Drumont himself was so affected by the death of Captain Mayer that he wrote it was the misfortune of France that such a courageous soldier should not have died on the battlefield fighting her enemies.[26]

The second event which brought the *Libre Parole* to the attention of Paris was a suit for libel instituted against Drumont by a well-known, popular deputy, Burdeau, whom Drumont had accused of accepting a bribe from Rothschild. The trial which followed revealed the flimsy foundation of Drumont's charges and presented Burdeau's attorney, Waldeck-Rousseau, a magnificent opportunity to condemn antisemitism. Drumont was forced to admit that he had only "moral proofs" of Burdeau's having been bribed, and as a consequence he received a sentence which included three months in prison and a fine of 1,000 francs.[27]

During the summer of 1892, the circulation of the newspaper managed to increase slowly, particularly in the provinces. Drumont and the staff were so dissatisfied with their progress, however, that August and September witnessed a new rash of duels. These tactics were not successful, but fall brought a great opportunity to the *Libre Parole* in the form of the Panama scandal.

The financing and construction of the Panama Canal had been a matter of interest and concern to the French people for almost fifteen years, and rumors of scandal had been particularly current since the Panama Company had crashed in 1889. Drumont himself in *La Dernière Bataille* in 1890 had covered one hundred and thirty-five pages with his account of the misery, waste, and corruption involved. Drumont then declared Ferdinand de Lesseps the responsible villain and considered the entire affair crushing evidence of French degeneracy and decadence. On September 20, 1892, however, the *Libre Parole* began a series of anonymous articles on the canal, charging unlimited corruption in the press and Chamber of Deputies, the corrupting agents being three notorious French Jews.[28]

It was a great error for the republican press to allow the privilege of unveiling such a great scandal to fall to an anti-republican paper. After a few weeks, the carefully-organized series began to be effective. The circulation soared, and the campaign began to attract wide interest, particularly as no one was able to deny the charges made. Finally, Baron Jacques de Reinach, who had helped to arrange the company's last loan and to provide favorable publicity for it, yielded valuable information to Drumont in an attempt to shield himself. Others tried the same practice, with the consequence that the *Libre Parole* obtained incriminating evidence on the newspapers and deputies involved.

The results were staggering. "At one blow, the *Libre Parole* became the most feared and widely read paper in Paris." Early in 1893, its daily circulation surpassed 200,000, and there was a frantic rush for it each afternoon as anxious and interested Frenchmen sought to discover the latest revelations. It is possible that had Drumont foreseen the course of events and planned his program carefully he might have emerged from the scandal a tremendously powerful figure in France. However, it is evident that the *Libre Parole* was simply using its classical tactics to increase its circulation and that Drumont failed to appreciate the political potential which able manipulation of this issue might have developed. At any rate, he chose November 1, 1892, to begin serving his three months' sentence for the Burdeau libel and spent these crucial days directing his newspaper from Sainte-Pélagie.[29]

For three or four months, Panama remained the center of the political stage in France. As the evidence was revealed, each newspaper, politician, and political group tried to wield the information as a club against its opponents. The Socialists saw it as proof of the inherent evils of capitalism, although most of them defended the republic, particularly when they saw the scandal being used against it by its enemies. The antisemites sought to prove the wickedness of the Jews, although Herz, Arton, and Reinach had become involved long after the major damage had been done. The Right, including such papers as *Univers, Croix, Autorité,* the *Gazette de France,* and *Cocarde,* tried to besmirch the republic and the republicans. As the facts appeared, however, each paper had to defend its own receipts with the theory of advertising costs, and so many politicians became involved that France discovered that virtue was the monopoly of no one party or group.[30]

Some politicians succeeded in repaying political grudges during Panama, but most of them were delighted with its disappearance. The suicide early in the affair of Jacques de Reinach and the successful escape of Arton, the intermediary for much of the corruption, added a touch of mystery and intrigue. The government's inability to find Herz and Arton and then to obtain their extradition gave the press an opportunity to digress from the real issues, and the distant Arton particularly was erected into a fabulous figure of tremendous knowledge and power.[31]

Panama gave the *Libre Parole* and Drumont a brief period of fortune, but from early 1893 until the arrest of Dreyfus was announced in November, 1894, the newspaper and the movement both declined perceptibly. Even Panama had become such a political football by February 1, 1893, that Drumont was greeted only by his staff when he left prison. When he ran for the Chamber of Deputies in Amiens in May, 1893, he was decisively routed. A new series of duels instigated to rouse interest during the summer of 1893 failed to attract attention, and at the same time Drumont's two principal lieutenants left the movement entirely.[32]

The most important political issues which faced France during the years 1892 through 1894 were *ralliement,* the growing power of the Socialists and syndicates, and the rash of anarchism. On each of these critical questions, particularly the third, Drumont was led by sentiment and temperament into a stand which cost the movement numbers of supporters. As a result, by the fall of 1894, organized antisemitism had reached its nadir in France and seemed ready to disappear completely.

Drumont originally hailed Leo XIII for his decision to ask French

Catholics to accept the republic, but by the summer of 1893 he had become the most bitter and venomous of the opponents of *ralliement*. He denounced the Pope as "the most poorly informed sovereign in Europe," a prelate who "with his Italian mentality, which is always Machiavellian, bows down before the republic only because it is victorious." At one time Drumont was so enraged at the program of the Pope that he prayed in an editorial for a "modern iron-fisted Nogaret for the modern Boniface VIII."

Drumont not only stormed at the policy of *ralliement,* but he ridiculed and insulted the Church and those Catholics who adopted it. When the marriage of a prominent Catholic was annulled, Drumont declared that the Church always granted special privileges to the wealthy and powerful and neglected the poor and faithful. The papal nuncio, Cardinal Ferrata, and Count Albert de Mun, an old friend of Drumont, were abused by the *Libre Parole* as though they were common criminals. An old opponent of the antisemites, Bishop Fuzet of Beauvais, was accused of having stolen tapestries from the cathedral, and Cardinal Bourret a short time later was charged with having accepted a cash bribe from the government to support submission to the *loi d'abonnement*. One antisemite, Father Charles Renaut, was so disturbed by Drumont's attacks upon the Pope and the Church that he became convinced Drumont was a disguised Jew using antisemitism to deceive the Catholics and ridicule the Church.[33]

The antisemites always posed as defenders of the poor, but conservative followers of Drumont who had not been thoroughly alarmed earlier by his "socialism" were seriously frightened by the economic views which appeared in the *Libre Parole* during 1893 and 1894. After the Panama scandal had disappeared as a political issue and the antisemitic campaign had begun to slacken, Drumont in the summer of 1893 began to write of socialism and the Socialists with increasing enthusiasm. Statements concerning the socialist views of antisemitism became more frequent, and one member of the editorial board even declared that the antisemites no longer recognized any distinction between Jewish and Christian capitalism.[34]

It was Drumont's stand on anarchism, however, which weakened antisemitism most. At a time when all Frenchmen were terrified by the wave of anarchist outrages which swept the country, Drumont alone defended the disciples of Bakunin and Kropotkin. He did this partly from friendship for some anarchists he had met in prison, but primarily because of his disappointment at the indifference with which France had greeted his own campaign. Nothing could have aroused the French people more in 1893 and 1894 than such a defense of terrorists.

The outstanding instances of anarchist activity were August Vaillant's throwing a bomb into the Chamber of Deputies in December, 1893, and the assassination of President Carnot in Lyon on June 24, 1894, by Santo Caserio. Drumont defended Vaillant first on the ground that he had not understood the teachings of anarchism and that, in any case, he had not killed or seriously injured anyone. Then he declared that society was guilty because of the materialism it preached. Finally, he upbraided the entire bourgeois world, declaring that the anarchists were merely putting into practice principles which the bourgeoisie themselves had applied a century earlier.[35]

When Drumont organized a subscription for Vaillant's daughter, Sidonie, and obtained a home for her, his actions in defending the anarchists were viewed somewhat less critically. However, the anti-semitic leader and his newspaper failed to heed the warning of the Vaillant case and continued to defend the anarchists in 1894. When Jean Grave was sentenced to two years in prison for his attacks on property and the family, Drumont ridiculed the decision by declaring that bourgeois property was only robbery and that the lay schools had already destroyed the respect in which the family had been held.

The assassination of President Carnot by Caserio brought what would probably have been the fatal eclipse of organized French anti-semitism, but for the arrest of Captain Dreyfus. When all the press joined to praise and lament the dead president, the *Libre Parole* denounced France for its attitude towards the grandson of the man who had murdered so many Frenchmen in 1793. Drumont compared the eminent Monsignor d'Hulst to Judas for having supported the rigid police and press laws which the anarchist actions had called forth, and during early July, 1894, his newspaper prosecuted an astonishing campaign against all those who resented the assaults of the terrorists. By the middle of July, Drumont was so alarmed by the reaction his stand had roused and so feared arrest and imprisonment that he fled to Belgium "to defend his freedom."[36]

Organized antisemitism during the summer and early fall of 1894 was at its lowest strength since 1886. Leading antisemites continually lamented their failure and prayed for five hundred resolute men or a batallion to rescue France from chaos. On March 24, 1894, the day on which Drumont had attacked Monsignor d'Hulst so unmercifully, Emile de Saint-Auban declared that "we antisemites are soldiers of the idea of democracy" and will succumb while struggling for it, "just as Jesus and Joan of Arc did." From Brussels in September, 1894, Drumont warned his followers that their common duty was to educate men for action to help train the coming generation. "It is our solemn obligation not to become discouraged and to retain belief in the power of our ideas."[37]

By the summer of 1894, the circulation of the *Libre Parole* had dropped to a few thousand, and both the *Libre Parole* and its illustrated weekly edition were in financial difficulty. Every newspaper trick was used to increase the circulation, with new contests and features each week. However, 1894 produced such a great dearth of news for the antisemites that the editors of the *Libre Parole* were forced to use incidents six and seven years old to fill the paper.

The *Libre Parole Illustrée* was reduced to half its original size in the fall of 1893, and in August, 1894, both it and the *Libre Parole* adopted a poorer grade of newsprint and finer, space-saving type. The 1894 dividend was only 1.5 percent, the lowest paid from 1893 through 1899. Drumont himself had lost hope, and during the summer of 1894 he made several attempts to sell the *Libre Parole* at a financial loss. Thus, the Dreyfus arrest was injected into the political scene at a time when Drumont, still in shelter in Brussels, was trying to promote the sale of his chief weapon against the Jews.[38]

NOTES

* *See* the author's, "Edouard Drumont and *La France juive*," in JEWISH SOCIAL STUDIES, vol. ix (1949), pp. 165–84.

[1] Drumont, Edouard, *Les Fêtes nationales à Paris* (Paris 1879).

[2] Drumont, Edouard, *La France juive* (Paris 1886), preface d–s; vol. i,

pp. 265–304, 440–49; vol. ii, pp. 72–85, 90–93, 107–108, 155–86, 283–88.

[3] Drumont, Edouard, *La Fin d'un monde* (Paris 1888), pp. 1881–84.

[4]*See* Szajkowski, Z., "Socialists and Radicals in the Development of Anti-semitism in Algeria (1884–1900)," in JEWISH SOCIAL STUDIES, vol. x, no. 3 (July 1948), pp. 257–80.

[5] Drumont, *La France juive*, vol. i, pp. 521–22; Drumont, *La France juive devant l'opinion* (Paris 1886), pp. 121–74.

[6] Drumont, *La Fin d'un monde*, pp. 263–66, 293–344, 379–417.

[7] *Ibid.*, pp. 1–40, 80–85, 98–180.

[8] *Ibid.*, pp. 158–63, 181–84, 187–236.

[9] Drumont, *La Dernière Bataille* (Paris 1890) pp. 53, 66–83 and *Le Testament d'un antisémite* (Paris 1891), pp. 382, 436–37; *Anti-Juif* (Algiers) March 13 and April 17, 1890; *Libre Parole Illustrée*, August 19, 1893.

[10] Bournand, François, (Jean de Ligneau, *pseud.*), *Juifs et antisémites en Europe* (Paris 1892) pp. 88–101. Laur had been a member of the *Parti Ouvrier Français* in 1882 (Compère-Morel, *Jules Guesde*, Paris, 1937, p. 252).

[11] *Revue Socialiste:* Tubiana, Henri, "Les Croisades au dix-neuvième siècle," vol. ii (1886), pp. 634–36, 959, 1131–33; Rouanet, Gustave, "La Vérité sur les chemins de fers Serbes," vol. i (1889), pp. 720–42; Rouanet reviews of *La Fin d'un monde*, vol. ii (1888), pp. 560, 662–64.

[12] Rouanet, Gustave, "La Question juive et la question sociale," in *Revue Socialiste*, vol. i (1890), pp. 219–34.

[13] *Revue Socialiste:* vol. i (1890) pp. 348–49; vol. ii (1891), pp. 641–45; Veber, Adrian, "L'Action catholique," vol. i (1892), pp. 230–47; Veber, "La Crise politique," vol. i (1892), 351–52; Veber, "Le Convent maçonnique," vol. ii (1892), pp. 478–80; Boz, Pierre, "Revue de la presse étrangère," vol. i (1893), p. 623; Rouanet, Gustave, "La Vérité sur le Panama," vol. ii (1892), pp. 646–58.

[14] Droulers, Charles, *Le Marquis de Morès, 1858–1896* (Paris 1932), pp. 102–104; Zévaès, Alexandre, *Jules Guesde, 1845–1922* (Paris 1929), pp. 109–111; Compère-Morel, *Jules Guesde* (Paris 1937), pp. 375–79.

[15] Drumont, *La France juive*, vol. i, pp. 139, 327; *id.*, *La France juive devant l'opinion*, pp. 287–90; *Congrès de Bucarest, août-septembre 1886 pour la fondation d'une Alliance anti-israélite universelle* (pamphlet), (Bucharest 1887), pp. 1–14; *Pas de guerre, Le Complot juif-allemand* (pamphlet) (Paris 1887), pp. 6, 13–21. de Biez, Jacques, *Le Complot financier des juifs allemands* (pamphlet) (Paris 1887); *Libre Parole Illustrée*, January 18, 1896.

[16] Drumont, *La Fin d'un monde*, pp. 312–319; Dansette, Adrien, *Le Boulangisme, 1886–1890* (Paris 1938), pp. 174–75, 320–22; Terrail, Gabriel (Mermeix, *pseud.*), *Les Antisémites en France* (Paris 1892), pp. 41–42; de Fleurance, Gustave, *Expulseurs et expulsés* (Paris 1888), preface by Drumont; Bahr, Hermann, *Der Antisemitismus. Ein internationales Interview* (Berlin 1894), p. 106.

[17] Bournand, François (Jean de Ligneau, *pseud.*), *Juifs et antisémites en Europe* (Paris 1892) pp. 88–101; Terrail, *Les Antisémites,* pp. 54–55; Levaillant, Isaac, "La Genèse de l'antisémitisme sous la troisième République," in *Revue des études juives,* vol. ii (1906–1907), p. 92; Viau, Raphaël, *Vingt Ans d'antisémitisme, 1889–1909* (Paris 1910), pp. 10–15; *Anti-Juif* (Algiers), February 20, 1890.

[18] *Univers,* January 15–January 29, 1890.

[19] Dansette, *Le Boulangisme,* pp. 347, 355–58; Terrail, *Les Antisémites,* pp. 55–58; Rouanet, Gustave, "La Question juive et la question sociale," in *Revue Socialiste,* vol. i (1890), p. 223.

[20] Drumont, *La Dernière Bataille* (Paris 1890), pp. 137–38, 154–89; Bournand, *Juifs et antisémites en Europe,* pp. 104–107.

[21] Drumont, *Le Testament d'un antisémite* (Paris 1891), pp. 91–92; Terrail, *Les Antisémites,* pp. 58–61; Viau, *Vingt Ans d'antisémitisme,* pp. 14–15; *Univers,* April 17–30, 1890.

[22] Drumont, *Le Testament d'un antisémite,* pp. 170–76; Drumont, *Le Secret de Fourmies* (Paris 1892), pp. 150–55; *Anti-Juif (Algiers),* May 29, 1890.

[23] Jacobs, Joseph, *The Jewish Question, 1875–1884. A Bibliographical Handlist* (London 1885), p. 57; Droulers, *Le Marquis de Morès,* p. 97; Gerredi, Marius, *Catholicisme et judaisme. Réponse à la France juive* (Paris 1888 xii); Debidour, Antonin, *L'Eglise catholique et l'Etat sous la troisième République, 1870–1906* (Paris 1906–1909), vol. i, p. 377; Levaillant, Isaac, "La Genèse de l'antisémitisme sous la troisième République," in *Revue des études juives* vol. lii (1906–1907), p. 87; Avenel, *Annuaire de la presse française,* vol. iii (1882), p. 64; vol. v (1884), XX-XXI, LX; vi (1885); XX; viii (1887), LXXIX; ix (1888), CXVI.

[24] Drumont, *Sur le Chemin de la vie. Souvenirs* (Paris 1914), p. 132; Gendrot, Alfred (Jean Drault, *pseud.*), *Drumont, La France juive et la Libre Parole* (Paris 1935), p. 89. Guérin, Jules, *Les Trafiquants de l'antisémitisme* (Paris 1906), pp. 17–33, 44–46, 54–59; Viau, *Vingt Ans d'antisémitisme,* p. 22; Reynaud, Léonce, *Les Français israélites* (Paris 1901), pp. 2–5; Avenel, *Annuaire de la presse française,* vol. viii (1887), p. 50.

[25] Viau, *Vingt Ans d'antisémitisme,* pp. 37–43, 61, 72, 112, 182–272; Gendrot, *Drumont, La France juive et la Libre Parole,* pp. 116, 191–92; Lecache, Bernard, *Séverine* (Paris 1930), p. 132–61; Missoffe, Michel, *Gyp et ses amis* (Paris 1932), pp. 147–54, 186. Drumont, *Sur le Chemin de la vie,* p. 299; *Libre Parole Illustrée,* February 24, 1894; *Vraie Parole,* February 28, 1893.

[26] Cremieu-Foa, Ernest, *La Campagne antisémitique. Les Duels. Les Responsibilités. Mémoire* (Paris 1892), pp. 24–72; Levaillant, Isaac, "La Genèse de l'antisémitisme sous la troisième République," in *Revue des études juives,* vol. lii (1906–1907), p. 95; Gendrot, *Drumont, La France juive et la Libre Parole,* pp. 113–17; Reinach (L'Archiviste, *pseud.*), *Drumont et Dreyfus.*

Etudes sur la Libre Parole de 1894 à 1895 (Paris 1898), pp. 13–19; Viau, *Vingt Ans d'antisémitisme*, p. 24–26; *Journal officiel*, June 26, 1892.

[27] Marion, Marcel, *Histoire financière de la France depuis 1715* (Paris 1914–1931), vol. vi, pp. 148–49. Viau, *Vingt Ans d'antisémitisme*, pp. 23–25, 34, 47; Gendrot, *Drumont, La France juive et la Libre Parole*, pp. 101–12; *Burdeau-Rothschild contre Drumont. Le Procès de Libre Parole. Débats complets* (pamphlet) (Paris 1892).

[28] Viau, *Vingt Ans d'antisémitisme*, p. 61; Bernanos, Georges, *La Grande Peur des bienpensants. Edouard Drumont* (Paris 1931), p. 293; Daudet, Léon, *Panorama de la troisième République* (Paris 1936), p. 127; Drumont, *La Dernière Bataille*, pp. 324–460. Batut, Guy de la, *Panama* (Paris 1931), p. 51.

[29] Frank, Walter, *Nationalismus und Demokratie im Frankreich der dritten Republik* (Hamburg 1933), pp. 276–80, 334; Barrès, Maurice, *Leur Figures. Le Roman de l'énergie nationale* (Paris 1902), pp. 25, 62–92; Gendrot, *Drumont, La France juive et la Libre Parole*, pp. 144–51; Viau, *Vingt Ans d'antisémitisme*, pp. 47–50. Bernanos, *Drumont*, pp. 285–93.

[30] Debidour, *L'Eglise catholique et l'Etat sous la troisième République*, vol. ii, pp. 94–99; Levaillant, "La Genèse de l'antisémitisme sous la troisième République," in *Revue des études juives*, vol. lii (1906–1907), pp. 97–98; Lucas, Auguste, *Précis historique de l'affaire du Panama* (Paris 1893), pp. 211–16; Gendrot, *Drumont, La France juive et la Libre Parole*, pp. 123–58, 384; Rouanet, Gustave, *Les Complicités du Panama* (Paris 1893), p. 161–281, 334; Ducray, Camille, *Paul Déroulède, 1846–1914* (Paris 1914), pp. 186–90; Batut, Guy de la, *Panama*, pp. 51–361; *Journal officiel*, November 20, 1892–March 30, 1893.

[31] Beaurepaire, Jules Quesnay de, *Le Panama et la République* (Paris 1899), pp. 118–67. *Univers*, November 1, 1892–March 30, 1893.

[32] Viau, *Vingt Ans d'antisémitisme*, pp. 57–61; Gendrot, *Drumont, La France juive et la Libre Parole*, p. 191.

[33] Father Charles Renaut, *L'Israélite Drumont et les sociétés secrètes actuellement* (Paris 1896), pp. 192–306; Dominique Cardinal Ferrata, *Mémoires. Ma Nonciature en France* (Paris 1922), p. 298–99; Father Edouard Lecanuet, *Les Signes avant-coureurs de la séparation, 1894–1910* (Paris 1930), pp. 30–31, 38–46, 67–68; Lecanuet, *La Vie l'Eglise sous Léon XIII* (Paris 1930), p. 576; *Libre Parole Illustrée*, May 16, 1895.

[34] Renaut, *L'Israélite Drumont*, p. 490; Suarez, Georges, *Briand. Sa Vie, son oeuvre* (Paris 1938–1941), vol. i, pp. 170–79, 216–18; *Libre Parole Illustrée*, June 1, 1895.

[35] Gendrot, *Drumont, La France juive et la Libre Parole*, pp. 197–98; Bernanos, *Drumont*, pp. 293–94; *Libre Parole Illustrée*, November 18–December 30, 1893.

[36] Viau, *Vingt Ans d'antisémitisme*, pp. 76–97; Bernanos, *Drumont*, pp. 295–302; Monsignor Alfred Baudrillart, *Vie de Monsignor d'Hulst* (Paris 1925),

vol. ii, pp. 405–07; Forain, Jean Louis, *Doux Pays* (Paris 1897), p. 9; *Libre Parole Illustrée,* January 6–July 23, 1894.

[37] Renaut, *L'Israélite Drumont,* pp. 483, 560–65; *Libre Parole Illustrée,* March 24, 1894.

[38] Gendrot, *Drumont, La France juive et la Libre Parole,* p. 175. Suarez, Briand, vol. i, p. 160; Astruc, Gabriel, *Le Pavillon des Fantômes. Souvenirs* (Paris 1929), pp. 150–51; Guérin, *Les Trafiquants de l'antisémitisme,* pp. 347, 364–67; *Libre Parole Illustrée,* January 6–November 2, 1894. In 1893, the *Libre Parole* dividend was 3 percent, in 1894 1.5 percent, in 1895, 2 percent, in 1896, 2.5 percent, in 1897, 4.3 percent, in 1898, 6 percent, and in 1899, 6.2 percent.

EDITORS' PREFACE

Arkady Kremer, Vladimir Medem, and the Ideology of the Jewish "Bund"

The small group of young Russianized Jews who started out to recruit Gentile workers to the anti-tsarist socialist revolutionary cause, but who organized a specifically Jewish revolutionary movement that contended with Lenin and today claims to be the party of "Doigkeit" (Here-ism), with its emphases on the diaspora and the Yiddish language, is the subject of Professor Pinson's essay, one of the earliest scholarly studies of the Bund in English, and for a long time almost the only one. Several English-language doctoral dissertations on the Bund have appeared within the past five years, a testimony to academic interest in the movement. This interest is, in part, a product of the expansion of Russian and Soviet studies and with them, also, of research on East European labor history. Also responsible are the increasing popularity of modern and East European Jewish history, and the ready availability of primary sources—thanks to dedicated people who moved the Bund archives from Paris to New York ahead of the Nazi troops.

The Bund was organized in 1897, after Jewish activists in Russia's Jewish Pale of Settlement discovered their failure to attract Gentiles to the revolutionary cause and, while working with Jews, began to question the feasibility of teaching Russian to Yiddish-speaking workers in order to enable them to read revolutionary publications. The answer was propaganda in Yiddish and a Jewish

283

movement. The Bund's founders set for themselves a two-fold task: the realization of the general political demands of the proletariat in Russia and the defense of the special interests of the Jewish workers, victims of both class and national oppression. In its initial phase, the Bund tried to ignore Jewish nationalism. However, closer acquaintance with the Yiddish-speaking proletariat and with the Yiddish language and its literature, a better understanding of the condition and moods of the Jewish masses, other competing Jewish ideologies, particularly autonomism and Zionism, and an intense desire for independence within the Russian and Polish socialist movements maneuvered the Bund into demanding cultural autonomy for Jews. The very minimal institutional demand for secular Yiddish schooling was adopted when the Bund had to compete on a practical basis for the allegiance of the masses under the German occupation of Poland in 1916.

As a socialist and trade-union movement in the orthodox-dominated Pale, the Bund had to battle religion and the religious establishment—in its own terminology, "clericalism." Thus it carried on the struggle for Haskalah and secularism, involving itself in battles with both the older generation and the Bund's contemporaries. The second front, as Pinson brought out, was the Bund's battle against assimilation. However, resisting assimilation meant upholding Jewish survival. The Bund was disinterested in the maintenance of the Jewish religion. The alternative was secular survival, but that could involve nationalism, a bad word in the socialist vocabulary of the period, even when modified by the adjective "cultural," which the Bund would not do. A course had to be steered between the pitfalls of assimilation and nationalism. Assimilation was condemned as the philosophical product of the bourgeoisie of the dominant nationality, and, therefore, unacceptable to the working class. On the other hand, for the Bund as for most socialists, Jewish nationalism was an artificially stimulated romanticism which enticed the proletariat away from its class interests.

The Bund leaders' solution was neutralism: no promotion of either assimilation or nationalism. Let life decide the choice between survival and disappearance of the Jews. Jewish survival was to be determined by social and political factors. However, the dialectics stopped here, as the ideologues refrained from considering the possibility that majority cultures might have some advantages in this struggle for continuity. To the Bund, Zionism, the chief spokesman for Jewish nationalism, was anathema, a symbol of despair, which diverted the masses from the realities of the class struggle and the revolution, the only solution to all problems. The Bund refused to accept the existence of one Jewish nation, or people, or of an entity known as world Jewry. It was concerned only with the Jews in Russia, Poland, and Lithuania, that is, in tsarist Russia. It defended Jewish cultural rights within the limits of the shifting Bundist ideology. The Bund leaders fought Lenin's centralism, both in the socialist movement and in the cultural mosaic of Russia. While the Bund followed the Austrian school of Marxism, it disagreed with that school's view that autonomy was to be determined on a territorial basis.

Pinson traces the development of the Bundist ideology in the life and writings of two of its leaders. Of the two, Medem was an expert on nationalism. The article is a good introduction to Marxist approaches to the Jewish problem and not only to the study of the Bund.

KOPPEL S. PINSON (1904–1961) was the first Managing Editor of JEWISH SOCIAL STUDIES and for several years was Vice President and President of the Conference on Jewish Social Studies, to which he devoted much of his time and talent. A graduate of the University of Pennsylvania and Gratz College in Philadelphia, he received the Ph.D. degree in history at Columbia University. He was Associate Editor of the *Encyclopedia of the Social Sciences,* editor of several volumes of the *Yivo Annual of Jewish Social Science,* served for a year as Educational Director for Displaced Jews in Germany and Austria for the Joint Distribution Committee, and was Professor of History at Queens College. He was author of *Pietism as a Factor in the Rise of German Nationalism; A Bibliographical Guide to Nationalism; Modern Germany: Its History and Civilization,* and of a number of articles. He also edited *Essays on Antisemitism* for the Conference on Jewish Social Studies.

Arkady Kremer, Vladimir Medem, and the Ideology of the Jewish "Bund"

by Koppel S. Pinson

The "Jewish Workers' Bund of Russia and Poland" represents one of the most important mass movements in modern Jewish history. From its inception in 1897 down to its heroic participation in the battle of the Warsaw ghetto and in the anti-nazi underground of our own day, it has occupied a stormy position in the life of east-European Jewry. At the same time, the prominent role played by the "Bund" in the founding of the Russian Social Democratic Party and in the subsequent history of the Russian labor and revolutionary movement makes' it a subject not only of Jewish, but of world historical significance. Nevertheless, the history of this movement has not yet been adequately and scientifically recounted; its importance has hardly been recognized in most works of Western Jewish scholarship, or, when treated, the accounts are usually so full of errors and inaccuracies as to make them entirely unreliable.[1] The ravages of World War II have caused the transfer of the central headquarters of the "Bund" to the United States, and the party leadership has now published two volumes which are of immeasurable value to the student of the history of the Jewish labor movement.[2] The volumes are devoted to two of the outstanding leaders in the history of the "Bund," Arkady Kremer and Vladimir Medem. They contain significant contributions by various leading figures of the Bundist movement as well as collections of the more

Reprinted from JEWISH SOCIAL STUDIES, Volume VII, 1945

important writings by Kremer and Medem. Alexander Kremer, better
known as Arkady, was the most outstanding political organizer in the
history of the "Bund" and the chief figure among its founders; while
Medem was undoubtedly its finest theoretician and scholar. Each
represents a different type of personality, a different segment of Jewish
life, and a different aspect of Jewish labor leadership. Their careers
as well as their leading ideas are well worth careful study and analysis
as representative of the dominant trends in the ideology of the
"Bund."[3]

I

The "Bund" represented the first great attempt at the organization
of the Jewish masses for secular and independent political activity. In
the last decades of the 19th century, Jewish life began to be fructified
by numerous cultural and national movements. *Haskalah,* Hebrew
renaissance, *Hoveve Tsiyyon* and Zionism, all began to stir the imagination and hopes of Jewish young men and women. But as for ardent
Jewish political activity in and for the Diaspora, it was left to the
"Bund" to become the fermenting and leavening factor in the Jewish
Pale. The mass of traditionally Orthodox Jews completely shunned
any revolutionary political action by Jews. Their attitude may be
illustrated by the irate proclamation which the Rabbi of Minsk issued
after the attempted assassination of the governor of Vilna by Hirsch
Lekert in 1902:

"A shudder passes over us," he wrote, "when we hear the terrible
story of what happened in the theatre. How do we Jews, who are
likened to a little worm—the worm of Jacob—come to get messed
up in such matters? How do we Jews, who, according to all sense
and reason, are always obligated to pray for the well-being of the
sovereign power, without whom we would long since have been
swallowed alive—how do we Jews dare to climb up to such high
places and meddle in politics? Oh, beware, Jewish children! Look
well at what you are doing! God only knows what you may bring
upon our unfortunate nation, upon yourselves, and upon your families. Our people always were proud of one thing—that they never

had any rebels among them; and now you desire to wipe out this virtue too. We hope you will think well about all this and you will not wish to place in jeopardy the happiness of our whole nation, your own fate and the fate of your parents and families."[4]

The idea of independent revolutionary activity by Jews in tsarist Russia had, it is true, been preached as early as the late 1870's by Aaron Liberman (1844–1880).[5] But Liberman remained a voice crying in the wilderness, and no organized Jewish labor movement resulted from his activities. Jewish intellectuals who did become engaged in revolutionary activity joined the incipient Russian groups of the Narodnaya Volya, and carried on their work among the Russian masses. Lazar Goldenberg, Solomon Chudnovsky, Semion Lurie, Lev Deitch, Pavel Axelrod, Liuba Axelrod, Aaron Zundelevich and a host of others occupy a prominent place in the annals of the Russian revolutionary movement. But their relation to the Jewish masses and to Jewish problems was negative, thoroughly assimilationist, and often even hostile. Vladimir Jochelson, one of the early pioneers of the Russian revolutionary movement, later described this attitude as follows:

We maintained a negative attitude toward the Jewish religion as to all religions. The [Yiddish] jargon we considered to be an artificial language, and Hebrew a dead language, of interest only to scholars. National beliefs, traditions and language in general did not seem valuable to us from the common standpoint of humanity. But we were sincere assimilationists, and it was to the Russian enlightenment that we looked for salvation for Jews. . . . One must also confess that Russian literature, which implanted in us love of culture and of the Russian people, also to some degree implanted in us a conception that Jews were not a people but a parasitic class. Such views were not rarely expressed also by radical Russian writers, and that, it seems to me, was one of the causes that explains our defection.[6]

The last decade of the 19th century witnessed the beginnings of active political agitation among Jewish workers. In part, this was due to the rapid spurt of industrialization which set in throughout Russia during that time. It was further inspired, however, by the growing policy of repression initiated by the tsarist government against the Jews. In Lithuania and White Russia, in particular, economic and political activities by Jewish workers began on a larger scale. Here, in the crowded urban centers of the Pale, among the Jewish workers in paint factories, the Jewish bristle makers, textile and tobacco operatives of Vilna, Bialystok, Smorgon, Grodno, and Minsk, as also among Jewish girls employed in tobacco and envelope factories, there emerged a group of class-conscious socialist workers and intellectuals.[7] Of all places Vilna stands out as the most important center for these movements. For this there were several reasons. In the first place, Vilna had a great concentration of Jewish artisans and workers. Secondly, it possessed a larger group of more enlightened Jews, from whom many of the early Jewish socialists came. Here was to be found a group of Jewish intellectuals who were free of the inferiority feeling so common among young Jews coming from the Pale into the general secular world. Ex-students of the Vilna Rabbinical School and students of the *Realschule* formed a large number of the leaders of the first revolutionary circles in Vilna.[8] In addition, there was a third important factor. It was to Vilna that many Jewish students came when they had been exiled from other parts of Russia on account of their political activity. Here, to be sure, they were kept under police surveillance and were supposed to refrain from participation in any political matters, but many managed to continue their revolutionary work in spite of all surveillance, and these formed a nucleus of leadership for many of the Jewish groups. Of such persons Juli Martov (Zederbaum) was no doubt the most famous.[9]

II

The earliest political activities were pursued in small "circles" or groups, and were designed to educate young men and women for further socialist leadership. Discussions and lectures were held on natural science, economics, socialist theory and Russian language and literature. As early as 1887, however, there came into being in Vilna a group of "Jewish Social Democrats" who engaged in even more organized activity. Their functioning is described in a report submitted by the later organized "Bund" to the International Socialist Congress in 1900:

> "The first Jewish Social-Democratic workers' groups," says this report, "were founded in Vilna about the year 1887. The first Jewish intellectuals who started to carry on propaganda among Jewish workers had no idea of creating a specifically Jewish labor movement. Confined to the Pale and not having the possibilities to dedicate their energies to the Russian labor movement, they were forced, willy-nilly, to start working among the Jews and thus at least quench to some degree their thirst for revolutionary activity. The Jewish labor movement occupies second place for them; they look chiefly to the Russian worker, upon whom they place all their hopes and from whom they expect also salvation for the Jewish proletariat. . . . Their propaganda is carried on in the Russian language."[10]

During the years 1893–1895 some of the leaders of such groups began to entertain doubts as to the efficacy of their work. A feeling developed that their field of activity should be broadened to include mass agitation, instead of being confined to small propaganda and educational groups. Among those who espoused this view, Arkady's pamphlet *On Agitation,* prepared in 1893, came to be regarded as the most important guide for the new type of mass agitation. We shall analyze this pamphlet later. For our present purpose, the important point to note is that this change from small circles engaged primarily in theoretical discussions to broader mass agitation resulted in bringing the Jewish social-democrats into closer contact with the Jewish masses and also with the Yiddish language and Jewish problems. A crucial turn in this direction is marked by the famous speech delivered by Martov on May 2, 1895, before a small group of agitators.[11]

Martov's speech contains in embryo the ideological basis for the later formation of the "Bund." In it he proclaims the need for the Jewish workers to act *as Jews* in the revolutionary struggle and to recognize the specifically Jewish problems and situations. He admits that the Jewish social-democrats had previously looked only to the Russian workers and had, therefore, merely glanced at specifically

Jewish problems. They carried on their agitation in Russian and thus "forgot to maintain contact with the Jewish masses who understand no Russian." But life, continued Martov, "forced us to change our tactics. The primary reason was that, while all our hopes were tied up with the general Russian movement, we, at the same time, although barely conscious of it, raised the Jewish movement to a level which the Russian movement had not yet attained." In changing their tactics to mass agitation, declared Martov, they were forced to adapt their propaganda to the masses, "and that meant making it more Jewish." Martov went on to make a point which later proved to be one of the most violent questions of dispute between the Bundists and the Polish Socialist Party,[12] and even more so between the Bundists and Lenin and the *Iskra* group in the years 1902–1907.[13] The Jewish proletariat, he contended, cannot rely solely on the Russian and Polish proletariat. It is always conceivable that, in order to gain their ends, non-Jewish proletarian leaders may be willing or obliged to make concessions at the expense of the Jews.[14] Accordingly, the Jewish proletariat must be prepared to fight as an organized Jewish group, alongside of the other groups, for "economic, civil and political liberty." "A working class that is content with the lot of an inferior nation," said Martov, "will not rise up against the lot of an inferior class. The national passivity of the Jewish masses, therefore, is also a bar to the growth of its class consciousness. The growth of national and class consciousness must go hand in hand."[15]

Out of these new developments in mass agitation came the organization of the "Bund." It was founded at a series of meetings held in Vilna on October 8, 9, 10, 1897. F. Kurski, formerly in charge of the "Bund" archives and the best living authority on facts relating to its history, lists the following thirteen persons as the participants in that historic event:[16] Noah Abramov (Vitebsk), Pavel Berman (Minsk), Leon Goldman (Warsaw), Rosa Greenblatt (Bialystok), Mere Zhaludski (Warsaw), John Mill (Warsaw), Abraham Mutnik (Vilna), Hirsch Saroka (Vilna), David Katz (Vilna), Hilel Katz (Bialystok), Israel Michel Kaplinski (Vilna), Vladimir Kossovsky (Vilna), and Arkady Kremer (Vilna).[17] John Mill, in his reminiscences regarding the founding of the "Bund," does well to point out that of these thirteen founders only five were intellectuals,[18] the others being artisans and factory workers. A sharp contrast to the composition of the other revolutionary groups in Russia, which consisted almost entirely of intellectuals, this active participation of workers in the leadership of the "Bund" was to continue to be a marked characteristic of its entire history, from its origin to the present day. This characteristic too was of the greatest importance in shaping the policies and destiny of the organization.

III

Of those active in the preliminary work as well as in the actual organization of the "Bund" it was Arkady Kremer who towered above all others as the guiding genius and authoritative leader.

"Arkady's political biography," remarks Raphael Abramovich,[19] "is not very sensational," and it provides no adequate clue to his remarkable personality. He was anything but a romantic figure; he did not organize terroristic acts nor was he a spellbinding orator. Yet, during the formative years of the "Bund," he came to be recognized clearly as the dominant figure of the movement. All his contemporaries, as well as all subsequent Bundist leaders, assign this position to him without reservation. Martov, Medem, Abramovich, Kopelsohn, John Mill and Kossovsky, all intimately acquainted with the early history of the "Bund," place Arkady in undisputed possession of the central place. In the early, illegal days of the movement, when the greatest need was for technical conspiratorial work, for organizing secret groups, for smuggling illegal literature over the border, for setting up secret printing presses and hectograph machines, it was Arkady's combination of solidity, sound common sense, organizing ability, sternness of character and utter dependability, together with scientific and technical knowledge, that made him the "central figure." His "unemotional and somewhat phlegmatic character," writes Martov, "and his lucid mind, his conspiratorial consistency and other virtues of an organizer of underground activity, provided him with the necessary authority for the role of leader."[20]

Arkady Kremer was born in 1865 in Svencyan, in the province of Vilna. His father was a religious Jew, but also a *maskil* who studied physics and geometry as well as the Talmud. As a teacher in the village school he received the princely salary of 23 rubles per month, which income he supplemented by a few additional *groschen* from private lessons at home. Arkady completed school in Svencyan and, at the age of 12, entered the Realschule in Vilna, taking up his quarters in the poverty-stricken home of his uncle. Pati, his future wife, poignantly describes the life of destitution and privation which he endured in Vilna. Many a day he would go to sleep at an early hour only in order to escape the gnawing feeling of hunger and the bitter pain of cold. After graduating from the Realschule, Kremer entered the Technological Institute in St. Petersburg, in 1885. Here he remained for one year. Then, after voluntary service in the army in Riga, he entered the Riga Polytechnicum in 1888. Arkady's revolutionary career began in Riga. Here he came into contact with Polish socialist groups, was arrested and served six months in the Warsaw "Pawiak," and then was sent to Vilna in 1889, to be kept for two years under police surveillance. It is here that his role as the organizing genius of Jewish workers began. Zemach Kopelsohn, who preceded him in the Vilna movement, recounts how, when Arkady arrived in 1889, "he gradually displaced me (Kopelsohn) and all the other workers in the movement, and assumed first place in our organization. He was then a fairly well-educated young man, wise, witty, good-hearted but often very strict, very able and untiring. His popularity grew rapidly, and practically all without exception accepted him as the leader of the organization."[21]

Arkady's chief interest at that time was directed towards the general Russian revolutionary movement and he never dreamed of founding a Jewish socialist mass party. Sentiments in favor of an independent Jewish party were already to be found among some of the active Jewish workers in the Vilna groups. Arkady himself, however, was at first interested only in getting a reservoir of good Jewish leadership material for use in the larger Russian industrial centers. Under his guidance, a center of active Jewish leaders began to function. Its activity consisted in holding weekly meetings, planning the work, drawing up programs of propaganda, setting up new groups, securing illegal literature for the organization, and hectographing and printing its own literature. "No practical understanding," recounts Nemansky, "especially of a conspiratorial nature, was ever carried out without

Alexander. He was the first at places of danger. Through his hands passed all transports of illegal literature, which he would carry from one house to another. If a brochure or a proclamation had to be hectographed, it was Alexander who participated in the job."[22] He was, himself, neither much of a writer nor an orator. Martov says that Arkady did not speak very often at meetings, that "he did not possess the talents of an agitator," and that "his own personal inclinations did not tend in the direction of the role of an agitator."[23] But when he did take the floor, his words carried great weight and his opinions, expressed in smaller gatherings, set the tone for the movement at large.

Kremer's sole important writing is his brochure *On Agitation,* which he wrote in Russian in 1893 and which he read before the group of Jewish social-democrats in 1894. It was distributed in written and hectographed copies and then published in Geneva in 1896 with a preface by Pavel Axelrod.[24] This brochure marked a significant turning point in the character of revolutionary activity in Russia.

The central idea of the essay was that political agitation should broaden its base by a greater appeal to the masses of the proletariat, that it should, therefore, cease being purely abstract and theoretical and, instead, embark on a program which would integrate thoroughly political and economic problems.[25] The tactics employed by the Russian social-democrats up to that time, argued Arkady, were erroneous in that they did not pay sufficient attention to the actual economic needs of the toiling masses. The working classes, he maintained, can only become fully conscious of the need for political liberty if they can be made to see that their own economic improvement is inextricably tied up with the struggle for it. "It is utopian," he wrote, "to believe that the mass of Russian workers can begin to carry on a political struggle unless they are enlightened, with properly conclusive arguments, that such a struggle is most important for their own interests." Arkady assailed the abstract concern of Russian socialists with the theories of scientific socialism. "The masses," he declared, "are drawn into the struggle not by theoretical speculation but by the objective logic of things, by the very course of events which push them into the struggle." Thus, for example, the political demand for freedom of speech and assembly can have meaning to the masses only if and when they are made to understand that freedom of assembly is a necessary instrument in the struggle for their own interests. It is the task of socialist propaganda, therefore, to reveal to the proletariat the intimate connection between the political demand for free speech and the betterment of their own economic position. In order to stimulate political consciousness, it is first of all necessary to show the workers the class conflict existing in capitalist society, and to start with smaller economic conflicts since such simpler manifestations are more apparent to them.

"The struggle engendered by such agitation," said Kremer, "will educate the workers to stand up for their demands, will raise their courage, will give them self-assurance in their own powers, the realization that it is necessary for them to unite, and ultimately it will pose for them more important problems demanding solution. Prepared in this way for a more serious struggle, the working class then concerns itself with the solution of these important problems, and the propaganda, revolving around these problems, must have as its goal the creation of class consciousness. This more conscious kind of class struggle creates the basis for political agitation and such agitation then sets up the goal to transform the existing political conditions in the interest of the working class."[26]

In order to carry out such mass propaganda, the revolutionary agitator must have several important qualifications. He must maintain constant contact with the masses; he must keep in intimate touch with the branches of industrial production; but he must also never lose sight of the final socialist goal. Theoretical grounding must go hand in hand with practical work. One without the other is useless. Socialist activity must emerge from its closed circle of autodidacts, engaged in cultural self-development and fine-spun theoretical abstractions, and go out to the broad masses with a propaganda literature adapted to their needs and mentality. "The intellectuals and the workers must also consider what should be put forth as an object of agitation in a given branch of production and in a given moment, taking as their point of departure the most common daily needs of the workers."[27]

Kremer's brochure contains not a single remark regarding specifically Jewish problems. It is directed to the general question of revolutionary agitation in the Russian movement at large. But its immediate objective was to silence the arguments of those Vilna Jewish socialists who were opposed to carrying on socialist agitation in Yiddish. Martov recounts that many of the Jewish workers in the socialist circles in Vilna violently opposed the move to change from propaganda in Russian to agitation in Yiddish. They considered such a move to be a "bar to their advance to a higher cultural level."[28] Pati, in her recollections of the period, gives a vivid description of the leader of this opposition, the engraver Abraham Gordon. "Gordon," writes Pati, "proceeded from the assumption that knowledge is power; therefore the workers must first of all acquire knowledge and only then proceed to fight for better economic conditions." Knowledge, he argued, can be obtained by the workers only through the small educational clubs and, since there was no literature in Yiddish, the Jewish workers must be taught Russian. Agitation, therefore, is undesirable. For in order to carry on mass agitation, Yiddish would have to be used and thus the workers would be deprived of the opportunity for education.[29] Kremer's views, however, were accepted by the group, and this meant the initiation of a program that soon brought about not only the formation of an autonomous Jewish socialist organization fighting for specifically Jewish as well as general political rights, but also revolutionary changes in the language, literature, education and social structure of the Jewish masses in eastern Europe.[30]

It is out of the combination of such events and trends of thought that the foundation of the "Jewish Workers Bund" was brought about in 1897. Arkady delivered the key-note speech. In it he described the aims of the new organization as follows:

A general union of all Jewish socialist organizations will have as its goal not only the struggle for general Russian political demands; it will also have the special task of defending the specific interests of the Jewish workers, carrying on the struggle for the civic rights of the Jewish workers and above all of carrying on the struggle against the discriminatory anti-Jewish laws. That is because the Jewish workers suffer not only as workers but also as Jews, and we dare not and cannot remain indifferent at such a time.[31]

From then on, Arkady's life and career became intimately bound up with the "Bund." He carried on his activity both inside Russia and as a political exile. He was taken into political custody in 1898, during the mass arrests of Zubatov, and not released until 1900. He left Russia and continued to represent the "Bund" both in the Russian Social-Democratic Party and at the congresses of the Second International. He returned illegally to Russia in April 1905 in time to participate in the revolutionary activities of that year, and he served with Mark Liber as a member of the St. Petersburg Soviet. Abramovich tells the interesting and revealing story of how, at the peak of the revolutionary successes of 1905–06, when the "Bund" was emerging from its illegal position, Kremer decided that his usefulness to the movement had come to an end. At a session of the Central Committee he arose and announced his resignation. Now, said Kremer, the party needed orators, writers, deputies, editors, and political leaders. He was no writer, orator, or scholar and he could not, he said, be either a parliamentary deputy or an editor of a paper. He could, therefore, be of no use to the Central Committee. He merely asked that he be allowed to become a machinist at the new printing press which the "Bund" had set up in Vilna. Arkady's resignation was not accepted, but, as Abramovich observes, it was apparent that he was bent on making a sharp change in his life.[32] And this he did. In 1912 he emigrated to France, and, at the age of 45, though burdened with the responsibility of supporting a wife and child, he matriculated at the Electrotechnic Institute of Toulouse, from which he was graduated in 1914. He returned to Vilna in 1921 as an instructor of mathematics at the Jewish Teachers Institute. Here he remained until his death, on September 20, 1935, honored and revered by the Jewish workers of Vilna until his end.

IV

As Arkady Kremer is the most representative practical and organizational leader of the "Bund" during its early and formative period, so Vladimir Medem stands out as its most brilliant theoretician and Marxist scholar during its years of maturity. His close identification with the Jewish masses presents an even more striking contrast to his own family tradition and upbringing than was the case with the partly assimilated Arkady. Medem was born in Libau, in 1879, into a completely assimilated Russian Jewish family. His father, David Medem, was one of the first Jews to graduate from the Army Medical Academy, and spent his mature years as an army doctor, completely divorced from Jewish life. All the children were baptized, the older ones into the Lutheran church, Vladimir, the youngest child, into the Orthodox church. Vladimir's childhood was happy and harmonious and not at all disturbed by the pains and fears of a child of the Jewish Pale. In 1897 he was graduated from the gymnasium of Minsk (where his father had been stationed) and entered the medical school of the University of Kiev. He soon changed his course of study to law, but meanwhile became interested in the controversies between Marxists and Narodniki, emerged as one of the leaders in a student strike, and was arrested and expelled from the university. He returned to Minsk, delved into the study of Marx's *Capital* and also, at the same time, began to show an interest in Jewish life. He became especially interested in the Bible. In his memoirs, Medem admits that he has no clear recollection of how he came to return to Jewish life.[33] He describes it as a very gradual process. But he was attracted to the group of Bundists in Minsk in 1900, began to work with them, and by 1901, when arrested and asked his nationality by the police, replied without hesitation "Jewish."[34] After several short-term arrests, he went to Bern, Switzerland, where he became involved in the controversies between the Bund and the *Iskra* group. He was one of the representatives of the former at the Conference of the Russian Social-Democratic Party in 1903, when it seceded from the Russian party on the issue of national autonomy. He returned to Kovno in 1913, but was arrested on the order of the Warsaw court and confined in the notorious "Tenth Pavilion." Transported in chains to Orel, in the interior of Russia, he was returned for trial to Warsaw, on May 3, 1915, and condemned to loss of civil rights and to four years of penal servitude. The evacuation of Warsaw by the Russians in the face of the German advance, however, opened the way for the liberation of political prisoners, and Medem was set free to resume his political activities. He began to issue a monthly periodical, *Lebensfragen,* in Warsaw and initiated his activities by the organization of Jewish schools and homes for children. After the Russian revolution of 1917, he was elected to the central committee of the "Bund", but could not get across the border to Russia. He remained active in Poland until 1920, but his very critical views of Bolshevism were not in line with the dominant trend in the Polish "Bund."[35] In 1921 he emigrated to the United States where he lived for two years until his death on January 9, 1923, at the age of 44.

Viktor Alter, surveying the evolution of Bundist ideology, lists the following as the three leading ideological battles waged by the "Bund" during the course of its history: (1) against the Jewish clericalism, (2) against assimilation, (3) against Zionism.[36] The last two are part of the general problem of nationalism. It is to the analysis of the national problem that Medem devoted his best talents and energies, and produced what remain to this day outstanding contributions to the study of the relationship between Marxism and nationalism, nationalism and internationalism, and nationalism and the Jewish problem. In these writings, in particular, Medem displays his subtle mind, his keen analytical sense, and his broad familiarity with all phases of the national problem.[37]

The evolution of Bundist thought on the problem of Jewish nationalism passed through four stages: (1) from the early beginnings to 1901, when the question was officially ignored; (2) from 1901–1905, when the party platform called for national self-determination;[38] (3) from 1905–1910, when the demand was changed to cultural autonomy, but without a concrete program;[39] and (4) from 1910 on, when the demand for cultural autonomy was implemented with a concrete program of national activities and demands.[40] Medem, too, in his own life and thought, passed through a similar process of development. His formal writings on the national question, however, are representative only of the latter two stages. Medem's first important work on this subject was his "Social Democracy and the National Question," which first appeared, in 1904, as a series of articles in the illegal Bundist periodical, *Vestnik Bunda*. The importance of this work to this day as a Marxist analysis of the problem of nationalism is attested by the fact that it was reprinted in Soviet anthologies on nationalism in 1923 and 1931, notwithstanding Medem's well-known anti-Bolshevik position.[41]

Despite changes in his attitude towards the Jewish question, there are several elements of Medem's thought on the national question which appear to be fairly constant. Throughout his writings he was first and above all the Marxist. "My views," he wrote in 1917 in the preface to a collection of his articles, "are based on the standpoint of scientific socialism, and my literary work in that field always had as its goal to bring the national question into the harmonious system of Marxist thought."[42] His treatment of nationalism and nationalist movements is always grounded in an analysis of economic conditions and social structure. Despite his sympathetic treatment of the national question, he never ceases to emphasize the primacy of the class struggle. National issues are never to be allowed to overshadow class conflicts. "Solidarity of the entire nation," he wrote, "means giving up the class struggle, means peace between proletariat and bourgeoisie, means spiritual and material enslavement of the proletariat."[43] The national question, like all other questions, is subordinate to "the supreme criterion of the class struggle."[44] With all his interest in the battle for Jewish national rights, he never ceases to believe that a final solution to the Jewish problem can be achieved only when the capitalist system of production has given way to a socialist society. Given this socialist goal, however, Medem consistently fought for a positive recognition of the importance of the national question at a time when most of the leading Marxists looked down upon it as being either of little importance or a mere creation of capitalist and bourgeois interests. The leading Russian social-democrats of the pre-war period, Plekhanov, Axelrod, Martov, Lenin, Trotsky, Riazanov, and Rosa Luxemburg (then active in the Polish socialist party of Russia), all adopted a negative attitude toward the national question, deriving much of their theoretical support from the writings of Karl Kautsky.[45] Only the Austro-Marxists, especially Karl Renner and Otto Bauer,[46] saw the tremendous significance of the problem of nationalism in the modern world and made an effort to get Marxists to take cognizance of this force. Medem and the "Bund" took their stand with the Austro-Marxists against the leading Russian Marxists. But it was not only the influence of the Austrian theorists that accounted for their interest in the national question. More important was the pressure exerted by the mass character of the "Bund's" activities and by its close identification with the Jewish masses of the tsarist Pale. These two

factors forced them to give increased attention to the national demands of the Jewish people. That is why, although they followed
the Austro-Marxists on the general aspects of the national problem,
they did not take over the negative attitude of the latter to the problem of Jewish national rights.

In his treatment of the national question Medem consistently
rejected both assimilation and national romanticism. The primacy of
the class struggle, he maintained, does not preclude the acceptance of
national differences. "All attempts to combat nationalism," he wrote
in 1909, "through the old method of ignoring and hushing up the
very facts of national differences and national character have proven
themselves to be useless, mouldy and outworn. We have long since
become alien to the mood of cosmopolitanism. . . . but we are also
no idolatrous worshippers of the national idea."[47] National differences are not to be identified, however, with an abstract concept such
as national spirit. National differences are merely the national forms
in which the class struggle goes on:

> A national culture as an independent entity, as a closed circle
> with peculiar content, does not exist at all. The national is the pe-
> culiar form into which the universally human content is poured.
> The contents of cultural life, which is generally the same all over,
> takes various colors and various national forms, as soon as it enters
> into different groups with different social relationships. These re-
> lationships, in which the social tasks are set and carried out, con-
> cerning which the social conflicts which accompany social life take
> place, these relationships in which the intellectual and spiritual
> currents mature—place a national stamp upon culture.[48]

Life develops in all its rich and varied forms, and when one national
organism is compared with another we find that in some respects they
are alike, in others they are different. "The language is not the same,
the psychology is different, the relationships of social forces are different; the body is the same, the outer skin is different." The class struggle, the basic principle of social development, "takes on various
national forms, becomes enveloped in a different veil and the ray takes
on one or another national color."[49] In this way, nationalities are
created which are realities and which cannot be ignored, yet which

are all subject to the universal laws of social development. In some ways Medem's analysis here is closely similar to the later formula adopted by the Soviet Union of "socialist in content and national in form."

With reference to Jews, such a view as that developed by Medem meant opposition to both assimilationism and national romanticism of all kinds, particularly Zionism. From the first, he completely rejected assimilationism. He viewed it as a product of modern industrialism, an artificial and coercive process, and he saw only too clearly that the philosophy of assimilation is but extreme nationalism turned inside out. "Nowhere does this striving to assimilate," said Medem, "bloom so profusely as among Jews."[50] Assimilationist philosophy, he holds, is entirely a product of the Jewish bourgeoisie. Whereas the non-Jewish bourgeoisie, in bringing about their revolutionary emancipation, could continue to remain within their own nationality, the Jew, whose emancipated rights came to him as a gift from the more powerful non-Jewish bourgeoisie and who was, therefore, in no secure position, felt that he had to assimilate himself to the dominant bourgeois nationality in order to retain the more prosperous position he had achieved. Medem draws a bitingly sarcastic comparison between the non-Jewish bourgeois, the established citizen, and the Jewish "stranger." The former, "sensing his strength, raised his head proudly; he appropriated to himself the rights of a world citizen, preserved them and used them, remaining at the same time the Frenchman or German he was before. The Jew, trembling and humiliated, accustomed to have other people spit in his face, found no other way to make his rights secure than by himself spitting at his own nation and renouncing his own national identity. In order to become a citizen of the world, he was forced to become a Frenchman, a German, etc."[51] The coming of emancipation and the opening of new economic opportunities for the Jew went hand in hand with the fostering of this tendency. Lured by the tremendously rich new market, the Jewish bourgeoisie became filled with greed.

"We must secure for ourselves a slice of the 'Leviathan,' and grab a place in this market," Medem has them saying. "But mere interrelationship is not enough for this, we must assimilate. We must not only break down the walls, but we must not allow a trace of memory to remain of all the differences. Everything that can possibly reveal the Jewish lining beneath the cosmopolitan exterior must be forgotten; everything which the established bourgeois, when he wakes up from his little slumber of liberalism, might use to prevent access to the 'Leviathan' must be effaced. The psychology of this weak and money-greedy bourgeoisie has created the slogan: Assimilate.

Assimilate! That means to throw off and exert all your energies to rid yourself of everything which distinguishes you from your fellow citizen of another nation. Religion is one of the differences —down with the Law of Moses, long live Christianity! Your own language must be banned! Your customs, clothing, manners, all bear witness to your ancestry—you must therefore try with all your power to get rid of these peculiarities. Take over foreign customs and wear the clothes that your neighbors wear.

Assimilate! Be like the others! Deny your ancestry! Heap ridicule on everything that bears a Jewish stamp upon it! Spit three times when you hear the dirty 'jargon'! and shout everywhere, as you beat your breast in confession, that there is no Jewish nation, that the Jews are not a nation but a religious association.

Assimilate! because only in this way will you get to share a fat and equal portion with the established bourgeoisie. Therefore, down with your ways and customs, long live the foreign ones!"[52]

At the same Medem rejected just as emphatically any sort of artificially stimulated Jewish national feeling. His analytical and coldly rational approach to human problems led him to spurn anything that smacked of national romanticism. Traditionalism, religious values, the Hebrew language and literature (this despite his interest in the Bible), all those elements out of which spring such concepts as national spirit, national culture, and national heritage—those elements which in one form or another provided the basis for the various types of Zionism and Diaspora nationalism—were completely repudiated by him. At the same time, his Marxist preoccupation with the class struggle and his exclusive concern with the immediate and concrete material needs of the masses, led him to reject any conception of nationalism as a goal or end in itself. He was, therefore, opposed to the creation of any movement intended solely to develop Jewish national self-consciousness:

"For," wrote he, "the development of national consciousness can never be an end in itself for any social movement. The consciousness of a social group develops in order to create the force capable of realizing certain of its tasks. National consciousness is developed only in order to realize certain national tasks. Whoever stops in his directives only with the goal of developing national self-consciousness, remains standing in the middle of the road. The chief question remains unanswered, *i.e.*, for what end is this self-consciousness to be developed? The entire character of the movement depends on this 'for what end?' "[53]

Medem's attempt to harmonize the Marxian concept of the class struggle with a positive attitude towards Jewish nationalism at first assumed the form of what came to be known as "neutralism." "Neutralism," in simple terms, meant saying this: we recognize the existence of a Jewish nationality with its own language, its own manners and customs and its own special problems as an incontestable fact; we oppose all forms of national oppression, including enforced assimilation; but we disclaim any capacity to predict the course of the future development of the Jewish people and hence do nothing to create a national will to continue to exist as a nation. In other words, we are neutral on the question of the future existence of the Jewish nation. Practically, the policy of neutralism was an attempt to avoid a clash between the more assimilationist tendencies of some of the older Bundists and the newer elements which were more deeply rooted in Jewish life and tradition and hence urged a more active national program for the organization.[54] But this point of view also had its theoretical foundation in a philosophy of materialistic determinism. Human events, held Medem, result from a complex of social and economic factors. We can patiently study and analyze these factors, unravel them, and hence possibly come to understand the direction in which society is heading. But we cannot set ourselves against these forces and cannot change them. The forms the class struggle assumes are "the result of a blind process over which we have no control."[55] Whether the Jewish nation will survive in the future or become assimilated depends on thousands of complex economic, political and cultural factors. A prognosis regarding the future of Jewry, declared Medem even in 1910, is impossible and, therefore, he added: "Our neutralism is a thousand times more honest than mystical nationalism."[56] In his earliest piece on the national question Medem refused to discuss any concrete national program for the Jews. "What are the tasks and the goals of a nation?" he wrote. "In what direction should the course of national development be steered? Such questions no more exist for us than do the class interests that posit them."[57] If it is the destiny of the Jews to become assimilated, he will not seek to oppose the process. But he also does not consider it his job to foster assimilation. In other words, he is not opposed to assimilation as a natural process, but he is opposed to the striving towards assimilation, towards assimilation as a goal and as a philosophy. If, on the other hand, the historical process is tending in the direction of the development of Jewish culture, he is neutral to that, too. All he was interested in at that time was that historical processes take place without coercion and force.[58] Even when he became interested in the concrete problems of the Yiddish language and Yiddish schools, Medem retained enough of his "neutralism" to point out that the motive behind such cultural demands is not some abstract "Judaism," but the real and living interests of the Jewish masses. He refused to attribute substance to any doctrine regarding the "essence" of Judaism. Similarly he denied validity to the question of *qiyyum ha-ummah* (the existence of the nation). "Nations do not assimilate or remain alive upon order," he wrote. "That is the joke on all those who pose the question: 'to be or not to be.' "[59]

Even during the period of "neutralism," however, Medem took the lead in championing the cause of national cultural autonomy for the Jews in Russia. It was on this question primarily that Medem and the "Bund" were pitted against the *Iskra* group of Russian social-democrats in the ideological battle that went on between 1901 and 1907, leading to the temporary secession of the "Bund" from the Russian party from 1903 to 1907, and continuing, even after 1907, to separate the "Bund" from the Russian social-democrats, particularly Lenin and Stalin.

From a practical party standpoint, the basic issue was the problem of a federative *vs.* a centralized party organization. The "Bund" desired to see the Russian Social-Democratic Party organized as a federation of autonomous parties representing the various nationalities in Russia. It envisaged the future constitution of Russia as that of a multi-national state with full rights of cultural autonomy for all its constituents. The Russian social-democrats, on the other hand, while willing to come out openly against the oppression of nationalities in Russia, were not willing to give their approval to a broad program of national cultural autonomy. This conflict merely reveals again the difference between the negative attitude of the Russian leaders and the positive attitude of Medem and the "Bund" towards the problem of nationalism. More specifically, however, it involved a basic difference in attitude toward the factors taken to distinguish a nationality, and especially those applying to the Jews.

In the controversy with the "Bund" a number of Russian socialists took part, Jews as well as non-Jews. There were Liuba Axelrod, Felix Dzherzhinsky, David Ryazanov, Rosa Luxemburg, Lenin, and Stalin. We shall take Lenin as representative of this approach. Lenin conceded that the socialist program must be directed against the oppression of one nationality by another and that Russian socialists must work for the granting of full civil and political rights to members of all nationalities; but he insisted that the main concern of socialists should be the liberation of the proletariat, not national autonomy.[60] Social democracy, "the party of the proletariat," he wrote, "sees as its chief positive task the furthering of self-determination not of nations and peoples, but of the proletariat of every nationality."[61] Economic progress and industrialization would bring about greater unity; hence he desired to discourage any national cultural programs which would emphasize cleavages and differences.[62] Granting the general existence of national differences, however, Lenin denied to the Jewish people any of the characteristics of a nationality. That is because he accepted the position of Kautsky that the two indispensable criteria of a nationality are language and territory. Ever since their dispersal, the Jews, wrote Lenin, have ceased to be a nationality because they no longer possess these characteristics. Ironically he added: "For the Bundists there remains perhaps only the task to work out the idea of a separate nationality of the Russian Jews, whose language is the jargon and whose territory is the Pale."[63] "The idea of a separate Jewish nation," continued Lenin, "is absolutely unfounded in a scientific sense and is reactionary in its political significance. . . . Throughout Europe, the breakup of medievalism and the development of political liberty went hand in hand with the political emancipation of the Jews, with the transition from their jargon to the language of the people among whom they lived, and in general with an unending progress of assimilation to their surrounding neighbors." There is no reason to think that Russia should be different, and the idea of a Jewish nationality "carries an openly reactionary character not only with its most consistent followers, the Zionists, but also with those who attempt to harmonize it with the ideas of social-democracy, the Bundists. The idea of a Jewish nationality is contradictory to the interests of the Jewish proletariat, in that it encourages directly and indirectly a 'ghetto mentality,' hostile to assimilation."[64]

It is against this position that Medem developed his best thinking on the national problem and laid the groundwork for the program of the "Bund" for national and cultural autonomy. Medem pointed out that in a multi-national state like Russia guarantees of individual personal freedom are not enough. Precisely in the cultural field, where national differences are most apparent, a violent struggle between the nationalities will ensue if all cultural problems are left in the hands of the central government. Only if they are removed entirely from the competence of the central state agencies and placed in the hands of juridically recognized bodies of the nationalities themselves will such a conflict of nationalities be avoided. This is what he meant by national cultural autonomy. It is "national self-administration in that area of problems in which the national life as such is expressed, *i.e.,* in the field of culture."[65] We are for such national self-administration, said he, because it underscores the idea that "individual freedom . . . is insufficient, that merely proclaiming the right does not get it. It is important to create the necessary collective agencies which alone can serve in a greater or lesser degree as guarantees of real equality of rights."[66]

Such national cultural autonomy, moreover, is not to be administered on a merely territorial basis. In his essay, "How to Pose the National Problem in Russia," first published in the *Vestnik Evropii* in August 1912, Medem elaborated a careful critique of the territorial view of nationalism. He presented a very keen analysis of the population of Russia, of majority-minority relationships as applied not only to numbers, but also to social and economic structure, and showed how any purely territorial identification of nationality is impossible since it always leaves millions of minority peoples subjected to a dominant nationality. In line with this reasoning, he held that national cultural autonomy must be administered by a body representing all the members of that nationality, no matter in what geographical location they may be.

The revolution of 1905 forced a change in the character of revolutionary strategy for both the non-Jewish as well as the Jewish socialist groups. With the beginning of open political activity, problems which hitherto had been purely speculative and abstract now became actual and practical. Such questions as Jewish communal activity, Jewish schools, election of Jewish representatives and the like did, for a while, become practical realities. Decisions had to be made, alternatives selected; more decisive attitudes towards not only the Jewish present but also the future had to be formulated. Out of these social and political circumstances came the change from "neutralism" to a more positive affirmation of the Jewish future. It was then that the "Bund" revised its program on cultural autonomy and began to participate in such general Jewish communal organizations as the *Hevrah Mefitse Haskalah* in St. Petersburg.

Medem's theoretical change from "neutralism" is first revealed in his essay "Natsionalism oder naitralism," published in 1910. But with all the changes brought about by the revolution of 1905, the field of secular and political activity by the Jewish communities was still very limited. This is reflected in the still wavering character of Medem's thought on the problems of planning for the Jewish future. Not until 1916, when the evacuation of Poland by the Russians opened the way for the initiation of a large-scale national program by the Jewish communities, did he shed the last vestiges of "neutralism." This complete break is revealed most clearly in his article "Tiefer in leben," published in that year. Here, for the first time, he admits that "neutralism" is not enough and that any sort of national program implies a national will to preserve something. In the question of schools, for example, he points out that a "neutral" position was possible "so long as the question of the national school had not yet assumed a practical form before the people. Once it becomes actual, however, the last remnants of the 'standing-on-the-sidelines' attitude received their final blow." Under the German occupation of Poland the issue of a secular Jewish school became a practical one, and Medem took the lead in organizing schools and children's homes, in planning textbooks for the former and in laying the basis for the educational program which later developed into the large network of Yiddish schools in Poland, known as Cysho.[67]

Within the Jewish community the chief target of attack of the "Bund" was Zionism. In this battle, too, Medem took a leading part. His opposition to Zionism runs through all his writings from his first essay on the national question to his last articles. Zionism, for him, is the Jewish equivalent of the aggressive bourgeois capitalist nationalism of the non-Jewish world. Zionism, with its emphasis on national solidarity, is like all other nationalist movements, the antithesis to the proletarian class struggle. It is the romantic element in Zionist nationalism, with its abstract concepts of national spirit and national tradition projected into a fantasy regarding the national future, that aroused Medem's greatest ire. The Zionist "aims to infuse a new life into his national 'spirit' upon his 'historical territory.' His fantasy creates an image of a Jewish state; and the word 'Jewish' sounds so beautiful and so glorious to him that he simply weeps from ecstasy when he utters the word 'Judaism.' "[68] Zionism is for Medem a symbol of Jewish weakness, of fear and national paralysis, a form of escapism from the hard realities of the struggle for Jewish rights. Here we come to the crux of the opposition of Medem and the "Bund" to Zionism. Zionism, Medem holds, means the abandonment of the Jewish masses, the frustrated surrender of the struggle for political and economic rights for the Jewish masses in the lands in which they reside. Zionism is in essence an ideology of weakness, of vassalage, and its father is desperation.[69] This same idea is already found in his earlier article on the national question:

The Zionist, cloaking his class interests with the mantle of national demands, does not even have the energy to fight for these demands; he can only let his fantasy run wild over them. He cannot look life straight in the eyes, he is too weak, tired, terrified, fearful of life; he dreams, dreams of independence and freedom; he dreams of his own territory on which he will get his own culture . . . his own market. He waxes eloquent with nationalist phrases, masking with high sounding and empty pomposity his own weakness and political bankruptcy.[70]

He essays a vivid and interesting psychological analysis of the Zionist type and the complex motivations that inspire the Zionist followers:

Zionism is a complex movement. I mean psychologically complex. Dozens of souls become tangled up into one colorful roll; the broken soul of an intellectual dreamer, the narrow and dull fanaticism of a desperate ne'er-do-well petty bourgeois, the ambitious pretensions of fantastic world reformers, the crooked mind of a *Yeshiva bochur,* and more and more. But over and above all these multicolored streams there is one main current, one dominant mood, one major feeling—the feeling of a man . . . who senses his loneliness and isolation and who is pushed aside from the main stream . . . it is a sort of chosen people idea turned inside out.[71]

A logical Zionist, he held, cannot maintain a consistent position on the need for Jewish rights in the Diaspora; Zionist activity, therefore, only weakens the Jewish forces in their daily battle for their rights.

Medem was no more gentle with the so-called Diaspora Jewish nationalists. He subjected Dubnow's theory of Jewish nationalism to a penetrating and searching analysis. Already in his earliest essay, "Social-Democracy and the National Question," he attacked the theories developed in Dubnow's *Letters Concerning Old and New Judaism* and placed their author and Bismarck in the same category of nationalists.[72] But his most elaborate analysis of this theory is found in his essay "Die alveltliche yidishe natsie," first published in Russian in 1911.[73] This bold and challenging article, extreme though it may be in many ways, presents a chain of reasoning that even today must be met by all who think and write on the Jewish problem. Medem here takes issue with the idea held by Dubnow, as well as by all other Jewish nationalists, that there is one Jewish nation throughout the world. Dubnow had based his notion of a world Jewry on the concept of *Kulturgemeinschaft* as the fundamental characteristic of a nationality. Jews throughout the world, held Dubnow, shared with each other a common set of cultural and historical traditions and ideas, and hence formed one nation, even though they were divided among different states. Medem rejects such a notion of a cultural community of world Jewry. There is no such *Kulturgemeinschaft,* he holds, between the French Jews and Polish or Bulgarian Jews. French Jews have become identified completely with French culture, whereas this is not true of Polish Jews. There is actually a deep gulf between the various Jewries of the world, and this is precisely because "there is no common and unified Jewish environment." Dubnow is right, he admits, in stressing the importance of history in fashioning a community of culture, but for the Jews that is true only of the past, not of the present. Historical destiny no longer operates in the same way upon all the Jews in the world:

> Our common history has bequeathed to us a series of impressions which cannot be eradicated. But since that time we have separated in different directions and we have been experiencing a subsequent history that is not a common one. This subsequent history also leaves impressions which cannot be erased and which become superimposed as a new layer upon the old. They become an integral part of the older structure, modifying it and bringing in new changes. Our common heritage evolves, and insofar as it evolves in divided forms, in the hands of different heirs, in different countries . . . in the milieu of different cultures—it is quite apparent as to what sort of destiny it will have. One or another heir may lose his heritage completely and move into an alien house; these we need not discuss. But even those who preserve the initial capital may well diverge in different directions; each will have his own home but one will be estranged from the other.[74]

It is too soon, held Medem, to speak *as yet* of several Jewish nations, but ever since the breakdown of the traditional ghetto, we can no longer speak of one unified Jewish nation. Interesting are his remarks regarding American Jewry which, although written in 1911, are equally apropos today. Obviously, he wrote, the immigrant Jew does not change immediately upon his arrival in the United States. "But," he continued, "take the same Jews who emigrated thirty years ago and look at their children, and you will cease to smile." And then what of the third and fourth generation? And what will happen as a result of a decrease in Jewish immigration? "The ideological ties with Russia become looser before our very eyes. The colossal American life, with its terrific intensity, envelops and refashions everything. This does not mean that the American Jews must necessarily be transformed into Yankees, but it does mean that a type of American Jewry is being formed which diverges more and more from Russian Jewry and which might well form a new national type."[75] There is no such thing as a real world Jewry, held Medem, and any attempt to think in such terms must resort to such things as traditional religion, the Hebrew language or abstract Jewish feeling. All such things are mere figments of romantic traditionalism—a traditionalism which tends only to foster neglect of the concrete needs of the Jewish masses and to create a dichotomy between "national" and "folk." "This dichotomy," concluded Medem, "destroys the national movement at its root, paralyzes the forces and kills the determination. It creates a cult of the past, creates a despicable sort of hypocrisy in the name of which men who are really free-thinking scoffers assume a mask of false piety."[76]

V

A. Litvak once characterized the Bundist type as one who is "before everything else a man of will, a man of deeds, a sober man."[77] Looking at the history of the "Bund" after close to fifty years of its activity, we are able to see both the strength and the weaknesses of the Bundist movement. Its strength and determination also assumed the form of Marxist dogmatism which has continued to this day to blind many of its leaders to the need for re-evaluating old ideologies in a swiftly changing world. Similarly, its sober rationalistic approach to human problems at the same time prevented them from grasping the deeper mystical and regenerative powers of religious piety. Particularly in the light of the tragic events of the last decade do we sense their failure to appreciate the fact that the capacity to endure endless privation and suffering is made all the greater by a romantic attachment to the Jewish past and a passionate hope in the Jewish future. The "Bund" continued a dogmatic opposition to Zionism at a time when Palestine has ceased to be an issue of inner Zionist politics and has become one of the essential elements in any disposition of the Jewish question. Contrary, therefore, to the frequent claims of its over-zealous champions, the "Bund" cannot be identified with the entire mass of eastern European Jewry. It represents but one aspect of Jewish life and thought. On the other hand, notwithstanding all the criticisms that can be leveled at it, the positive achievements of the "Bund" stand out as a luminous page in the tragic history of the Jews of Russia and Poland. More than any other Jewish group, the "Bund" developed the dignity and self-consciousness of the Jewish proletarian; it helped tremendously in stimulating the development of the Yiddish language, the Yiddish press and Yiddish literature; it provided the Jewish youth with a will to resist oppression, even to the point of heroic martyrdom. But more than anything else, the "Bund" may be considered to be the most emphatic expression of that trend of Jewish thought which repudiates the notion that Jews (remaining Jews) are strangers in the lands in which they dwell. With dogged determination, it affirmed the identity of the best interests of the state with the best interests of the Jews, and repudiated the notion that the latter must bow to the nazi tide of hate and leave their homes and emigrate from hate-ridden Europe. It was this passionate conviction that has guided it in its heroic participation in the Polish underground resistance movement. It was this same conviction that breathed through the proclamation issued by its Warsaw central committee for May Day of 1944:

Comrades! Notwithstanding the terrible tragedy and suffering which we, the surviving remnants, have endured in the terrible past, and which we continue to endure in the concentration camps, prisons, forests and other places, we do not indulge in lamentations. True to the great commands of life we must be active, and, within the limits of our modest forces, we will continue to be active.

In keeping with our glorious tradition, we are bound to the working people of Poland and other lands through our common destiny in the common struggle against our common enemy for our common ideals of liberty. These ideals are today the slogans and the postulates of our common labor holiday, the First of May.[78]

NOTES

[1] The most recent example of such crude handling is the article "Bund" in vol. ii of the *Universal Jewish Encyclopaedia*. A competent brief survey is to be found in the articles by A. Menes and R. Abramovich in the *Yiddish Encyclopaedia*, vol. iii of the series *"Yidn"* (New York 1942).

[2] *Arkady: Zamlbukh zum ondenk fun grinder fun "bund" Arkady Kremer* (1865–1935) (Arkady: A Collective Book in Memory of the Founder of the "Bund" Arkady Kremer [1865–1935]) (New York, Farlag Unzer Zeit, 1942); *Vladimir Medem zum tsvantsikstn yorzeit* (Vladimir Medem on the Twentieth Anniversary of His Death) (New York, American Representation of the General Jewish Workers' Union of Poland, 1943).

[3] In addition to Arkady and Medem, the following are to be mentioned as prominent figures in the history of the "Bund"; among the pioneers—Gozhansky, Zemach, Kopelsohn, Yudin-Eisenstadt, Vladimir Kossovsky and John Mill; for the middle period—also Mark Liber, Raphael Abramovich and A. Litvak; for the post-war period in Poland—Henryk Ehrlich and Viktor Alter.

[4] *Die arbeter shtime,* no. 27, June 1902.

[5] *See* Weinryb, D., "Darko ha-rayonith shel A. S. Liberman," in *Zion,* vol. iv (1939), pp. 317–48; *see also* the interesting memoirs of Morris Vinchevsky in *Zeit fragen* (Vilna 1910).

[6] Quoted in *Vos geven* by A. Litvak (Vilna 1925). Aaron Zundelevich, in a letter to B. Frumkin in 1910 (also cited by Litvak), expresses the same views regarding the assimilationist tendencies of these early Jewish revolutionaries in Russia. A. Menes, in his brilliant introductory article to the Arkady volume, takes issue with this general characterization. As proof he cites a most interesting passage from Stepniak's *Career of a Nihilist,* in which David (a character intended to represent Zundelevich) expresses sentiments of the warmest attachment for the Jewish people. He says to the hero, Andrey, that as soon as Russia is liberated, "I shall expatriate myself forever and settle somewhere in Germany," for "we Jews are outcasts among the nations," and "German working people are educated, and are on the way towards better feelings, and Germany is the only land where we are not total strangers" (Eng. trans. New York 1889, p. 47). Zundelevich's letter to Frumkin, however, as well as the entire record of his career seems to substantiate Jochelson. The passage from Step-

niak's novel, even if literally accurate, would prove at most that Zundelevich retained his warm feelings for Jews, that he felt strange in the completely Russian environment and that he placed greater hopes on the German social-democrats than upon the Russian masses. It does not provide any basis, however, for a conception of the Jews as a separate national group. For the best treatment of Zundelevich *see* the article by David Shub in the anthology *Vilna,* edited by E. H. Jeshurin (New York 1935), pp. 96–126. For the more general treatment of the subject of Jewish participation in the revolutionary movement in tsarist Russia *see* Deitch, L. *Yidn in der rusisher revoluzie* (Berlin 1924); Shub, D., *Helden un martyrer,* 2 vols. (Warsaw 1938) and "Yidn in der russisher revoluzie," in the *Zukunft,* vol. xlix (1944), pp. 360–68; and, above all, the voluminous collection of material in vol. iii of the *Historishe shriftn,* issued by the Yiddish Scientific Institute (Vilna 1939).

⁷ *See* Buchbinder, N. A., *Die geshichte fun der yiddisher arbeter bavegung in Rusland* (Vilna 1931) and Rafes, M. G., *Kapitlen geshichte fun Bund* (Kiev 1929).

⁸ Among such ex-students of the Rabbinical Seminary were the leaders of the Vilna revolutionary circle of 1875, Liberman, Zundelevich, Weiner, Jochelson and Lieb Davidovich. Nine of the members of the circle of 1876 were likewise ex-students of this Rabbinical Seminary (*see* reports of police archives in Vilna in *Historishe shriftn,* vol. iii, pp. 256–82). From the *Realschule* came Arkady Kremer, Samuel Peskin, John Mill, and Jacob Notkin.

⁹ Martov in his memoirs relates that it was not until after the revolution of 1917 and the opening of the secret police archives that he discovered how effectively concealed was the conspiratorial work in Vilna. He cites a Vilna police report to the effect that for a period of two and a half years the Vilna police force found "nothing to compromise" him. Yet during this entire period, says Martov, "I was in constant contact with many people who, together with me, were engaged in conspiratorial work" (Martov, L., *Zichroines fun a sotsialdemokrat* [Berlin 1922], also cited in *Arkady,* p. 127).

¹⁰ Quoted in Frumkin, K., "Der Bund un seine gegner," in *Zukunft,* vol. ii (1903), p. 281.

¹¹ This address was entitled "Concerning the Theoretical and Practical Achievements of the Movement." It was first published in 1900 in the original Russian and also in Yiddish translation, under the title, *Die naye epoche in der yiddisher arbeter bavegung.* It is most readily available in a reprint of the Yiddish version in the *Arbeter luach,* vol. iii (Warsaw 1922), pp. 71–90.

¹² *See* the pamphlet issued by the Bund, *Die milchome fun der poilisher sozialistisher partei gegen dem yiddishen arbeter Bund* (n.p. 1898).

¹³ *See* the collection of articles by Lenin against the "Bund," ed. by S. Agurski, and issued by the White Russian Scientific Academy (Minsk 1933). For those who do not read Russian, but who read German, *see* the German edition of Lenin's *Sämtliche Werke,* vols. iv, v and vi, with helpful notes by the

editors. [The cited Yiddish book is: V. I. Lenin and I. V. Stalin, *Kegn "Bund"* (Against the Bund). Eds].

[14] An interesting analysis of this point is found in D. Shub's article in *Zukunft*, cited above.

[15] Martov later changed his views on this question, joined the Russian Social Democratic Party and became, with Lenin, one of the editors of *Iskra*. There is a crying need for a full-length study of the life and thought of this brilliant Jewish socialist and leading theoretician of the Mensheviks. [*Cf.* Boris Sapir's review of Getzler, Israel, *Martov, A Political Biography of a Russian Social Democrat*, JEWISH SOCIAL STUDIES, vol. xxx, no. 4 (October 1968), pp. 282 f. Eds.]

[16] *Arkady*, p. 89.

[17] Israel Cohen, in his *Vilna* (Philadelphia 1943), erroneously gives the number as 11, and lists only 3 instead of 6 members as coming from Vilna. Completely fantastic, of course, is the implication in Weinryb's article in the *Universal Jewish Encyclopaedia*, vol. ii, p. 588, that "Martov, Zederbaum and Liessin" were the founders of the Bund. Martov and Zederbaum are, of course, one and the same person. [Weinryb has publicly disavowed this article. Eds.]

[18] *Arkady*, pp. 161–62. The reader will please note the *corrigenda* in pagination in the volume for these pages.

[19] *Ibid.*, p. 238.

[20] *Zichroines fun a sotsial-demokrat*, p. 153.

[21] Kopelsohn, Zemach, "Die ershte shprotzungen," in *Arbeter luach*, vol. iii (1922), p. 63.

[22] Nemansky, A., in *Arbeter shtime*, no. 45. September 27, 1917.

[23] *Op. cit.*, p. 153.

[24] A Yiddish translation of this brochure is published in *Arkady*, pp. 293–321.

[25] This idea, in a much more extreme form, was taken up later by some Russian social-democrats and received the label "economism." These socialists argued in favor of giving up long-range political goals and concentrating solely on demands for the economic improvement of the working classes. Lenin's *What Is to Be Done?* is a sharp and violent assault upon this current of thought. Kremer and the leaders of the "Bund" never adopted this extreme view, although they were so accused by Lenin. (*See* Lenin's *Sämtliche Werke*, vol. v, p. 335).

[26] *Arkady*, pp. 309–310.

[27] *Ibid.*, p. 318.

[28] *Op. cit.*, pp. 179–80.

[29] *Arkady*, pp. 52–53.

[30] Arkady's pamphlet also exerted a great influence on the Russian social-democrats. It was published by them in 1896 with an introduction by Pavel Axelrod, and the methods initiated by Arkady were imitated by the Russian

groups in many respects, although Plekhanov successfully opposed the publication by the Russian group of three other mass-agitation pamphlets prepared under Kremer's direction (see Mill, John, in *Arkady*, pp. 155–56). Arkady himself was also one of the initiators of the founding of the Russian Social-Democratic Party in Minsk in 1898 and was selected as a member of the first Central Committee of the R.S.D.P.

[31] *Arkady*, p. 164.

[32] *Ibid.*, pp. 237–38.

[33] *Fun mein leben*, 2 vols. (New York 1923), vol. i, p. 171.

[34] *Ibid.* Medem, in a volume of earlier memoirs, states that he was able to understand some Yiddish in his youth, but could not carry on a conversation in Yiddish. During the first years of his activity in the "Bund," his articles for the Yiddish press had to be translated from the Russian. His first speech in Yiddish was at the 8th conference of the "Bund" in 1910, and his first public address in Yiddish before a large audience was given in Warsaw in 1915 *(see* Medem, V., *Zichroines un artiklen,* Warsaw 1917).

[35] For his critique of Russian Bolshevism, see especially the articles reprinted in *Fun mein notizbuch* (Warsaw 1920).

[36]"Oif bundishe temes," in *Unser zeit,* vol. i (1927).

[37] Medem's most important writings on the national problem are the following: "Social Democracy and the National Question" (1904), "National Movements and National Socialist Parties in Russia and Poland" (1908), "The Jewish Question in Russia" (1911), "How to Pose the National Question in Russia" (1912), all published in Yiddish translation in *Vladimir Medem;* to those should be added: "Die alveltliche yiddishe natsie" (1911), "Natsionalism un naitralism" (1910), and "Tiefer in leben" (1916), all reprinted in *Zichroines un artiklen,* and "Vegen rusishen natsionalen gesicht," in *Die naye zeit,* no. 7 (Vilna 1909). It should be noted here that, in addition to Medem, Vladimir Kossovsky was also very important in the formulation of the "Bund's" national program.

[38] The resolution adopted at the 4th Conference of the "Bund" in 1901 declared as follows: "The Conference holds that it is against the sense of the social-democratic program to allow for the oppression of one class by another, of citizens by the government, and also of one nationality by another and one language by another. The conference holds that a state such as Russia, consisting as it does of many nationalities, should, in the future, be reconstructed as a federation of nationalities with complete national autonomy for each nationality, independent of the territory in which it is located. The conference holds that the term 'nation' is also to be applied to the Jewish people. In the light of existing circumstances, however, it is still too soon to put forth the demand for national autonomy for Jews and hence the conference holds that for the time being the struggle is to be carried on only against all discriminatory laws directed against Jews, publicize and protest against any suppression of the Jewish nationality, but at the same time to be careful not to fan

into a flame the national feeling, for that will only obscure the class consciousness of the proletariat and lead to chauvinism."

[39] The 6th Conference of the "Bund," in October 1905, made the demand for national cultural autonomy for Jews a definite part of its program.

[40] The 8th Conference of the "Bund," in 1910, was the first in which the deliberations were held exclusively in Yiddish, at which the first resolution on Yiddish was adopted by the "Bund," and at which a program calling for the organization of Jewish cultural groups and agencies was adopted.

[41] See Cherkaski, Ravich, ed., *Marxism and the National Question* (Kharkov 1923). The last part of the essay is also reprinted in Velikovski, M. and Levin, I., *Nationalnii vopros* (Moscow 1931).

[42] *Zichroines un artiklen*, p. 68.

[43] "Social Democracy and the National Question," in *Vladimir Medem*, p. 186.

[44] "National Movements and National Socialist Parties," in *Vladimir Medem*, pp. 220–21; *see also* pp. 186–87.

[45] During a heated discussion of Russian social-democrats at Karlsruhe in 1903, Medem was engaged in a tilt with Leon Trotsky on the Jewish national question. Medem turned to Trotsky and said: "As for your own person, you cannot ignore the fact that you belong to a definite nation. You consider yourself, I take it, to be either a Russian or a Jew." Trotsky shot back quickly: "No, you are wrong! I am a social-democrat, and that's all" (quoted in *Vladimir Medem*, pp. 10–11 n.).

[46] Renner, Karl, *Der Kampf der Nation um den Staat* (Vienna 1902) and *Grundlagen und Entwicklungsziele der östereichisch-ungarischen Monarchie* (Vienna 1906) and Bauer, Otto, *Die Nationalitätenfrage und die Sozial-Demokratie* (Vienna 1907, 2nd ed. Vienna 1924).

[47] In *Die naye zeit*, no. 7 (1909), p. 47.

[48] *Vladimir Medem*, p. 188.

[49] *Ibid.*, p. 189.

[50] *Ibid*, p. 175.

[51] "Social Democracy and the National Question," p. 176.

[52] *Ibid.*, p. 177.

[53] *Die naye zeit*, no. 7 (1909), pp. 47–48.

[54] One of the best examples of this type was A. Helfand, better known as Litvak. *See* his unfinished but most absorbing volume of memoirs and collection of articles, *Vos geven* (Vilna 1925). Litvak became one of the most able writers in the socialist Yiddish press, first in Russia and later in the United States. Abraham Liessin was another and older representative of this trend in the "Bund."

[55] *Vladimir Medem*, p. 189.

[56] "Natsionalism oder naitralism," in *Zichroines un artiklen*, p. 116.

[57] *Vladimir Medem*, p. 187.

[58] Here Medem failed to see the contradiction between his deterministic conception of the historical process and his opposition to the intrusion of coercion and force into this process. Are not coercion and force, in themselves, part of this blind historical process?

[59] "Natsionalism oder naitralism," p. 130.

[60] *See* his "Das Manifest der armenischen Sozialdemokraten," in *Sämtliche Werke*, vol. v.

[61] "Die nationale Frage in unserem Program," *ibid.*, p. 478.

[62] *See* Lenin's article on cultural national autonomy, directed against the Austro-Marxists, published December 11, 1913 in *Pravda;* also in Yiddish translation in S. Agurski, *Kegn Bund."*

[63] "Die Stellung des 'Bund' in der Partei," in *Iskra,* October 22, 1903, reprinted in *Sämtliche Werke,* vol. vi, p. 106.

[64] *Ibid.*, p. 106. It is important to point out that the whole problem of the position of the Jews in the Soviet Union cannot be properly understood unless these views of Lenin are taken into consideration. While it is true that Stalin entertained somewhat different views regarding the general problem of nationalism from those of Lenin, his basic emphasis on territory and language as the distinguishing marks of nationality remained the same as that of Lenin. His attitude towards the "Bund" and its national program was also the same. It is my opinion that the entire collapse of Jewish cultural life in the Soviet Union during the last ten years, the attempt to provide a territorial foundation for the Jews in Biro-Bidjan, and the tremendously rapid rate of assimilation among the Jews of Russia and the Ukraine are all evidences of the essentially negative attitude on the part of Stalin and the Russian communists towards Jewish national cultural rights. In this respect they are merely carrying out the views held by Lenin before World War I. There is a great deal of confusion regarding the status of Yiddish culture and Jewish cultural rights in the Soviet Union. An accurate and objective account of this whole subject still awaits doing.

[65] *Vladimir Medem,* p. 217.

[66] *Ibid.*

[67] This subject is ably treated by H. S. Kazdan in *Vladimir Medem,* pp. 160–69.

[68] *Vladimir Medem,* p. 182.

[69] "Die farblondzete," written in 1919 and reprinted in *Fun mein notizbuch,* p. 111. Precisely the same characterization is made almost a decade later by Viktor Alter in *Unser zeit,* vol. i (1927), p. 51.

[70] *Vladimir Medem,* p. 183.

[71] *Fun mein notizbuch,* pp. 110–11.

[72] *Vladimir Medem,* pp. 184–85.

[73] Reprinted in Yiddish translation in *Zichroines un artiklen.*

[74] *Ibid.*, pp. 93–94.

[75] *Ibid.*, pp. 100–101.
[76] *Ibid.*, p. 106.
[77] Litvak, *op. cit.*, p. 136.
[78] *The Forward,* September 12, 1944.

EDITORS' PREFACE

The Founder of Modern Political Antisemitism: Georg von Schönerer

Von Schönerer, as Dr. Karbach points out, has been dismissed by Jewish historians as a "mere common or garden-type Jew-baiter, and the real significance both of himself and of his movement for the history of modern antisemitism tends to be ignored." However, the number of important antisemitic ideologues and activists who have not received the attention of Jewish scholars is quite sizeable, for there are many lacunae in the research on the history of Jew-hatred.

The essential implication of the article is that not only the Nazi racist theory, but also the tactics for the attainment of power, preceded the Weimar Republic, with nineteenth and early twentieth century Austria as the proving grounds.

Schönerer began his political career as a liberal pan-German who dreamed of a greater Germany under Prussia. He became convinced of antisemitism's efficacy in seducing Germans, both in Austria and Germany, and proceeded accordingly. The essential first step was to banish the emancipationist notion that Jews are human beings. They were, therefore, constantly and consistently portrayed as a subhuman race and as Germany's and civilized mankind's eternal foes and destroyers.

323

Half a century before Willy Muenzberg's creation of the Stalinist satellite system, Schönerer organized his followers, women, students, farmers, even bicyclists, along occupational and interest lines. Those functioned as his front organizations. His tactics called for the relentless presentation of the Jewish issue before the public, principally by making demands that could not be met in a parliamentary state. Schönerer's followers continually proposed anti-Jewish legislation in parliament. Refusal to accept such demands served to label the state, the Church, and other institutions as lackeys of the Jews and offered more opportunities for propaganda. Legislation proposed in 1903 called for the abrogation of the citizenship and legal equality of all Jews and their descendants, even baptized ones, until the third generation. It demanded the establishment of ghettoes in the larger towns; exclusion from all occupations, except trade and handicrafts; prohibition of ownership of landed property outside the ghettoes, of employment of Gentiles, of attendance at non-Jewish schools, of service in the armed forces; and other exclusionary and restrictive measures. An examination of Nazi legislation proves that Hitler borrowed not only his tactics, but also his ideas, from Schönerer.

Karbach reports the reaction of Jews to these counter-emancipationist efforts. Only the old-timers who had some taste of pre-emancipation conditions took the threats seriously. The post emancipation generation lost its ability to comprehend the significance of antisemitism and often even sensitivity to its manifestations, and dismissed its threats. By underestimating their importance, Jewish leadership found itself incapable of devising even adequate theoretical weapons against the racist attacks.

Karbach also deals with dilemma of the Catholic Vatican-oriented Christian Socialists who opposed racism. Their leadership feared that antisemitic legislation would bring about protective mass baptism. The Church, unable to reject the converts, no matter how insincere, would then be attacked as a shelter for Jews. Christian Socialist antisemitism was therefore defensive and vague, tending to join in the attack against the Jews, at the very least in order to steal some of Schönerer's thunder. This was not always understood by Jews. Karbach also touches very briefly on the success of Lueger, the first antisemitic   mayor of Vienna, who became the most powerful Austrian of his day.

Dr. Karbach's article is essential for the serious study of antisemitism, politics, and mass movements.

OSCAR KARBACH, a student of Jewish political problems, was a native of Vienna. He was active in the Jewish Association for the League of Nations in Austria, and participated in international gatherings on minority protection. He emigrated to the United States in 1939. From 1941 until his death in 1973 he was associated with the World Jewish Congress and its Institute of Jewish Affairs, serving as Head of the Division for the Prosecution of Nazi Crimes since 1964. Karbach was the author of papers on the protection of minorities, Jewish political thought, and antisemitism, and co-author of *Were the Minority Treaties a Failure?* (New York, Institute of Jewish Affairs, 1943).

The Founder of Modern Political Antisemitism: Georg von Schönerer

by Oscar Karbach

Adolf Hitler has himself acknowledged that much of his antisemitic technique was derived from Georg von Schönerer, leader of the German irredentists in Austria during the latter half of the 19th century.[1] Nevertheless, von Schönerer continues to be dismissed by Jewish historians as a mere common or garden-type Jew-baiter, and the real significance both of himself and of his movement for the history of modern antisemitism tends to be ignored. The reason for this is not far to seek. If von Schönerer be judged solely on the strength of his personal character or the immediate effectiveness of his policies, he must certainly cut a sorry, even a ridiculous, figure. His public activities, his oratorical achievements, his propagandistic innovations, may safely be left to oblivion. Nor can his peculiar brand of Pan-Germanism or the several constitutional "reforms" which he advocated in support of it lay claim to such originality as would give him distinction. All of them were already formulated in their essentials before he came upon the scene, while even in his radical and racial antisemitism he was but a convert to an already current ideology. The fact is, however, that, in the long view, all of these things are secondary, and it is not upon them that history's appraisal of von Schönerer's significance should properly be based. Von Schönerer is important because he was the first to perceive the possibilities of

Reprinted from JEWISH SOCIAL STUDIES, Volume VII, 1945

antisemitism as an instrument for forcing the direction of foreign policy and disrupting, for partisan ends, the internal structure of the state. Von Schönerer was the first to hit upon the idea of using the Jews not only as a political scapegoat but also as a political catalyst, or—to change the metaphor—of isolating the Jews as a distinctive political unit for the purpose of using them as a king's pawn on the chessboard of domestic and foreign intrigue. He was thus, to a large extent, the "onlie begetter" of a tactic to which national socialism has since given worldwide currency, and the application of which, as a matter of general policy, has been mainly responsible for the Jewish tragedy of our own day. As such, his activities merit fresh examination and appraisal, particularly in the light of the political milieu in which they took place. Such an examination shows clearly that the setting of von Schönerer's labors in the German-speaking areas of Austria was no freak of chance. It attests once more the basic truth of Bishop Hudal's shrewd observation that nazi antisemitism "is, in a sense, nothing but the problem of the east-German borderland transferred to the Reich."[2]

I

Von Schönerer's antisemitism was part of a wider policy aimed at the reunion of Austria with Germany. This was the continuation and development of a movement which had been steadily gaining ground in Europe since 1870. The events of that year, even more than the Austro-Prussian War of 1866, had changed the entire attitude of statesmen towards the Hapsburg monarchy. "It's existence," wrote Lord Salisbury to Disraeli in 1876, "is no longer of the importance to us that it was in former times. Its vocation in Europe has gone. It was a counterpoise to France and a barrier against Russia: but France is gone, and the development of Russia is chiefly in regions where Austria could not, and if she could, would not help to check it. We have no reason, therefore, for sharing Austria's tremor. . . ."[3] Thus, with a disinterested Great Britain, a conquered and isolated France, and with the three other great European powers in the role of rejoicing heirs, the question was not whether, but how and when the dissolution of the Dual Monarchy would be effected. At the same time, however, with Austria excluded from the German reconstruction, it was but to be expected that the center of gravity might shift toward the Austrian Slavs who formed the majority of the population, a tendency which gradual democratization could only hasten.

In face of this situation, it is not surprising that as early as 1868 Austro-German groups began openly to voice claims which could only be described as subversive from the point of view of official Austrian policy. A program issued on February 15th of that year, for example, demanded "reunion with Germany of those parts of Austria which had belonged to the German Federation" without premature interference with the internal affairs of Germany and "a close alliance of Austria with Germany, that is, with the leading German State [Prussia], against any foreign foe."[4] Similarly, in the summer of the same year a speaker said bluntly: "If the devil can unite us, we will go with the devil";[5] while in 1870, a manifesto issued by the Deutscher Volksverein of Vienna on the occasion of the elections of the Diet of Lower Austria already foreshadowed what were later to become the main points of von Schönerer's foreign policy. In vehement terms it attacked "the so-called European, cosmopolitan or purely humanitarian democracy" and maintained that the most important problem for German Austria was the struggle of the non-German nationalities against Germanism. "We believe," declared this document, "that the most favorable solution of this problem from the point of view of the German people in Austria is not a question of law, but of power." In line with this view, the manifesto demanded separation of Galicia and Dalmatia by granting them autonomy, formation of a common parliament for those provinces which formerly belonged to the German Federation[6] and immediate reunion of them with Germany by a close alliance. "It will take a national disaster," ran the warning, "or severe political oppression to rouse the innocent, complacent Viennese to a sense of their duty towards the common fatherland and the purified national spirit."[7]

Such was the setting for the appearance of Georg von Schönerer on the political stage.

II

Matthias Schönerer, the father of our "hero," was a remarkable man.[8] It was with his help that the first horse-driven railway on the

European continent had been constructed—the line between the border of Bohemia and Gmunden in the Upper Austrian Salzkammergut. This railway carried the products of the Alpine salt-works to the great waterways of the Danube and of the Moldau-Elbe. In 1838 he visited the United States and brought back with him the first steam-locomotive ("Philadelphia") ever seen in Austria. During the following two decades, he was connected with all of the important railroads then being constructed in Austria as well as with the first Austrian plant to build railroad locomotives and cars. During the war of 1848–49 he was responsible for the transportation of the Austrian forces to the Italian and Hungarian fronts. In 1860, after his commercial enterprises had brought him considerable wealth, he and his whole family were knighted by the Emperor.

His son Georg was born on July 17, 1842, at his home in the terminus building of the Southern Railroad in Vienna. The boy attended school in Vienna, but in 1856 came into conflict with the Catholic priest who taught religion, and consequently left to continue his studies in Dresden. We may rightly assume that the most severe punishment, the expulsion from *all* Austrian schools, was inflicted upon the "unruly" youngster. He thus came to spend his formative years in Germany, devoting himself to agricultural and commercial studies. Not until 1863 did he return to his fatherland. Three years later, when war broke out, he quietly continued his agricultural studies on one of the large estates of the Archduke Albrecht, while his employer commanded the Austrian army in Italy. After two years of travel, he settled down in 1869 at the old castle and estate of Rosenau (near Zwettl in Lower Austria, close to the Bohemian border) which his father had bought for his son's establishment.

Well provided with funds, the new squire soon ingratiated himself with the local population by his practical interest in the creation of useful institutions; he is said to have been connected with no less than 200 fire-brigades and 130 agricultural associations. On October 14, 1873, at the age of thirty-one, he was elected deputy by the district of Zwettl and Waidhofen-on-the-Thaya. He joined the Progressive Club, one of the groups within the German Liberal Party.

III

Even his friends never attributed unlimited gifts to von Schönerer. His strength lay in his ability to anticipate political developments and to crystallize them in effective slogans. As speaker and propagandist he was undeniably gifted, sharing this talent with a familiar type of top-flight nazi in our own day. But in print his speeches bring more torture than edification, since he had a habit of "blending high-flown expressions of idealism with mere banalities."[9] One of his nazi biographers maintains that "he did not acknowledge the practical importance of interdependence in international politics,"[10] and the leader of the Pan-Germans in the Reich, the well-known Heinrich Class, said of him that "unfortunately this highly gifted and educated man, who is endowed with definite political instinct, has been seduced by oratorical success into mere propaganda, and has thus become unproductive."[11]

Being financially independent, von Schönerer could afford to indulge in extravagant attacks on royalty, the state, the Church, and the industrial leaders of the nation. Thus he attracted first the interest and then the adherence of the masses, both white-collar and others, who had been merely bemused by the high-flown, intellectual oratory of the old-time liberal spokesmen.[12] During the initial years of his activity nobody doubted his sincere attachment to the Liberal cause. Even as late as 1877 he was the recipient of a formal testimonial signed by such unimpeachable progressive politicians as J. Ofner and J. Kopp.[13] When, therefore, after two re-elections, he began, in 1880, to consider the foundation of a new political party, the *Deutsche Volkspartei,* he had inevitably to face the opposition and hostility of the old forty-eighters and their followers.[14] To balance this, however, he soon secured the enthusiastic indorsement and support of the best men among the young generation. For a short time, von Schönerer seemed to be the unquestioned future leader of the Austrian Germans. Gentiles and Jews alike, who a few years later were instrumental in the shaping of all the other new political parties or their programs, gathered around him: Engelbert Pernerstorfer and Victor Adler, Otto Steinwender and Julius Sylvester, Heinrich Friedjung and Hermann Bahr.[15] Finally, in the fall of 1882, and mainly with Friedjung's help, he propounded his famous "Linz Program."[16] Its main points were (1) dissolution of the union with Hungary (only the ruler should remain a common one); (2) annexation of Dalmatia and the recently occupied Turkish provinces of Bosnia and Hercegovina to Hungary; (3) autonomy, or union with Hungary, for Galicia and Bukovina; (4) closer alliance with Germany; (5) establishment of a customs union with Germany, Hungary and the Balkan States; (6) dominance of the German language; (7) reform of the franchise; (8) disbarment from parliamentary candidature of priests, civil servants and executives of stock companies; (9) "a good and progressive education" for the young; (10) a series of new anti-capitalist taxes; (11) "a quick and inexpensive administration of justice," including the foundation of penal settlements—probably the origin of the German concentration camps; and (12) far-reaching protection of farmers, very similar to the provisions of later nazi legislation.

Except for the fact that there was as yet no reference to the Jewish question, the Linz Program may be taken as a fair indication of von Schönerer's attitude toward Austrian problems during his whole public career. Its phrasing, however, was relatively temperate, when compared with the even far more radical language in which he indulged both before and after its publication. Thus, for example, on December 18, 1878 he had created something of a furor in parliament by boldly expressing the wish that "Austria already belonged to the German Empire." Four years later, in a speech at Breslau, he dared to speak of the "fruits of the immortal harvest of Sedan,"[17] and to voice his longing for "the day, when a German army will invade Austria and put an end to her." Similarly, on March 18, 1902 he proposed three cheers for the Hohenzollern dynasty at a session of the Austrian parliament.[18]

Von Schönerer made no bones about it; he advocated the destruction of his own fatherland. "The position of Austria as a Great Power must cease," he said, "if we possess no means of maintaining it. . . ."[19] "We can cheerfully renounce our position as a Great Power, because we will have closer economic relations with the co-national German Empire and an alliance with it."[20]

In order to secure permanent dominance for the German element in the restricted Austria the way he saw it, he suggested, as early as 1882, a representation of the people by estates[21] on the grounds that "universal and direct franchise is everywhere only a transitional state."[22] His utterances are suggestive, indeed, of many a familiar modern slogan: "We do not pay homage to Roman Law, according to which man is but a commodity."[23] "I wish men would soon get accustomed to putting the common weal above individual interest."[24] "The state has to intercede particularly in favor of Labor and not of Capital."[25]

Nor was it only in point of ideology that von Schönerer anticipated nazi doctrines. He was also the forerunner of standard nazi propaganda techniques. He was indefatigable in devising new vehicles for popularizing his movement: it was the first in Austria to attract the interest of the "little man" by propaganda songs, post-cards, Schönerer beer-mugs, walking-sticks and matches. He even presented the inn-keepers of his electoral district with special signboards gaudily inscribed with such suggestive names as "German Home," "Watch on the Rhine," "Germania" and the like.[26] He initiated the technique of a camouflaged network of subversive associations with ostensibly harmless purposes. He had his own Pan-Germanic organizations of workers, farmers, merchants, teachers, students, gymnasts, bicyclists, women, as well as choral and historical societies. If any one of them closed down, its members promptly withdrew to another, "in order to continue their activities even less disturbed, under the cover of its allegedly non-political tendency."[27]

In yet another strange way von Schönerer anticipated and satisfied an indispensable need of the German soul, the idolization of a Führer. Never regarding himself as a leader of *all* the Germans, far less as *the* Pan-German leader, but merely as a kind of *Gauleiter* of Austria, he turned his and his followers' admiration and veneration toward a very unwilling object, Bismarck. The Iron Chancellor, "faithful servant of his old Emperor" at home and carefully restricting himself abroad to the conventional role of a prime minister, did all in his power to curb the exuberance of the "Schönerereans" who besieged him with deputations and overwhelmed him with presentations. He succeeded, significantly, in never seeing his fervent Austrian admirer, but could not prevent him from ending his public addresses and signing his tracts with the slogan, *Heil Bismarck,* or from telling his audiences that "We are resolved to be a people of Bismarckian stalwarts" or from sum-

ming up his life-long convictions in the political "swan-song" (1913):
"Heil the Bismarck of the Future, Savior of the Germans and Founder
of Greater Germany!"

Von Schönerer's novel methods of propaganda were bound, of
course, to have their effect on the electorate, especially on the young
people. "His political credo," says an Austrian statesman,[28] "that
mixture of Bismarck-veneration, longing for Hohenzollern rule, worship of Odin and other pagan, anti-Christian idols, was accepted as
gospel by the citizens and students of Graz." Similar, too, is the
testimony of Count Felix Lichnowsky, temporarily in charge of the
German Embassy in Vienna. "The German national movement,"
wrote he to von Bülow, "has embraced ever-widening circles. . . . The
whole of the intelligensia, the university graduates, the merchants, nay,
even a part of the farmers, are affected by it. Professors and students
of the universities and high-schools are followers of Schönerer. The
only exception is the Catholic priest. The latter is regarded by his
pupils as an enemy, and his moral influence has completely diminished. The slightest allusion to nationalism at once unleashes a
positive frenzy of enthusiasm, and Tacitus' *Germania* is being
devoured fervently."[29]

IV

Especially bitter and irreconcilable was the struggle of the Austrian
Pan-German movement against the Catholic Church. Here again, von
Schönerer—like the nazis—did nothing more than adopt and exploit
a time-honored liberal tradition. European liberalism, especially in
Catholic countries, has always been bound up with anti-clericalism.
In Austria, in particular, the tremendous influence of the Church upon
the masses gave solid backing to the Hapsburgs and to the maintenance of their Empire. The disappearance of what still remained of
the Holy Roman Empire in 1866, the Prussian-Protestant dominance
over the new political structure of Bismarck and his *Kulturkampf*
during the seventies, the creation of the then strongly anti-clerical
Italian kingdom, the developments in republican France—all of these
things could not but foster a stronger attachment to the Dual Monarchy, the last of the Catholic great powers, on the part of all who

espoused the Catholic cause. Resolved to destroy this Empire, von Schönerer was bound to intensify the old anti-Catholic tradition in the direction of outright radicalism.

For several decades he waged incessant war on the influence of the Church. Under the slogan of "Away from Rome," he advocated and organized a movement aiming at mass conversion to Protestantism. Although the actual results were none too impressive—altogether about 85,000 persons left the Church within ten years[30]—the bearing of this campaign on the disintegration of Catholic life should not be underestimated. Von Schönerer viewed his efforts solely from the standpoint of politics. As early as 1878 he had pronounced the opinion that "Protestantism was desirable because it corresponds to Germanism."[31] Later he expressed his purpose more bluntly in true nazi fashion: "We are Christians," he said, "but wherever Germanism and Christianity conflict with each other, we are, of course, first of all Germans!"[32] And when representatives of the German Evangelic Federation tried to persuade him to implement his battle-cry "Away from Rome" with the joyous summons "Forward to the Gospels," he reminded them that "even the Protestant communion is not free from clericalism." As a Protestant writer pointedly observes, von Schönerer and his followers chose Protestantism "merely as the lesser evil."[33] He was, indeed, the first to wean considerable portions of the population from adherence to Catholicism—and this at a time when they had not yet come under the spell of a thoroughgoing Marxist ideology. Even his opponents were influenced in this direction. And well he knew how useful it was to this struggle to attack the Bible as the "disgusting Jew book."

V

All of the foregoing serves as the indispensable background for a correct evaluation of von Schönerer as the father of modern political antisemitism. Without that background it is impossible to answer the basic question whether he was a deranged fanatic or a shrewd politician, or to explain the most striking feature of the whole bewildering picture: why just in Austria radical antisemitism arose from within a liberal, progressive and anti-clerical party, one which had the whole-hearted support of practically all the German-speaking Jews, whereas everywhere else it was associated with essentially reactionary movements.

Von Schönerer's primary aim was to destroy the state in which he lived. He was, however, the first to discover the tremendous possibilities of undermining its structure by attacking and crushing the Jews. He did not, primarily, become the protagonist of modern political antisemitism because influence in the Dual Monarchy was vested in men of an "alien race" nor even because it was utilized in support of his hated fatherland. The true reason was that he saw clearly—before anyone else had grasped the fact—that elimination of the Jewish element would disrupt the whole fabric of the state.

While his fellow Jew-baiters wanted either to prevent Jewish emancipation (as in tsarist Russia or Rumania) or to abrogate it (as in Germany) von Schönerer was astute enough to realize that the very fact that the Jews had achieved equality provided in itself unheard of possibilities for a new revolutionary, or counter-revolutionary, tactic. He realized that the Jewish group, while indeed a constituent part of the population, could nevertheless be recognized as a distinctive entity or, in the case of baptism or mixed parentage, could still be determined as such if only the appropriate criteria were devised. A concentration of attacks upon the Jews—directed in reality against the State, its constitution, its political and economic structure and against the Church—would find no appreciable resistance. The Jews were no longer to be attacked as a more or less isolated group, but as the weakest spot in the totality of citizens, and the attack was to be launched under cover of a shrewd propaganda which would conceal the real objective by pointing up the "exotic strangeness" of the Jewish group.

This tactic, however, could be successful only under two conditions. First, the Jew had to be "built up" as the eternal, implacable foe, with whom it was impossible to come to terms and who must ultimately be driven from the territory of the State. Second, adherence to the Jewish group had to be regarded as final and unalterable. No one was to be allowed to escape it. To this end, the philosophy of racism had to be introduced into politics. Antisemitism was to be injected not only into nations to which the Jew migrated, but also into those smaller units of society—community, congregation and family—into which he was received by baptism or intermarriage.

Consistent with these two assumptions, practical anti-Jewish demands had to be given such a scope as to make their adoption impossible within the existent framework of the legal and economic structure of the State, particularly in Austria, where for their own sake, the non-German nationalities would vigorously oppose such innovations. Accordingly, the demands would have to include: abrogation of citizenship, ghettoization, prohibition of mixed marriages, extension of anti-Jewish legislation to baptized Jews and to the children of mixed marriages, etc. Once von Schönerer had succeeded in mustering sufficiently strong support, he would gain a key position, enabling him to influence and even paralyze the State, the Church, and the other political parties, even if they were still stronger than his own. Should they accept his anti-Jewish proposals, they would destroy themselves, the State (by disintegrating its constitution and very basis, namely, the cooperation of numerous nationalities on an equal footing), and the Church (by yielding to the principle of racism). Should they try to accommodate themselves to the newly created situation by partial adoption of anti-Jewish measures and especially by attempting to restrict them to actually professing Jews, the situation would be practically the same; but wholesale baptism, which could be reasonably expected as the consequence of such a policy, would enable the racists to attack the Church as a Jew shelter, would sow discord within the Catholic camp and possibly induce an embargo on Jewish admission into the fold of the Church, *i.e.,* it would permit interference in its purely spiritual affairs. Incidentally, too, it would eliminate any organized Jewish resistance. Finally, if State, Church and political parties rejected his anti-Jewish proposals, von Schönerer would attack them as lackeys of the Jews. They would have, perforce, to answer the charge, and this would mean either that they would resort to antisemitism themselves, or that they would ignore the attacks, or—finally—that they would come out openly on behalf of the Jews. By any of these courses, von Schönerer stood to gain.

Once this is realized, it becomes unnecessary to seek subtle psychological explanations of why von Schönerer suddenly changed his attitude towards the Jews.

Although as early as 1879 he had once spoken against the "Semitic dominance of money and empty phrases,"[34] three years later there were three Jews on the Committee of Fifteen which he convoked for the preparation of the Linz Program.[35] Nevertheless, on July 1, 1883, in a statement of aims published in the first issue of his new periodical, *Unverfälschte Deutsche Worte,* von Schönerer already insinuated the Jewish issue. "We have," he wrote, "to wage the bitter struggle between ourselves and the Slavs without using the Jews. If some of the Jews want to join our ranks, they may do so for aught I care, but only as simple privates, not in any leading position."[36]

The election of 1885 formed the turning-point of von Schönerer's attitude towards the Jews. On May 1st of that year he added a further point to the Linz Program, declaring that "the elimination of Jewish influence from all spheres of public life is an indispensable condition for the accomplishment of our reforms." This thesis subsequently became a plank in the platform of this group, now renamed the German National Party. "We Pan-Germans," he was now able to announce, "regard antisemitism as the mainstay of our national ideology, as the most essential expression of genuine popular conviction and thus as the major national achievement of the century."[37]

Although von Schönerer thenceforth combined his denunciation of the Jews with general attacks on economic liberalism and once declared that "to a large extent, the social question is nothing but the Jewish question," his political-minded nazi biographer of 1935 was undoubtedly right when he maintained that he "found supreme justification for his struggle [against the Jews] in the fact that he waged it for the salvation of his German people. Thus he progressed to national, racial antisemitism."[38] "The Jews," he wrote, "are an alien and hostile nation and race, who regard it as the prerogative of their tribe to exploit and enslave us."[39] And the quintessence of his attitude on the subject was finally summed up in that notorious slogan to which the nazis were later to give new currency: *In der Rasse liegt die Schweinerei.*

VI

The anti-Jewish development of von Schönerer's policy did not remain on an academic plane. In 1882, when the Russian pogroms sent a wave of Jewish refugees pouring into the neighboring countries, the Austrian agitator was not slow to realize the opportunity which this presented for pushing the party "line." In short order, parliament was inundated with petitions against admitting the immigrants or even permitting them transit. "It looks," von Schönerer told that body on May 11, "as though the Jewish émigrés will also turn perforce to Austria. They are an element of the population which has already excited indignation and hostility, even disturbances, in their own country, and that the reason lies within their own nature is amply borne out by the numerous statements of the Russian government."[40] The House, however, turned a deaf ear to these representations. Five years later, but with no greater success, he urged the passing of a law prohibiting immigration to Jewish refugees from Russia and Rumania. As a parallel to the proposed measure, he adduced the American Anti-Chinese Bill and at the same time hinted darkly that "in our opinion, native Jews will likewise be subjected before long to special legislation."[41] On another occasion, he asked the Minister of Public Worship to investigate the question whether the Talmud could be reconciled with the laws of the State. So too, when an amendment to the Law on Primary Schools came up for debate, he seized the opportunity for giving expression to his newly acquired anti-Jewish philosophy. "There is a real antithesis," he said, "between Christianity and Judaism."[42] "I must insist on the segregation of Jewish children and on the complete exclusion of Jewish teachers, even if baptized, from the schools of our race."[43] "We do not desire," he added, "to attain the exclusion of the Jews from our schools merely by indirect means. Accordingly, we cannot agree with the principle of dividing our schools according to Christian denominations. We regard German Catholics and German Protestants as equal co-nationals, but want to specify the Jews in the School Law and declare them unfit for attendance and education at Christian Aryan schools." "His aim," said one of his biographers, "was the division of the school into a Christian and a Jewish section—both taken not in a religious, but in an ethnic sense."[44] He also spoke in Parliament against the employment of Jews in government service.

His followers were even more radical. As early as April 1882, a meeting of Christian tradesmen in Vienna passed a resolution, moved by one of their leaders, Holubek, which aimed to abrogate the emancipation of the Austrian Jews and reduce them to their former restricted legal status. Only a limited number of Jews would be "tolerated" after payment of a special tolerance tax; likewise, only a small number of licenses for Jewish marriages would be granted annually. The right of residence would be confined to a certain city and temporary absence would be permitted at most for a period of two weeks, and then only on payment of a fee. Permanent change of domicile would depend on the approval of the authorities and be subject to a special tax. Jews would not be permitted to acquire real estate either in the cities or in rural areas; they would be excluded from all public office, and their rights as burghers, merchants and tradesmen would be restricted by law. Holubek wanted also to forbid the employment of Christian women by Jews.

But racial criteria were still absent, and few overall economic restrictions were proposed. The liberal professions, with the exception of public office, were not mentioned. Twenty-odd years later, however, Hitler's legislation was completely anticipated. On May 1, 1903 the independent Pan-German deputy Josef Herzog introduced two drafts of bills in the Austrian Parliament; and the difference between Holubek's and Herzog's proposals may well be regarded as the result of Schönerer's "enlightenment" of the public. The first of the Herzog bills was an amendment to the Basic Constitutional Law of 1867 abrogating Austrian citizenship and legal equality for "all members of the Jewish race, irrespective of their religion, whose descent from a Jew or a Jewess could be proved either from the paternal or maternal side in the first, second or third generation." The second was a law "to regulate the civil rights of members of the Jewish race." It provided the institution of ghettos, to be set up in townships of more than 10,000 inhabitants for all persons belonging to the Jewish "race" without any denominational distinction. This category of persons was to be excluded from all occupations with the single exception of trade and handicraft and was not to be permitted to acquire landed property outside the ghettos, to employ gentiles (men as well as women), to attend non-Jewish schools or universities, to serve in the armed forces, to become physicians, judges, lawyers, publishers, or editors of or contributors to non-Hebrew publications. Mixed marriages were to be forbidden, violations of this law being punishable by expulsion from Austrian soil, a sinister precursor of the practice of the Third Reich.[45]

As early as 1882, social discrimination against Jews, practically unknown during the seventies ("No antisemitic movement existed after the great financial crash of 1873," says Charmatz[46]), had already caused the German Club in Vienna to exclude baptized Jews and persons of mixed parentage. Moreover, the burghers and students added their voice to the antisemitic clamor, even though they were not unconditionally in favor of Schönerer's program.

Nevertheless, among the Pan-Germans there were soon wild quarrels, the varying factions vying with one another to modify, qualify, and otherwise circumscribe the antisemitic program, thus forcing von Schönerer more and more into the position of a rabid extremist. The independent Pan-German deputy Dr. Freissler, for instance, wanted to combat "only the excessive, not the legitimate influence of the Jews,"[47] while in its election program of 1891 the German National Union permitted its members to determine for themselves what attitude they wanted to adopt toward antisemitism. "There was thus neither uniformity nor clarity," says Molisch, "about that basic issue of German national racial antisemitism: whether or not the Jews were to be regarded as Germans."[48] Similarly, an attempt to establish cooperation with the Slavonic nationalities of Austria on the basis of a common anti-Jewish program failed significantly.[49]

How did the Jews and their liberal friends react to this sudden liquidation of the peaceful seventies, with their atmosphere of unconditional equality? Significantly enough, the only expression of sound political judgment was to be found in the utterances of the older generation, the revolutionary "forty-eighters" whose political experience enabled them to sense the dangers of the proposed counterrevolution. Although but recently elected to the freedom of the city, Ignaz Kuranda (1812–84), from 1861 to 1881 a distinguished member of the Reichsrat, had the vision and courage to impart to the guests of a Vienna banquet, arranged in honor of his seventieth birthday, his fear that "tomorrow will destroy what we have together created;"[50] while the well-known poet and humanitarian, Ludwig

August von Frankl (1810–94), said outrightly: "I have lost any hope for an improvement of the situation."[51] The younger generation, however, those who had been reared in an atmosphere of tranquil complacence, had already lost the faculty for "spotting trends." When von Schönerer fulminated in Parliament, the liberal press could but bleat smugly that "the speech of this rabid, fierce Jew-baiter merely unleashed storms of laughter in the House. His motion was, of course, defeated, only about a dozen Rightist deputies having the pitiful hardihood to share in the strange sport of the Squire of Rosenau."[52] (About forty years later, be it noted, the liberal press tried likewise to laugh off Adolf Hitler with ponderous humor.)

For the rest, counter-measures were singularly ineffective. To be sure, in 1884 an Österreichisch-Israelitische Union was founded by such prominent Jewish leaders as Chief Rabbi Moritz Güdemann (1835–1918) and Rabbi Joseph S. Bloch (1850–1923) in order "to oppose and dispel widespread fallacies about the Jews and prejudices against them, and to combat the efforts instituted to increase the severity of the religious and racial opposition to them." But since von Schönerer and his followers did not intend to let them destroy the new weapon, which consisted in the utilization of just those fallacies and prejudices, the effectiveness of such efforts were necessarily restricted. The free legal aid which the Union provided for Jewish groups and individuals whose rights had been infringed was in many cases certainly useful, but could scarcely affect the real motives and aims of the anti-Jewish campaign. Similarly, in 1891, a few prominent liberals founded a Verein zur Abwehr des Antisemitismus, but its activities are fittingly summarized by Dubnow in the statement that "from time to time it convoked public meetings."[53]

For a long time, as Molisch rightly observes, the Jews "tried to shift the whole issue to the denominational field, because there the struggle against antisemitism could be waged more easily."[54] Indeed, as late as 1907 the liberal writer Charmatz proved his complete failure to grasp the essence of political antisemitism by propounding the view that "where there are no 'Semites' there can obviously be no antisemitism." Certain Austrian provinces, like Salzburg, Carinthia, the Tyrol and Vorarlberg, he contended, had practically no Jews so that antisemitism as the basis of a political party could have no attraction there.⁵⁵ As a matter of fact, however, even at the time he wrote, those provinces were hotbeds of antisemitic sentiment, while later they played a leading role in the agitation against the Jews.

VII

Von Schönerer's downfall was due to a spectacular blunder—the more interesting because it is typical not only of his own species of mentality but also of the methods and techniques of political antisemitism in general.

On March 8, 1888, Emperor Wilhelm I lay on his deathbed at his palace in Berlin. But he was not yet dead. Despite his ninety-one years, the old soldier was still fighting. Nevertheless, he was sinking rapidly, and when a particularly sharp attack of weakness ensued during the day, word flew around that the end had finally come. The report was flashed at once to the four ends of the earth, and in short order "extras" appeared on the streets of Vienna announcing that the first emperor of the new Reich had entered eternity. Shortly afterwards, however, the news came through that he was still alive; and "late final editions" cancelled the previous report.⁵⁶

It was past midnight, and von Schönerer was sitting with his cronies in Skoda's beer-hall "mourning" the passing of Bismarck's master. Suddenly, in the midst of this gay scene, when the "sorrows" of the company had been well-nigh drowned, a copy of the "late final" was thrust into his hands. The old campaigner made a swift decision. He decided, under the guise of an antisemitic demonstration, to stage a spectacular exhibition of allegiance to the Hohenzollern dynasty and to the ideal of union with the German empire right under the noses of Francis Joseph, his government and his police. With a gang of his followers, he rushed from the beer-hall to the offices of the *Neues Wiener Tagblatt,* a local liberal newspaper. Armed with clubs, knives and pistols, they forced entry and proceeded to hurl threats and insults at the members of the staff, most of whom were, in fact, gentiles. "This," screamed the ringleader, "is the day of vengeance. No mercy for the Jewish devils. On your knees, you Jews, and beg pardon! By spreading lying reports you have tried to make capital out of the death of His Germanic Majesty!"⁵⁷

The whole thing was, of course, a colossal blunder. Von Schönerer was playing right into the hands of his political adversaries. By representing his action as disorderly conduct and by punishing him ostensibly for an antisemitic outrage, they could discredit him and eliminate the influence of one whom they rightly regarded as the personification of high treason. And this was the line they took. "At 12:30 last night," wrote the liberal Crown Prince Rudolph to his consort the next day, "von Schönerer and his henchmen forced burglarous entry into the newspaper offices,"[58] while a leading Austrian statesman is said to have declared openly to his friends: "Now we've trapped the beast!"

The competent committee of the Reichsrat lost no time in delivering von Schönerer to justice. Within two months (on May 5, 1888) he was arraigned on charges of assault and battery and was condemned to four months' imprisonment. The sentence carried with it automatic disenfranchisement and an enjoinder against serving as a parliamentary deputy or running for election for a period of five years. It also liquidated his patent of nobility.

As was but to be expected, von Schönerer's followers tried at once to make a martyr of the defendant. When the verdict was returned, troops had to be stationed in the streets to prevent disturbances. Nevertheless, noisy demonstrations occurred. A parade was organized to express sympathy with von Schönerer's wife, although it had been proved a year before that the lady was partly of Jewish descent.[59] When the marchers reached the Maria Theresa Memorial (due to be unveiled the following day) loud cheers were raised for the Hohenzollerns, and there were demonstrations against the Hapsburg dynasty.[60]

Von Schönerer's power was now definitely broken. When he returned to Parliament in 1897, he had lost contact with the Pan-German groups, and these had already been split among themselves. For the following ten years, he was, at best, the radical elder statesman of a moderately sized political party; he was no longer the potential future leader of the country.

VIII

The Austrian Pan-Germans have always maintained that the temporary elimination of von Schönerer contributed essentially to the rise of the Christian Socialist Party. This contention, however, is scarcely valid. For while it is certainly true that this political group (which was to become a factor of the first magnitude for the next fifty years) scored its initial great success during the period of the involuntary retirement of the squire of Rosenau, it is more than doubtful whether things would have turned out differently had he still been at large. The fact is that by the end of the eighties, the disintegration of the Austrian empire had not yet proceeded so far as to frustrate any organized reaction against the centrifugal forces. Moreover, even after the collapse of the Dual Monarchy, some appropriate representation of the traditional interests of the Catholic farmers and small middle class was still a political necessity.

Able organizers and propagandists, astute in foreign affairs—the weak side of all other Austrian political parties, including the Social-Democrats—the Christian Socialists soon became the backbone of the State. Under the single banner of the Cross they succeeded in maintaining harmony between a wide variety of divergent ideologies. Consequently, they were able to act as the bulwark of the monarchy in the times of Lueger, the "Super and Chief Royalist," as Sieghart calls him; to assist efficiently at the founding of the Republic in 1918 by such men as Mgr. Hauser and the gifted peasant leader Jodok Fink; to pave a way later to a more dynamic period by the powerful intervention of Ignaz Seipel, the most brilliant of their priestly politicians; and finally to institute a dictatorship of their own under Dollfuss and Schuschnigg, the latter a nephew and disciple of a well-known co-founder of the Party, Baron Kathrein.[61] Experts in the intricacies of the Austrian parliamentary system, they took their place in almost every coalition cabinet both of the Empire and Republic, and contrived somehow to sponsor the interests of the urban and rural "little man" without resigning their role as the protectors of free enterprise and banking.

Any evaluation of their attitude toward the Jews—a problem which at the time of the founding of their party had already assumed the form of attitude toward the utilization of political antisemitism—has to start from the fact that from the point of view of *Grosspolitik,* the Christian Socialists owed their very *raison d'être* to their basic antagonism to Pan-Germanism. The rules of the parliamentary game made both political bed-fellows for years of the struggle against socialism; but from the very first day of the co-existence of the two parties, fifty years before the murder of Dollfuss and the incarceration of Schuschnigg, their ways were bound to end in fratricidal uproar and sanguinary civil war.

Strictly Catholic, the Christian Socialists regarded an independent Austria as an essential asset of the Church. They were therefore deeply interested in maintaining the Hapsburg dynasty, the last great ruling house of the Catholic faith and the scions of a family whose chiefs had borne the crown of the Holy Roman Empire for centuries. Thus, after thirty years of Austrian parliamentarianism, they became the first avowedly "patriotic" party, and even in 1918, when the monarchy collapsed, this did not altogether cut the ground from under their feet. They devoted equal zeal to maintaining the truncated post-war State as a transalpine foothold of the Church.

Why, then, did they attack the Jews? Both Jewish and general historians have given various answers. Some have attempted to resolve the seeming paradox by exaggerating the factor of religious antagonism; others have overemphasized economic considerations.[62] But this is superficial and the real truth lies elsewhere.

From the moment they entered the political arena, the Christian Socialists found themselves in an extremely delicate position. Even though they never openly admitted it, their whole attitude shows how well they realized that von Schönerer's agitation against the Jews was in fact directed against the Church and themselves. Confronted as they were with the antisemitic clamor of the Pan-Germans, they could not risk ignoring the Jewish question completely. At the same time, as a Catholic party fighting liberalism and in turn attacked by it, they could not very well come out for Jewish rights without being branded by von Schönerer as "lackeys of the Jews." On the other hand, they were unable to compete with him in antisemitic demonstrations; they realized that any anti-Jewish activity must inevitably lead to proposals for discriminatory legislation and that the introduction of such laws would presuppose a rigid definition of the term "Jew." They were thus in a cleft stick. They could never think of adopting the racial theories of their antagonists without destroying with their own hand the doctrines of the Church on which their philosophy and party program were built. They could not restrict their antisemitism to professing Jews, since that would merely provoke a rush to the baptismal font and thus throw the whole thorny problem right into their own lap. Moreover, they could not obstruct such a rush without compromising their own Catholic convictions.

The Christian Socialists realized that something had to be done; and out of this realization there issued that anti-Jewish policy which, by and large, they retained for half a century. It was characterized, however, as much by vagueness as by insistence, as much by inefficiency of performance as by stridency of utterance. They never attempted seriously to introduce basic discriminatory legislation. As a last desperate measure to stave off a victory of the Pan-Germans they tried to divert public opinion to their own program, hoping thereby to avoid any discussion of the thorny problem as to how to define a Jew and at the same time to suppress any discussion of racism in general. Their antisemitism had thus a clearly defensive character. Circumstances being what they were, any other policy was scarcely conceivable. Nevertheless, it enabled them to steal much of von Schönerer's thunder.

About ten years ago, I asked the then chairman of the Christian Socialist Party, Emmerich Czermak, how his group had defined the term "Jew" in the early period of its history. He answered, after some hesitation, that it had never occupied itself with the problem—an answer, which, though probably untrue, is none the less significant. The attitude which it evinces corresponds exactly with the well-known dictum of Lueger, "Who is and is not a Jew, is for *me* to decide." The statement, it should be noted, is double-edged and far less naive than many contemporary politicians suppose. It implies clearly that the author regarded the problem as embarrassing, but realized at the same time that he could not evade it and must therefore devise some sort of technique for its ventilation in public. In its Statement of Policy issued on February 24, 1895, the Christian Socialist Party expressly refused to adopt radical antisemitism, and, as Molisch observes, since that date its anti-Jewish program "has never been taken seriously by the Pan-Germans."[63]

Even Dubnow, who criticizes the Christian Socialists sharply, charges them with nothing more than "pin-pricking at Galician-

Jewish peddlers," unsuccessfully attempting to segregate school-children according to their religion and "refusing to waive the fees of Jewish pupils at Vienna high-schools."[64]

Lueger's tactical ability enabled him to hoist his opponents upon their own petard; in the municipal elections of 1895 he proposed to them the conquest of Vienna by means of a common antisemitic front called the "United Christians." The Pan-Germans agreed—against the advice of von Schönerer. The result was a smashing success. The Christian Socialists now gained entrance to the influential keypoint of the City Hall, while for Lueger the road was opened to the mayor's parlor. From this comparatively modest position, which he held from 1897 until his death in March 1910, the "first successful demagogue of constitutional Austria" bossed his party, pulled parliamentary strings, made and unmade Cabinet Ministers, carried on secret government negotiations abroad and became, in short, the most powerful Austrian of his day.

When the Pan-Germans woke up, they found that they now retained but a handful of seats in the City Council, while their supporters among the electorate had stampeded to the new party. "What we have done," wailed Neuschäfer, "is to boost our dangerous enemy, Lueger, to power."[65] Embittered by this failure, von Schönerer retired, in June 1895, from the leadership of the "mutinous party."[66] Outsmarted, he could not but concede defeat.

IX

But it was not only the allegiance of the German-speaking Austrians to the dynasty and the Church, nor the undoubted organizational genius of "handsome Charlie"—as Lueger was called by the Viennese —that were responsible for these successes. During the few years of von Schönerer's eclipse, Europe had witnessed more important changes. When the Pan-Germanist, after a postponement of the execution of the sentence, presented himself for his jail term on August 20, 1888, Germany already had her third emperor after the hundred days' reign of Frederick III. One and a half years later, Kaiser Wilhelm II "dropped the pilot"; and with Bismarck gone, German relations with Russia soon took a turn for the worse.

These developments had a profound effect on the Pan-German movement in Austria and, as a direct consequence of the fate of this most radical antisemitic center, also on the situation of the Austrian Jews. Indeed, there are few instances in the political history of the Jews where a direct dependence upon foreign politics can be more clearly shown; and this fact gives von Schönerer's story general and lasting significance.

An irredentist movement can never achieve its goal—union with a co-national foreign state—without the latter's unreserved support. As soon as the "motherland" begins to regard the movement as a hindrance and an embarrassment, pan-nationalistic tendencies are bound to lose their importance. Just that happened after Bismarck had left the political arena; and, curiously enough, his successors, the men of the "New Course," otherwise busy in destroying the threads so skillfully woven by the Iron Chancellor, not only followed his lead in this respect, but were obliged even to intensify the policy of aloofness from Austria's domestic developments in general.

Throughout his political career, Bismarck had stubbornly maintained that "Vienna cannot be governed from Berlin." He had persistently discouraged any Pan-German tendencies among the German-speaking subjects of Francis Joseph.[67] Even after his resignation, when he was at daggers drawn with the Kaiser and the men of the "New Course," he studiously avoided ovations from his Austrian admirers; while in 1894 the *Hamburger Nachrichten* wrote, significantly, against "misguided politicians who are prepared to sacrifice our good relations with Austria and even to force this state *manu militari* to carry through the decisions of the [Austrian] Pan-German Union."[68]

Bismarck's successors had to face an even more threatening world. The alienation of Germany from Russia resulted very soon in the Russo-French alliance; Germany was encircled. Depending on her only trustworthy ally, the highest interests of the Hohenzollern Empire demanded a policy which would ensure the cooperation of all the armed forces of the Dual Monarchy in the event of a European war. Any weakening of the structure of this State and its army, composed as it was of a dozen nationalities, had to be avoided at any price. Accordingly, the attitude of Berlin toward the embarrassing co-

national irredentists of the South became clearly hostile. Even the
German Pan-Germans, the radical chauvinists and imperialists, otherwise always at loggerheads with the government, fell in line with this
policy, albeit for reasons of their own. Significant of their attitude was
the declaration of their extremist leader, Ernest Hasse. He advocated
a "firm dependence of the entire Dual Monarchy on the Reich," and
warned that "the disintegration of Austria . . . would be a revolutionary event without parallel in history. It would involve us in
endless wars." At the same time he criticized the separative tendencies
of his Austrian colleagues as embodied in the Linz Program, and
observed that "The secession of Bukovina seems to us unjustified. The
German element has surely gained a firm footing there."[69]

The German Pan-Germans were also embarrassed by von Schönerer's "away-from-Rome" policy which threatened to alienate their
own Catholic fellow-citizens. In addition, they feared the Magyariza-
tion of two million Germans in Hungary and the loss of "living space,"
markets, and future possibilities for German settlement. They even
advocated the extension of "the Hapsburg Great Power to the Mediterranean *via* Salonica."

The result of this common front in the "motherland" was a complete isolation of von Schönerer and of Austrian Pan-Germanism in
general; and it is this that explains the rise to power of the Christian
Socialists. Freed from the pressure of their dangerous rivals, they were
only too glad to be able to limit themselves to mere Jew-baiting slogans without facing the necessity of legally defining the Jew or of
attacking Holy Writ.

For the Jews of Austria this meant that they were now, more or
less, out of the wood. The way was paved for that "golden age" which
ensued during the two decades immediately preceding the First World
War. Before the eyes of those who had followed Lueger and von
Schönerer, Austrian Jewry enjoyed a prosperity without parallel in its
economic history. Lueger was now mayor of Vienna, a city with a
predominantly German population and with the third-largest Jewish
community in Europe. But even in the civil service and in the field
of public education, Jews were now better represented than under the
former liberal dispensation, though still not entirely in proportion to
their numbers. In recording this fact historians have attributed it to

such factors as personal intervention by the emperor, or else they have restricted themselves to such laconic and enigmatic statements as Charmatz's dictum that "their [the Austrians'] antisemitism gradually lost its fury; the Jacobins' caps disappeared"[70] or that Austrian antisemitism had "put away childish things." How superficial and erroneous such judgments are is shown by the fact that after the revolutionary changes of 1918, the old tendencies soon reappeared—unimpaired.

X

Von Schönerer returned for a decade (1897–1907) to Parliament. He fought desperately against the introduction of universal and equal suffrage, realizing that this would give the Slavonic nationalities a majority in the Reichsrat. After it had been adopted on December 1, 1906, he declared the struggle for the German cause in Austria as hopeless, and, after a final speech in Parliament on January 26, 1907, retired to his castle at Rosenau. Already in July 1904 he had himself dissolved his Pan-German Union, which meanwhile had deteriorated by numerous quarrels, secessions and desertions. But the Pan-German ideal was by this time well represented by several groups and had gained a firm hold on the German-speaking intelligentsia everywhere and on the broad masses of the Germans, at least in the linguistic border districts, where national animosity was always rampant. Schuschnigg gives a true picture of conditions at the time of the beginning of the First World War. "Bismarck Squares," he writes, "and Bismarck Streets were ubiquitous, while only here and there a monument to Emperor Joseph II reminded one of Austrian history."[71] Inscriptions on the Deutsches Haus in Celje, Southern Styria, read: "This house was built by Slovene arrogance" and "the iron keel must break through," indicating clearly that even in 1906, when this *Trutzburg* was built, men were already dreaming Pan-German dreams of a penetration of the Reich to the Adriatic Sea and thus to the Mediterranean.[72]

Von Schönerer disappeared from the public scene. Many did not even know that he was still alive. In 1917, when it was found necessary to placate the German elements after the amnesty of certain

Czech leaders sentenced for high treason, the Emperor Charles seized the opportunity of the Pan-German's seventy-fifth birthday to restore his patent of nobility, twenty-nine years after it had been withdrawn. Von Schönerer, however, was far from reconciled by this gesture. On the contrary, he was embarrassed by it; and the following year he was among those who hailed the final collapse of the Dual Monarchy.

He was now too old to participate in the post-war resuscitation of the Pan-German cause. On August 14, 1921, at the age of seventy-nine, he passed away at Rosenau, a forgotten man; and in accordance with his will, his remains were transferred the following spring to a plot in the Sachsenwald close to the tomb of his idol, Bismarck.

NOTES

[1] Immediately after the *Anschluss* a street in the Jewish section of Vienna was named for von Schönerer, while at the centenary of his birth a memorial exhibition was held in Vienna in honor of the "proclaimer and pioneer of Greater Germany" *(Deutsche Zeitung für Ostland,* September 9, 1942).

[2] *Die Grundlagen des Nationalsozialismus* (Leipzig and Vienna 1937), p. 83.

[3] Cecil, Lady Gwendolen, *Life of Robert Marquis of Salisbury* (London 1921), vol. ii, pp. 85 ff.

[4] Pichl, Eduard, *Georg Schönerer* (Oldenburg and Berlin 1938), vol. i, p. 9.

[5] *Ibid.,* p. 11.

[6] This implied permanent outnumbering of the local non-German nationalities, *i.e.,* the Czechs and the Slovenes.

[7] Pichl, *op. cit.,* p. 12.

[8] *Ibid.,* p. 21 ff.

[9] Bilgeri, Ferdinand, *Niederösterreichische Biographie* (Vienna 1928), vol. v, pp. 82 ff.

[10] Neuschäfer, Fritz Albrecht, *Georg Ritter von Schönerer* (Hamburg, 1935), p. 62.

[11] *Ibid.,* p. 41.

[12] Charmatz, Richard, *Deutsch-Österreichische Politik* (Leipzig 1907), p. 94: "Austrian liberalism lived isolated from the masses."

[13] Pichl, *op. cit.,* vol. i, p. 31. Five years later, Kopp acted as counsel for Rabbi Josef Bloch in the famous lawsuit against Rohling; *cf.* Dubnow, S. M., *Weltgeschichte des jüdischen Volkes* (Berlin 1929), vol. x, p. 81.

[14] Even Adolf Fischhof tried, in the summer of 1882, to found a rival group under the same name. Pichl, *op. cit.,* vol. i, p. 105.

[15] In 1879 Friedjung was, in fact, ousted from his professorship for being a

follower of von Schönerer; *cf.* Molisch, Paul, *Geschichte der deutsch-nationalen Bewegung in Österreich* (Jena 1926), p. 144.

[16] The program is so named because it was to have been proclaimed at a mass meeting in Linz on September 24, 1882. The police, however, prohibited the gathering; *cf.* Pichl, *op. cit.,* vol. i, p. 105.

[17] Pichl, *op. cit.,* vol. i, pp. 27 ff.

[18] Neuschäfer, *op. cit.,* p. 29.

[19] At the Third Lower Austrian Party Rally, June 25, 1876; *cf.* Pichl, *op. cit.,* vol. i, p. 90.

[20] *Ibid.,* p. 32.

[21] *Ibid.,* p. 130.

[22] *Ibid.,* p. 131.

[23] Neuschäfer, *op. cit.,* p. 38.

[24] Pichl, *op. cit.,* vol. ii, p. 253.

[25] *Ibid.,* vol. iii, p. 420.

[26] *Ibid.,* vol. vi, p. 545.

[27] Neuschäfer, *op. cit.,* pp. 44 ff.

[28] Polzer-Hoditz und Wolframitz, Arthur Graf, *Kaiser Karl* (Zürich-Leipzig, Vienna 1929), p. 96.

[29] Neuschäfer, *op. cit.,* p. 28.

[30] Von Schönerer himself became a Protestant in 1900 and later instituted a non-denominational chapel in his castle at Rosenau.

[31] Neuschäfer, *op. cit.,* p. 29.

[32] Pichl, *op. cit.,* vol. iv, p. 502.

[33] Witte, Leopold, *Wie der Evangelische Bund zu seiner österreichischen Arbeit gekommen ist* in *Daheim-Kalender* (1914), p. 93.

[34] Pichl, *op. cit.,* vol. i, p. 82.

[35] One of them was Victor Adler (1852–1918), later the founder of the Austrian Social-Democratic movement; another was the historian Heinrich Friedjung (1851–1920) whose essential contribution to the shaping of the program of the *Deutsche Volkspartei* and of the Linz Program even the nazi writers acknowledge. It was Friedjung who in 1880 had formulated the points demanding autonomy for Galicia, dominance of the German language, reform of the franchise, and an indissoluble alliance and customs union with Germany "in order to enable the Balkan States to join the great Central European Union without concern for their political freedom and without fear of annexation" (Pichl, *op. cit.,* vol. i, pp. 101 ff). The Linz Program was based on drafts submitted by Schönerer and Friedjung.

[36] Charmatz, *op. cit.,* p. 100.

[37] Neuschäfer, *op. cit.,* p. 24.

[38] *Ibid.*

[39] Pichl, *op. cit.,* vol. i, p. 190.

[40] *Ibid.,* vol. i, pp. 161 ff. Curiously enough, these very allegations were

revived in 1943 in the U.S. House of Representatives when Congressman William P. Elmer, a Missouri Democrat, opposed the abrogation of the Chinese Exclusion Act and cited as an analogy the fact that "since nearly every nation of Europe chased out the Jews, there must have been some compelling reason for their actions."

[41] *Ibid.,* p. 321.

[42] *Ibid.,* p. 185.

[43] *Ibid.,* p. 189.

[44] *Ibid.,* p. 193.

[45] *Ibid.,* vol. vi, pp. 450 ff.

[46] Charmatz, *op. cit.,* p. 93.

[47] *Ibid.,* p. 97.

[48] Molisch, *op. cit.,* p. 143.

[49] *Ibid.,* p. 144.

[50] Grunwald, Max, *Geschichte der Wiener Juden bis 1914* (Vienna 1926), p. 67; *cf.* also Part Two, ch. 2 above.

[51] *Ibid.,* p. 54.

[52] Pichl, *op. cit.,* vol. i, p. 165.

[53] Dubnow, *op. cit.,* vol. x, p. 88.

[54] Molisch, *op. cit.,* p. 145.

[55] Charmatz, *op. cit.,* p. 101.

[56] The circumstances of Wilhelm's death are, of course, reported in all of the numerous contemporary memoirs. According to Prince Philipp zu Eulenburg-Hertefeld *(Aus 50 Jahren* [Berlin 1923], p. 162) even the Prince of Wales, brother of the new empress, telegraphed his condolences at a time when Wilhelm I was still alive.

[57] Pichl, *op. cit.,* vol. ii, pp. 435 ff.

[58] *Ibid.,* vol. vi, p. 435.

[59] She was the great-granddaughter of one Schmul Leeb Kohn of Pohrlitz, Moravia (1762–1832), known after his baptism as Leopold Provander; *cf.* Sieghart, Rudolf, *Die letzten Jahrzehnte einer Grossmacht* (Berlin 1932), pp. 307 ff.

[60] Significantly enough, it is an influential statesman of Jewish origin, Rudolf von Sieghart, who maintains that "even those who were loyal and well-disposed to the dynasty doubted whether it was wise thus to make a martyr"; *ibid.*

[61] Schuschnigg, Kurt, *My Austria* (New York 1938), p. 23.

[62] The prevalent view is perhaps best expressed by Sieghart who contends that Lueger "used antisemitism as a means of catching the middle class vote" *(op. cit.,* p. 315).

[63] Molisch, *op. cit.,* p. 144.

[64] Dubnow, *op. cit.,* p. 86. The latter assertion is clearly an error since the city never maintained any high schools.

[65] Neuschäfer, *op. cit.,* p. 27.

[66] *Ibid.*

[67] When, in his Berlin student days, the writer Hermann Bahr went with his political friends to pay a visit of homage to Bismarck, the chancellor told him, through an official spokesman, that "Germany counts on you but in Austria. A powerful Austria is a vital necessity to Germany." Similarly, on another occasion, an Austrian Pan-German was advised that "there is no better way of showing your goodwill towards your compatriots in the western German Empire than by fostering good relations with your own imperial household" (*ibid.*, pp. 57 ff.).

[68] *Ibid.*

[69] As Neuschäfer rightly observes, "even the German Empire, particularly the leading circles, opposed him" (*ibid.*, p. 33).

[70] Charmatz, *op. cit.*, p. 97.

[71] Schuschnigg, *op. cit.*, p. 29.

[72] League of Nations, *Official Journal,* vol. xiv (1933), 1315 and following documents.

EDITORS' PREFACE

Selected Bibliography on Jewish Emancipation and Counter-Emancipation

by Abraham G. Duker

Emancipation is a process extending over three centuries. Its harbingers can be traced to the Marrano settlement in West-Central Europe. The term goes back to 1828. In many circles, the term, in addition to connoting the attainment of equality for the individual Jew, also implies the acquisition of such status for the Jewish people as a national, ethnic or religious-national group in the enjoyment of its peoplehood, religion, culture, languages, and ways of life, on the basis of minority rights, autonomy, territorial concentration, and even independent statehood, as well as the internationl recognition of such rights by representative bodies of the nations of the world. There is also the problem of equal status for Judaism as a religion. These group approaches have given new meanings to the concept of Jewish Emancipation, but have also aroused objections on the part of the Neo-Emancipationists, the advocates of the original limited view of individual Emancipation.

The march of Emancipation has been frequently checked by Counter-Emancipation, namely, efforts to exclude or limit the participation of Jews in the life of the surrounding society or in the state, or even to eliminate them altogether, as seen in the prime example,

357

the antisemites' world-wide assault on the physical survival of the Jewish people in the twentieth century.

In colloquial usage, the term "Emancipation" also carries the implication of "liberation" of an individual or group from a traditional way of life. It therefore involves the acculturation of Jews into the dominant culture of the environing society, or ruling or fashionable stratum, and at the same time their estrangement from their own culture and its abandonment: de-Judaization to the extent of assimilation and disappearance.

This Bibliography follows the broader approach. It attempts to cover many aspects of Jewish Emancipation that go beyond legal developments. It includes readings and studies on the multi-faceted struggle for Emancipation of the individual and of the group, as well as the social, religious, cultural, economic, political, and psychological impact of Emancipation within the Jewish communities and to some extent also in the environing societies.

The Bibliography is intended to serve readers and students in a number of ways. It is hoped that it will supply ideas and references for supplementary readings, term papers, assignments, and theses, and thus encourage research in a field that needs it. Because of limitations of space, the Bibliography is restricted to publications in English. Fortunately, many works, particularly articles, are available in that language, and regrettably, too few publications in Hebrew and other languages have been translated into English. To mention but a few important publications in Hebrew that deserve translation, Yehezkel Kaufman's classic *Golah ve-nekhar*; most of Ben Zion Dinur's essays gathered in his *B'mifne ha-dorot*; Simon Rawidowicz's *Yerushalaim u-bavel*; and on the more popular level, Jehiel Halpern's *Ha-mahapekha ha-yehudit*.

The perusal of the Bibliography and the Index will reveal that coverage is fullest for Germany. Obviously, the six years between the Nazi take-over and the outbreak of World War II afforded escape to many Jews, including persons interested in the moral stock-taking of Emancipation experiences. Other important factors are the tradition of modern Jewish scholarship and the sense of organization of German Jews, at the very least as testified by the publication, *The*

Year Book of the Leo Baeck Institute, a unique source and guide. Neglected are the East European Jewries. Very little has been published in English on the struggle for Emancipation in Poland and Russia, and even less on Hungary, the Balkans, and Baltic countries. It would also seem that American scholars tend to neglect secular ideologies, economic and socio-cultural trends, and legal developments in favor of theology. Generally, the emphasis in the Bibliography has been on interpretation and secondary studies rather than on original sources. In some areas, as for instance, the arts, community organization, and life style, a few items are listed in order to call attention to connections with Emancipation or Counter-Emancipation. It was found impossible to give them fuller coverage within the covers of this book. Indeed, a more extensive bibliography of works on the two major themes of this *Reader* in all languages is very much in order.

The Index to the Bibliography is merely a guide to major topics and to some personalities treated at length in the entries. No attempt has been made to list or index all the articles in collective volumes and in collected works. Such books are identified by a dagger (†). Source collections carry paragraph signs (¶); while works containing more extensive bibliographies are marked by an asterisk (*).

ABBREVIATIONS

AJA—American Jewish Archives.

AJHQ—American Jewish Historical Quarterly.

AJYB—American Jewish Year Book.

BSEEJA—Bulletin on Soviet and East European Jewish Affairs.

BSJA—Bulletin on Soviet Jewish Affairs.

CCAR—Central Conference of American Rabbis.

Essays . . . Baron—Essays on Jewish Life and Thought Presented in Honor of Salo Wittmayer Baron, Edited by Joseph L. Blau, Philip Friedman, Arthur Hertzberg and Isaac Mendelsohn, New York, Columbia University Press, 1959.†

Freedom and Reason—Freedom and Reason, Studies in Philosophy and Jewish Culture in Memory of Morris Raphael Cohen, edited by Salo W. Baron, Ernest Nagel and Koppel S. Pinson, New York, Conference on Jewish Relations, 1951.

HJ—Historia Judaica.

HUCA—Hebrew Union College Annual.

IYHR—Israel Yearbook on Human Rights.

JHSE, *Mis.*—Jewish Historical Society of England, *Miscellanies.*

JHSE, *Tr.*—Jewish Historical Society of England, *Transactions.*

JJS—Journal of Jewish Sociology.

JPSA—Jewish Publication Society of America.

JQR—Jewish Quarterly Review.

JQR, NS—Jewish Quarterly Review, New Series.

JSS—Jewish Social Studies.

JYIL—The Jewish Year Book of International Law.

LBIYB—Leo Baeck Institute Year Book.

PAAJR—Publications of the American Academy for Jewish Research.

PAJHS—Publications of the American Jewish Historical Society.

SLBI—Studies of the Leo Baeck Institute, Edited by Max Kreutzberger, New York, Ungar, 1967.

SR—Studia Rosenthaliana.

YAJSS—YIVO Annual of Jewish Social Science.

BIBLIOGRAPHY

Abrahamsen, Samuel, "The Exclusion Clause of Jews in the Norwegian Constitution of May 17, 1814," *JSS,* XXX, 1968, pp. 67–88. [1]

Acculturation and Integration, 130.

Adler, Cyrus and Aaron M. Margalith, *With Firmness in the Right. American Diplomatic Action Affecting Jews,* 1840–1945, New York, The American Jewish Committee, 1946 (Based on Adler's "Jews in the Diplomatic Correspondence of the United States," *PAJHS,* XXXVI, 1943). [2]

Adler, H. G., *The Jews in Germany from the Enlightenment to National Socialism,* Notre Dame, Indiana, University of Notre Dame Press, 1960. [2a]

Ages, Arnold, *French Enlightenment and Rabbinic Tradition,* Frankfurt a.M., V. Klostermann, 1970. [3]

Agus, Jacob B., *Guideposts in Modern Judaism: An Analysis of Current Trends in Jewish Thought,* New York, Bloch, 1954. [4]

———, *The Meaning of Jewish History,* New York, Abelard-Schuman, 1963, 2 vols. [5]

———, *Modern Philosophies of Judaism: A Study of Recent Jewish Philosophies of Religion,* New York, Behrman, 1941. [6]

Ahad Ha'am, 318.

Ainsztein, R., "Poland's New Antisemitism," *The Bridge* (Sidney), IV, No. 2, pp. 3–20. [7]

Alter, Robert, "Emancipation, Enlightenment and All That," *Commentary,* LIII, No. 2, F, 1972, pp. 62–68. [7a]

Altfeld, E. Milton, *The Jew's Struggle for Religious and Civil Liberty in Maryland,* New York, DaCapo Press, 1970. [8]

Altholz, Josef, L., "A Note on the English Catholic Reaction to the Mortara Case," *JSS,* XXIII, 1961, pp. 111–18. [9]

Altmann, Alexander, "The New Style of Preaching in Nineteenth-Century German Jewry," in Altmann, Alexander, Ed., *Studies in Nineteenth Century Jewish Intellectual History,* Cambridge, Mass., Harvard University Press, 1964, pp. 65–116.† [10]

———, *Moses Mendelssohn: A Biographical Study,* University, Alabama, University of Alabama Press, 1973.* [11]

———, 429.

Altmann, Berthold, "Jews and the Rise of Capitalism: Economic Theory and Practice in a Westphalian Community," *JSS,* V, 1943, pp. 163–85. [12]

Altschuler, M., "The Attitude of the Communist Party of Russia to Jewish National Survival, 1918–1930," *YAJSS,* XIV, 1969, pp. 68–86. [13]

American Jewish Committee, 236a.

American Jewish Historical Society, *Publications,* 284.

———, *Migration . . .,* 412.

Anon., "The Secession from the Frankfurt Jewish Community under Samson Raphael Hirsch," *HJ,* V, 1948, pp. 99–122. [14]

Angress, Werner T., "Prussia's Army and the Jewish Reserve Officer Controversy Before World War I," *LBIYB,* XVII, 1972, pp. 19–42. [15]

Arendt, Hannah, "From the Dreyfus Affair to France Today," *JSS,* IV, 1942, pp. 195–240. [16]

———, "The Jew as Pariah: A Hidden Tradition," *JSS,* VI, 1944, pp. 99–122. [17]

———, *The Origins of Totalitarianism,* New York, Harcourt, Brace, and World, 1966. [18]

———, *Rahel Varnhangen: The Life of a Jewess,* Translated . . . by Richard and Clara Winston, London, East and West Library and Leo Baeck Institute, 1957. [19]

Arkin, Marcus, "West European Jewry in the Age of Mercantilism," *HJ,* XII, 1960, pp. 85–104. [20]

Aronsfeld, C. C., 95.

Aronson, Gregor [Gregory], 173.

Aronson, Gregor, Jacob Frumkin, et al., Eds., *Russian Jewry 1917–1967,* Translated by Joel Carmichael, New York, Yoseloff, 1969.† [21]

Aronson, Gregory, "Jews in Russian Literary and Political Life," in Aronson, Ed., *Russian Jewry (1860–1917),* I, pp. 253–99. [22]

Asch, Adolph and Philippson, Johanna, "Self-Defence in the Second Half of the Nineteenth Century: The Emergence of the KC," *LBIYB*, III, 1958, pp. 122–139. [23]

Association of Latvian and Esthonian Jews in Israel, 85.

Atlas, Samuel, "Solomon Maimon: The Man and His Thought," *HJ*, XIII, 1951, pp. 109–20. [24]

Avineri, Shlomo, "A Note on Hegel's Views on Jewish Emancipation," *JSS*, XXV, 1963, pp. 145–51. [25]

———, "Marx and Jewish Emancipation," *Journal of the History of Ideas*, XXV, 1964, pp. 445–50. [26]

Axinn, Sidney, "Kant on Judaism," *JQR*, NS, LIX, 1968–69, pp. 9–23. [27]

Baeck, Leo, *This People Israel: The Meaning of Jewish Existence*, Translated with an Introductory Essay by Albert H. Friedlander, Philadelphia, JPSA, 1965. [27a]

Baer, Yitzhak [J. F.], *A History of the Jews in Christian Spain . . .* , Philadelphia, JPSA, 1966, 2 vols. [28]

———, *Galuth,* New York, Schocken Books, 1947. [29]

Balla, Erzsebet, "The Jews of Hungary: A Cultural Overview," *Hungarian-Jewish Studies,* II, pp. 85–136. [30]

Bamberger, Fritz, "Zunz's Conception of History: A Study of the Philosophic Elements in Early Science of Judaism," *PAAJR,* XI, 1941, pp. 1–25. [31]

Banks, Arthur, 182.

Barnard, Frederick M., "Herder and Israel," *JSS*, XXVIII, 1966, pp. 25–33. [32]

Barnett, R. D., Ed., *The Sephardi Heritage. Essays on the History and Cultural Contribution of the Jews of Spain and Portugal,* Vol. I, *The Jews in Spain and Portugal Before and After the Expulsion of 1492,* New York, Ktav, 1971.† [33]

Baron, Jeannette Meisel, 36.

Baron, Salo Wittmayer, *Ancient and Medieval Jewish History. Essays,* Edited with a Foreword by Leon A. Feldman, New Brunswick, N. J., Rutgers University Press, 1972. [33a]

———, "Bibliography of Jewish Social Studies, 1938–39," *JSS,* II, 1940, pp. 305–88, 481–605; Published as book under the same title, revised, with index: New York, Jewish Social Studies, 1941.* |34]

———, "Church and State Debates in the Jewish Community of 1848," *Mordecai M. Kaplan Jubilee Volume on the Occasion of His Seventieth Birthday,* New York, Jewish Theological Seminary of America, 1953, pp. 49–72. [35]

———, "The Emancipation Movement and American Jewry," in his *Steeled by Adversity. Essays and Addresses on American Jewish Life,* Edited by Jeannette Meisel Baron, Philadelphia, JPSA, 1971, pp. 81–105.† [36]

————, "Ghetto and Emancipation," *Menorah Journal*, XIV, 1928, pp. 515–26. [37]

————, *History and Jewish Historians: Essays and Addresses*, Compiled . . . by Arthur Hertzberg and Leon Feldman, Philadelphia, JPSA, 1964.† [38]

————, *The Jewish Community; Its History and Structure*, Philadelphia, JPSA, 1942, 3 vols.* [39]

————, "Jewish Emancipation," *Encyclopedia of the Social Sciences*, New York, Macmillan Co., 1935, VIII, pp. 394–99. [40]

————, "Medieval Heritage and Modern Realities in Protestant-Jewish Relations," *Diogenes*, No. 61, 1968, pp. 32–51. [41]

————, "The Modern Age," in *Great Ages and Ideas of the Jewish People*, edited by Leo W. Schwarz, New York, Random House, 1956, pp. 315–484.† [42]

————, "Modern Capitalism and Jewish Fate," *Menorah Journal*, XXX, 1942, pp. 116–38, Also in his *History and Jewish Historians*, pp. 43–64. [43]

————, *Modern Nationalism and Religion*, New York, Harper and Brothers, 1947. [44]

————, "Nationalism and Intolerance," *Menorah Journal*, XVI, 1929, pp. 405–15. [45]

————, "Newer Approaches to Jewish Emancipation," *Diogenes*, No. 29, Spring 1960, pp. 56–81. [46]

————, "Newer Emphases in Jewish History," *JSS*, XXV, 1963, pp. 235–48. [47]

————, "The Revolution of 1848 and Jewish Scholarship," *PAAJR*, XVIII, 1948–49, pp. 1–66; XX, 1951, pp. 1–100. [48]

————, *The Russian Jew under Tsars and Soviets*, New York, Macmillan, 1964.* [49]

————, *A Social and Religious History of the Jews*, New York, Columbia University Press, II, 1937, pp. 164–261.* [50]

————, *A Social and Religious History of the Jews*, Ed. 2, New York, Columbia University Press; Philadelphia, JPSA, 1952–1973+, esp. vols. 11–15.* [51]

Baron, Salo W., 62a, 80.

[*Barou, Noah . . . Essays in Memory of . . . 632*]

Baroway, Israel, "Toward Understanding Tudor-Jacobean Hebrew Studies," *JSS*, XVIII, 1956, pp. 3–24. [52]

Barth, Aron, *The Modern Jew Faces Eternal Problems*, Jerusalem, Jerusalem Post Press, 1956. [53]

Barzilay, Isaac E., *Between Reason and Faith, Antirationalism in Italian Jewish Thought, 1250–1650*, The Hague, Muton and Co., 1967. [54]

————, "The Italian and Berlin Haskalah," *PAAJR*, XXIX, 1960–61, pp. 17–54. [55]

——, "John Toland's Borrowings from Simone Luzzatto," *JSS*, XXXI, 1969, pp. 75–81. [56]

——, "Moses Mendelssohn (1729–1786), *JQR*, NS, LII, 1961, pp. 69–93; 175–86. [57]

——, "National and Anti-National Trends in the Berlin Haskalah," *JSS*, XXI, 1959, pp. 165–68. [58]

——, *Shlomo Yehudah Rapoport [SHIR] (1790–1867) and His Contemporaries. Some Aspects of Jewish Scholarship of the Nineteenth Century*, Jerusalem, Massada Press, 1969. [59]

Barzilay, *see also* Eisenstein-Barzilay.

Bea, Augustin, *The Church and the Jewish People*, New York, Harper & Row, 1966. [59a]

Bein, Alex, "Modern Anti-Semitism and Its Place in the History of the Jewish Question," in *Between East and West, Essays Dedicated to the Memory of Bela Horovitz*, London, Horovitz Publishing Co., 1958, pp. 164–93.† [60]

——, "Notes on the Semantics of the Jewish Problem with Special Reference to Germany," *LBIYB*, IX, 1964, pp. 3–40. [60a]

——, "The Origin of the Term and Concept 'Zionism'," *Herzl Year Book*, II, 1959, pp. 1–27. [61]

Beinart, Haim, "The *Converso* Community in 15th Century Spain," and "The *Converso* Community in 16th and 17th Century Spain," in Barnett, R.D., Ed., *The Sephardi Heritage*, London, 1971, pp. 425–56; 457–58. [61a]

Benardete, Mair Jose, *Hispanic Culture and Character of the Sephardic Jews*, New York, Hispanic Institute in the U. S., 1952. [61b]

Ben Horin, Meir, *Common Faith—Uncommon People: Essays in Reconstructionist Judaism*, New York, Reconstructionist Press, 1970. [62]

——, *Max Nordau. Philosopher of Human Solidarity*, with a Foreword by Salo W. Baron, New York, Conference on Jewish Social Studies, 1956. [62a]

Bennett, A. and Herz, A., "French Speaking Jews in Quebec Face Crisis in Identity," *Jewish Digest*, XVI, No. 12, 1970, pp. 9–16. [63]

Ben-Sasson, H. H., and S. Ettinger, Eds., *Jewish Society Through the Ages*, New York, Schocken, 1971 (Contains articles published in the *World History through the Ages*).† [64]

Berger, Elmer, *Emancipation: The Rediscovered Ideal*, Philadelphia, American Council for Judaism, 1945. [65]

——, *The Jewish Dilemma*, New York, Devin-Adair, 1945. [66]

——, *Judaism or Jewish Nationalism; The Alternative to Zionism*, New York, Bookman, 1957. [67]

Berkovits, Eliezer, *Judaism: Fossil or Ferment?*, New York, Philosophical Library, 1956. [68]

————, *Faith after the Holocaust,* New York, Ktav, 1973. [68a]

Berlin, Charles, 386.

Berlin, Isaiah, "Benjamin Disraeli, Karl Marx and the Search for Identity," *JHSE, Tr., Session 1968–1969,* XX, 1970, pp. 1–20. [69]

Berline, Paul, "Russian Religious Philosophers and the Jews," *JSS,* IX, 1947, pp. 271–318. [70]

Berman, Jeremiah J., *Shehitah: A Study in the Cultural and Social Life of the Jewish People,* New York, Bloch, 1941.* [71]

Berman, Louis A., *Jews and Intermarriage: A Study in Personality and Culture,* New York, Yoseloff, 1968.* [72]

Bernards, Solomon S., Ed., *Who is a Jew? A Reader,* New York, Anti-Defamation League of B'nai B'rith, 1966.† [73]

Bernstein, Herman, *The Truth about "The Protocols of Zion"* . . . , Introduction by Norman Cohn, New York, Ktav Publishing House, 1971 (Reprint of 1935 Edition). [74]

Bernstein, Peretz, *Jew-Hate as a Sociological Problem,* New York, Philosophical Library, 1951. [75]

Birmingham, Stephen, *The Grandees: America's Sephardic Elite,* New York, Harper and Row, 1971. [75a]

Blau, Bruno, "Nationality among Czechoslovak Jewry," *HJ,* X, 1948, pp. 147–54. [76]

Blau, Joseph L., *Modern Varieties of Judaism,* New York, Columbia University Press, 1966. [77]

————, "Robert Burton on the Jews," *JSS,* VI, 1944, pp. 58–64. [78]

————, *The Story of Jewish Philosophy,* New York, Random, 1962. [78a]

Blau, Joseph L., Ed., *Reform Judaism: A Historical Perspective: Essays from The Yearbook of the Central Conference of American Rabbis,* New York, Ktav, 1973.† [79]

Blau, Joseph L., and S. W. Baron, Eds., *The Jews of the United States, 1790–1840: A Documentary History,* New York, Columbia University Press, 1963, 3 vols.¶ [80]

Bleich, J. David, "Survey of Recent Halakhic Literature," *Tradition,* IX, No. 3, 1967, pp. 103–19; X, No. 2, 1968, pp. 72–120; XI, No. 1, 84–98; XI, No. 2, 1970, pp. 91–102; XII, No. 1, 1971, pp. 81–100; XIII, No. 1, 1971, pp. 111–21; XIII, No. 1, 1972, pp. 143–54; XIII, No. 2, 1972, pp. 127–41. [80a]

Bloch, Josef Samuel, *Israel and the Nations,* Berlin, B. Harz, 1927. [81]

Bloom, Herbert I., *The Economic Activities of the Jews of Amsterdam in the Seventeenth and Eighteenth Centuries,* Williamsport, Pa., Bayard Press, 1937. [82]

————, "Felix Libertaté and the Emancipation of Dutch Jewry," *Essays . . . Baron,* pp. 105–22. [83]

Bloom, Solomon, "Karl Marx and the Jews," *JSS*, IV, 1942, pp. 3–16. [84]

Bobe, M., Levenberg, I. et al., Eds., *The Jews in Latvia*, Tel Aviv, Association of Latvian and Esthonian Jews in Israel, 1971.† [85]

Bober, Arie, Ed., *The Other Israel: The Radical Case Against Zionism*, Garden City, N. Y., Doubleday, 1972. [85a]

Bokser, Ben Zion, *Judaism and Modern Man; Essays in Jewish Theology*, New York, Philosophical Library, 1957. [85b]

Borochov, Ber, 129.

Borowitz, Eugene, *A New Jewish Theology in the Making*, Philadelphia, Westminster Press, 1968. [86]

————, "Judaism and the Secular State," *Journal of Religion*, XLVIII, 1968, pp. 12–34. [87]

Braham, Randolph L., Ed., *Hungarian-Jewish Studies*, World Federation of Hungarian Jews, New York, 2 vols., 1966, 1969. [88]

Braunstein, Baruch, *The Chuetas of Majorca: Conversos and the Inquisition of Majorca*, Reprinted with a new Prolegomenon by the Author, New York, Ktav, 1972. [89]

Breines, Paul, "The Jew as Revolutionary—The Case of Gustav Landauer," *LBIYB*, XII, 1967, pp. 75–84. [89a]

Buber, Martin, *A Believing Humanism: My Testament, 1902–1695*, Translated and edited by Maurice Friedman, New York, Simon and Schuster, 1967. [90]

Burton, William L., "Protestant America and the Rebirth of Israel," *JSS*, XXVI, 1964, pp. 203–14. [91]

Byrnes, Robert F., *Anti-Semitism in Modern France*, Volume I. *The Prologue to the Dreyfus Affair*, New Brunswick, N. J., Rutgers University Press, 1950; New York, Fertig, 1969.* [92]

————, "Jean-Louis Forain: Antisemitism in French Art," *JSS*, XII, 1950, pp. 246–56. [93]

Cahnman, Werner J., "Adolf Fischof and His Jewish Followers," *LBIYB*, IV, 1959, pp. 111–39. [93a]

Cahnman, Werner J., Ed., *Intermarriage and Jewish Life: A Symposium*, New York, Herzl Press and Reconstructionist Press, 1963.† [93b]

Cang, Joel, "The Opposition Parties in Poland and Their Attitude Towards the Jews and the Jewish Problem," *JSS*, I, 1939, pp. 241–56. [94]

Carsten, F. L., 98.

Caspar, Ċ., 95. [*Castro, Americo, Collected Studies in Honor of . . . 649*]

Caspar, C. (pseud.) [Aronsfeld, C. C.], "Mein Kampf—A Best Seller," *JSS*, XX, 1958, pp. 3–16. [95]

CCAR, *Yearbook*, 79.

CCAR, *Yearbook*, XX, 1910 (Abraham Geiger issue).† [96]

CCAR, *Yearbook*, XXIX, 1919 (Isaac M. Wise issue).† [97]

Carsten, F. L., "The Court Jews. A Prelude to Emancipation," *LBIYB*, III, 1958, pp. 140–56. [98]

Central Yiddish Culture Organization (CYCO), 264a.

Chouraqui, Andre N., *Between East and West: A History of the Jews of North Africa*, Philadelphia, JPSA, 1968. [99]

Chyet, Stanley P., *Lopez of Newport, Colonial American Merchant Prince*, Detroit, Wayne State University Press, 1970. [99a]

————, "The Political Rights of the Jews in the United States: 1776–1840," *AJA*, X, No. 1, April 1958, pp. 14–75. [100]

Coen, 312.

Cohen, Arthur A., *Arguments and Doctrines: A Reader of Jewish Thinking in the Aftermath of the Holocaust*, Philadelphia, JPSA, and New York, Harper and Row, 1970. [100a]

————, *The Natural and the Supernatural Jew. A Historical and Theological Statement*, New York, Pantheon, 1962. [100b]

Cohen, Carl, "The Road to Conversion," *LBIYB*, VI, 1961, pp. 259–79. [101]

Cohen, Haim H., Ed., *Jewish Law in Ancient and Modern Israel*, New York, Ktav, 1971. [101a]

Cohen, Hermann, *Religion of Reason Out of the Sources of Judaism*, Translated with an Introduction by Simon Kaplan; Introductory Essay by Leo Strauss, New York, Frederick Ungar, New York, 1972. [101b]

Cohen, Israel, *Contemporary Jewry*, London, Methuen and Co., 1950. [102]

————, *Jewish Life in Modern Times*, New York, Dodd, Mead, and Co., 1914. [103]

————, *The Zionist Movement*, New York, Zionist Organization of America, 1946. [104]

Cohen, Jack J., *The Case for Religious Naturalism; A Philosophy for the Modern Jew*, New York, The Reconstructionist Press, 1958. [104a]

Cohen, Mark R., "Leone de Modena's *Ritti:* A Seventeenth Century Plea for Liberation of Jews," *JSS*, XXXIV, 1972. [105]

Cohen, Martin A., "Antonio Diaz de Caceres; Marrano Adventurer in Colonial Mexico," *AJHQ*, LX, 1970–71, pp. 169–84. [106]

————, "The Religion of Luis Rodriguez Carvajal," *AJA*, XX, No. 1, April 1968, pp. 33–62. [107]

————, "Some Misconceptions about the Crypto-Jews in Colonial Mexico," *AJHQ*, LXI, 1972, pp. 277–93. [108]

Cohen, Martin A., 645.

Cohn, Norman, *Warrant for Genocide: The Myth of the Jewish World-Conspiracy and the Protocols of the Elders of Zion*, New York, Harper & Row, 1966 (Harper Torchbooks, 1969). [109]

Cohn, Willy, "Christian Wilhelm von Dohm," *HJ*, XIII, 1951, pp. 101–08. [110]

Cohon, Samuel S., "Zunz and Reform Judaism," *HUCA*, XXXI, 1960, pp. 223–50. [111]

Commentary Magazine, Editors of, Ed., *The Condition of Jewish Belief: A Symposium*, New York, Macmillan, 1966 (first appeared in *Commentary*, XLII, No. 2, August 1966).† [112]

Corre, Alan D., "Heroes, Heretics, and Hidalgos," *JSS*, XXVIII, 1966, pp. 99–107. [113]

Corti, Egon Caesar, *The Reign of the House of Rothschild, 1830–1871*, New York, Cosmopolitan Book Corporation, 1928. [114]

——, *The Rise of the House of Rothschild*, New York, Cosmopolitan Book Corporation, 1928. [115]

Coser, Lewis A., 651a.

Cranfield, G. A., "The London Evening Post and the Jew Bill of 1753," *The Historical Journal*, VIII, 1965, pp. 16–30. [116]

Curtiss, John, *An Appraisal of the Protocols of Zion*, New York, Columbia University Press, 1942. [117]

Davidsohn, Joseph, "The Problem of George Brandes' Jewishness," *YAJSS*, II-III, 1947–48, pp. 118–39. [118]

Davis, Moshe, *The Emergence of Conservative Judaism: The Historical School in 19th Century America*, Philadelphia, JPSA, 1963.* [119]

——, "Mixed Marriage in Western Jewry: Historical Background to Jewish Response," *JJS*, X, 1968, pp. 177–220. [120]

Dawidowicz, Lucy S., *The Golden Tradition: Jewish Life and Thought in Eastern Europe*, New York, Holt, Rinehart and Winston, 1967.† [121]

Deak, Istvan, *Weimar Germany's Left-Wing Intellectuals: A Political History of the Weltbuehne and Its Circle*, Berkeley, University of California Press, 1968. [122]

Decter, Moshe, 651a.

Deutscher, Isaac, *The Non-Jewish Jew and Other Essays*, Edited with an Introduction by Tamara Deutscher, London, Oxford University Press, 1968. [123]

Deutscher, Tamara, 123.

Diamond, Malcolm I., *Martin Buber: Jewish Existentialist*, New York, William Ganon, 1971. [123a]

Dinstein, Y., "The International Human Rights of Soviet Jewry." *IYHR*, II, 1972, pp. 194–210. [123b]

Dinur, Ben Zion, *Israel and the Diaspora*, with an Introduction by Yitzshak Baer, Philadelphia, JPSA, 1969. [124]

Dinur, Ben Zion, et al., "Emancipation," *Encyclopedia Judaica*, VI, 1972, pp. 696–718. [125]

Dubnov [-Dubnow], Simon, *History of the Jews* . . . Translated from the Russian . . . by Moshe Spiegel, South Brunswick, N. J., Yoseloff, vols. III, IV, and V, 1969–73. [125a]

——, *History of the Jews in Russia and Poland,* Philadelphia, JPSA, 1916–20, 3 vols. [126]

——, *Nationalism and History: Essays on Old and New Judaism,* Edited by Koppel S. Pinson, Philadelphia, JPSA, 1958. [127]

Duchinsky, Eugene, 376.

Duker, Abraham G., "Anti-Semitism," in Dunner, Joseph, Ed., *Handbook of World History: Concepts and Issues,* New York, Philosophical Library, 1967, pp. 47–64. [128]

——, "The Background: An Introductory Chapter," in Weinryb, 658 [128a]

——, "Ber Borochov's Theories and Their Place in the History of the Jewish Labor Movement," Introduction to Borochov, Ber, *Nationalism and the Class Struggle. A Marxian Approach to the Jewish Problem,* New York, Poale Zion, 1937, pp. 17–55. ¶ [129]

——, "Cultures in Transition. A Jewish Survivalist View," in *Acculturation and Integration, A Symposium* . . . [with Harold Isaacs and Louis Guttman], New York, American Histadrut Cultural Exchange Institute, 1965, pp. 143–76, 205–11, 224–25. [130]

——, *Jewish Survival in the World Today,* New York, Hadassah, The Women's Zionist Organization of America, 1939 (particularly Parts IIA and IIB and appropriate Source Books).¶† [131]

——, "Jewish Territorialism: An Historical Sketch," *Contemporary Jewish Record,* II, No. 2, March-Apr. 1939, pp. 14–30. [132]

——, "The Lafayette Committee for Jewish Emancipation," in *Essays* . . . *Baron,* pp. 169–82. [133]

——, "The Polish Emigré Christian Socialists and the Jewish Problem," *JSS,* XIV, 1952, pp. 317–42. [134]

——, "The Polish Insurrection's Missed Opportunity: Mochnacki's Views on the Failure to Involve the Jews in the Uprising of 1830/31," *JSS,* XVIII, 1968, pp. 212–32. [135]

——, "The Polish Political Émigrés and the Jews in 1848," *PAAJR,* XXIV, 1955, pp. 69–102. [136]

——, "Prince Czartoryski, the Émigré, and the Jewish Problem," in *The Joshua Bloch Memorial Volume. Studies in Booklore and History,* New York, New York Public Library, 1960, pp. 165–79. [137]

Dunner, Joseph, 128.

Eban, Abba, *My People; The Story of the Jews,* New York, Behrman House and Random House, 1968. [138]

Eckardt, Roy A., *Elder and Younger Brothers: The Encounter of Jews and Christians,* New York, Scribner's, 1967. [139]

————, "Theological Approaches to Anti-Semitism," *JSS*, XXXIII, 1971, pp. 272–84. [139a]

Eichhorn, David Max, *Conversion to Judaism: A History and Analysis*, New York, Ktav, 1965. [140]

Eisenstaedt, Shmuel Noah, *Israeli Society*, New York, Basic Books, 1967. [140a]

Eisenstein, Ira, *Judaism under Freedom*, New York, The Reconstructionist Press, 1956. [141]

Eisenstein, Miriam, *Jewish Schools in Poland 1919–39: Their Philosophy and Development*, New York, King's Crown Press, 1950. [142]

Eisenstein-Barzilay, Isaac, "The Background of the Berlin Haskalah," *Essays, . . . Baron*, pp. 183–97. [143]

————, "The Ideology of the Berlin Haskalah," *PAAJR*, XXV, 1956, *pp.* 1–37. [144]

————, "The Treatment of the Jewish Religion in the Literature of the Berlin Haskalah," *PAAJR*, XXIV, 1955, pp. 30–68. [145]

————, *see also* Barzilay.

Eitches, Edward, "Maryland's Jew Bill," *AJHQ*, LX, 1970–71, pp. 258–79. [146]

Elazar, Daniel, "American Political Theory and the Political Notions of American Jewry; Convergences and Contradictions," *JJS*, IX, 1967, pp. 5–24. [147]

Elazar, Daniel J., and Stephen R. Goldstein, "The Legal Status of the American Jewish Community," *AJYB*, LXX, 1972, pp. 3–93. [148]

Elbogen, Ismar, *A Century of Jewish Life*, Philadelphia, JPSA, 1945.* [149]

Emmanuel, I. S., "New Light on Early American Jewry," *American Jewish Archives*, VII, 1955, pp. 3–64. [150]

————, *Precious Stones of the Jews of Curacao*, New York, Bloch, 1957. [150a]

Emmanuel, Isaac S. and Suzanne A., *History of the Jews of the Netherlands Antilles*, Cincinnati, American Jewish Archives, 1970, 2 vols. [151]

Emmanuel, Suzanne A., 151.

Engelman, Uriah Zevi, *The Rise of the Jew in the Western World: A Social and Economic History of the Jewish People of Europe*, New York, Behrman, 1944. [152]

Epstein, Klaus, *The Genesis of German Conservatism*, Princeton, N. J., Princeton University Press, 1968. [152a]

Estreicher, John M., 617.

Ettinger, Shmuel, "The Beginnings of the Change in the Attitude of European Society Towards the Jews," *Scripta Hierosolymitana*, VII, 1961, pp. 193–219. [153]

————, "Russian Society and the Jews," *BSJA*, No. 5, May 1970, pp. 36–43. [154]

Ettinger, Shmuel, 64.

Fackenheim, Emil L., *Encounters between Judaism and Modern Philosophy; A Preface to Future Jewish Thought*, New York, Basic Books, 1972.† [155]

————, *Quest for Past and Future. Essays in Jewish Theology*, Bloomington, Ind., University of Indiana Press, 1968.† [156]

————, "Samuel Hirsch and Hegel: A Study of Hirsch's *Religionsphilosophie der Juden* (1842)," in Altman, Ed., *Studies*. [157]

Feinberg, Nathan, "The Jewish Question at the Congress of Aix-la-Chapelle," *IYHR*, II, pp. 176–93. [157a]

————, "The National Treatment Clause in Historical Perspective (A Controversy with Czarist Russia)," *Recueil d'etudes de droit international, en hommage à Paul Guggenheim*, Geneva, 1968, pp. 44–69. [157b]

————, "The Recognition of the Jewish People in International Law," *JYIL*, 1948, pp. 1–26. [158]

Feingold, Henry L., "German Jewry and the American Jewish Condition: A View from Weimar," *Judaism*, XX, No. 1, Winter 1971, pp. 108–19. [158a]

Feldman, Leon A., 33a, 38.

Feuer, Lewis Samuel, *Spinoza and the Rise of Liberalism*, Boston, Beacon, 1965. [158b]

Finestein, Israel, "Anglo-Jewish Opinion during the Struggle for Emancipation (1828–1858)," JHSE, *Tr.*, *Sessions 1959–61*, XX, pp. 113–43. [159]

Fisch, Harold, *The Dual Image: The Figures of the Jew in English and American Literature*, New York, Ktav, 1971. [159a]

Fishman, Joshua A., Ed., *Studies in Modern Jewish History . . . from YIVO Annual of Jewish Social Science*, New York, Ktav Publishing House and YIVO Institute for Jewish Research, 1973.‡ [160]

Flusser, David, "A New Sensitivity in Judaism and the Christian Message," *Harvard Theological Review*, LXI, 1968, pp. 107–27. [160a]

Fraenkel, Josef, Ed., *The Jews of Austria: Essays on Their Life, History and Destruction*, London, Vallentine, Mitchell, 1969.† [161]

Frankenstein, Ernst, "The Meaning of the Term, 'National Home for the Jewish People'," *JYIL*, 1948, pp. 27–41. [162]

Freehof, S., 437.

Friedberg, Maurice, "Antisemitism as a Policy Tool in the Soviet Bloc," *AJYB*, LXXI, 1970, pp. 123–40. [163]

Friedenberg, Albert M., *The Sunday Laws of the United States and Leading Judicial Decisions Having Special Reference to the Jews*, Philadelphia, JPSA, 1908. [164]

Friedenwald, Harry, "Montaigne's Relation to Judaism and the Jews," *JQR*,

NS, XXXI, 1940–41, pp. 141–48. [165]

Friedman, Elisha M., *Survival or Extinction: Social Aspects of the Jewish Question,* New York, Thomas Seltzer, 1924. [166]

Friedman, Georges, *The End of the Jewish People?,* New York, Doubleday, 1967. [167]

✓ Friedman, Lee M., *Jewish Pioneers and Patriots,* Philadelphia, JPSA, 1942.† [168]

———, *Pilgrims in a New Land,* Philadelphia, JPSA, 1948.† [169]

Friedman, Norman L., "The Problem of the Runaway Jewish Intellectuals: Social Definition and Sociological Perspective," *JSS,* XXXI, 1969, pp. 3–19. [170]

Friedman, Philip, "Polish-Jewish Historiography between the Two Wars (1918–1939)," *JSS,* XI, 1949, pp. 373–408.* [171]

Friedman, Theodore H., Ed., "My Jewish Affirmation (Symposium)," *Judaism,* X, 1961, pp. 291–52.† [172]

Frumkin, Jacob, 21.

Frumkin, Jacob, Gregor Aronson, and Alexis Goldenweiser, Eds., *Russian Jewry (1860–1917),* Translated by Mirra Ginsburg, New York, Yoseloff, 1966.† [173]

Fuchs, Lawrence H., *The Political Behavior of American Jews,* Glencoe, Ill., Free Press, 1956.* [174]

Gal, Allon, *Socialist-Zionism: Theory and Issues in Contemporary Jewish Nationalism,* Cambridge, Mass., Schenkman Publishing Company, 1973. [175]

Galliner, Arthur, "The Philanthropin in Frankfurt. Its Educational and Cultural Significance for German Jewry," *LBIYB,* III, 1958, pp. 169–86. [176]

Gamoran, Emanuel C., *Changing Conceptions in Jewish Education,* New York, Macmillan Co., 1924. [177]

Gay, Peter, *The Berlin-Jewish Spirit; A Dogma in Search of Some Doubts,* New York, Leo Baeck Institute, 1972. [178]

———, *Weimar Culture: The Outsider as Insider,* New York, Harper and Row, 1968. [178a]

Gelber, Nahum M., "The Intervention of German Jews at the Berlin Congress 1878," *LBIYB,* V. 1960, pp. 221–48. [179]

———, "The Sephardic Community in Vienna," *JSS,* V. 1948, pp. 359–96. [180]

Geltman, Max, *The Confrontation: Black Power, Anti-Semitism, and the Myth of Integration,* Englewood Cliffs, N. J. Prentice-Hall, 1970. [180a]

Getzler, Israel, *Neither Toleration nor Favour: The Australian Chapter of Jewish Emancipation,* Carlton, Victoria, Melbourne University, 1970. [180b]

Gilman, Stephen, "The Conversos and the Fall of Fortune," *Castro Volume* [as in 649], pp. 127–36. [181]

Gilbert, Martin, *Jewish History Atlas,* Cartography by Arthur Banks, London, Weidenfeld and Nicolson, 1969. [182]

Ginzberg, Asher, 318.

Ginzberg, Louis, *Students, Scholars and Saints,* Philadelphia, JPSA, 1928. [182a]

Gitelman, Zvi Y., *Jewish Nationality and Soviet Politics: The Jewish Sections of the CPSU, 1917–1930,* Princeton, N. J., Princeton University Press, 1972.†* [183]

Glatzer, Nahum N., "The Beginnings of Modern Jewish Studies," in Altmann, Ed., *Studies,* pp. 27–45. [184]

——, Ed., *The Dynamics of Emancipation: The Jew in the Modern Age,* Boston, Beacon Press, 1965.¶ [185]

Glatzer, Nahum N., *Franz Rosenzweig, His Life and Thought,* New York, Schocken, 1961 (paperback). [186]

——, *The Judaic Tradition,* Boston, Beacon Press, 1969.¶ [187]

——, *Leopold and Adelheid Zunz: An Account in Letters, 1815–1885,* London, East and West Library for the Leo Baeck Institute, 1958. [188]

Glazer, Nathan, "Social Characteristics of American Jews, 1654–1954," *AJYB,* LVI, 1954–1955, pp. 3–41. [189]

Goldberg, Harvey, "Jean Jaures and the Jewish Question: The Evolution of a Position," *JSS,* XX, 1958, pp. 67–94. [190]

Goldberg, Nathan, *et al., The Classification of Jewish Immigrants and Its Implications; A Survey of Opinion; 140 Replies to a Questionnaire and Papers by Nathan Goldberg, Jacob Lestchinsky and Max Weinreich,* New York, Yivo, 1945.¶† [191]

Goldelman, Solomon I., *Jewish National Autonomy in Ukraine 1917–1920,* Chicago, Ukrainian Research and Information Institute, 1968. [192]

Goldenweiser, Alexis, "Legal Status of Jews in Russia," *Russian Jewry (1860–1917),* pp. 85–119. [193]

Goldenweiser, Alexis, 173.

Goldin, Judah, Ed., *The Jewish Expression,* New York, Bantam, 1970 (paperback).¶† [194]

Goldman, Lazarrus Morris, *The History of the Jews in New Zealand,* Wellington, New Zealand, Reed, 1958. [195]

Goldstein, Moritz, "German Jewry's Dilemma before 1914," *LBIYB,* II, 1957, pp. 236–54. [196]

Goldstein, Sidney, "American Jewry, 1970: A Demographic Profile," *AJYB,* LXXII, 1971, pp. 3–88. [197]

Goldstein, Stephen R., 148.

Goldstuecker, Eduard, "Jews between Czechs and Germans around 1848," *LBIYB,* XVII, 1972, pp. 61–71. [198]

Golomb, Abraham I., "Jewish Self-Hatred," *YAJSS,* I, 1946, pp. 250–59. [199]

Goodman, Abram V., *American Overture: Jewish Rights in Colonial America*, Philadelphia, JPSA, 1947. [200]

Gordis, Robert, *Judaism in a Christian World*, New York, McGraw-Hill, 1966. [201]

Gordon, Albert I., *Jews in Transition*, Minneapolis, University of Minneapolis Press, 1949. [202]

✓ Gordon, Milton M., *Assimilation in American Life. The Role of Race, Religion, and National Origins*, New York, 1964. [203]

Graeber, Isacque, Ed., *Jews in a Gentile World; The Problem of Anti-Semitism*, New York, Macmillan, 1942.† [204]

Graetz, Heinrich, *History of the Jews from the Earliest Times to the Present Day*, Philadelphia, JPSA, 1891, vols. 4–6. [205]

Grayzel, Solomon, *A History of the Jews: From 1900 to the Present*, New York, Meridian Books; Philadelphia, JPSA, 1960. [206]

Greenbaum, Alfred Abraham, *Jewish Scholarship in Soviet Russia*, Boston, (privately published), 1959 (mimeographed). [207]

——, "Nationalism as a Problem in Soviet Jewish Scholarship," *PAAJR*, XXX, 1962, pp. 61–99. [208]

——, "Religion and History According to Samuel Hirsch," *HUCA*, XLIII, 1972, pp. 103–24. [209]

——, "Samuel Hirsch, Jewish Hegelian," *Revue des Etudes Juives-Historia Judaica*, CXXIX, 1970, pp. 205–15. [210]

Greenberg, Hayim, *The Inner Eye; Selected Essays*, New York, Jewish Frontier Association, 1964, 2 vols. [211]

——, *The Hayim Greenberg Anthology*, Edited by Marie Syrkin, Detroit, Wayne State University Press, 1968. [212]

Greenberg, Louis, *The Jews in Russia*, New Haven, Conn., Yale University Press, I, 1944; II, Edited by Mark Wischnitzer, 1951 (Also later edition by Ktav). [213]

Greenberg, Simon, *Foundations of Faith*, New York, Burning Bush Press, 1968. [213a]

Gringauz, Samuel, "Jewish National Autonomy in Lithuania (1918–1925)," *JSS*, XIV, 1952, pp. 225–46. [214]

——, "The Jewish National Autonomy in Lithuania, Latvia and Estonia," in *Russian Jewry 1917–1967*, pp. 58–71. [215]

Greenleaf, Richard E., *The Mexican Inquisition of the 16th Century*, Albuquerque, University of New Mexico, 1969. [216]

Gross, Felix, 651.

Gruenewald, Max, "The Modern Rabbi," *LBIYB*, II, 1957, pp. 85–97. [217]

Grunfeld, Isidor, *Three Generations: The Influence of Samson Raphael Hirsch on Jewish Life and Thought*. London, Jewish Post Publications, 1958. [218]

Grunwald, Kurt, "Europe's Railways and Jewish Enterprise," *LBIYB*, XII, 1967, pp. 163–209. [219]

[*Guggenheim, Paul, Recuell . . . en hommage . . .* , 157b]

Gutstein, Morris Aaron, *To Bigotry No Sanction; A Jewish Shrine in America, 1658–1958,* New York, Bloch, 1958. [220]

———, *The Story of the Jews of Newport 1658–1908,* New York, Bloch, 1936. [221]

Guttman, Louis [on identity], 130.

Guttmann, Julius, *Philosophies of Judaism. The History of Jewish Philosophy from Biblical Times to Franz Rosenzweig.* Introduction by R. J. Zwi Werblowsky. Translated by David W. Silverman, Philadelphia, JPSA; New York, Holt, Rinehart and Winston, 1964. [222]

Hailperin, Herman, 459.

Haliczer, Stephen H., "The Castillian Urban Patriciate and the Jewish Expulsions of 1480–92," *American Historical Review,* LXXVIII, 1973, pp. 35–63. [222a]

Halkin, Abraham S., "A *Contra Christianos* by a Marrano," *Kaplan Jubilee Volume* [as in 35], pp. 399–416. [223]

Halkin, Simon, *Modern Hebrew Literature: From the Enlightenment to the Birth of the State of Israel; Trends and Values,* New York, Schocken, 1971. [223a]

Halperin, Samuel, *The Political World of American Zionism,* Detroit, Wayne State University Press, 1961. [224]

Halpern, Ben, *The Idea of the Jewish State,* Cambridge, Mass., Harvard University Press, 1961. [224a]

Hamburger, Ernest, *Jews, Democracy and Weimar Germany,* New York, Leo Baeck Institute, 1972. [225]

———, "Jews in Public Service under the German Monarchy," *LBIYB*, IX, 1964, pp. 206–38. [226]

———, "One Hundred Years of Emancipation," *LBIYB,* XIV, 1969, pp. 3–66. [227]

Handlin, Oscar, "Jews in the Culture of Middle Europe," *SLBI*, pp. 157–75. [228]

Handlin, Oscar and Mary F., "Acquisition of Political and Social Rights by the Jews in the United States," *AJYB*, LVI, 1954–1955, pp. 43–98. [229]

Handlin, Mary F., 229.

Harcave, Sidney S., "The Jewish Question in the First Russian Duma," *JSS,* VI, 1944, pp. 155–76. [230]

Harris, M. H., "The Dangers of Emancipation," CCAR, *Yearbook,* II, 1893, pp. 55–63. [231]

Hartog, John, "The Honen Daliem Congregation of St. Eustatius," *AJA*, XIX, No. 1, April 1967, pp. 60–77. [232]

Hay, Malcolm, *The Foot of Pride. The Pressure of Christendom on the People of Israel for 1900 Years*, Boston, Beacon, 1951 (published in paperback as *Europe and the Jews*.* [233]

————, *The Prejudices of Pascal Concerning in Particular the Jesuit Order and the Jewish People*, London, Neville Spearman, 1962. [234]

Heinemann, Isaac, "Supplementary Remarks on the Secession from the Frankfurt Jewish Community under Samson Raphael Hirsch," *HJ*, X, 1948, pp. 123–34. [235]

Heller, Max, "Place of the Jew in a Racial Interpretation of the History of Civilization," CCAR, *Yearbook*, XXIII, 1913, pp. 304–39. [236]

Henkin, Louis, Ed., *World Politics and the Jewish Condition: Essays Prepared for a Task Force on the World of the 1970s of the American Jewish Committee*, New York, Quadrangle Books and the Institute of Human Relations Press, 1972.† [236a]

Henriques, Henry Straus Quixano, "The Civil Rights of English Jews," *JQR*, XVIII, 1906, pp. 40–83. [237]

————, *The Jews and the English Law*, Oxford, Hart, 1908. [238]

————, *The Political Rights of English Jews*, JQR, XIX, 1907, pp. 298–341, 751–99. [239]

————, "The Jewish Emancipation Controversy in 19th Century Britain," *Past and Present*, XL, 1968, pp. 126–46. [240]

Herberg, Will, *Judaism and Modern Man*, Garden City, N. Y., Anchor, 1951. [241]

————, *Protestant, Catholic, Jew*, Ed. 2, Garden City, N. Y., Doubleday Anchor Books, 1960 (paperback). [241a]

Herrman, Simon, *Israelis and Jews: The Continuity of an Identity*, Philadelphia, JPSA, 1971.* [242]

Hertzberg, Arthur, *The French Enlightenment and the Jews*, Philadelphia, JPSA, 1968 (also in paperback). [243]

————, *The Zionist Idea: A Historical Analysis and Reader*, New York, Atheneum, 1969 (also in paperback).¶† [244]

Hertzberg, Arthur, 38, 63.

Herz, A., 63.

Heschel, Abraham J., *Between God and Man: An Interpretation of Judaism from the Writings of Abraham Heschel*, Edited by Fritz A. Rothschild, New York, The Free Press, 1959. [245]

————, *God in Search of Man; A Philosophy of Judaism*, New York and Philadelphia, Meridian Books and JPSA, 1959. [246]

Heyman, Jan, "The Conflict between Jewish and Non-Jewish Population in Bohemia before the 1541 Banishment," *Judaica Bohemiae*, VI, 1970, pp. 39–53. [246a]

Hilberg, Raul, *The Destruction of the European Jews*, Chicago, Quadrangle

Books, 1961 (Quadrangle Paperback, 1967). [247]

Himmelfarb, Milton, *The Jews of Modernity*, New York, Basic Books, 1973.† [248]

——, 112.

Hirsch, Samson Raphael, *Fundamentals of Judaism: Selections from the Works of S. R. Hirsch and Outstanding Torah-true Thinkers*, New York, Feldheim, 1949.† [249]

Hoenig, Sidney B., 357.

Hollander, Jacob H., "The Civil Status of the Jews in Maryland 1634–1776," *PAJHS*, II, 1893, pp. 33–44. [250]

——, "The Naturalization of Jews in the American Colonies under the Act of 1740," *PAJHS*, VII, 1897, pp. 102–17. [251]

Holtz, Louis, 536.

Homa, Bernard, *Orthodoxy in Anglo-Jewry, 1880–1940*, London, The Jewish Historical Society of England, 1969. [252]

Horak, Stephan, *Poland and Her National Minorities, 1919–39, A Case Study*, New York, Vantage, 1961. [253]

Hornik, M. P., 649.

[Horovitz, Bella, *Between East . . . Dedicated to . . .* 429.]

Hoselitz, Bert F., 593.

Huhner, Leon, *Jews in America in Colonial and Revolutionary Times: A Memorial Volume*, New York, Gertz Brothers, 1959. [254]

Hungarian-Jewish Studies, 88.

Hurwitz, Edith, 256.

Hurwitz, Henry, "Heritage and Allegiance," *The Menorah Journal*, XLV, Nos. 1 and 2, 1959, pp. 1–60. [255]

Hurwitz, Samuel J., and Edith, "The New World Sets an Example for the Old: The Jews of America and Political Rights, 1661–1831," *AJHQ*, XLV, 1965–66, pp. 37–56. [256]

Hyamson, Albert M., "The Lost Tribes and the Return of the Jews to England," *JHSE, Tr., Sessions 1902–05*, V, pp. 115–47. [257]

——, *The Sephardim of England*, London, Methuen & Co., 1951. [257a]

Hyman, Louis, *The Jews of Ireland from Earliest Times to the Year 1910*, London-Jerusalem, The Jewish Historical Society of England and Israel Universities Press, 1972. [258]

Hyman, Paula E., "Joseph Salvador: Proto-Zionist or Apologist for Assimilation?" *JSS*, XXXIV, 1972, pp. 1–22. [259]

Idelsohn, A. Z., *Jewish Music in its Historical Development*, New York, Holt, 1929. [260]

Infeld, Henrik, F., 632.

Isaac, Jules, *The Teaching of Contempt: Christian Roots of Antisemitism*,

Translated . . . by Helen Weaver, New York, Holt, Rinehart and Winston, 1964. [260a]

Isaacs, Harold, "For a Redefinition of the Jew," [as in 130]. [260b]

Jacobowitz, Emanuel, *Jewish Law Faces Modern Problems,* New York, Yeshiva University, 1965. [260c]

Jacobs, Noah J., "Salomon Maimon's Relation to Judaism," *LBIYB,* VIII, 1963, pp. 117–35. [260d]

Janowsky, Oscar I., *The Jews and Minority Rights, 1898–1919,* New York, Columbia University Press, 1933.* [261]

———, Ed., *The American Jew: A Reappraisal,* Philadelphia, JPSA, 1964.† [262]

Janowsky, Oscar I., and Melvin M. Fagen, *International Aspects of German Racial Policies,* New York, Oxford University Press, 1937. [262a]

Jehouda, Josue, *The Five Stages of Jewish Emancipation.* Translated by Eva Jackson, Brunswick, N. J., Yoseloff, 1966. [263]

Jenks, William A., "The Jews in the Hapsburg Empire, 1879–1918," *LBIYB,* XVI, 1971, pp. 155–62. [264]

———, 662.

Jewish Historical Society of England, 412, 467.

The Jewish People: Past and Present, New York, Jewish Encyclopedic Handbooks, Central Yiddish Culture Organization (CYCO), 1948, 4 vols.† [264a]

The Jews in Latvia, 333.

The Jews of Austria, 161.

The Jews of Czechoslovakia: Historical Studies and Surveys, Philadelphia, JPSA, and New York, Society for the History of Czechoslovak Jews, 2 vols., 1968, 1971. [265]

Johnpoll, Bernard K., *The Politics of Futility: The General Jewish Workers Bund of Poland, 1917–1943,* Ithaca, N. Y., Cornell University Press, 1967. [266]

Jospe, Alfred, Ed., *Tradition and Contemporary Experience. Essays on Jewish Thought and Life,* New York, Schocken Books for the B'nai B'rith Hillel Foundations, 1970.† [267]

Jospe, Alfred, 383b.

Judaism magazine, 172.

Juhn, Erich, "The Jewish Sports Movement in Austria," in *Jews of Austria,* pp. 161–64. [268]

Jung, Leo, Ed., *Guardians of Our Heritage,* New York, Bloch, 1958.† [269]

———, *Jewish Leaders 1750–1940,* New York, Bloch, 1953.† [270]

———, *Men of Spirit,* New York, Kymson, 1964.† [271]

———, *Judaism in a Changing World,* New York, Oxford University Press, 1939.† [272]

Kahane, Meir, *Never Again*, Los Angeles, Nash, 1971; New York, Pyramid, 1972. [272a]

Kahler, Erich, "The Jews and the Germans," *SLBI*, pp. 17–44. [273]

Kallen, Horace M., "The Bearing of Emancipation on Jewish Survival," *YAJSS*, XII, 1958–59, pp. 9–35. [274]

————, *"Of Them Which Say They Are Jews": And Other Essays on the Jewish Struggle for Survival,* Edited by Judah Pilch, New York, Bloch, 1954. [275]

————, *Judaism at Bay; Essays Toward the Adjustment of Judaism to Modernity,* New York, Bloch, 1932. [276]

Kamen, Henry, *The Spanish Inquisition,* New York, New American Library, 1965. [276a]

Kann, Robert A., "Assimilation and Antisemitism in the German-French Orbit," *LBIYB*, XIV, 1969, pp. 92–115. [277]

————, "Hungarian Jewry During Austria-Hungary's Constitutional Period, (1867–1918)," *JSS*, VII, 1945, pp. 357–86. [278]

Kaplan, Mordecai Menahem, *The Greater Judaism in the Making: A Study of the Modern Evolution of Judaism,* New York, Reconstructionist Press, 1960. [279]

————, *Judaism as a Civilization. Toward a Reconstruction of American Jewish Life,* New York, Macmillan, 1934; Yoseloff, 1957. [280]

————, *Judaism without Supernaturalism; The Only Alternative to Orthodoxy and Secularism,* New York, Reconstructionist Press, 1958. [281]

————, *The Religion of Ethical Nationhood; Judaism's Contribution to World Peace,* New York, Macmillan, 1970. [282]

————, *The New Zionism,* New York, Herzl Press, 2nd ed., 1959. [283]

Kaplan, Simon, 101b.

Karp, Abraham J., Ed., *The Jewish Experience in America. Selected Studies from the Publications of the American Jewish Historical Society,* Waltham, Mass., American Jewish Historical Society, 1969, 4 Vols.† [284]

Katz, Jacob, *Emancipation and Assimilation: Studies in Modern Jewish History,* Farnborough, Hants, Gregg International Publishers, 1972.† [285]

————, "The German-Jewish Utopia of Social Emancipation," *SLBI*, pp. 61–80. [286]

————, "The Impact of Jewish Emancipation on the Concepts of Galut and Geulah—Exile and Redemption," CCAR, *Yearbook,* LXXX, 1970, pp. 119–33. [287]

————, "The Influence of Religion and Society on Each Other at the Time of the Emancipation," *European Judaism,* I, No. 1, Summer 1966, pp. 20–29. [288]

————, *Jews and Freemasons in Europe (1723–1739),* Cambridge, Mass., Harvard University Press, 1970. [289]

————, "Judaism and Christianity against the Background of Modern Secularism," *Judaism*, XVII, 1968, pp. 299–315. [290]

————, *Out of the Ghetto: The Social Background of Jewish Emancipation, 1770–1870*, Cambridge, Harvard University Press, 1973. [291]

————, "Samuel Hirsch — Rabbi, Philosopher and Freemason," *REJ-HJ*, CXXV, 1966, pp. 113–26. [292]

————, "A State within a State: The History of an Anti-Semitic Slogan," The Israel Academy of Sciences and Humanities, *Proceedings*, IV, 1971, pp. 79–196. [293]

————, "The Term 'Jewish Emancipation': Its Origins and Historical Impact," Altmann, Ed., *Studies* [as in 10], pp. 1–26. [294]

————, *Tradition and Crisis: Jewish Society at the End of the Middle Ages*, Glencoe, Ill., The Free Press, 1961; New York, Schocken Paperback Books, 1971. [295]

Katz, Shlomo, Ed., *Negro and Jew: An Encounter in America; A Symposium Compiled by Midstream Magazine*, New York, Macmillan, 1966.† [295a]

Katz, Shlomo, 571b.

Katzburg, Nathaniel, "Hungarian Jewry in Modern Times: Political and Social Aspects," *Hungarian-Jewish Studies*, New York, 1966, pp. 137–70. [296]

Kautsky, Karl, *Are the Jews a Race?* . . . Translated from the Second German Edition, New York, International Publishers, 1926. [297]

Kestenberg-Gladstein, Ruth, "The Jews between Czechs and Germans in the Historic Lands, 1848–1918," *Jews in Czechoslovakia*, I, pp. 21–71. [298]

Kiell, N., *The Psychodynamics of American Jewish Life; an Anthology*, New York, Twayne, 1967.†* [298a]

Kisch, Guido, *The Jews in Medieval Germany*, Chicago, University of Chicago Press, 1949. [298b]

————, "Linguistic Conditions among Czechoslovak Jewry," *HJ*, VII, 1946, pp. 19–32. [299]

Klein, Bernard, "Hungarian Politics and the Jewish Question in the Inter-War Period," *JSS*, XVIII, 1966, pp. 79–98. [300]

Klein, Charlotte Lea, "The Changing Image of the Jew in Modern English Literature," *Patterns of Prejudice*, V, No. 2, March-April, 1971, pp. 22–31. [301]

Klineberg, Otto, et al., *Aspects of French Jewry*, London, Vallentine, Mitchell, 1969.† [302]

Kober, Adolf, "Emancipation's Impact on the Education and Vocational Training of German Jewry," *JSS*, XVI, 1954, pp. 3–32, 151–76. [303]

————, "The French Revolution and the Jews in Germany," *JSS*, VII, 1945, pp. 291–322. [304]

————, "Jewish Preaching and Preachers. A Contribution to the History of the Jewish Sermon in Germany and America," *HJ*, VII, 1945, pp. 103–34. [305]

———, "The Jewish Theological Seminary of Breslau and 'Wissenschaft des Judentums'," *HJ*, XVI, 1954, pp. 85–122. [306]

———, "Jews in the Revolution of 1848 in Germany," *JSS*, X, 1948, pp. 135–64. [307]

———, "150 Years of Religious Instruction," *LBIYB*, II, 1957, pp. 98–118. [308]

———, "The Seminary of Breslau," *HJ*, XVII, 1954, pp. 121–42. [309]

Kobler, Franz, Ed., *A Treasury of Jewish Letters: Letters from the Famous and the Humble*, London, East and West Library; New York, Farrar, Straus and Young, 1952, 2 vols.¶ [310]

Kochan, Lionel, Ed., *The Jew in Soviet Russia since 1917*, London, Oxford University Press, 1970.†* [311]

Koen (Coen), E. M., and W. Chr. Pieterse, "Notarial Records in Amsterdam Relating to the Portuguese Jews in that Town up to 1639," *Studia Rosenthaliana*, I, No. 1, January 1967, pp. 109–15 (continued in subsequent issues under Coen). [312]

Kohler, Max J., "Civil Status of the Jews in Colonial New York," *PAJHS*, VI, 1897, pp. 81–106. [313]

———, "The Doctrine that Christianity Is a Part of the Common Law and Its Recent Judicial Overthrow in England, with Particular Reference to Jewish Rights," *PAJHS*, XXI, 1928, pp. 105–34. [314]

———, "Educational Reforms in Europe in Their Relations to Jewish Emancipation, 1778–1878," *Jewish Forum*, II, 1919, pp. 704–15, 775–88. [315]

———, *Jewish Rights at the Congress of Vienna (1814–1815) and Aix-la-Chapelle (1818)*, New York, American Jewish Committee, 1918 (reprinted from *PAJHS*, XXVI, 1918). [315a]

———, "Phases in the History of Religious Liberty in America, with Particular Reference to the Jews, I-II," *PAJHS*, XI, 1903, pp. 53–73; XIII, 1905, pp. 7–36. [316]

Kohler, Kaufman, "The Mission of Israel and Its Application to Modern Times," CCAR, *Yearbook*, XXIX, 1919, pp. 265–305. [317]

Kohn, Hans, "Introduction," to Ginzberg, Asher, *Nationalism and the Jewish Ethic. Basic Writings of Ahad Ha'am*, Edited by Hans Kohn, New York, Herzl Press, 1962. [318]

Kolatt, I., "Theories on Israeli Nationalism," *In the Dispersion*, No. 7, 1967, pp. 13–50. [318a]

Koltun, Liz, Ed., *The Jewish Woman: An Anthology*, Waltham, Mass., Response, 1973 (*Response*, No. 18, Summer 1973).†* [318b]

Kopald, Louis J., "The Friendship of Moses Mendelssohn and Lessing and its Relation to the Good Will Movement between Jews and Non-Jews,"

CCAR, *Yearbook,* XXXIX, 1929, pp. 370–401. [319]

Korn, Bertram Wallace, *The Early Jews of New Orleans,* Waltham, Mass., American Jewish Historical Society, 1969. [319a]

Kramer, Meyer, "Is America a Christian Country? Sunday Closing Laws vs. Sabbath Observing Jews," *Tradition,* IV, No. 1, 1951, pp. 5–20. [319b]

Kranzler, George, *Williamsburgh: A Jewish Community in Transition,* New York, Feldheim, 1961. [319c]

Kreutzberger, Max, *see, SLBI.*

Kuhn, Arthur K., "Hugo Grotius and the Emancipation of the Jews in Holland," *PAJHS,* XXXI, 1928, pp. 173–80. [320]

Kurzweil, Z. E., *Modern Trends in Jewish Education,* New York, Thomas Yoseloff, 1964. [321]

Ladd, Everett Carill, Jr., 353.

Lamberti, Marjorie, "The Attempt to Form a Jewish Bloc; Jewish Notables and Politics in Wilhelmian Germany," *Central European History,* III, 1970, pp. 73–93. [322]

Lamin, N., "The Ideology of the Neturei Karta, According to the Satmarer Version," *Tradition, XII,* No. 2, Fall 1971, pp. 38–53. [323]

Landa, M. J., *The Jew in Drama,* London, P. S. King & Son, 1926. [324]

Landau, Jacob M., *Jews in Nineteenth Century Egypt,* New York, New York University Press, 1969. [325]

Landman, Leo, *Jewish Law in the Diaspora: Confrontation and Accommodation,* Philadelphia, Dropsie College, 1968. [325a]

Langmuir, Gavin I., "Majority History and Post-Biblical Jews," *Journal of the History of Ideas,* XXVII, 1966, pp. 343–64. [326]

———, "Tradition, History, and Prejudice," *JSS,* XXX, 1968, pp. 157–68. [327]

Langnas, Isaak A., and Barton Shalad, *Studies in Honor of Mair Jose Bernadete: Essays in Hispanic and Sephardic Culture,* New York, La America, 1965.† [327a]

Laqueur, Walter, "The German Youth Movement and the Jewish Question," *LBIYB,* VI, 1961, pp. 193–205. [328]

———, *A History of Zionism,* New York, Holt, Rinehart and Winston, 1972. [329]

———, *Out of the Ruins of Europe,* New York, Library Press, 1971. [330]

Laqueur, Walter Ze'ev and George L. Mosse, Eds., *The Left-Wing Intellectuals between the Wars, 1919–1939,* New York, Harper Torchbooks, 1966 (First published as Vol. I, No. 2, 1966 of the *Journal of Contemporary History*). [331]

Lasswell, W. D., 481.

Lazerson, Max M., "The Jewish Minorities in the Baltic Countries," *JSS,* III, 1941, pp. 273–84. [332]

————, "The Jews and the Latvian Parliament," *The Jews in Latvia*, pp. 21–77. [333]

Lehrmann, Chanan, "The Image of the Jew Portrayed in Literature," *Proceedings of the Fifth World Congress of Jewish Studies, 3–11 August 1969*, Jerusalem, World Union of Jewish Studies, III, 1972, pp. 17–25.† [334]

Leiser, Joseph, *American Judaism: The Religion and Religious Institutions of the Jewish People in the United States*, New York, Bloch, 1925. [334a]

Lelyveld, Arthur, *Atheism is Dead: A Jewish Response to Radical Theology*, Cleveland, World, 1968. [334b]

Lendvai, Paul, *Antisemitism without Jews: Communist Eastern Europe*, New York, Doubleday, 1971. [335]

Lenin, Vladimir I., *Lenin on the Jewish Question*, New York, International Publishers, 1934. [336]

Lenn, Theodore, *Rabbi and Synagogue in Reform Judaism*, New York, Central Conference of American Rabbis, 1972. [336a]

Leo Baeck Institute, *Studies, see SLBI.*

Leon, Abram, *The Jewish Question: A Marxist Interpretation*, New York, Merit, 1970. [336b]

Leschnitzer, Adolf, *The Magic Background of Modern Anti-Semitism. An Analysis of the German-Jewish Relationship*, New York, International University Press, 1956. [337]

Lestchinsky, Jacob, "The Anti-Jewish Program: Tsarist Russia, the Third Reich and Independent Poland," *JSS*, III, 1941, pp. 141–58. [338]

————, *Crisis, Catastrophe and Survival*, New York, World Jewish Congress, 1948. [339]

————, 191.

Levenberg, I., 85.

Levine, Ephraim, Ed., *The Jewish Heritage; A Symposium*, London, Valentine Mitchell, 1955.† [339a]

Levy, Felix, "Moses Mendelssohn's Ideals of Religion and their Relation to Reform Judaism," CCAR, *Yearbook*, XXXIX, 1929, pp. 351–69. [340]

Levy, Harry W., 448a.

Levin, Nora, *The Holocaust: The Destruction of European Jewry 1933–1945*, New York, Thomas Y. Crowell, 1968.* [341]

Levitats, Isaac, *The Jewish Community in Russia, 1772–1844*, New York, Columbia University Press, 1943.* [342]

Levy, Hyman, *Jews and the National Question*, (Revised American edition), New York, Cameron Associates, 1958. [343]

Levy, Isaac Jack, Ed., *American Society of Sephardic Studies: Series I, 1968–1969*, New York, Yeshiva University, Sephardic Studies Program, 1969.† [343a]

Lewin, Kurt, *Resolving Social Conflict*, New York, Harper and Row, 1948.† [344]

Lewkowitz, Albert, "The Significance of 'Wissenschaft des Judentums' for the Development of Judaism," *HJ*, XVI, 1954, pp. 81–84. [345]

Lichtheim, George, "Socialism and the Jews," *Dissent*, XV, 1958, pp. 314–42. [346]

Liebeschutz, Hans, "German Radicalism and the Formation of Jewish Political Attitudes during the Early Part of the Nineteenth Century," Altmann, Ed., *Studies* [as in 10], pp. 141–70. [347]

———, "Max Wiener's Reinterpretation of Liberal Judaism," *LBIYB*, V, 1960, pp. 35–57. [348]

———, "Treitschke and Mommsen on Jewry and Judaism," *LBIYB*, VII, 1962, pp. 153–82. [349]

Liebman, Seymour B., "Anti-Semitism in Martinique in the 17th Century," *Tradition*, X, No. 4, Fall 1969, pp. 40–47. [350]

———, *The Jews in New Spain: Faith, Flame and the Inquisition*, Coral Gables, Fla., University of Miami, 1970. [351a]

Lipman, V. D., *Social History of the Jews in England, 1850–1950*, London, Watts and Co., 1954. [352]

Lipset, Seymour Martin, "The Socialism of Fools; the Left, the Jews and Israel," *Encounter*, XXXIII, December 1969, pp. 24–35. [353]

Lipset, Seymour Martin, and Everett Carill Ladd, Jr., "Jewish Academics in the United States: Their Achievements, Culture and Politics," *AJYB*, LXXII, 1970–71, pp. 89–128. [353a]

Lipton, Marcus, "The Jewish Question in Anglo-Swiss Diplomacy," JHSE, *Tr., Sessions 1921–1923*, X, pp. 207–20. [354]

Liptzin, Solomon, *Germany's Stepchildren*, Philadelphia, The Jewish Publication Society of America, 1948.* [355]

Littmann, Ellen, "Saul Ascher: First Theorist of Progressive Judaism," *LBIYB*, V, 1960, pp. 107–21. [356]

Litvin, Baruch, Comp., *Jewish Identity: Modern Responsa and Opinions on the Registration of Children of Mixed Marriages; David Ben-Gurion's Query to Leaders of World Jewry; A Documentary Compilation*, Edited by Sidney B. Hoenig, New York, Feldheim, 1965.† [357]

Loewenstein, Rudolph M., *Christians and Jews: A Psychoanalytic Study*, New York, International Universities Press, 1951. [357a]

Longworth, Philip, Ed., *Confrontations with Judaism: A Symposium*, London, A. Blond, 1967.† [358]

Lowenthal, Marvin, *The Jews of Germany*, New York, Longmans, Green, 1936; reprint, Russell and Russell, 1970. [359]

Lumer, Hyman, *Zionism: Its Role in World Politics*, New York, International Publishers, 1973. [359a]

Luzzati, Luigi, *God in Freedom. Studies in the Relations between Church and State,* New York, Macmillan, 1930. [360]

[Magnus, Laurie], *Aspects of the Jewish Question by a Quarterly Reviewer,* London, J. Murray, 1902; New York, Bloch, 1902. [361]

Margalith, Aaron M., 2.

McCagg, W. O., *Jewish Nobles and Geniuses in Modern Hungary,* New York, Columbia University Press, 1972. [361a]

Mahler, Raphael, *A History of Modern Jewry, 1780–1815,* New York, Schocken, 1971.* [362]

————, *Jewish Emancipation: A Selection of Documents,* New York, American Jewish Committee, 1941.¶ [363]

Malachy, Yonah, "Seventh-Day Adventists and Zionism," *Herzl Year Book,* VI, 1964–65, pp. 265–301. [364]

Manor, Alex, Ed., *The Jews and the National Question,* Tel Aviv, Ichud Habonim, 1964.

Maor, I., "The Communal Image of Latvian Jewry," *The Jews in Latvia,* pp. 78–93. [365]

Marcus, Jacob R., *The Colonial American Jew, 1492–1776,* Detroit, Wayne State University Press, 1970, 3 vols.* [366]

————, *The Jew in the Medieval World: A Source Book,* Cleveland, Meridian Press, 1961¶ [367]

————, "The Modern Religion of Moses Hart," *HUCA,* XX, 1947, pp. 585–615. [368]

Margolis, Max L., "The Mendelssohnian Programme," *JQR,* XVII, 1905, pp. 531–544. [369]

Marmorstein, Emile, *Heaven at Bay: The Jewish Kulturkampf in the Holy Land,* London, Oxford University Press, 1969. [369a]

Marrus, Michael R., *The Politics of Assimilation: A Study of the French Jewish Community at the Time of the Dreyfus Affair,* New York, Oxford University Press, 1971.* [370]

Martin, Bernard, Ed., *Contemporary Reform Jewish Thought,* Chicago, Quadrangle, 1968.† [371]

————, *Great Twentieth Century Jewish Philosophers with Selections From Their Writings,* New York, Macur, 1969.† [372]

Marx, Alexander, "Societies for the Promotion of the Study of Jewish History," *PAJHS,* XX, 1911, pp. 1–9. [373]

Massing, Paul W., *Rehearsal for Destruction: A Study of Political Anti-Semitism in Imperial Germany,* New York, Harper and Brothers, 1949.* [374]

Mayer, Gustav, "Early German Socialism and Jewish Emancipation," *JSS,* I, 1939, pp. 409–22. [375]

Mayer, Peter; Bernard D. Weinryb; Eugene Duchinsky; and Nicholas Sylvain,

The Jews in the Soviet Satellites, Syracuse, Syracuse University Press, 1953.† [376]

Medding, P. Y., *From Assimilation to Group Survival: A Political and Sociological Study of an Australian Jewish Community,* Melbourne, F. W. Cheshire, 1968.* [377]

Meijer, Jacob, "Hugo Grotius' Remonstrantie," *JSS,* XVII, 1955, pp. 91–104. [378]

Meissner, Frank, "German Jews of Prague: A Quest for Self-Realization," *AJHQ,* L, 1960–61, pp. 98–120. [379]

Melber, Jehuda, *Hermann Cohen's Philosophy of Judaism,* New York, Jonathan David, 1968. [380]

Memmi, Albert, *The Liberation of the Jew,* New York, Orion Press, 1966. [381]

Mendelsohn, Ezra, "Jewish Assimilation in Lvov; The Case of Wilhelm Feldman," *Slavic Review,* XXVIII, 1969, pp. 577–90. [382]

———, "The Jewish Socialist Movement and the Second Internationale, 1899–1915; The Struggle for Recognition," *JSS,* XXVI, 1964, pp. 131–45. [383]

———, "The Politics of Agudas Yisroel in Inter-War Poland," *Soviet Jewish Affairs,* II, No. 2, 1972, pp. 47–60. [383a]

Mendelssohn, Moses, *Jerusalem and Other Jewish Writings,* Translated and Edited by Alfred Jospe, New York, Schocken, 1969. [384]

Menes, A., "The Conversion Movement in Prussia 'During the First Half of the 19th Century," *YAJSS,* VI, 1951, pp. 187–205. [385]

Meyer, Michael A., "Christian Influence on Early Reform Judaism," in *Studies in Jewish Bibliography, History and Literature in Honor of I. Edward Kiev,* Edited by Charles Berlin, New York, Ktav, 1971, pp. 289–303.† [386]

———, "The Great Debate on Antisemitism: Jewish Reaction to New Hostility in Germany, 1879–81," *LBIYB,* XI, 1966, pp.137–70. [387]

———, *"The Origins of the Modern Jew; Jewish Identity and European Culture in Germany, 1749–1824,"* Detroit, Wayne State University Press, 1967.* [388]

Meyer, Paul H., "The Attitude of the Enlightenment towards the Jew," *Studies on Voltaire and the Eighteenth Century,* XXVI, 1963, pp. 1163–1205. [388a]

Michaeli, Z., "The Cultural Autonomy and Jewish School System," *The Jews in Latvia,* pp. 186–216. [389]

Midstream magazine, 295.

The Midstream Reader, 571b.

Migration and Settlement, 412.

Millgram, Abraham Ezra, Ed., *Great Jewish Ideas,* Washington, D. C., B'nai B'rith, 1969.‡ [389a]

Modder, Montague Frank, *The Jew in the Literature of England to the End of the Nineteenth Century*, Philadelphia, JPSA, 139. [389b]

Montefiore, Claude G., "Assimilation: Good and Bad," *Contemporary Jewish Record*, VII, 1944, pp. 211–24. [390]

Morgenthau, Hans J., "The Tragedy of German-Jewish Liberalism," *SLBI*, pp. 45–58. [391]

Morgenstern, Friedrich, "Hardenberg and the Emancipation of Franconian Jewry," *JSS*, XV, 1953, pp. 253-74. [392]

Morin, Edgar et al., *Rumour in Orleans*, New York, Pantheon, 1971. [393]

Morris, Maxwell H., "Roger Williams and the Jews," *American Jewish Archives*, III, No. 2, January 1951, pp. 24–27. [394]

Morton, Frederic, *The Rothschilds: A Family Portrait*, New York, Atheneum, 1962. [395]

Moskovits, Aaron, *Jewish Education in Hungary (1848–1948)*, New York, Bloch Publishing Company for Dropsie College, 1964. [395a]

Mosse, George L., *The Crisis of German Ideology: Intellectual Origins of the Third Reich*, New York, Grosset and Dunlap, 1964. [396]

——, "German Socialists and the Jewish Question in the Weimar Republic," *LBIYB*, XVI, 1971, pp. 123–51. [397]

——, *Germans and Jews. The Right, the Left, and the Search for a "Third Force" in Pre-Nazi Germany*, New York, Howard Fertig, 1970. [398]

——, "The Image of the Jew in German Popular Culture: Felix Dahn and Gustav Freytag," *LBIYB*, II, 1957, pp. 218–27. [399]

——, "Left-Wing Intellectuals and the Jewish Problem in the 'Thirties and in the 'Sixties," *Dispersion and Unity*, No. 17–18, Jerusalem, 1973, pp. 106–16. [400]

Mosse, George L., 331.

Mosse, Werner E., "A. F. Kerensky and the Emancipation of Russian Jewry," *BSJA*, No. 6, Dec. 1970, pp. 33–38. [401]

——, "The Conflict of Liberalism and Nationalism and its Effect on German Jewry," *LBIYB*, XV, 1970, pp. 125–39. [402]

Myers, Maurice, "Some Miscellaneous Sidelights on Anglo-Jewish Emancipation," JHSE, *Tr., Sessions 1908–1910*, 1912, pp. 240–46. [403]

Namier, L. B., *Conflicts: Studies in Contemporary History*, New York, Macmillan, 1943.† [403a]

Narkiss, Bezalel, 507.

Necheles, Ruth F., "The Abbé Gregoire and the Jews," *JSS*, XXXIII, 1971, pp. 120–40. [404]

Nedava, Joseph, *Trotsky and the Jews*, Philadelphia, JPSA, 1972. [405]

Netanyahu, B., *Don Isaac Abravanel, Statesman and Philosopher*, Philadelphia, JPSA, 1953. [406]

——, Introduction to, Pinsker, Leo, *Road to Freedom. Writings and*

Addresses, New York, Scopus Publishing Co., 1944.¶ [407]

————, *The Marranos of Spain from the Late XIVth to the Early XVIth Century According to Contemporary Hebrew Sources,* New York, American Academy for Jewish Research, 1966. [408]

Neuman, Abraham A., *The Jews in Spain,* Philadelphia, JPSA, 1961; New York, Octagon Books, 1970, 2 vols. [408a]

Neusner, Jacob, Ed., *The Study of Judaism: Bibliographical Essays,* New York, Anti-Defamation League of B'nai B'rith and Ktav, 1972.* [409]

————, *Understanding Jewish Theology: Classical Issues and Modern Perspectives,* New York, Ktav and Anti-Defamation League of B'nai B'rith, 1973.† [410]

Newman, Aubrey, "The Expulsion of the Jews from Prague in 1745 and British Foreign Policy," JHSE, *Tr., Sessions 1968–69,* XXII, 1970, pp. 30–37. [411]

Newman, Aubrey, Rapporteur, *Migration and Settlement, Proceedings of the Anglo-American Historical Conference held in London jointly by the Jewish Historical Society of England and the American Jewish Historical Society, July 1970,* London, The Jewish Historical Society of England, 1971. [412]

Newman, Louis Israel, *Jewish Influences on Christian Reform Movements,* New York, Columbia University Press, 1925. [412a]

Niewyk, Donald L., "The Economic and Cultural Role of the Jews in the Weimar Republic," LBIYB, XVI, 1971, pp. 163–73. [413]

————, *see also* 537, 662.

Noveck, Simon, Ed., *Contemporary Jewish Thought,* Washington, D. C., B'nai B'rith Department of Adult Jewish Education, 1963.† [414]

————, *Great Jewish Thinkers of the Twentieth Century,* Washington, D.C., B'nai B'rith Department of Adult Jewish Education, 1960.† [415]

Oelsner, Toni, "The Place of the Jews in Economic History as Viewed by German Scholars," LBIYB, VII, 1962, pp. 183–212. [416]

Oppenheim, Samuel, "The Early History of the Jews in New York, 1654–1664 . . . ," PAJHS, XVIII, 1909, pp. 1–91.¶ [417]

————, "More About Jacob Barsimson, the First Jewish Settler in New York," PAJHS, XXIX, 1925, pp. 39–52.¶ [418]

Orlinsky, Harry, "On Toynbee's Use of the Term *Syriac* for One of His Societies," *In the Time of Harvest. Essays in Honor of Abba Hillel Silver on the Occasion of his Seventieth Birthday,* Edited by Daniel Jeremy Silver et al., New York, Macmillan, 1963, pp. 255–69. [419]

Osborne, Sidney, *Germany and Her Jews,* London, Soncino, 1939.* [420]

Osterman, Nathan, "The Controversy over the Proposed Readmission of the Jews to England (1655)," JSS, III, 1941, pp. 301–28. [421]

Ottenheimer, Hilde, "The Disappearance of Jewish Communities in Germany, 1900–1938," *JSS*, III, 1941, pp. 189–206. [422]

Ozer, Charles L., "Jewish Education in the Transition from Ghetto to Emancipation," *HJ*, IX, 1947, pp. 75–94. [423]

Parkes, James, *Anti-Semitism: A Concise World History*, Chicago, Quadrangle, 1960. [424]

———, *Conflict of the Church and the Synagogue: A Study in the Origins of Anti-Semitism*, Cleveland, World; Philadelphia, JPSA; New York, Quadrangle Paperback, 1961. [424a]

———, *The Emergence of the Jewish Problem 1878–1939*, Westport, Conn., Greenwood Press, 1970 (reprint of 1946 ed.). [425]

Patai, Raphael, "The Iglesia de Dios and Zionism," *Herzl Year Book*, VI, 1964–65, pp. 303–10. [426]

———, *Tents of Jacob; The Diaspora Yesterday and Today*, Englewood Cliffs, N. J., Prentice-Hall, 1971. [427]

———, Ed., *Encyclopedia of Zionism and Israel*, New York, Herzl Press, 1971, 2 vols.† [428]

Patinkin, Don, "Mercantilism and the Readmission of the Jews to England (1665), *JSS*, VIII, pp. 161–78. [429]

Patterson, David, "Moses Mendelssohn's Concept of Tolerance," in *Between East and West. Essays Dedicated to the Memory of Bella Horovitz*, Edited by A. Altmann, London, East and West Library, 1958, pp. 149–63. [430]

Pelli, Moshe, "The Impact of Deism on the Hebrew Literature of the Enlightenment in Germany," *Eighteenth Century Studies*, VI No. 1, Fall 1972, pp. 35–59. [431]

———, "Intimations of Religious Reform in the German Hebrew Haskalah Literature," *JSS*, XXXII, 1970, pp. 3–13. [431a]

Perry, T. W., *Public Opinion, Propaganda, and Politics in Eighteenth Century England: A Study of the Jew Bill of 1753*, Cambridge, Mass., Harvard University Press, 1962.* [432]

Peskin, Alan, "England's Jewish Naturalization Bill of 1753," *HJ*, XIX, 1957, pp. 3–28. [433]

Petuchowski, Jacob J., "The Limits of 'People-Centered' Judaism," *Commentary*, XXVII, 1959, pp. 387–94. [434]

———, "Manuals and Catechisms of the Jewish Religion in the Early Period of Emancipation," Altmann, Ed., *Studies* [as in 10], pp. 47–64. [435]

———, *Prayerbook Reform in Europe: The Liturgy of European Liberal and Reform Judaism*, New York, World Union for Progressive Judaism, 1968.* [436]

Pieterse, 312.

Philipson, David, *The Reform Movement in Judaism*. A Reissue with an Introduction by Solomon B. Freehof, New York, Ktav, 1967. [437]

Philipson, Johanna, 23.

Phillips, Henry E. I., "An Early Stuart Judaising Sect," JHSE, *Tr., Sessions 1939–1945*, XV, pp. 63–72. [438]

Pilch, Judah, 275.

Pinsker, Leo, 407.

Pinsker, Polly, "English Opinion and Jewish Emancipation (1830–1860)," *JSS*, XIV, 1952, pp. 51–96. [439]

Pinson, Koppel S., "German Pietism and the Jews," in *Freedom and Reason*, pp. 397–412. [439a]

———, "The National Theories of Simon Dubnow," *JSS*, X, 1948, pp. 335–58. [440]

———, Ed., *Essays on Anti-Semitism*, New York, Conference on Jewish Relations, 1942; 2nd Ed., 1946.† [441]

———, 127.

Plaidy, Jean, *The Spanish Inquisition: Its Rise, Growth and End*, New York, Citadel, 1967. [442]

Pool, David de Sola, *Portraits Etched in Stone*, New York, Columbia University Press, 1952. [443]

Pool, David de Sola and Tamar, *An Old Faith in the New World: Portraits of Shearith Israel 1654–1954*, New York, Columbia University Press, 1955. [443a]

Plaut, W. Gunther, *The Rise of Reform Judaism*, New York, World Union for Progressive Judaism, 1965. [444]

Poliakov, Leon, *The History of Antisemitism*, Translated by Richard Howard, New York, Vanguard, 1965. [445]

Polish, David, *The Higher Freedom: A New Turning Point in Jewish History*, Chicago, Quadrangle, 1965. [445a]

Poll, Solomon, *The Hassidic Community of Williamsburgh*, New York, Free Press of Glencoe, 1962. [445b]

Pool, David de Sola, *see supra*, 443, 443a.

Pool, Tamar, [446.]

Poor, Harold L., *Kurt Tucholsky and the Ordeal of Germany, 1914–1935*, New York, Scribner's, 1968. [447]

Popkin, R. H., "The Historical Significance of Sephardic Judaism in 17th Century Amsterdam," *The American Sephardi*, V, No. 1–2, Autumn 1971, pp. 18–27. [448]

Porter, Jack Nusan, and Levy, Harry W., Eds., *Jewish Radicalism: A Selected Anthology*, New York, Grove, 1973.† [448a]

Posener, Solomon V., *Adolphe Cremieux: A Biography*, Philadelphia, JPSA, 1940. [449]

———, "The Immediate Economic and Social Effects of the Emancipation of the Jews in France (On the Occasion of the 150th Anniversary of the French Revolution)," *JSS,* I, 1939, pp. 281–93. [450]

Priluker, Yakov, *The New Israelite, or Rabbi Shalom on the Shores of the Black Sea,* London, Simkin Marshall, et al., 1903. [451]

———, *Under the Czar and Queen Victoria; The Experiences of a Russian Reformer,* London, J. Nisbet and Co., 1895. [452]

Prinz, Joachim, *The Dilemma of the Modern Jew,* Boston, Little, Brown, 1962. [453]

Pulzer, P. G. J., "The Development of Political Antisemitism in Austria," in *Jews of Austria,* pp. 429–43. [454]

———, *The Rise of Political Anti-Semitism in Germany and Austria,* New York, John Wiley, 1964.* [455]

Quarterly Reviewer, The, 361.

Rabinowicz, Aharon Moshe, "The Jewish Minority [in Czechoslovakia]," *Jews in Czechoslovakia,* I, pp. 155–265. [456]

Rabinowicz, Harry M., *The Legacy of Polish Jewry 1919–1939: A History of Polish Jews in the Inter-War Years 1919–1939,* New York, Yoseloff, 1965. [457]

Radcliffe, Barrye M., "Some Jewish Problems in the Early Careers of Emile and Isaac Perèyre," *JSS,* XXXIV, 1972, pp. 189–206. [458]

Raisin, Jacob I., *Gentile Reactions to Jewish Ideas with Special Reference to Proselytes,* Edited by Herman Hailperin, New York, Philosophical Library, 1953. [459]

Raisin, Jacob S., *The Haskalah Movement in Russia,* Philadelphia, JPSA, 1913; Westport, Conn., Greenwood Press, 1972. [460]

Rawidowicz, Simon, "Israel: The Ever-Dying People," *Judaism,* XVI, 1967, pp. 423–33. [461]

Reichmann, Eva G., *Hostages of Civilization; The Social Sources of National Socialist Anti-Semitism,* Boston, Beacon Press, 1951; Westport, Conn., Greenwood Press, 1970.* [462]

Reissner, Hanns G., "The German-American Jews (1800–1850)," *LBIYB,* X, 1965, pp. 57–116.

———, "Rebellious Dilemma: Case Histories of Eduard Gans and Some of His Partisans," *LBIYB,* II, 1957, 179–93. [464]

Reitlinger, Gerald, "The Changed Face of English Jewry at the End of the Eighteenth Century," *JHSE, Tr., Session 1969–1970,* XXIII *and Mis.,* Part VIII, 1971, pp. 34–43. [465]

———, *The Final Solution: The Attempt to Exterminate the Jews of Europe, 1939–1945,* South Brunswick, N. J., A. S. Barnes, 1965. [466]

Remember the Days. Zekhor yemot olam; Essays on Anglo-Jewish History Presented to Cecil Roth by Members of the Council of The Jewish His-

torical Society of England, Edited by John M. Shaftesley, London, JHSE, 1966. [467]

Rhee, *see* Song Nai Rhee.

Ricks, Eldin, "Zionism and the Mormon Church," *Herzl Year Book,* V, 1963, pp. 147–74. [468]

Richards, Bernard G., "Correspondence: Jewish National Minority Rights," *JQR,* NS., XXXVI, 1945–46, pp. 89–98; Reply by Solomon Zeitlin, pp. 98–103. [469]

Rinott, Moshe, "Gabriel Riesser—Fighter for Jewish Emancipation," *LBIYB,* VII, 1962, pp. 11–38. [470]

Rischin, Moses, "The Early Attitudes of the American Jewish Community to Zionism (1906–1922)," *AJHQ,* XLIX, 1959–60, pp. 188–201. [471]

———, "The Jews and the Liberal Tradition in America," *AJHQ,* LI, 1961, pp. 4–29. [472]

Rivkin, Ellis, "The Diaspora: Its Historical Significance," *SLBI,* pp. 265–318. [473]

———, *Leon Da Modena and Kol Sakhal,* Cincinnati, Hebrew Union College Press, 1952. [474]

———, *The Shaping of Jewish History: A Radical New Interpretation,* New York, Scribner's, 1971. [475]

Roback, A. A., *Jewish Influence in Modern Thought,* Cambridge, Mass., Sci-Art, 1929. [476]

Robinson, Jacob, "From Protection of Minorities to Promotion of Human Rights," *JYIL,* 1948, pp. 115–51. [477]

Robinson, Jacob, et al., *Were the Minorities Treaties a Failure?,* New York, Institute of Jewish Affairs, 1943. [478]

Robinson, Nehemia, "Reparations and Restitution in International Law as Affecting Jews," *JYIL,* 1948, pp. 186–205. [479]

Rodinson, Maxime, *Israel, a Colonial-Settler State?,* New York, Monad Press, 1973. [479a]

Rogger, Hans, "The Beilis Case; Anti-Semitism and Politics in the Reign of Nicholas II," *Slavic Review,* XXV, 1966, pp. 215–29. [480]

Rogow, Arnold A., Ed., *The Jew in a Gentile World: An Anthology of Writings about Jews by Non-Jews,* with an Introduction by C. P. Snow and an Epilogue by Harold W. D. Lasswell, New York, Macmillan, 1961.†¶ [481]

Rose, Constance H., "New Information on the Life of Joseph Nasi, Duke of Naxos; The Venetian Phase," *JQR,* NS, LX, 1970, pp. 330–44. [481a]

Rose, Peter I., Ed., *The Ghetto and Beyond; Essays on Jewish Life in America,* New York, Random, 1969.† [481b]

Rosenbaum, Eduard, "Ferdinand Lassalle—A Historiographical Meditation," *LBIYB,* IX, 1964, 122–30. [482]

————, "Miscellany: Sephardim at the Lower Elbe," *LBIYB*, IV, 1959, pp. 260–72. [483]

Rosenberg, Edgar, *From Shylock to Svengali: Jewish Stereotypes in English Fiction,* Stanford, Cal., Stanford University Press, 1960. [484]

Rosenberg, Stuart E., *America Is Different: The Search for Jewish Identity,* New York, Nelson, 1964. [484a]

————, *The Jewish Community in Canada:* Vol. I: *A History,* Toronto, McClelland Stewart, 1970. [484b]

Rosenblum, Noah H., "Hegelian Juridicial Dialectics as a Matrix for Jewish Law," *REJ-HJ,* CXXII, 1963, pp. 75–122. [485]

————, "Religious and Secular Co-Equality in S. R. Hirsch's Educational Theory," *JSS,* XXIV, 1962, pp. 223–47. [486]

Rosenheim, Jacob, "The Historical Significance of the Struggle for Secession from the Frankfurt Jewish Community," *HJ,* X, 1948, pp. 135–46. [487]

Rosenstock-Huessy, Eugen, Ed., *Judaism Despite Christianity: The Letters on Christianity and Judaism between Eugen Rosenstock Huessy and Franz Rosenzweig,* University, Alabama, University of Alabama Press, 1969. [488]

Rosenthal, Erich, "Trends in the Jewish Population in Germany, 1910–1939," *JSS,* VI, 1944, pp. 233–74. [489]

Rosenthal, Frank, "The Rise of Christian Hebraism in the Sixteenth Century," *HJ,* VII, 1945, pp. 167–91. [490]

Rosenzweig, Franz, 488.

Rosmarin, Trude Weiss, *Judaism and Christianity: The Differences,* New York, Jonathan David, 1968. [491]

Rotenstreich, Nathan, "An Examination of Jewish Auto-Emancipation," *Forum for the Problems of Zionism, World Jewry and the State of Israel,* No. 2, April 1956, pp. 7-18. [492]

————, "For and Against Emancipation; The Bruno Bauer Controversy," *LBIYB,* IV, 1959, pp. 3–36. [493]

————, "Hegel's Image of Judaism," *JSS,* XV, 1953, pp. 33–52. [494]

————, *Jewish Philosophy in Modern Times, From Mendelssohn to Rosenzweig,* New York, Holt, Rinehart and Winston, 1968. [495]

————, "Mendelssohn's Political Philosophy," *LBIYB,* XI, 1966, pp. 28–41. [496]

————, *The Recurring Pattern: Studies in Anti-Judaism in Modern Thought,* New York, Horizon Press, 1964. [497]

————, "The Revival of the Fossil Remnant—or Toynbee and Jewish Nationalism," *JSS,* XXIV, 1962, pp. 131–43. [498]

————, *Tradition and Reality: The Impact of History on Modern Jewish Thought,* New York, Random House, 1971. [499]

Roth, Cecil, "Are the Jews Unassimilable?" *JSS,* III, 1941, pp. 3–14. [500]

————, *Essays and Portraits in Anglo-Jewish History*, Philadelphia, JPSA, 1962.† [501]

————, *Gleanings*, New York, Bloch, 1967.† [501a]

————, *A History of the Jews in England*, ed. 3, London, Oxford-Clarendon Press, 1964. [502]

————, *The History of the Jews of Italy*, Philadelphia, JPSA, 1946. [503]

————, *A History of the Marranos*, Philadelphia, JPSA, 1959. [504]

————, *The House of Nasi: Dona Gracia*, Philadelphia, JPSA, 1947. [505]

————, *The House of Nasi: Duke of Naxos*, Philadelphia, JPSA, 1948. [506]

————, *Jewish Art, An Illustrated History*, Revised edition by Bezalel Narkiss, Greenwich, Conn., New York Graphic Society, 1971. [507]

————, *The Jewish Contribution to Civilization*, Cincinnati, Union of American Hebrew Congregations, 1938. [508]

————, "The Jews in the English Universities," JHSE, *Mis.*, IV, 1942, pp. 102–15. [509]

————, *The Jews in the Renaissance*, Philadelphia, JPSA, 1959. [510]

————, "The Jews of Malta," JHSE, *Tr.*, XII, *Sessions 1928–1931*, pp. 187–251. [511]

————, *A Life of Menasseh Ben Israel*, Philadelphia, JPSA, 1934. [512]

————, *The Magnificent Rothschilds*, London, R. Hale, 1939. [513]

————, "Marranos and Racial Antisemitism," *JSS*, II, 1940, pp. 239–48. [514]

————, *The Resettlement of the Jews in England in 1656*, London, Jewish Historical Society of England, 1960. [515]

————, *The Spanish Inquisition*, London, 1937; New York, W. W. Norton, 1964. [515a]

————, "Were the Sephardim Hidalgos?" *Commentary*, XX, 1955, pp. 125–31. [516]

————, Ed., *Anglo-Jewish Letters (1158–1917)*, London, Soncino, 1938. [517]

————, 467, 678.

Roth, Leon, *Jewish Thought as a Factor in Civilization*, Paris, UNESCO, 1954. [518]

Rothenberg, Joshua, *The Jewish Religion in the Soviet Union*, New York, Ktav; Waltham, Mass., Brandeis University, 1972. [518a]

Rothkirchen, Livia, "Slovakia: I, 1848–1918," and "Slovakia: II, 1918–1938," in *Jews in Czechoslovakia*, I, pp. 72–124. [519]

Rothkoff, Aaron, *Bernard Revel, Builder of American Jewish Orthodoxy*, Philadelphia, JPSA, 1972. [520]

Rothmuller, Aron Marko, *The Music of the Jews*, New York, The Beechhurst Press, 1954. [521]

Rothschild, Fritz, and Seymour Siegel, "Modern Jewish Thought," in Neusner, Ed., *The Study of Judaism*, pp. 113–84 (A Bibliography).* [522]

Rubin, Israel, *Satmar: An Island in the City*, New York, Quadrangle Books, 1972. [523]

Rubinstein, Richard L., *After Auschwitz*, New York, Bobbs-Merrill Co., 1966. [523a]

Rudavsky, David, *Modern Jewish Religious Movements: A History of Emancipation and Adjustment*, New York, Behrman, 1967 (paperback). [524]

Runes, Dagobert, Ed., *The Hebrew Impact on Western Civilization*, New York, Philosophical Library, 1951.† [525]

———, *The Hebrew Impact on Western Civilization*, Abridged Edition, New York, Philosophical Library, 1957.† [526]

Rürup, Reinhard, "Jewish Emancipation and Bourgeois Society," *LBIYB*, XIV, 1969, pp. 67–91. [527]

Ruppin, Arthur, *The Jewish Fate and Future*, London, Macmillan & Co., 1940. [528]

———, *The Jews in the Modern World*, London, Macmillan and Co., 1934. [529]

———, *The Jews of To-Day*, New York, Henry Holt, 1913. [530]

Russian Jewry, 173, 193.

Sachar, Howard, *The Course of Modern Jewish History*, New York, Dell, 1958 (Delta Paperback, 1968).* [531]

Sack, B. G., *History of the Jews in Canada*, Translated by Ralph Novek, Montreal, Harvest House, 1965. [532]

Salaman, Redcliffe N., "The Jewish Fellows of the Royal Society," JHSE, *Mis.*, V, 1948, pp. 146–75. [533]

Salomon, H. P., "The Portuguese Inquisition and its Victims in the Light of Recent Polemics," *Journal of the American Portuguese Cultural Society*, Summer-Fall, 1971, pp. 19–28, 50–55. [533a]

Samuel, Edgar Loy, "Portuguese Jews in Jacobean London," JHSE, *Tr., Sessions 1953–1955*, XVIII, pp. 143–70. [534]

Samuel, Maurice, *The Professor and the Fossil: Some Observations on Arnold J. Toynbee's "A Study of History,"* New York, Knopf, 1956. [535]

Saron, Gustav, and Louis Holtz, Eds., *The Jews in South Africa: A History*, Oxford University Press, New York, 1956.* [536]

Sauer, Wolfgang, "Comments on the Paper of Donald L. Niewyk" [-Niewyk. "Economic and Cultural Role of the Jews in the Weimar Republic"], *LBIYB*, XVI, 1971, pp. 178–81. [537]

Schaeder, Grete, *The Hebrew Humanism of Martin Buber*, Detroit, Wayne State University, 1973. [537a]

Schappes, Morris U., *A Documentary History of the Jews in the United States, 1654–1875*, New York, Citadel, 1950 (3rd ed., 1971).*¶ [538]

Schechtman, Joseph, "Jewish Community Life in Ukraine (1917–1918)," in *Russian Jewry 1917–1967*, pp. 39–57. [539]

Schlesinger, Benjamin, *The Jewish Family; A Survey and Annotated Bibliography*, Toronto, University of Toronto Press, 1971.†* [540]

Schleunes, Karl Albert, *The Twisted Road to Auschwitz; Nazi Policy Toward German Jews 1933–1939*, Urbana, University of Illinois Press, 1970.* [541]

Schlochauer, Ernest J., "Thomas Wale: Forgotten Champion of English Jewry," *JSS*, XIII, 1951, pp. 227–34. [542]

Schmelz, Oscar and R. Shebath, *Jewish Demography and Statistics: Bibliography for 1920–1960*, Jerusalem, Hebrew University, 1961. [542a]

Schmidt, H. D., "The Terms of Emancipation, (1781–1812)," *LBIYB*, I, 1956, pp. 28–48. [543]

Schoeps, Hans Joachim, *The Jewish-Christian Argument: A History of Theologies in Conflict*, New York, Holt, Rinehart and Winston, 1963. [544]

———, "Philosemitism in the Baroque Period," *JQR*, NS, XLVIII, pp. 139–44. [545]

Scholem, Gershom, *Major Trends in Jewish Mysticism*, New York, Schocken, 1954.* [546]

———, *The Messianic Idea in Judaism, and Other Essays on Jewish Spirituality*, New York, Schocken Books, 1971. [547]

Schorsch, Ismar, *Jewish Reactions to German Anti-Semitism 1870–1914*, Philadelphia, JPSA, 1972.* [548]

———, "Moritz Güdemann, Rabbi, Historian and Apologist," *LBIYB*, XI, 1966, pp. 42–66. [549]

———, "The Philosophy of History of Nachman Krochmal," *Judaism*, X, 1961, pp. 237–45. [550]

Schorske, Carl E., "Politics in a New Key: An Austrian Triptych," *Journal of Modern History*, XXXIX, 1967, pp. 343–86. [551]

Schulman, Elias, *A History of Jewish Education in the Soviet Union*, New York and Waltham, Ktav and Brandeis University, 1971. [552]

Schwab, Hermann, *The History of Orthodox Jewry in Germany*, London, Mitre Press, 1950. [553]

Schwarcz, Moshe, "Religious Currents and General Culture," *LBIYB*, XVI, 1971, pp. 3–17. [554]

Schwartz, Arnold, "Intermarriage in the United States," *AJYB*, LXXI, 1969–1970, pp. 101–21. [555]

Schwartz, Solomon M., *The Jews in the Soviet Union*, Syracuse, Syracuse University Press, 1951.* [556]

Schwarz, Karl, *Jewish Artists of the Nineteenth and Twentieth Centuries*, New York, Philosophical Library, 1949. [557]

Schwarz, Leo W., 42.

Schwarz, Robert, "Antisemitism and Socialism in Austria, 1918–62," in *Jews of Austria*, pp. 445–66. [558]

Schwarz, Walter, "Frederick the Great—His Jews and His Porcelain," *LBIYB*, XI, 1966, pp. 300–05. [559]

Schweid, Eliezer, *Israel at the Crossroads*, Philadelphia, The Jewish Publication Society of America, 1973. [560]

Scult, Mel, "English Missions to the Jews: Conversion in the Age of Emancipation," *JSS*, XXXV, 1973, pp. 3–18. [561]

Segal, Simon, *The New Poland and the Jews*, with a Foreword by Arthur Swift, Jr., New York, Lee Furman, 1938. [561a]

Seiden, Morton Irving, *The Paradox of Hate; A Study of Ritual Murder*, South Brunswick, Yoseloff, 1967. [562]

Selzer, Michael, Ed., *Zionism Reconsidered; The Rejection of Jewish Normalcy*, London, Collier-Macmillan, 1970.† [563]

Shaftesley, John M., 467.

Shalad, Barton, 327a.

Shapiro, Harry Lionel, *The Jewish People: A Biological History*, Paris, UNESCO, 1960. [564]

Shatzky, Jacob, "Alexander Kraushar and His Road to Total Assimilation," *YAJSS*, VII, 1952, pp. 146–74. [565]

———, "Jewish Ideologies in Austria during the Revolution of 1848," in *Freedom and Reason*, pp. 397 412. [566]

———, "Warsaw Jews in the Polish Cultural Life of the Early 19th Century," *YAJSS*, V, 1950, pp. 41–54. [567]

Shepard, S., "The Background of Uriel Da Costa's Heresy; Marranism, Scepticism, Karaism," *Judaism*, XX, 1971, pp. 341–50. [568]

Sherman, C. Bezalel, *Bund, Galuth, Nationalism, Yiddishism*, New York, Herzl Press, 1958. [569]

Shulvass, Moses, *From East to West. The Westward Migration of Jews from Eastern Europe during the Seventeenth and Eighteenth Centuries*, Detroit, Wayne State University Press, 1971.* [570]

———, *The Jews in the World of the Renaissance*, Leiden, Brill, 1973. [571]

Shumsky, Abraham, *The Clash of Cultures in Israel: A Problem for Education*, Westport, Conn., Greenwood Press, 1972. [571a]

Sicroff, A. A., "The Spanish Obsession," in *The Midstream Reader*, Edited by Shlomo Katz, New York, Yoseloff, 1960, pp. 296–314.† [571b]

Siegel, Seymour, 522.

Sigal, Phillip, "Whither Diaspora Judaism?," *Conservative Judaism*, XIV, No. 4, Summer, 1960, pp. 35–45. [572]

Silberg, Moshe, *Talmudic Law and the Modern State*, translated by Ben Zion Bokser, edited by Marvin S. Wiener, New York, The Burning Bush Press, 1973. [573]

[*Silberman, Curt G., Jubilee Volume*], 613.

Silberner, Edmund, "Anti-Jewish Trends in French Revolutionary Syndicalism," *JSS*, XV, 1953, pp. 195–202. [574]

———, "The Attitude of the Fourierist School Towards the Jews," *JSS*, IX, 1947, pp. 339–62. [575]

———, "Austrian Social Democracy and the Jewish Problem," *HJ*, XIII, 1951, pp. 121–40. [576]

———, "British Socialism and the Jews," *HJ*, XIV, 1952, pp. 27–52. [577]

———, "Charles Fourier on the Jewish Question," *JSS*, VIII, 1946, pp. 245–66. [578]

———, "Ferdinand Lassalle: From Maccabeism to Jewish Anti-Semitism," *HUCA*, XXIV, 1952–53, pp. 151–86. [579]

———, "French Socialism and the Jewish Question," *HJ*, XVI, 1954, pp. 367–84. [580]

———, "German Social Democracy and the Jewish Problem Prior to World War I," *HJ*, XV, 1953, pp. 3–48. [581]

———, "Pierre Leroux's Ideas on the Jewish Problem," *JSS*, XII, 1950, pp. 367–84. [582]

———, "Was Marx an Anti-Semite?," *HJ*, XI, 1949, pp. 3–52. [583]

———, *Western European Socialism and the Jewish Problem, 1800–1918; A Selective Bibliography*, Jerusalem, Hebrew University, 1955.* [584]

Silver, Jeremy, 419.

Simmel, Ernst, Ed., *Anti-Semitism; A Social Disease*, New York, International Universities Press, 1946.† [585]

Simon, Walter B., "The Jewish Vote in Austria," *LBIYB*, XVI, 1971, pp. 97–122. [586]

Sklare, Marshall, *America's Jews*, New York, Random House, 1971.* [587]

———, *Conservative Judaism: An American Religious Movement*, Glencoe, Ill., The Free Press, 1955.* [588]

———, Ed., *The Jews: Social Patterns of an American Group*, Glencoe, Ill., 1958.† [588a]

Snow, C. P., 481.

Snyder, Charles R., *Alcohol and the Jews: A Cultural Study of Drinking and Sobriety*, Glencoe, The Free Press, 1958.* [588b]

Snyder, Louis L., *The Dreyfus Case: A Documentary History*, New Brunswick, N. J., Rutgers University Press, 1973. [588c]

Society for the History of Czechoslovak Jews, 265.

Sokolow, Nahum, *History of Zionism 1600–1918*, with Introduction by Arthur Hertzberg, New York, Ktav, 1969 (reprint of 1919 London edition.)* [589]

Sole, Aryeh, "Subcarpathian Ruthenia: 1918–1938," *Jews in Czechoslovakia*, I, pp. 123–54. [590]

Soloveitchik, Joseph B., "Confrontation," *Tradition*, VI, No. 2, 1964, pp. 5–29. [591]

Song Nai Rhee, "Jewish Assimilation: The Case of the Chinese Jews," *Comparative Studies in Society and History*, XV, 1972, pp. 115–26. [591a]

Sonne, Isaiah, "Leon Modena and the DaCosta Circle in Amsterdam," *HUCA*, XII, 1949, pp. 1–28. [592]

Sombart, Werner, *The Jews and Modern Capitalism*, translated by M. Epstein, with an Introduction . . . by Bert F. Hoselitz, New York, Collier Books, 1962. [593]

Spicehandler, Ezra, "Joshua Heschel Schorr: Maskil and Eastern European Reformist," *HUCA*, XXXI, 1960, pp. 181–222. [594]

Spiegel, Shalom, *Hebrew Reborn*, New York, Macmillan, 1930 (paperback, Meridian, 1962).* [595]

Starr, Joshua, "Italy's Antisemites," *JSS*, I, 1939, pp. 105–24. [596]

———, "Jewish Citizenship in Rumania (1878–1940)," *JSS*, III, 1941, pp. 60–65. [597]

Steiner, George, *In Bluebeard's Castle: Some Notes towards the Redefinition of Culture*, New Haven, Yale University Press, 1971. [597a]

Sterling, Eleanor O., "Anti-Jewish Riots in Germany in 1819; A Displacement of Social Protest," *HJ*, XII, 1950, pp. 105–58. [598]

———, "Jewish Reaction to Jew-Hatred in the First Half of the Nineteenth Century," *LBIYB*, III, 1958, pp. 103–21. [599]

Stern, Fritz, *The Politics of Cultural Despair. A Study in the Rise of the Germanic Ideology*, Berkeley, University of California Press, 1961. [600]

Stern (Stern-Taeubler), Selma, *The Court Jew: A Contribution to the History of the Period of Absolutism in Central Europe*, Philadelphia, JPSA, 1950.* [601]

———, "The First Generation of Emancipated Jews," *LBIYB*, XV, 1970, pp. 3–40. [602]

———, "The Jew in the Transition from Ghetto to Emancipation," *HJ*, II, 1940, pp. 102–19. [603]

———, "The Jews in the Economic Policy of Frederick the Great," *JSS*, XI, 1949, pp. 129–52. [604]

———, *Josel of Rosheim: Commander of Jewry in the Holy Roman Empire of the German Nation*, Philadelphia, JPSA, 1965. [605]

Stillschweig, Kurt, "International Protection of Human Rights and Fundamental Freedoms," *HJ*, IX, 1947, pp. 35–56; X, 1948, pp. 43–60. [606]

———, "Jewish Assimilation as an Object of Legislation," *HJ*, VII, 1946, pp. 1–18. [607]

———, "Jewish Nationhood as a Factor in Law," *HJ*, IV, 1942, pp. 38–50. [608]

————, "The Jews of Germany as a National Minority," *HJ*, XI, 1949, pp. 53–76. [609]

————, "Nationalism and Autonomy among Eastern European Jewry: Origin and Historical Development up to 1939," *HJ*, VI, 1944, pp. 27–68. [610]

Stitskin, Leon D., Ed., *Studies in Torah Judaism*, New York, Yeshiva University Press-Ktav, 1969.† [611]

Stonequist, Everett V., *The Marginal Man*, New York, Scribner's, 1937. [612]

Strauss, Herbert A., "Liberalism and Conservatism in Prussian Legislation for Jewish Affairs, 1815–1847," *Jubilee Volume Dedicated to Curt C. Silberman*, New York, American Federation of Jews from Central Europe, 1969, pp. 114–32. [613]

————, "Pre-Emancipation Prussian Policies Towards the Jews, 1815–1847," *LBIYB*, XI, 1966, pp. 107–36. [614]

Strauss, Leo, 101b.

Strauss, Raphael, "The Jewish Question as a Problem of Nationalism," *HJ*, XII, 1950, pp. 3–20. [615]

————, "The Jews in the Economic Evolution of Central Europe," *JSS*, III, 1941, pp. 15–40. [616]

Studies of the Leo Baeck Institute, see SLIB.

Swift, Arthur, Jr., 561a.

Sylvain, Nicholas, 376.

Synam, Edward A., *The Popes and the Jews in the Middle Ages*, Preface by John M. Estreicher, New York, Macmillan, 1965. [617]

Syrkin, Marie, 212.

Szajkowski, Z., "Demands for Complete Emancipation of German Jewry during World War I," *JQR*, NS, LV, 1965, pp. 350–63. [618]

————, "Internal Conflicts in French Jewry at the Time of the Revolution of 1848," *YAJSS*, II-III, 1947–48, pp. 100–17. [619]

————, *Jews and the French Revolutions of 1789, 1830, and 1848*, New York, Ktav, 1970 (contains many items).†¶* [620]

————, *Jews, Wars, and Communism*, Vol. 1, *The Attitude of American Jews to World War I, the Russian Revolutions of 1917 and Communism (1914–1945)*, New York, Ktav, 1972.* [621]

————, "The Marranos and Sephardim of France," *The Abraham Weiss Jubilee Volume*, New York, Yeshiva University, 1964, pp. 107–27. [622]

————, "Protestants and Jews in the Fight for Emancipation 1789–1791," *PAAJR*, XXV, 1956, pp. 119–36. [623]

————, "Socialists and Radicals in the Development of Antisemitism in Algeria (1884–1900)," *JSS*, X, 1948, pp. 257–80. [624]

Szechtman, Joshua, "Voltaire on Isaac of Troki's *Hizzuk Emunah*," *JQR*, XLVII, 1957–58, pp. 53–57. [625]

Tager, Alexander B., *The Decay of Czarism: The Beiliss Trial. A Contribution to the History of the Political Reaction during the Last Years of Russian Czarism,* Philadelphia, JPSA, 1935. [626]

Tal, Uriel, "Liberal Protestantism and the Jews in the Second Reich, 1870–1914," *JSS,* XXV, 1963, pp. 23–41. [627]

———, *Religious and Anti-Religious Roots of Modern Anti-Semitism,* New York, Leo Baeck Institute, 1971. [628]

Talmon, Jacob L., "Suggestions for Isolating the Jewish Component in World History," *Midstream,* XVII, No. 3, March 1972, pp. 8–26. [630]

———, "European History—Seedbed of the Holocaust," *Midstream,* XIX, No. 5, May, 1973, pp. 3–25. [629]

———, *The Unique and the Universal; Some Historical Reflections,* New York, George Brazillier, 1965.† [631]

Tanenbaum, Marc H., and R. J. Zwi Werblovsky, Eds., *Colloquium on Religion, Peoplehood, Nation, and Land, Jerusalem Colloquium . . . Proceedings, Oct. 30–Nov. 8, 1970,* Jerusalem, The Hebrew University, American Jewish Committee and Israel Interfaith Committee, 1972.† [631a]

Tartakower, Arieh, "Diaspora Jewry Today: Outline of a Sociology," in *Essays in Jewish Sociology, Labour and Cooperation in Memory of Dr. Noah Barou, 1889–1955,* Edited by Henrik F. Infeld, New York, Thomas Yoseloff and World Jewish Congress, 1962, pp. 73–78. [632]

———, "Hitler's Heritage," *In the Dispersion,* No. 5–6, Spring 1966, pp. 77–138. [633]

———, "The Jewish Problem in the Soviet Union," *JSS,* XXXIII, 1971, pp. 285–306. [634]

Teller, Judd L., *Scapegoat of Revolution,* New York, Scribner's, 1954. [635]

Tenenbaum, Joseph, *Race and Reich; The Story of an Epoch,* New York, Twayne, 1956.* [636]

Tillich, Paul, "The Jewish Question: Christian and German Problem," *JSS,* XXXIII, 1971, pp. 253–71. [637]

Tobias, Henry J., *The Jewish Bund in Russia from its Origins to 1905,* Stanford, Cal., Stanford University Press, 1972.* [638]

Toury, Jacob, "The Jewish Question; A Semantic Approach," *LBIYB,* XI, 1966, pp. 85–106. [639]

Trachtenberg, Joshua, *The Devil and the Jews: The Medieval Conception of the Jew and its Relation to Modern Antisemitism,* Cleveland, World; Philadelphia, JPSA, 1943.* [640]

Tramer, Hans, "Prague—City of Three Peoples," *LBIYB,* IX, 1964, pp. 305–39. [641]

Trotsky, Leon, *On the Jewish Question,* New York, Pathfinder Press, 1970.¶ [642]

Tuchman, Barbara W., *Bible and Sword: England and Palestine from the*

Bronze Age to Balfour, New York, New York University Press, 1956.*
[643]

Tuchman, Hyman, "Review of Halakhic Periodical Literature," *Tradition,*
I, No. 1, 1958, pp. 117–24; I, No. 2, 1958, pp. 230–43; II, No. 1, 1959,
pp. 145–54; III, No. 1, 1960, pp. 73–81. [644]

Union of Russian Jews, 21, 22.

Usque, Samuel, *Consolation for the Tribulations of Israel* . . . , Translated from
the Portuguese by Martin A. Cohen, Philadelphia, JPSA, 1965.¶* [645]

Valentin, Hugo, *Antisemitism Historically and Critically Examined,* New York,
Viking, 1936. [646]

Van der Veen, H.R.S., *Jewish Characters in Eighteenth Century Fiction and
Drama,* Gronningen, J. B. Walters, 1935; New York, Ktav, 1973.* [646a]

Verètè, M., "The Restoration of the Jews in English Protestant Thought, 1790–
1840," *Middle Eastern Studies,* VIII, No. 1, Jan. 1972, pp. 3–50. [647]

Viewpoints, IV, No. 3, 1969, issue on "The Jew in French Canada." [647a]

Vilensky, M., "The Royalist Position Concerning the Admission of Jews to
England," *JQR,* NS, XLI, 1950–51, pp. 397–409. [648]

———, 668

Villaneuva, Francisco Marques, "The Converso Problem: An Assessment,"
in *Collected Studies in Honor of Americo Castro's Eightieth Year,* Editor
M. P. Hornik, Oxford, Linombe Lodge Research Library, 1965, pp. 317–
34. [649]

Vishniac, Mark, "An International Convention against Antisemitism," New
York, Research Institute of the Jewish Labor Committee, 1946.* [650]

Vlavianos, Basil J., and Feliks Gross, *Struggle for Tomorrow: Modern Political
Ideologies of the Jewish People,* New York, Arts, Inc., 1954.† [651]

Voronel, Alexander, and Viktor Yakhot, Eds., *I Am a Jew; Essays on Jewish
Identity in the Soviet Union,* Edited and with a Foreword by Moshe
Decter, Introduction by Lewis A. Coser, New York, Academic Committee
on Soviet Jewry and the Anti-Defamation League of B'nai B'rith, 1973.
[651a]

Vorspan, Albert, *Jewish Values and the Social Crisis; A Casebook for Social
Action,* New York, Union of American Hebrew Congregations, 1968.
[651b]

Waldman, Mark, *Goethe and the Jews; A Challenge to Hitlerism,* New York,
London, G. P. Putnam's Sons, 1934. [651c]

Waldman, Morris, *Nor by Power,* New York, International Universities Press,
1953. [652]

Wallach, Luitpold, "The Beginnings of the Science of Judaism in the Nineteenth Century," *HJ,* VII, 1946, pp. 33–60. [653]

———, "The Scientific and Philosophical Background of Zunz's 'Science of
Judaism'," *HJ,* IV, 1942, pp. 51–70. [654]

Waxman, Meyer, *History of Jewish Literature from the Close of the Bible to Our Own Days*, Ed. 2, New York, Yoseloff, 1960, 5 vols.* [655]

Waxman, Mordecai, Ed., *Tradition and Change: The Development of Conservative Judaism*, New York, Burning Bush Publications, 1958.† [655a]

Weiler, Gershon, "Fritz Mauthner—A Study in Jewish Self-Rejection," *LBIYB*, IV, 1959, pp. 136–48. [656]

Weinreich, Max, 191.

Weinryb, Bernard D., "Enlightenment and German Haskalah," *Studies on Voltaire and the Eighteenth Century*, XXVII, 1963, pp. 1817–47. [657]

——, *Jewish Emancipation under Attack: Its Legal Recession until the Present War*, New York, American Jewish Committee, 1942.¶ [658]

——, *Jewish Vocational Education; History and Appraisal of Training in Europe*, New York, J.T.S.P. [Jewish Teachers' Seminary], University Press, 1948.* [659]

——, 376.

Werblovsky, R. J. Zwi, 222.

West, Benjamin, *Struggle of a Generation: Jews Under Soviet Rule*, Tel Aviv, Massada, 1959. [660]

Weyl, Nathaniel, *The Jew in American Politics*, New Rochelle, Arlington House, 1968.* [661]

Whiteside, Andrew G., "Comments on the Papers of William A. Jenks and Donald L. Niewyk," [Jenks: "Jews in the Hapsburg Empire, 1879–1918"; Niewyk: "Economic and Cultural Role of the Jews in the Weimar Republic"], *LBIYB*, XVI, 1971, pp. 174–77. [662]

Wiener, Marvin S., 573.

Wiener, Max, *Abraham Geiger and Liberal Judaism: The Challenge of the Nineteenth Century*, Philadelphia, JPSA, 1962.* [663]

——, "Abraham Geiger's Conception of the 'Science of Judaism'," *YAJSS*, XI, 1956–57, pp. 142–62. [664]

——, "The Conception of Mission in Traditional and Modern Judaism," *YAJSS*, II-III, 1947–48, pp. 9–24. [665]

——, "The Ideology of the Founders of Jewish Scientific Research," *YAJSS*, V, 1950, pp. 184–96. [666]

——, "John Toland and Judaism," *HUCA*, XVI, 1941, pp. 215–42. [667]

Wilensky, Mordecai L., "Thomas Barlow's and John Dury's Attitude towards the Readmission of the Jews to England," *JQR*, NS, L, 1959–60, pp. 167–75, 256–68. [668]

——, 648.

Wilhelm, Kurt, "The Jewish Community in the Post-Emancipation Period," *LBIYB*, II, 1957, pp. 47–75. [669]

Wischnitzer, Mark, *To Dwell in Safety: The Story of Jewish Migrations since 1800*, Philadelphia, JPSA, 1948.* [670]

————, *A History of Jewish Crafts and Guilds*, New York, Jonathan David, 1965.* [671]

Wistrich, Robert S., "Karl Marx, German Socialists and the Jewish Question, 1880–1914," *Soviet Jewish Affairs*, III, No. 1, 1973, pp. 92–97. [672]

Wiznitzer, Arnold, "Crypto-Jews in Mexico during the Seventeenth Century," *AJHQ*, LI, 1962, pp. 168–214, 222–68. [673]

————, "The Exodus from Brazil and Arrival in New Amsterdam of the Jewish Pilgrim Fathers, 1654," *PAJHS*, XLIV, 1954, pp. 80–97. [674]

————, *Jews in Colonial Brazil*, New York, Columbia University Press, 1960. [675]

Wolf, Arnold Jacob, Ed., *Rediscovering Judaism: Reflections on a New Theology*, Chicago, Quadrangle, 1965.† [675a]

Wolf, Lucien, "American Elements in the Re-Settlement," JHSE, *Tr., Sessions 1896–1898*, III, pp. 76–99. [676]

————, "Crypto-Jews under the Commonwealth," *JHSET, Session 1893–94*, I, pp. 55–88. [677]

————, *Essays in Jewish History* . . . Edited by Cecil Roth, London, JHSE, 1934.† [678]

————, "Jews in Elizabethan England," JHSE, *Tr., Sessions 1924–1927*, XI, pp. 1–91. [679]

————, *Notes on the Diplomatic History of the Jewish Question*, London, Jewish Historical Society of England, 1919. [679a]

————, "The Zionist Peril," *JQR*, XVII, 1905, pp. 1–25. [680]

World Jewish Congress, Institute of Jewish Affairs, *The Institute Anniversary Volume, 1941–1961*, New York, 1962.† [681]

Wurzburger, Walter S., "Alienation and Exile," *Tradition*, VI, No. 1, 1964, pp. 42–52. [682]

Wynot, Edward D., Jr., " 'A Necessary Cruelty': The Emergence of Official Anti-Semitism in Poland, 1936–69," *American Historical Review*, LXXVI, 1971, pp. 1035–58. [682a]

Yakhot, Viktor, 651a.

Yerushalmy, Yosef Hayim, *From Spanish Court to Italian Ghetto; Isaac Cardoso: A Study in Seventeenth Century Marranism and Jewish Apologetics*, New York, Columbia University Press, 1971.* [683]

YIVO Annual of Jewish Social Science, 160.

YIVO Institute for Jewish Research, 191.

Zangwill, Israel, "Mr. Lucien Wolf on 'The Zionist Peril'," *JQR*, XVII, 1905, pp. 397–425. [684]

————, *The Voice of Jerusalem*, London, William Heinemann, 1920.† [685]

Zeitlin, Solomon, "The Jews: Race, Nation or Religion—Which?," *JQR*, NS, XXVI, 1935–36, pp. 313–46. [686]

————, "Who Is a Jew? A Halachic Historic Study," *JQR*, NS, XLIX, 1959, pp. 241–70. [687]

————, 469.

Zimmels, H. J., *Ashkenazim and Sephardim: The Relations, Differences, and Problems as Reflected in the Rabbinical Responsa*, London, Oxford University Press, 1958.* [688]

Zitt, Hersch L., "The Jew in the Elizabethan World-Picture," *HJ*, XIV, 1952, pp. 53–60. [689]

Zucker, Stanley, "Ludwig Bamberger and the Rise of Anti-Semitism in Germany, 1848–1893," *Central European History*, III, 1970, pp. 332–52. [690]

Zuckerman, Nathan, *The Wine of Violence; An Anthology on Anti-Semitism*, New York, Association Press, 1947.†¶* [691]

Zukerman, William, *The Jew in Revolt: The Modern Jew in the World Crisis*, London, Secker and Warburg, 1937. [692]

————, *Voice of Dissent; Jewish Problems, 1948–61*, New York, Bookman, 1964. [693]

Subject Index to Selected Bibliography

407